Southern Poets

REPRESENTATIVE SELECTIONS, WITH
INTRODUCTION, BIBLIOGRAPHY, AND NOTES

BY
EDD WINFIELD PARKS

AWS

AMERICAN BOOK COMPANY
*New York · Cincinnati · Chicago
Boston · Atlanta*

COPYRIGHT, 1936, BY

AMERICAN BOOK COMPANY

All rights reserved

———

PARKS'S SOUTHERN POETS

W. P. I.

MADE IN U.S.A.

PREFACE

Certain questions which have troubled the editor, in the preparation of this volume, may also prove troublesome to the readers. What is the South? That question can be answered only by implication, not by precise definition. In the Introduction, I have attempted to trace the development and partial disintegration of the causes and emotions which have made the South a unified section, and have set it somewhat apart from the nation. The background of general thought out of which a poet writes, or against which he revolts, has an immediate bearing upon the literature which the man, or the section, may produce. With this in mind, I have tried to adumbrate the indebtedness of Southern poets to men, living and dead, in other sections and nations; to point out their elements of kinship as well as their dissimilarities.

What is a Southern poet? This puzzling question required an immediate, if rough and approximate, answer. Local patriotism has frequently led editors of state and sectional anthologies to claim any person who might stray into that region. I have preferred a straiter definition; for the purposes of this anthology, I considered as Southerners mainly those persons who were born in the South, or who lived in the South for many years and came to think of themselves as native to the region.

Thus, Mr. John Gould Fletcher, who was born in Arkansas but who expatriated himself temporarily in England, is included here because since 1930 he has lived in the South and in his writing he has revealed Southern qualities and interests; Mr. Conrad Aiken, who was born in Georgia but has not lived in the South since his childhood, is not included because the accident of birth did not seem sufficient reason for arbitrarily defining either the poet or his work as Southern. In a very few instances, where the subject matter seemed a justification, I have deviated from this rule: for example, in the case of Dan D. Emmett and his version of "Dixie."

This volume makes no pretense of being a local-color exhibit. Some poems have become a heritage of the people; they are here included without apology, for most of them are good as literature and all of them have definite values and validity. This selection of poems on historical grounds has rarely interfered with my first intention: to present the best poems by Southerners that I could find, regardless of subject. This choice was necessarily limited by the physical scope of the volume; in a few cases it was limited by circumstances over which the editor had no control.

It is a pleasure to record my indebtedness to the friends who have aided me in the preparation of this volume. The general editor of the series, Harry Hayden Clark, made many wise, useful, and occasionally provocative suggestions. Lloyd and Jessie Wells Miller, Mr. V. V. Palma of the Library of Congress, Miss Isabel Howell, Mrs. D. C. Cabeen, and Mrs. Brainerd Cheney of the Vanderbilt University Library, and Dr. William S. Knickerbocker contributed liberally of their time and knowledge, and helped me in many ways. To three men, witty and profound students of Southern life and thought—Donald Davidson, Frank L. Owsley, and John Donald Wade—I am deeply indebted for direct aid and indirect suggestions which have enriched this book. Most of all, I am indebted to Aileen Wells Parks, who has worked with me constantly and whose name should, in justice, be on the title page with my own.

                                                                    E. W. P.

ACKNOWLEDGMENTS

For permission to reprint material from the works of the authors listed below, the editor is under grateful obligations to publishers and individuals as indicated:

JOHN PEALE BISHOP: selection from *Now with His Love*, by permission of Charles Scribner's Sons, publishers; "The Mothers," by permission of the author.

JAMES BRANCH CABELL: selection from *From the Hidden Way*, by permission of Robert M. McBride & Company, publishers.

MADISON CAWEIN: selections, by permission of The Macmillan Company, publishers.

OLIVE TILFORD DARGAN: selection from *Lute and Furrow*, by permission of Charles Scribner's Sons, publishers.

DONALD DAVIDSON: selections from *An Outland Piper* and from *The Tall Men* (Houghton Mifflin Company, publishers) and a prose selection, all used by permission of the author.

JOHN GOULD FLETCHER: selections from *Preludes and Symphonies*, *Breakers and Granite*, and *The Black Rock* (The Macmillan Company, publishers), all used by permission of the author.

PAUL HAMILTON HAYNE: selections, by permission of the estate of William Hamilton Hayne (Lothrop, Lee & Shepard Company, publishers).

WILLIAM HAMILTON HAYNE: selection from *Sylvan Lyrics*, by permission of Mr. Hayne's estate.

DUBOSE HEYWARD: selections from *Carolina Chansons* and *Jasbo Brown and Other Poems* (copyright 1922, 1931), by permission of Farrar & Rinehart, publishers.

SIDNEY LANIER: selections from poems and an excerpt from *The Science of English Verse*, by permission of Charles Scribner's Sons, publishers.

JOHN TROTWOOD MOORE: "Sam Davis," by permission of Mrs. John Trotwood Moore.

MERRILL MOORE: selections from *The Noise That Time Makes*, by permission of Harcourt, Brace and Company, publishers.

vii

WILLIAM ALEXANDER PERCY: selections from *In April Once* and *Levkas*, by permission of Yale University Press, publishers.

JOSEPHINE PINCKNEY: selections from *Sea-Drinking Cities*, by permission of Harper & Brothers, publishers.

JOHN CROWE RANSOM: selections from *Chills and Fever* and *Two Gentlemen in Bonds*, by permission of Alfred A. Knopf, Inc., publishers; "Autumn Love," by permission of the author.

LIZETTE WOODWORTH REESE: selections from *Selected Poems* (copyright 1926), by permission of Farrar & Rinehart, publishers.

CALE YOUNG RICE: selections from *Collected Poems*, by permission of D. Appleton-Century Company, publishers.

IRWIN RUSSELL: "Christmas Night in the Quarters," by permission of D. Appleton-Century Company, publishers.

ABRAM JOSEPH RYAN: selections from poems, published by J. P. Kennedy & Sons.

ALEC B. STEVENSON: "Icarus in November," by permission of the author.

JESSE STUART: selections from *Man With the Bull-Tongue Plow*, published and copyrighted by E. P. Dutton & Company, New York.

JOHN BANISTER TABB: selections from poems (Dodd, Mead and Company, publishers), by permission of Dr. Francis A. Litz.

ALLEN TATE: "Ode to the Confederate Dead" and "The Cross" from *Poems, 1928–1931*, by permission of Charles Scribner's Sons, publishers; "Mr. Pope" (from *Mr. Pope and Other Poems*, published by Minton, Balch and Company), "John Brown," and "Shadow and Shade," by permission of the author.

ROBERT PENN WARREN: "Kentucky Mountain Farm," by permission of the author.

CONTENTS

SOUTHERN POETS: INTRODUCTION

    I. The Background, xvii
   II. Poetic Theory, xlvi
  III. The Poetry, lxxxii

SELECTED BIBLIOGRAPHY

    I. Anthologies, cxxxi
   II. General, cxxxiii
  III. Authors, cxxxvi
  IV. Negro Songs and Spirituals, cxlvii

SELECTIONS

  EARLY BALLADS, SONGS, AND POEMS
    JOHN SMITH: The Sea Mark, 3
    ANONYMOUS: The Brown Girl or Fair Ellender, 4
    ANONYMOUS: Bacon's Epitaph, Made by His Man, 5
    WILLIAM BYRD: Long Has the Furious Priest, 6
    A GENTLEMAN OF VIRGINIA: Epigram, 7
    ANONYMOUS: The Battle of King's Mountain, 7
    JOHN SHAW: Song ("Who has robbed the ocean cave"),
      9
    ST. GEORGE TUCKER: Resignation, 9
    FRANCIS SCOTT KEY: The Star-Spangled Banner, 11

  RICHARD HENRY WILDE, 12
    Stanzas ("My life is like the summer rose"), 14
    To the Mocking-Bird, 14
    To Lord Byron, 15
    A Farewell to America, 15

  SAMUEL HENRY DICKSON, 16
    "I Sigh for the Land of the Cypress and Pine," 17

  EDWARD COOTE PINKNEY, 18
    Song ("We break the glass"), 19
    The Voyager's Song, 19
    Serenade ("Look out upon the stars"), 21
    A Health ("I fill this cup"), 22

Song ("Day departs"), 23
The Widow's Song, 23
Self-Esteem, 24
On Parting, 24
Melancholy's Curse of Feasts, 24

WILLIAM GILMORE SIMMS, 25
The Swamp Fox, 28
The Edge of the Swamp, 31
The Lost Pleiad, 33
'Tis True That Last Night I Adored Thee, 35
The Grape-Vine Swing, 36
The Decay of a People, 37
Song in March, 37
Sonnet ("We are a part"), 38

THOMAS HOLLEY CHIVERS, 38
Faith, 40
Georgia Waters, 41
Song of Adoration to God, 41
The Crucifixion, 43
Sonnet: Grief, 43
Isadore, 44
To Allegra Florence in Heaven, 49
Burdens of Unrest: Mary's Lament for Shelley Lost at
Sea, 52
Song to Isa, 54
The Chaplet of Cypress: An Elegy on the Death of My
Sister, 55
Apollo, 57
The Voice of Thought, 58
Lily Adair, 58
To Idealon, 60

EDGAR ALLAN POE, 60
To Science (A Prologue to "Al Aaraaf"), 62
Romance, 63
To Helen, 63
The City in the Sea, 64
Israfel, 66
To One in Paradise, 67
The Coliseum, 68

The Haunted Palace, 70
The Conqueror Worm, 71
The Raven, 72
Lenore, 77
Ulalume, 78
Annabel Lee, 81
Eldorado, 82

PHILIP PENDLETON COOKE, 83
Florence Vane, 84
Life in the Autumn Woods, 85
From The Power of the Bards, 87

THEODORE O'HARA, 88
The Bivouac of the Dead, 89
The Old Pioneer, 91

JAMES MATHEWES LEGARÉ, 93
On the Death of a Kinsman, 94
To a Lily, 95
Haw-Blossoms, 95
Flowers in Ashes, 97
The Reaper, 98

HENRY TIMROD, 99
Why Silent, 101
Sonnet ("I know not why"), 101
Sonnet ("Most men know love"), 102
Ethnogenesis, 102
The Cotton Boll, 106
A Cry to Arms, 110
Carolina, 112
Spring, 115
Charleston, 117
Christmas, 119
The Unknown Dead, 121
Ode, 123
Sonnet ("At last"), 124

PAUL HAMILTON HAYNE, 124
Shelley, 125
My Study, 126
The Pine's Mystery, 126

Vicksburg. A Ballad, 127
Aspects of the Pines, 128
The Snow-Messengers, 129
To Longfellow (On Hearing He Was Ill), 133
To W. H. H., 133
A Little While I Fain Would Linger Yet, 134
In Harbor, 135

CIVIL WAR BALLADS, SONGS, AND POEMS
    DAN D. EMMETT: Dixie, 136
    ALBERT PIKE: Dixie, 138
    JAMES RYDER RANDALL: Maryland, My Maryland, 140
    HARRY McCARTHY: The Bonnie Blue Flag, 142
    INNES RANDOLPH: I'm a Good Old Rebel, 144
    FRANCIS ORRAY TICKNOR: The Virginians of the Valley,
        146
    FRANCIS ORRAY TICKNOR: Little Giffen, 146
    HENRY LYNDON FLASH: Zollicoffer, 148
    JOHN REUBEN THOMPSON: Lee to the Rear, 148
    JOHN WILLIAMSON PALMER: Stonewall Jackson's Way, 151
    MARGARET JUNKIN PRESTON: The Shade of the Trees, 153
    ANONYMOUS: "The Brigade Must Not Know, Sir!" 154
    JOHN ESTEN COOKE: The Band in the Pines, 155
    JOHN DICKSON BRUNS: The Foe at the Gates, 155
    JOSEPH BLYTH ALLSTON: Stack Arms, 156
    WILLIAM GORDON McCABE: Dreaming in the Trenches,
        158
    DANIEL BEDINGER LUCAS: The Land Where We Were
        Dreaming, 159

ABRAM JOSEPH RYAN, 162
    The Conquered Banner, 162
    The Sword of Robert Lee, 164
    A Land without Ruins, 165
    Song of the Mystic, 166

SIDNEY LANIER, 168
    Song for "The Jacquerie," 170
    The Symphony, 171
    Song of the Chattahoochee, 181
    The Stirrup-Cup, 182
    The Revenge of Hamish, 183

Hymns of The Marshes
    I. Sunrise, 188
    II. Individuality, 194
    III. Marsh Song—At Sunset, 197
    IV. The Marshes of Glynn, 197
A Ballad of Trees and the Master, 201

JOHN BANISTER TABB, 201
    Kildee, 203
    Compensation, 203
    The Departed, 203
    Evolution, 204
    The Snow-Bird, 204
    My Secret, 204
    Matins, 205
    Going Blind, 205

IRWIN RUSSELL, 205
    Christmas-Night in the Quarters, 206

LIZETTE WOODWORTH REESE, 214
    April Weather, 215
    Tears, 215
    Waiting, 216
    Spicewood, 216
    Old Saul, 216
    Today, 218

MADISON JULIUS CAWEIN, 222
    Snow, 222
    Aubade, 223
    Prototypes, 224
    The Winds, 224
    Ku Klux, 225
    The Man Hunt, 226
    Deserted, 227
    The Mountain Still, 228

WILLIAM ALEXANDER PERCY, 229
    Overtones, 229
    The Wanderer, 229
    Chorus, 231
    In New York
        1. On Sunday Morning, 231
        2. The Song You Love, 232

    3. Weariness, 232
    4. In the Night, 233
    5. Home, 233
DuBose Heyward, 234
    Dusk, 235
    Prodigal, 236

Single Poems
    James Barron Hope: Our Anglo-Saxon Tongue, 236
    William Hamilton Hayne: To My Father, 237
    John Trotwood Moore: Sam Davis, 237
    Walter Malone: Opportunity, 239
    Olive Tilford Dargan: Lute and Furrow, 240
    James Branch Cabell: One End of Love, 242
    Alec B. Stevenson: Icarus in November, 244

Cale Young Rice, 245
    From a Felucca, 246
    Daniel Boone's Last Look Westward, 246
    The Contessa to Her Judges, 248

John Gould Fletcher, 249
    White Symphony, 250
    Down the Mississippi, 256
    Earth, 259
    The Swan, 262
    The Black Rock, 263
    The House to the Man, 268

John Crowe Ransom, 269
    Spectral Lovers, 270
    Here Lies a Lady, 271
    Judith of Bethulia, 271
    Blue Girls, 273
    Our Two Worthies, 273
    Autumn Love, 275

John Peale Bishop, 276
    Beyond Connecticut, Beyond the Sea, 277
    The Mothers, 279

Donald Davidson, 280
    Redivivus, 281
    The Tall Men (Section of *The Tall Men*), 281

Fire on Belmont Street (Epilogue to *The Tall Men*), 289
Southward Returning, 292
Lee in the Mountains, 292

JOSEPHINE PINCKNEY, 296
Street Cries, 297
Sea-Drinking Cities, 299

ALLEN TATE, 300
Mr. Pope, 300
Ode to the Confederate Dead, 301
The Cross, 304
John Brown, 304
Shadow and Shade, 305

MERRILL MOORE, 306
The Noise That Time Makes, 306
Shot Who? Jim Lane! 307

ROBERT PENN WARREN, 307
Kentucky Mountain Farm
    I. Rebuke of the Rocks, 308
    II. At the Hour of the Breaking of the Rocks, 308
    III. History Among the Rocks, 309

JESSE STUART, 310
Young Kentucky (a sonnet sequence), 310

NEGRO SONGS AND SPIRITUALS, 313
John Henry, 315
The Boll Weevil Song, 316
Water-Boy, 318
Go Down, Moses, 318
Steal Away, 319

APPENDIX: THEORIES OF POETRY BY SOUTHERNERS
W. G. SIMMS: Letter to T. H. Chivers, 321
T. H. CHIVERS: Letter to W. G. Simms, 322
T. H. CHIVERS: Preface to *Nacoochee*, 325
T. H. CHIVERS: Preface to *Memoralia*, 327
T. H. CHIVERS: From Preface to *Virginalia*, 332
E. A. POE: From "The Poetic Principle," 332
E. A. POE: "The Philosophy of Composition," 338
P. P. COOKE: Extracts from Letters, 349
HENRY TIMROD: From "A Theory of Poetry," 351

W. H. Hayne: Paul Hamilton Hayne's Methods of Composition, 353

Sidney Lanier: From *The Science of English Verse*, 355

DuBose Heyward and Hervey Allen: From "Poetry South," 360

J. G. Fletcher: Preface to *Preludes and Symphonies*, 364

Allen Tate: "Note on Southern Poetry," 368

Donald Davidson: "The Southern Poet and His Tradition," 369

Notes, 377
Index, 400

SOUTHERN POETS

I. THE BACKGROUND

When Captain John Smith arrived in Jamestown in 1607, he brought with him an English attitude which distrusted all things foreign to his own race and tradition. He noted with a curious eye the customs of the Indians, who seemed to him and to his successors heathen savages, either to be exterminated, or Christianized and made into peaceful servants. Whatever culture these Indians had made no impression upon the doughty captain, who had a neat taste for literature himself and in later years occasionally spiced the fabric of his descriptive prose with a verse that, if not particularly good in itself, was at least in the best Elizabethan manner.[1] The highly conventionalized poetry (the tribal chants and death songs, for example) of the Indians[2] made no impression then or later upon what we have come to think of as Southern poetry.[3]

---

[1] W. G. Simms, in *Life of Captain John Smith* (1902 ed.), compares him with John Davies and Philip Quarles, and speaks of the "peculiar quaintness of tone which marked the verses of the Elizabethan period," 326–7. Of "The Sea Mark" he writes, "they are better lines than those of his eulogists," 327. But Smith seems more definitely (as J. G. Fletcher suggests in *John Smith—Also Pocahontas*) a minor edition of Sir Walter Raleigh, having more kinship with him than with any other contemporary. Smith, in the Preface to *True Travels*, well expressed his feeling: "Many of the most eminent warriors, what their swords did, their pens writ. Though I be never so much their inferior, yet I hold it no great error to follow good examples."

[2] See Louis Untermeyer, *American Poetry from the Beginning to Whitman*, 687–704.

[3] The intrinsic value of Indian poetry and its influence upon the Southwest deserve, in any study of American literature as a whole, more consideration than has been given to it, but it does not seem to come within the scope of this volume. W. G. Simms, at least, was not unmindful of this literature and he suggested an anthology of Indian poetry; cf. his "Literature and Art among the American Aborigines," in *Views and Reviews*, 102–17. T. H. Chivers also knew the poetry of the Cherokees, but I am unable to find any record that he used this knowledge in his prosody. He

To John Smith, Virginia was only the lengthened shadow of England.[4]

For more than a century the South remained in spirit and in fact a continuation of England. Richard Rich wrote in 1610 that "wee hope to plant a nation where none before hath stood"[5] but the context shows clearly that he meant an English colony. A man like George Sandys found it a temporary haven, a place where as treasurer he must spend some years of his life.[6] But his desires centered about the London from which he felt himself in temporary exile, and it was for men in London that he polished so carefully his classical translation of Ovid's *Metamorphoses*.[7] Most men of position felt themselves temporary residents in the new land. Yet, inevitably, a dual allegiance came into being. A Virginia planter like William Byrd, educated at the Middle Temple and with a wide acquaintance in London, might consider himself an English gentleman, might complain of English friends that "distance they reckon the same as death"[8]—but he found that distance too great to traverse, and he found also that it led to constant governmental misunderstandings which fretted him and his friends mightily.

On the seaboard a colonial aristocracy developed rapidly.

did write on Indian subjects; "The Chickamauga Indian's Conversion" reveals his first-hand knowledge.

[4] The best edition of Smith's works is that edited by Edward Arber: *Captain John Smith, Works* (1884).

[5] "Newes from Virginia," by Richard Rich. A. C. Gordon, Jr., *Virginian Writers of Fugitive Verse*, discusses the poem, 25–6, quoting the preface, and giving the text, 138–43. Gordon's book is very valuable for its presentation of early Virginia poetry.

[6] Gordon, *op. cit.*, 28, quotes one stanza of a contemporary ballad to show that Sandys did not neglect his duties:

Stout Master George Sandys upon a night did bravely venture forth
And mong'st the savage murtherers did forme a deed of worth
For finding many by a fire to death their lives did pay
Set fire of a towne of theirs and bravely came away.

[7] Published in London, 1626, with a dedication which describes the hardships of writing in Virginia. Sandys was included by Thomas Fuller in his *Worthies of England*, and his translation was praised by Dryden and Pope.

[8] R. C. Beatty, *William Byrd of Westover*, 116.

Indentured servants, after they had secured freedom by work, and free men with little money, tended to move west and take up land, leaving a settled landed gentry which in turn imported more servants or more slaves. In a land where social lines had not become strait and well-defined, this gradual transformation was not unusual, although it was, naturally, limited to the shrewdest and most capable men. The number of *bona fide* members of the English aristocracy was numerically small: "A thin sprinkling of the genteel class came from England until Cromwell's time, when fairly numerous opponents of the Roundheads sought asylum in the colonies."[9] More important was the idea of aristocracy, which from the beginning was firmly planted in the Southern colonies. To men at that time this ideal way of life was most nearly approximated by William Byrd with his thousands of acres, his slaves, his fine house, and his library of four thousand choice volumes.[10] If few men could do that well, they were at least headed in the same direction.[11]

The settled country and the frontier[12] had divergent interests

[9] U. B. Phillips, *Life and Labor in the Old South*, 26. Phillips gives an excellent picture in small compass of the development of Virginia, 14–41.

[10] Beatty, *op. cit.*, 184–8. A catalogue of Byrd's books is given in J. S. Bassett, *Writings of William Byrd*, 413–43. Bassett's introduction is particularly good on Byrd's part in Virginia politics.

[11] T. J. Wertenbaker, *Patrician and Plebeian in Virginia*, 28: "Beyond doubt, the most numerous section of the Virginia aristocracy was derived from the English merchant class." Phillips, *op. cit.*, 39–40, adds that "Byrd's pace was too fast," and quotes from Landon Carter, who wrote in 1770 (*William and Mary College Quarterly*, XIII, 47), "I believe everybody begins to laugh at English education; the general importers of it nowadays bring back only a stiff priggishness with as little good manners as possible." But in spite of some discontent, Phillips considers the ideal of a Virginian was to be a planter, but cautions that "the planters included by courtesy many who might equally well have been termed farmers" (*ibid.*, 41).

[12] The term *frontier* is used throughout this essay according to the definition of Frederick Jackson Turner in his "Significance of the Frontier in American History," in *The Frontier in American History* (1920): "The most significant thing about the American frontier is, that it lies at the hither edge of free land. In the census reports it is treated as the margin of that settlement which has a density of two or more to the square mile. The term is an elastic one. . . ."

and were often in opposition. Only a few times did these differences lead to open and dramatic conflict, as in 1676 when Nathaniel Bacon rebelled against Governor Berkeley and organized the frontiersmen to fight against the Indians,[13] or as in 1785 when John Sevier and his fellows west of the mountains revolted against North Carolina and organized the short-lived State of Franklin.[14] Such outbreaks are rare and incidental; a truer picture can be gained by a comparison of the sections in quieter times.

The seaboard South had an established religion; such a religion did little to encourage thought or writing. The Episcopal church was in authority and ministers saw little need to defend it. They were not, as were the Puritans, "leading a great body of men out of this castellated state of mind";[15] they were rather set upon holding to traditional ways and beliefs. The racial and religious homogeneity of this powerful aristocracy was not fully broken up until after the Civil War. But it received before that time many a rude jolt. The waves of population brought Huguenots to South Carolina after the Edict of Nantes (1685);[16] the founding of Georgia as an asylum for dissenters and outcasts in 1732 brought Lutherans, Moravians, and Salzburgers, and brought, along with the English, the propagation of Methodism;[17] but, most important of all, the years brought a steady stream of Scotch-Irish to the frontier. The seaboard welcomed these immigrants, partially for the mercenary reason that landowners could sell farms to them, but more because of the reason advanced by Governor Gooch of Virginia in 1738:

[13] P. A. Bruce, *The Virginia Plutarch*, I, gives a sketch of Sir William Berkeley, 71–86, and a good account of the rebellion in a sketch of Bacon, 86–102.

[14] Carl S. Driver, *John Sevier*, 79–98, gives an excellent brief account. The standard work is Samuel Williams, *The Lost State of Franklin*.

[15] N. S. Shaler, quoted in M. J. Moses, *The Literature of the South*, 12.

[16] A. H. Hirsch, *The Huguenots of Colonial South Carolina*. Scholarly and adequate, with an extensive bibliography.

[17] John Donald Wade, *John Wesley*, 63–81, shows the influence of the Moravians on Wesley.

that the Presbyterians would serve as a buffer between the seaboard and the Indians.[18]

Since it influenced the leaders primarily, and through them
permeated in diluted form the thought of most men, the influence of deism[19] and rationalism in the latter part of the eighteenth century was important, although not so important as it
was in the Middle Colonies; it contributed, along with the
views of the Presbyterians, Baptists, and Methodists, to American independence and to the separation of church and state
in the new republic.[20] Not until Revolutionary days did these
sects and these philosophies displace the established church,
but they did succeed in helping to make it conservative and
lifeless.[21] While Cotton Mather wrote his four hundred books,
and Puritan divines produced before 1750 a body of work tremendous in volume and not unimpressive in quality, the

[18] Moses, *op. cit.*, 9. See also H. J. Eckenrode's *Separation of Church and
State in Virginia from 1776 to 1861*, especially chap. III, "The Dissenters."
Although the Presbyterians had opened the way for religious freedom,
they became relatively conservative after the Revolution, and the Baptists of the piedmont and tidewater sections embodied the chief threat to
the established order.

[19] G. A. Koch, *Republican Religion: The American Revolution and the
Cult of Reason;* H. M. Morais, *Deism in 18th Century America.* Morais remarks, wisely, that not all Jeffersonians were deists, nor all Federalists
orthodox (p. 144); W. D. Gould, "The Religious Opinions of Thomas
Jefferson," *Mississippi Valley Historical Review*, XX, 191–209 (1933).

[20] For scholarly studies, see C. H. McIlwain's *The Struggle of Prot-
estant Dissenters for Religious Toleration in Virginia*, and especially Wesley
M. Gewehr's excellent *The Great Awakening in Virginia, 1740–1790.* The
latter proves that by 1785 the Baptists, Presbyterians, and Methodists were
the most powerful religious factors in the state, that they were the most
ardent of the revolutionists, and that it was their support which secured
the passage of Jefferson's Bill for the Establishment of Religious Freedom.
It is important to remember that dissenters were influential in the South
as well as in the North.

[21] Phillips, *op. cit.*, 30, writes: "Despite the Bacchic lives of some of the
clergy, the Anglican church was a dignifying influence." Note, however,
Monroe's opinion as expressed in a letter to Bradford, of Philadelphia, in
April, 1774: "That liberal, catholic, and equitable way of thinking, as to
the rights of conscience, which is one of the characteristics of a free people,
and so strongly marks the people of your province, is little known among
the zealous adherents to our hierarchy." (Quoted by Moses, *op. cit.*, 10.)

12 Episcopalians wrote almost nothing; it is perhaps not without significance that today men blame many of our evils upon the Puritans, but neither blame nor praise is given to the Episcopalians.

The Puritan also had turned to education as one form of betterment and had founded schools. The Southern gentleman preferred to educate his children at home under supervision of a tutor, and then to send his sons to England for college or legal education.[22] There was considerable opposition to free schools. Governor Berkeley in 1670 had expressed the dictatorial spirit regarding education, when he declared: "I thank God there are no free schools nor printing [in Virginia], and I hope we shall have none these hundred years, for learning has brought disobedience and heresy and sects into the world, and printing has divulged them and libels against the best of governments."[23] Schools and newspapers soon became common enough,[24] but the true Southerner continued to look to England for his education, when the family's resources would permit.

Education in newly settled regions was of necessity fragmentary. Thus John Marshall received almost no formal schooling until in 1780 he temporarily left the army to study law for six weeks under George Wythe, the greatest lawyer in Virginia, at William and Mary.[25] And Wythe, although called by Thomas Jefferson the best Greek and Latin scholar in Virginia, was entirely self-educated. Fairly typical of the education given to sons

[22] Moses, *op. cit.*, 101–6. See also Isaac S. Harrell, *Loyalism in Virginia.*
[23] Frequently quoted; here taken from Gordon, *op. cit.*, 33.
[24] Bruce, *op. cit.*, I, 75, states that free schools then existed in Symmes and Eaton, less than a day's ride from Richmond. Apparently the first newspaper established in Virginia was *The Virginia Gazette*, published by William Parks at Williamsburg in 1736. The first college, William and Mary, was founded in 1693.
[25] A. J. Beveridge, *John Marshall*, I, 42–4, 148–55. Books were difficult to transport into the frontier regions. The only books known to have been in Thomas Marshall's library were the Bible and the works of Alexander Pope, although Justice Story thought he owned Milton's, Dryden's, and Shakespeare's works. Before he was twelve, John had copied every word of Pope's *Essay on Man.*

of well-to-do planters was that given to Jefferson. His father was almost entirely self-taught, but Peter Jefferson was a capable mathematician who enjoyed the works of Addison, Swift, Pope, and Shakespeare, and desired that his son have a classical education. Thomas was educated in private English and Latin schools conducted by clergymen until in 1760 he entered William and Mary. Then he studied law under Chancellor Wythe. His nephew, Peter Carr, went to Edinburgh; Thomas Randolph to France.[26] Over and over these stories could be repeated in the lives of other men. In the years that followed came the gradual founding and development of state and sectarian universities. Schools like the universities of Virginia and of North Carolina gained a favor which did not extend to elementary public schools, however, until the nineteenth century, and in most Southern states not until after the Civil War.[27]

The Southerner largely copied the educational system of England. Equally he looked to England for his literature. The seventeenth-century Southerner read the Elizabethan dramatists and the Restoration wits; in the eighteenth century his

[26] Jefferson's correspondence is a mine of information about every phase of life in the South, and is especially useful with regard to education and reading. His admiration for Wythe was unbounded. He wrote some notes to John Sanderson for a sketch of Wythe (*Memoirs . . .*, ed. T. J. Randolph, I, 91–4), and he was frequently sending Wythe editions of Latin or English books. Jefferson's ideas on education are discussed, and significant essays collected together in appendices, in R. J. Honeywell, *The Educational Work of Thomas Jefferson*, and C. F. Arrowood, *Thomas Jefferson and Education*. Of particular interest is the reading list which Jefferson prepared for his nephew Peter Carr (*Writings*, ed. A. A. Lipscomb, V, 82–7). A partial list of the authors recommended includes: Herodotus, Thucydides, Xenophon (Anabasis), Vergil, Anacreon, Theocritus, Homer, Plato, Cicero (all to be read in the original), Milton, Shakespeare, Ossian, Pope, and Swift. Jefferson prepared equally detailed plans for Madison, Monroe, Bernard Moore, his grandson, and others. For Jefferson's own reading, see G. Chinard's *The Literary Bible of Thomas Jefferson* and *The Commonplace Book of Thomas Jefferson*.

[27] See Honeywell and Arrowood, as noted above; Honeywell gives an excellent bibliography. Also H. B. Adams, *Thomas Jefferson and the University of Virginia*, which includes sketches of other Virginia colleges. The best treatment of the development of elementary education is E. W. Knight's *Public Education in the South*.

descendants turned to Dryden, Pope, Fielding, Swift, Johnson, and Goldsmith. More and more, however, the planters and lawyers studied the works of the philosophers, of Hume and Hooker and Harrington and, particularly, Locke. As men became more interested in governmental theory they tended to abandon *belles-lettres* and to concentrate upon political philosophy.[28] The lawyer and the plantation-owner were alike respected; men returned from London or Princeton to sit under Chancellor George Wythe of Virginia,[29] and receive a training at once broad and intensive. Such training took for granted a thorough knowledge of Latin literature: a man was expected to quote his Horace or his Cicero as readily and correctly as his Locke or Pope.[30] This development was natural enough in regions controlled by the aristocracy. The frontier regions at once emulated it and revolted against it; the struggles of Patrick Henry against privileged classes in Virginia is best known, but his attitude and his contentions could be matched in every other colony.[31]

[28] A. C. Gordon, Sr., "Some Lawyers in Colonial Virginia," in *Men and Events*, 91–113; see also Chinard, *op. cit.*

[29] John Sanderson, "George Wythe," in *Biography of the Signers to the Declaration of Independence*, II, 175–6. These men included Jefferson, John Marshall, James Madison, and Henry Clay. Jefferson, in 1787, advised Thomas Randolph to remain in France until he completed his study there, to make a tour of Europe, and "return then to Virginia and pass a year in Williamsburg under the care of Mr. Wythe, and you will be ready to enter on the public stage, with superior advantages." (*Writings*, ed. P. L. Ford, IV, 405.) At that time Peter Carr was studying under Wythe.

[30] A. C. Gordon, Jr., *op. cit.*, 73, relates this anecdote about Wirt, taken from J. P. Kennedy's *Life of Wirt:* that two lawyers, Hay and Wickham, were opposed to each other, and Wickham trapped Hay in a dilemma. Wickham remarked: "The gentleman may take whichever horn he pleases." Jock Warden, another lawyer who knew Hay's hasty temper, remarked "Take care of him; he has Hay upon his horn." Wirt, appreciating Warden's classical witticism, drew upon Horace's satire for an impromptu quatrain:

> Wickham was tossing Hay in Court
> On a dilemma's horns for sport;
> Jock, rich in wit and Latin too,
> Cried "Habet fornum in cornu!"

[31] M. C. Tyler, *Patrick Henry*, 271–317.

The aristocratic yet acquisitive planter of the seventeenth century had largely been replaced by the lawyer. If William Byrd can be cited as the ideal of early Virginia and of the early South, equally can Chancellor Wythe be considered the ideal of the eighteenth century.[32]

The Revolution almost seemed to remove definite barriers. Before that time only three small areas were settled;[33] immediately after the war, wave after wave of men crossed the mountains. Along the eastern coast the farmer was pushed out or absorbed by the plantation-owner; he "found it of no advantage to live within hail of ocean-going ships; and most of those who owned tidewater farms sold them to neighboring planters and moved inland."[34] The Virginia planter depended upon tobacco, and would traffic with no middleman, but shipped directly to England; around Charleston and Savannah, in the rich indigo and rice—and later cotton—districts, there developed a system of marketing through towns. Geography caused the relative poverty of North Carolina, with its poorer soil and broken topography.[35] From these sections largely, after the Revolution, men moved into the west, and they sought, primarily, land. "The possession of land is the aim of all action, generally speaking, and the cure of all social evils among men in the United States."[36] By 1836 the South was formed, in so far as its human geography was concerned.[37] But the process of its settlement has less importance, as background for literature, than some of the conditions which arose in that process.

[32] Parrington, *op. cit.*, 28, 142. Jefferson wrote to Sanderson (*Memoirs*, ed. Randolph, I, 93): "No man ever left behind him a character more venerated than George Wythe."

[33] The best brief account of the settling of the South is in R. B. Vance, *Human Geography of the South*, chap. III.

[34] U. B. Phillips, *Plantation and Frontier*, I, 76. The documents in these two volumes are extremely valuable; in this connection, see the section on Migration, II, 185–201.

[35] Vance, *op. cit.*, 49, 56, 31–4.

[36] Harriet Martineau, *Society in America*, I, 292.

[37] Vance, *op. cit.*, 53. Arkansas was admitted as a state in 1836. Texas is here considered as Southwestern rather than Southern.

These new states, contrary to modern belief, were not unified either sectionally or nationally. Certain definable influences can be traced, certain beliefs and trends and ways of life. But this tracing results in over-simplification, when, as here, only the broad outlines can be drawn.[38]

The most important unit was the state. It took precedence over the nation, and men resigned from the United States Senate to serve as governors of their state. Even the state, in early days, was insufficient: John Sevier and his fellows west of the mountains, in 1785, calmly seceded from North Carolina and established the state of Franklin;[39] just as calmly, after Tennessee was admitted to the Union, its citizens proceeded to negotiate with Spanish governors of Louisiana in a manner little short of treasonable.[40] "These United States" was the term used, in its literal sense; Alexander Stephens employed a significant phrase when he wrote that Calhoun "would like to see this Confederacy abolished."[41] Yet this independence of states and localities can easily be overdrawn: it was a Tennessean who wrecked Nullification, and some of the bitterest foes

[38] Holland Thompson, "The Coming of Industry to the South," *Annals of the American Academy of Political and Social Science*, CLIII, p. 11, neatly contrasts the diverse elements in the ante-bellum South: "There was a South of the plantation, and of the upland farm; of the Coastal Plains and of the mountains; the South with lands almost incredibly fertile and the barren South where living was hard; the civilized South, and nearby the South ignorant and rude; the austere Calvinist South, and the South of romance; the haughty aristocratic South and the democratic South."

[39] Driver, *op. cit.*, 79–98. See also C. W. Alvord, "Virginia and the West: An Interpretation," *Mississippi Valley Historical Review*, III, and Thomas P. Abernethy, *From Frontier to Plantation in Tennessee: A Study in Frontier Democracy*.

[40] A. Henderson, "The Spanish Conspiracy in Tennessee," *Tennessee Historical Magazine*, III, 229–43. A valuable chapter on another phase of independent western citizens is J. S. Bassett's "Jackson and Burr," in his *Andrew Jackson*, I, 37–54.

[41] Quoted in George Fort Milton, *The Eve of Conflict*, 46. This belief in a confederacy, and of the supremacy of the individual state, is the thesis behind Stephens's *Constitutional View of the War Between the States*. In the first volume he shows definitely that a majority of the Constitutional Convention held this view.

of Nullification were South Carolinians.[42] "It is the North that has changed, and not the South, and the nationality that sits so easily upon us would have seemed ominous to the simpler world that determined the ideals of the Old Dominion. The southern mind has grown old-fashioned, but it is native and of long and honorable descent. It derived its singularity from the eighteenth century in which it took shape; and it retained the clear impress of its origins long after the eighteenth century had become an anachronism in America. . . . this political agrarianism, parochial in its outlook rather than national, suffices to explain the singularity of the southern mind in the eyes of a later industrialized America."[43]

Before the South did become a unified section (chiefly through the welding force of outside attacks made upon it, and even then less completely than is generally realized), it was influenced chiefly by three philosophies: of physiocratic agrarianism, developing through Jefferson; of imperialism which, under Calhoun, took the ideal of a Greek democracy; and of the frontier.[44] These divergent philosophies finally took shape to form the Southern mind, a political and economic mind which

---

[42] The fullest discussions of Nullification are D. F. Houston's *Nullification in South Carolina* and C. S. Boucher's *The Nullification Controversy in South Carolina*. Among the Unionists were J. L. Petigru, H. S. Legaré, and D. E. Huger. The best account of Calhoun's political philosophy can be found in Gaillard Hunt's *John C. Calhoun*. The reactions of various Southern sections are treated in A. C. Cole's *The Whig Party in the South* and E. P. Powell's *Nullification and Secession in the United States*.

[43] V. L. Parrington, *Main Currents in American Thought*, II, 3. It is a pleasure to record here my general indebtedness to Parrington's analysis of Southern thought (pp. 3–179). The divergence from his interpretation is plain enough and needs no particular commentary. Parrington's lack of personal knowledge of the South led him to overemphasize the plantation tradition, and to discount too much the continuing influence of Jeffersonian agrarianism; and he misunderstood the local causes which made Jackson a regional aristocrat but a national democrat. On physiocratic agrarianism, see also Dumas Malone, *Correspondence Between Thomas Jefferson and Pierre Samuel du Pont de Nemours, 1798–1817*, and G. Chinard, *Correspondence of Jefferson and Du Pont de Nemours*.

[44] *Ibid.*, 3–179. See also W. E. Dodd, *Statesmen of the Old South*.

liberals like William P. Trent partially misunderstood and called feudal.[45] He considered only the planters.

The superficial aspects of the life of the plantation owner are well-known. His tradition became in the hands of romancers the Southern tradition: a stately house surrounded by broad fields, with a dignified, goateed master and good-looking, capable mistress, with daughters at once beautiful, pure, and flirtatious, with sons wild yet noble, and with slaves contentedly working in house or fields. Here hospitality reigned supreme and good living was ennobled until it became an art.[46] Such is the novelist's conception of the South—a conception not without elements of truth.[47] But this picture omits from consideration the yeoman farmer; as John Spencer Bassett discerningly notes: "This class of men has received but little attention from those who have written of Southern society, and yet it was the backbone of that society. There was little that was ideal about such men. They were humdrum, but they were honest, pious, and substantial, and they were numerous."[48] Some

[45] W. P. Trent, *William Gilmore Simms*, 21–37. Trent wrote seriously that the South "ignored the fact that while Chivalry was a good thing in its day, modern civilization is a much higher thing" (p. 36). Aside from the very questionable truth of the general thesis involved here (and many would question the *fact* of the higher quality of modern civilization), his statement reveals a strong tendency toward over-simplification, and a concentration upon the superficial aspect of Southern planters who revived Governor Spottswood's "Knights of the Golden Horseshoe," and it neglects the political and social ideas which evolved in the South. That mind was definitely conservative, but, as Parrington reveals, it was conservatism based on definite philosophies of life.

[46] F. P. Gaines, *The Southern Plantation*, 1–5. Gaines's sharp and interesting contrast between the plantation life of tradition and that of reality has clarified many problems concerning the Old South.

[47] *Ibid.*, 143–236. Parrington, *op. cit.*, II, 29: "It is not so much that the worst did not get into the romantic tradition—shortcomings in Virginia life which even Wirt hints at—as that the best did not get in. The plantation master of the romantics falls grossly short of the reality that Virginia provided. The simple dignity of John Taylor, the ingrained Puritanism of Lee and Jackson, the Catholic culture and fine integrity of George Wythe, have been left out of the tradition. The Virginian created by the romantics is absurdly inferior to such men. . . . "

[48] J. S. Bassett, *Slavery in the State of North Carolina*. His third chapter gives an excellent account of the power of the yeoman farmer. That

owned a few slaves; more of them worked their fifty or one hundred acres entirely by themselves; they shaded, as a class, from small plantation owners to poverty-stricken farmers. With the exception of the mountaineers, however, all of these men were distinctly Southern in sympathy, when war came. The reason for that attitude must be traced to the heritage of Jeffersonian agrarianism[49]—a heritage which did much to form the mind of the South.

The political idea of democracy had evolved in American minds primarily from John Locke;[50] the economic and later political doctrine of the South came largely from Quesnay and the French Physiocrats. Although Franklin introduced physiocratic agrarianism to this country, Jefferson first gave the philosophy a wide currency among a receptive audience[51]—and

Southern people could be divided into three classes—planters, poor whites, and slaves—has long been proved false. Nearly six of the eight million whites in the South owned no slaves, but relatively few were desperately poor. These shadings are well described in Phillips, *Life and Labor in the Old South*, chap. VIII ("The Plain People"). But no better appraisal of the Southern middle class can be found than D. R. Hundley's *Social Relations in Our Southern States* (1860), 121: "As we view it, respectability is one thing and gentility or fashion quite another. It is respectable to labor . . . but where, we should like to know, is it considered genteel or fashionable." His book is an invaluable record of ante-bellum life and thought.

[49] See D. H. Gilpatrick, *Jeffersonian Democracy in North Carolina, 1789–1816*.

[50] Carl Becker, *The Declaration of Independence*. H. J. Eckenrode, *The Revolution in Virginia*, argues that the Revolution in the South was in origin more political than economic. See also Edward McCrady, *South Carolina in the Revolution, 1775–1783*. That democracy and equality were not the same, and that controlling classes intended to stay in power, is shown in C. A. Beard's *The Economic Origin of the Constitution*. Particularly useful for its study of the use of Locke's works as textbooks in American colleges is P. E. Aldrich's "John Locke and the Influence of His Works in America," in *Publications of the American Antiquarian Society*, April, 1879, pp. 22–39. Locke was by no means the sole influence; for Richard Hooker's influence, see C. M. Gayley's misleadingly titled work, *Shakespeare and the Founders of Liberty in America*, chap. V, "Richard Hooker, and the Principles of American Liberty."

[51] C. A. Beard, *The Economic Origins of Jeffersonian Democracy;* well summarized in regard to Jefferson's thought in Parrington, *op. cit.*, II, 10–19. Valuable general material can be found in Gide and Rist, *History*

in John Taylor of Caroline he found an agrarian economist who could elaborate and expound this doctrine. Briefly, the Physiocrats believed that "agriculture is the single productive form of labor, that from it alone comes the *produit net* or ultimate net labor increment,"[52] and that all manufacturers and middlemen are parasites. But Jefferson and his followers rejected the benevolent despotism advocated by the French philosophers, and replaced it with the more congenial idea of democracy. To this he added "the doctrine of the terminable nature of contract," a doctrine which he amplified to include the view "no society can make a perpetual constitution, or even a perpetual law."[53] In this was the origin of the theory of states' rights; in this can be found one of the germinal ideas which later governed Southern thought. Long before slavery became an issue, John Taylor in 1814 pointed out that there was created "a fundamental conflict between the capitalistic and agrarian interests which was the origin of parties in the United States."[54]

This agrarianism was never abandoned; it remained a determining factor in Southern thought. But it was elaborated

---

of *Economic Doctrines* (trans. Smart and Richards), and in G. Weulersse, *Le Mouvement Physiocratique*.

[52] Parrington, *op. cit.*, II, 11.

[53] Quoted, *ibid.*, II, 12.

[54] A summary of Taylor's ideas, in C. A. Beard, *op. cit.*, 351. Beard thinks Taylor's *Inquiry into the Principles and Policies of the Government of the United States* "among the two or three really historic contributions to political science which have been produced in the United States" (p. 323). A remarkable analysis of Taylor's thought and its influence is Andrew Nelson Lytle's "John Taylor and the Political Economy of Agriculture," *American Review*, Sept.-Oct.-Nov., 1934. See also H. H. Simms's comprehensive *Life of John Taylor: The Story of a Brilliant Leader in the Early Virginia State Rights School*, and B. F. Wright's "The Philosopher of Jeffersonian Democracy," *American Political Science Review*, XXII, 870 ff. (1928). Other relevant scholarly studies on frontier and agrarian influences in the South are V. W. Crane's *The Southern Frontier, 1670–1732*; C. H. Ambler's *Sectionalism in Virginia from 1776 to 1861*; U. B. Phillips's "The South Carolina Federalists," *American Historical Review*, XIV; W. A. Schaper's "Sectionalism and Representation in South Carolina," *American Historical Association Annual Report*, 1901, I; Henry M. Wagstaff's *State Rights and Political Parties in North Carolina, 1776–1861*.

and subtly transformed until the ideal of a Greek democracy replaced the humanitarian Virginia concept of Jeffersonian democracy, and the definite belief in the right of a state veto replaced the looser idea of a terminable contract. This was largely the work of two political philosophers—John C. Calhoun and Alexander H. Stephens—who rationalized the position of the South, and gave to that section a clear-cut philosophy. When slavery, after 1820, became too profitable to be voluntarily exterminated,[55] and added this economic factor to equally vital philosophic considerations, Calhoun shifted the argument to democratic imperialism, which denied the natural rights theory of the Declaration of Independence, and held that democracy is possible only in a society which recognizes inequality as a law of nature. Liberty was "a reward to be earned, not a blessing to be gratuitously lavished on all alike."[56] Calhoun also distrusted the merchant class, and he argued with sustained logic that slavery was preferable to wage servitude. To the "checks and balances" in the Constitution he added also the checking power of each state, and it was on this principle that South Carolina attempted Nullification. Logically, also, he turned to a strict construction of the letter of the Constitution, for he argued that "Two powers are necessary to the existence and preservation of free States: a power on the part of the ruled to prevent rulers from abusing their authority, by compelling them to be faithful to their constituents, and which is effected through the right of suffrage; and a power to compel the parts of society to be just to one another, by compelling them to consult the interest of each other—which can only be effected . . .

---

[55] Vance, *op. cit.*, 177–204, gives a clear picture of the rise of "The Cotton Economy." Not only the invention of the cotton gin (1793), but improvements in manufacturing made possible the growth of cotton economy, and the rise of "King Cotton."

[56] J. C. Calhoun, "A Disquisition of Government," in *Works*, I, 55. Interesting contemporary essays by a man not always sympathetic with Calhoun are H. S. Legaré's "The Democracy of Athens" and "The Public Economy of Athens," in his *Writings*, I, 367–442, and II, 502–58.

by requiring the concurring assent of all the great and distinct interests of the community to the measures of the Government."[57]

This ideal of Greek democracy, with its center in the plantation system, ran counter to frontier influence. For the constantly moving frontier was in a state of flux, which led men into contradictory positions. Thus, Andrew Jackson was instantly willing to disregard the orders of the federal government, when he attacked Florida;[58] he said of John Marshall's decision on the Georgia Indians that "he has made his decision, now let him enforce it,"[59] but he also delivered the famous toast that the union must be preserved.[60] Lawless and law-abiding, according to the particular question at issue—such was the frontiersman. And Jackson, who is confusedly regarded as a democrat, illustrates another point: there were several kinds of democracy on the frontier. Jackson represented the acquisitive landowning class, the gentry; he was never one of the "wool-hat

---

[57] Calhoun, *Works*, VI, 189–90.

[58] James Parton, *Andrew Jackson*, I, 618–26. Parton's biography, though old-fashioned, is still the best life of Jackson. J. S. Bassett's *Andrew Jackson* is generally reliable, and C. G. Bowers's *Party Battles of the Jackson Period* is valuable for clearing up the political struggles, but weak on the philosophical ideas back of those struggles. The latest biographer (Marquis James, *Andrew Jackson, the Border Captain*) gives a fine picture of Jackson as man and soldier—but James's historical background is shaky and unreliable.

[59] Bassett, *Andrew Jackson*, II, 690–91. It is not certain that these words were uttered by Jackson; they were credited to him by Horace Greeley, *The American Conflict*, I, 106. Certainly Jackson did refuse to execute the judgment of the Supreme Court, which left the Cherokees at the mercy of Georgia, and led to their deportation to western Indian lands in 1835–38. One defense made by Jackson was that he had received Monroe's orders.

[60] A. S. Colyar, *Andrew Jackson*, II, 709–11, gives a dramatic account of Jackson's toast: "Our Federal Union—it must be preserved." But Calhoun's response stated the position of many Southerners: "The Union—next to our liberty the most dear—may we all remember that it can only be preserved by respecting the rights of the states, and distributing equally the benefit and burthen of the Union." Martin Van Buren, *Autobiography*, 415, says that R. Y. Hayne caused the insertion of the word *Federal* after the toast had once been delivered.

boys."[61] The democratic frontiersman is better personified in
David Crockett,[62] the opponent of Jackson on the Public Lands
question. Although Jackson might seem, and be, nationally the
defender of the plain man, his real philosophy was that of the
land speculator and frontiersman grafted on to the agrarian
beliefs of Thomas Jefferson.[63] His attack upon the National
Bank was a direct attack upon consolidation of government,
upon the growing power of capitalism. In that respect he
agreed (though he probably would never have admitted such
agreement) with Calhoun and South Carolina, but Jackson and
the frontier generally never recognized the true basis of contention. And by 1836 the frontier had progressed westward beyond the boundaries of the South. A new question came then
to plague Southern leaders: what would happen, in a government run by a numerical majority, when the South had become
a hopeless minority?[64]

Slavery, right or wrong, was ever-present, and it offered a
convenient moral weapon with which to attack the South. But
the basic conflict was between diverse systems—and the Civil
War, eventually, was not fought over slavery. That was only
a superficial cause, but its tangibility, in the propaganda of

[61] The term used here was a common one on the frontier and in the gulf
region. Phillips, *op. cit.*, 350, gives as partial equivalents elsewhere "Tar
Heel in North Carolina, hill-billy, red neck in the gulf region." One biographer of Jackson, Gerald W. Johnson, subtitles his work "An Epic in
Homespun." Nothing could be farther from the truth; Jackson was a frontier gentleman, and fought duels according to the code to prove it. A good
portrayal of the shifting status of individuals on the frontier can be found
in Abernethy, *op. cit.*

[62] Constance Rourke's *David Crockett*, although intended for children,
gives the best account of Crockett. He was in every way representative
of the frontier, except in his friendliness for the Indians. His opposition
to Jackson on the Public Lands question expressed the general sentiment
of the frontier, to which Jackson in 1832 had mainly ceased to belong.

[63] Parrington, *op. cit.*, II, 145–52. But Parrington does not sufficiently
recognize the fact that Jackson also belonged to the ruling class, for all
his dislike of "aristocratical establishments."

[64] This fear was ever-present in the South from 1830 to 1861, and per-
vades the speeches of Southern congressmen, and the books by ante-
bellum writers. See Calhoun, *Works*, III.

abolitionists, made it appear to overshadow all other issues. The conflict developed out of two entirely different philosophies of government which in turn had evolved from different economic systems: narrowly and immediately, a conflict between local and national sovereignty; basically, a conflict between agrarianism and industrialism. The Southern mind was a conservative, agrarian mind; the small farmer and the large planter, the yeoman and the slaveholder, were eventually forced into the same position because their philosophies possessed definite elements of kinship, and were at complete variance with the philosophy of industrialism.[65] Always the Southerner remained loyal to the Union as he interpreted the Union, and Alexander Stephens late in life could truly declare that "no stronger or more ardent Union man ever lived than I was"[66]—but the majority of Southerners, like Stephens, thought of the country as a confederacy, and the majority also, like Robert E. Lee, felt that first allegiance went not to the nation but to the state.

A religious transformation came over the South after 1800— a change which can be traced partially to the Calvinistic beliefs of the Scotch-Irish. Men like Calhoun and Jackson were hard, upright, honest, unbending; they lacked pliability; they might break but never bend. Deism had ceased to be largely influential. Methodism had spread throughout the Old Southwest. Perhaps the Biblical defense of slavery (which led Alexander Stephens to write: "To maintain that Slavery is *in itself sinful*, in the face of all that is said and written in the Bible upon the subject, with so many sanctions of the relation by the Deity

---

[65] For a brief, forceful discussion from this point of view, see Frank L. Owsley's "The Irrepressible Conflict," in *I'll Take My Stand*. A. C. Cole's *The Irrepressible Conflict, 1850–1865*, containing elaborate bibliographies, is especially valuable for its survey of the social backgrounds in all their phases.

[66] Quoted in Parrington, *op. cit.*, II, 84. L. B. Pendleton's *Alexander Stephens* gives a good picture of this gentle slaveholder, brilliant political philosopher, and advocate of peace, who, as Vice-President of the Confederacy, acted as watchdog for states' rights in the new nation.

himself, does seem to me to be little short of blasphemous!")[67] completed this transformation of a cavalier religion into a puritanical religion. In Charleston, particularly, this attitude assumed a moral rather than a theological cast.

It made generally true the Southern contention that actual slavery was more civilized and decent than wage slavery. "There was clearly no general prevalence of severity and strain in that regime . . . little of the curse of impersonality and indifference which too commonly prevails in the factories of the present-day world where power-driven machinery sets the pace, where the employers have no relations with the employed outside of work hours."[68] The plantation was a community and that community was part of a stabilized order, a conservative way of life: if a man owned land and slaves, he accepted the personal obligation which such ownership imposed upon him and did not take refuge in an abstract relationship known as freedom. Not always, certainly; an imposing array of cases can be cited to show cruelty, mismanagement, illicit sexual relationships, and general lack of consideration for the Negroes. But an even more imposing list of exceptionally merciful masters can be drawn up, and there seems little reason to disagree with the verdict of Gaines that "In the large, the Negro who did his share of the work received a modest sufficiency of life's necessities and was not often subjected to any form of physical torture, either of punishment or of over-work."[69]

Most Southerners had, in truth, grown blind to the evils of slavery; gone were the days before 1810 when Southern leaders fondly hoped and expected that slaves could be emancipated. As a result of Abolitionist attacks and of Nat Turner's Rebel-

[67] A. H. Stephens, *Constitutional View of the Late War*, II, 83.

[68] U. B. Phillips, *American Negro Slavery*, 307. See also Gaines, *op. cit.*, 223–36. U. B. Phillips, "The Plantation as a Civilizing Factor," *Sewanee Review*, XII, 262 (April, 1904), says, "We find records of many instances where planters hired *Irish* immigrants to dig ditches and do other straining work."

[69] Gaines, *op. cit.*, 231.

lion,[70] they had been forced to defend their "peculiar institution," and they had developed a theory of government upon it. But that imperialistic theory was only superimposed upon the Jeffersonian theory of physiocratic agrarianism and of local sovereignty—and it is well to remember that the great majority of Southerners fought rather for agrarianism than for slavery, and that three states did not secede until Lincoln called for volunteers to invade the South.

The "irrepressible conflict" had been years in the making. In 1850 secession had seemed inevitable, and only a specious compromise held the Union together for a decade. The lines had become tautly drawn until Southern fire-eater and Northern abolitionist alike were ready for war. From the Southern point of view the ominous specter of the Republican party, with its strictly sectional policies, overshadowed all other matters and seemed to end a voluntary compact.[71] The immediate issue was clearly defined, the basic issue thoroughly beclouded, when in 1858 Abraham Lincoln delivered his famous "house divided" speech.[72] The following year the fanatical John Brown threw

[70] J. E. Cooke, *Virginia: A History of the People*, 485–6. In an uprising under Turner, August, 1831, fifty-five white persons were killed—mostly women and children. This uprising greatly changed the attitude of Southern people; Turner's rebellion is not given the significance it deserves by modern historians of the period 1830–61.

[71] George Fort Milton, in *The Eve of Conflict*, has brought forth much new material to show that war might have been avoided. The influence of Southern fire-eaters on Buchanan, the splitting of the Democratic party, and the conduct of Lincoln after his election were all unfortunate, even tragic; but whether war could have been prevented or not is questionable. A point often overlooked is that Lincoln would have been elected, because the electoral college voted by states, even if Douglas had received every vote cast for the three opponents of Lincoln.

[72] Effective politically, the speech was not inevitable true. Douglas spoke prophetically when he answered it on July 9th: "Uniformity is the parent of despotism the world over . . . [if Lincoln's plan is followed] then the States will all be slave or all be free; then the Negroes will vote everywhere or nowhere; then you will have a Maine liquor law in every State or none; then you will have uniformity in all things, local and domestic, by the authority of the Federal Government. But when you attain that uniformity, you will have converted these thirty-two sovereign, independent States

the South into a panic with his raid on Harper's Ferry. After Lincoln's election in 1860 seven states seceded and formed the Confederate States of America. Even then war might have been prevented or postponed, but the efforts of Douglas and Crittenden came to nothing while the president-elect and his party attended to their political fences.[73] In April, 1861, Fort Sumter was fired on. War had come.

The story of that war is too well-known to need retelling here.[74] The South began with high hopes of quick and complete victory, and the first year of conflict seemed to bear out these hopes. But it was the weaker section, and it was fighting a defensive war. Victories in Virginia were nullified by unspectacular but effective Federal campaigns in the west. Gradually the South was hemmed in, with one part—Texas, Louisiana, and Arkansas—cut off from the main body. The club of "King Cotton Diplomacy," confidently expected to force European intervention on the South's behalf, failed when England found our war a most profitable enterprise for her citizens.[75] Even the states' rights theory operated against the successful prosecution of the war.[76] After four years of dogged, gallant fighting General Lee surrendered at Appomattox, and the Confederacy collapsed.

The war had taken a horrible toll. While the North prospered and grew rich, the South served as battleground.[77] Men who had gone into war jubilantly lived to see houses and prop-

---

into one consolidated empire, with the uniformity of despotism reigning triumphantly throughout the length and the breadth of the land." (Milton, *op. cit.*, 312.)

[73] Milton, *op. cit.*, 522–44.

[74] An excellent one-volume account from the Southern point of view is Robert Henry's *The Story of the Confederacy*.

[75] Frank L. Owsley, *King Cotton Diplomacy*. This supplements, if indeed it does not replace, the older idea that dependence on Western wheat prevented European intervention.

[76] Frank L. Owsley, *States Rights in the Confederacy*.

[77] J. T. Adams draws in brief compass a fine contrast between the sections at the end of the war, in *The Epic of America*, 274–6.

erty destroyed, relatives and friends killed, and their section
ruined. In part this destruction was the natural result of the
war being fought on Southern soil; in part it was due to a deliberate policy of destruction on the part of men like General
Sherman, in his far-flung campaign, and like General Butler in
New Orleans.[78] Whether caused by military policy, as in
Sherman's case, or simply by unintelligent brutality, as in Butler's,
this deliberate destruction has left far more bitterness in its wake
than all the horrors of legitimate war.[79]

More horrible even than Sherman's march was reconstruction. Truly it deserves the titles of *The Tragic Era* and *The
Age of Hate*.[80] The Confederate soldiers had returned to raise
crops on lands sown with bullets, and to patch up twisted and
broken lives. The Negroes were free, but no provision had
been made for them. All was confusion. Then to sectional
despair was suddenly added a national confusion when John
Wilkes Booth assassinated Abraham Lincoln. Death removed
the one man who might have controlled the Republican politicians.[81] To his place succeeded an honest and capable Union-
ist Democrat, Andrew Johnson of Tennessee—but Johnson
had no power over Congress, and narrowly escaped impeach-
ment at its hands. Government became strictly a party affair,
the Southern states (the fact of whose secession the North had

[78] Henry, *op. cit.*

[79] Many personal incidents and illustrations of losses suffered by various
poets are given later, either in connection with their works, or in the
biographical sketches.

[80] Claude G. Bowers's *The Tragic Era* is a thoroughly documented and
vivid account of Reconstruction. George Fort Milton's *The Age of Hate*
deals with the same period, but his narrative is woven more closely around
the career of Andrew Johnson.

[81] One of the fascinating *Ifs* of history is what Lincoln might have done,
or been able to do. Adams, *op. cit.*, 285: "The vindictiveness of Stevens
and the fanaticism and egotism of Sumner combined to despoil the nation
of that peace which Lincoln would have brought." This seems much too
strong; Lincoln might have tempered the treatment greatly, but he was an
excellent politician and might have used an obvious advantage. For an argument that his assassination was greatly to the advantage of his reputation,
see Milton, *The Age of Hate*, chap. 1.

refused to admit) merely conquered territories to be governed by military rule until Congress decided that they could safely be re-admitted to the Union. Dominating that Congress were fanatical Thaddeus Stevens and vindictive Charles Sumner— party politicians bent primarily on keeping the Republican party safely in office.

The South was divided into military districts, and ruled by army generals. The local governments were taken over by white carpetbaggers, by Southern unionists who generally deserved their title of "scalawags," and by the freed Negroes. These men sat in legislative halls, represented their states in Congress, and made a travesty of government. Corruption was everywhere, until state and city debts became unbearable. Only the hooded terror of the Ku Klux Klan, under the leadership of General Nathan Bedford Forrest, held the carpetbaggers and Negroes partially in check.[82]   A temperate historian, not overkind to the South generally, has written: "There is no parallel for the situation in the history of modern civilized nations, and it is almost incredible that it occurred within our own country. No civilized victor was ever more ungenerous. The war had left the South prostrate; Reconstruction left it maddened."[83]

Hardly less irritating was the attitude of Northerners who meant to be kind. The spirit of the South must be changed; President Wayland of Brown University "regarded the South as 'the new missionary ground for the national school-teacher,' and President Hill of Harvard looked forward to the task for the North 'of spreading knowledge and culture over the regions that sat in darkness.' "[84] So Northern historians wrote *error* across the ideals of the lost cause, and Northern missionaries prepared to re-make one of the authentic cultures which this nation had possessed.

[82] The best account is W. L. Fleming's *The Ku Klux Klan*.
[83] Adams, *op. cit.*, 286.
[84] Frank L. Owsley, "The Irrepressible Conflict," in *I'll Take My Stand*.

Thus was born the "Solid South." Except for occasional periods when local emotions or economic conditions have caused it to split, the section has remained closely unified. The free Negro was as much of a problem as the slave: one experience of his political control was more than enough. And the South, generally, has remained agrarian; it has suffered, as it suffered before the Civil War, but in greater degree, from high tariffs and protectionist policies. But its life and society have grown increasingly complex. For ten years, after the war, little could be done by native men. Schools were founded by the new "missionaries," and businesses established by them. In that decade the one significant change in the section was the growth of cities.

The ante-bellum South had little need for cities. Farm and plantation were really small communities, almost entirely self-sustaining. But the dangers of Reconstruction forced men to band closely together, and towns grew mightily almost overnight. Since few men possessed money, a system of tenant-farming or share-cropping developed, with the farms taken over by Negroes or poor whites; in many cases the owner superintended the farm work by day and returned to town at nightfall. The sons of these men knew little of farming, and that little was unpromising. They tended to move from the towns to the rapidly developing cities.[85]

By 1880 the period of stagnation was over. If money could not be made from raising cotton or tobacco, it could from the manufacture of products from these crops. The South must be revived, men said, "not with cotton in the fields, but cotton in the mills."[86]

[85] A. M. Schlesinger, *The Rise of the City*, 1–22 (a work containing valuable critically annotated bibliographies); E. W. Parks, "Southern Towns and Cities," in *Culture in the South*, 501–18.

[86] Holland Thompson's *From the Cotton Field to the Cotton Mill* gives an excellent account of the growth of this spirit, especially in North Carolina; see also Broadus Mitchell, *The Rise of Cotton Mills in the South*.

Cities sought eagerly for these new industries. New towns like Birmingham were founded, with the development of coal and iron ore as their main objective.[87] At first these industries were financed by local men, and their progress seemed heart-breakingly slow. But, significantly, they were founded to utilize local products, chiefly tobacco and cotton and iron ore, and they might have grown integrally out of the structure of society. These industries succeeded so well that Northern capitalists, like Northern missionaries of twenty years earlier, became interested. Andrew Carnegie and his competitors bought into the Alabama iron industries, and capitalists invested in new industries in many places.[88]

By 1900 the period of self-development had largely passed and the era of exploitation had begun. But long before that time two schools of thought contested for supremacy in the South: the old school conservative and agrarian, the new school progressive and industrialistic. The composite mind of the South since the Civil War has been torn between these two philosophies, but it has turned more and more to the group which advocates the development of industrialism.

A term was coined by the progressive leaders: "The New South." There had been an old South of slavery and secession, but that, said Henry Grady, was dead.[89] A new order had come, a new and better way of life. If only his section could be awakened from its lethargy, if only it would become progressive and industrialized, then all would be well and prosperity would come again. Grady's early death soon silenced his prophetic voice, but able men were not lacking to carry his message. Publicists like Walter Hines Page excoriated the "Southern

[87] Birmingham was founded in 1871, and intended from the beginning as a manufacturing town. (Holliday, *The Story of Birmingham*.)

[88] Schlesinger, *op. cit.*, 12–15. He writes without intentional irony that "It was only after the path had been blazed and the certainty of profits demonstrated that Northern investors began to show an active interest."

[89] Henry Grady, "The New South," in J. C. Harris, *Life of Henry W. Grady, Including His Writings and Speeches*.

mummies" who were stubbornly agrarian—which in his eyes
meant backward—in thought. In 1879 he wrote an article
called "An Old Southern Borough."[90] He portrayed a sleepy
North Carolina town inhabited by Southern gentlemen, living
in the past, unconscious of the present. They read Horace,
Vergil, Addison; above all, they read Sir Walter Scott, and continued, as their fathers had done, to pattern their conduct on his
bookish notions of chivalry. In contrast to these idlers, Page
pictured the new order which had arisen; young men who
advocated a burial of dead issues, a united country. These
young men envisioned a South cured of all its troubles by three
agencies: education, industrialism, and science. That message
Page hammered home relentlessly, in articles and editorials, even
in a novel which is no more than propaganda. Nicholas Worth[91]
was confronted by three ghosts which dominated Southern
life: the ghost of the Confederacy, the ghost of religious ortho-
doxy, the ghost of negro domination. In the end he abandoned
teaching and politics to manage a cotton mill, convinced that
the salvation of the South depended on economic progress—
which in life, as well as in Page's mind, was most often synony-
mous with mere activity.

 Grady and Page are here used as representative of a powerful
school of thought in the South. They did much to call attention
to the "Forgotten Man,"[92] to interest philanthropic and educational agencies in Southern problems, and most valuable of all,
to stimulate local activity in many fields.[93] This stimulus led—

[90] W. H. Page, "An Old Southern Borough," *Atlantic Monthly*, Sept.,
1879.
[91] W. H. Page, *Nicholas Worth, Southerner*. A standard work is B. J.
Kendrick's, *The Life and Letters of Walter Hines Page* (4 vols.). For an
analysis of Page from the agrarian point of view, see E. W. Parks, "Judas
or Messiah," *Harvard Graduates' Magazine*, Sept., 1932.
[92] Page coined the phrase in a speech before the North Carolina State
Normal College for Women in 1897. One man in every four, he said, in
the South would receive no education, no chance in life; he was the South's
"forgotten man."
[93] Edwin Mims's *The Advancing South* gives an excellent account of this
development from the point of view of a liberal and progressive South-

as was inevitable in a world of men—to fully as much harm as good. The public school system, established in most states immediately after the Civil War, developed rapidly, but it came, as public school systems seem always to come, to spread factual knowledge more and more thinly as it touched a greater number of people, while it inexorably crowded out such excellent private academies as were established about the same time by men like W. Gordon McCabe in Virginia and Sawney Webb in Tennessee.[94] The classics were slightly taught, or not taught at all, in the schools; the reading of an educated and curious person in Nashville would not differ greatly from that of a person elsewhere. There was a certain lag in this as in other respects; men turned more slowly from Vergil and Shakespeare to Darwin (or to popularizers of Darwinian theory) and Dreiser—but they were, after all, human, and even the influence of a cultural tradition, combined with inertia, could not long hold them from the way of a world which came ever nearer to each man's doorstep. The benefits of science brought also the philosophic doubts which accompany that learning when it forsakes facts and becomes speculative. The impact of science upon religious thought led, contradictorily enough, to laws which denied the truth of evolution and at the same time to a loosening of the religious structure.[95] In short, the South as it lost its autonomy

erner. Of less value is Virginius Dabney's *Liberalism in the South*, but Dabney gives an unusually complete bibliography. Cf. J. H. Dillard, "Fourteen Years of the Jeanes Fund," *South Atlantic Quarterly*, July, 1923.

[94] E. W. Knight, *Public Education in the South*. The analysis of an intelligent Southerner who opposes the public school system is not without point; see J. G. Fletcher, "Education, Past and Present," in *I'll Take My Stand*, 114-5.

[95] Contrast such an article as O. K. Armstrong's "Bootleg Science in Tennessee," *North American Review*, Feb., 1929, with John Crowe Ransom's *God Without Thunder*. The Tennessee legislature in 1925 passed a bill prohibiting the teaching of the theory of evolution in the state schools; at the trial of John T. Scopes, with William Jennings Bryan assisting the prosecution and Clarence Darrow the leading lawyer for the defense, Scopes was convicted and fined $100. See also S. G. Cole, *The History of Fundamentalism*, and R. Maury, *The Wars of the Godly*.

became more like New York and Nebraska—as Atlanta tended to become more like New York City, Birmingham like Pittsburgh. Civilization and thought followed, though more slowly than in other sections, the American current toward urbanization, mechanization, and standardization.

The progressives, while always speaking reverently of the past, repudiated that past as rapidly as possible. But there were other men who saw that more than a war had been lost—that, in truth, a philosophy of life had been destroyed.[96] The geographic South was defeated, said Richard L. Dabney after Appomattox, but the spiritual South could yet be saved by a wholesale migration to Brazil. Not many men cared to go to that extreme, but men were not lacking who recognized that picturesque values (more easily discernible than philosophical values) were rapidly vanishing. Local colorists set about the task of preserving on paper the customs and idiosyncrasies of unstandardized localities. A Henry Grady could attempt to make the sections love each other, a Sidney Lanier could sing the paeans of a new and mighty nationalism in his "Psalm of the West,"—but a Thomas Nelson Page could see that this world around him was a grossly materialistic world, and he went back to one where abstract principles counted for less than personal relationships. Joel Chandler Harris, who with Grady had attempted to advance progress and reconciliation, came in his later years to doubt the value of that progress, came to doubt the application if not the inherent truth of the New South doctrine, "put business above politics"—and he turned to writing directly of neighbor-knowledge and of personal kindness and of all the intangible values which he had indirectly put into his stories of Uncle Remus.[97]

[96] J. D. Wade, "New Wine in an Old Bottle," *Virginia Quarterly Review*, March, 1935. In this excellent article, which relates to present conditions the beliefs of Dabney, Bledsoe, and Jones, Wade has clarified the psychological change which came over the South in the 1880's.

[97] J. D. Wade, "Profits and Losses in the Life of Joel Chandler Harris,"

Not all men were blind to philosophical values. In one mighty, old-fashioned sentence, C. C. Jones of Augusta struck to the root of the question: "Under the absurd guise of a New South, flaunting the banners of utilitarianism, lifting the standards of speculation and expediency, elevating the colours whereon are emblazoned consolidation of wealth and centralization of government, lowering the flag of intellectual, moral and refined supremacy in the presence of the petty guidons of ignorance, personal ambition and diabolism . . . not a few there are who, ignoring the elevating influence of heroic impulses, manly endeavour, and virtuous sentiments, would fain convert this region into a money-worshipping domain; and, careless of the landmarks of the fathers, impatient of the restraints of a calm, enlightened, conservative civilization . . . would counsel no oblation save at the shrine of Mammon."[98] These leaders were mainly old, bewhiskered, and indubitably clerical; they were of an age rapidly passing, Jeffersonian democrats in a nationalistic country fast abandoning both Jeffersonianism and democracy. Such men could readily be discredited with opprobrious titles like "professional Southerner." For allies they had, primarily, the patriotic organizations, and, queerly, the Populists; they had on their side, also, inertia. Inertia could be overcome; the patriotic organizations seemed also buried in the past; the Populists,[99] after several active campaigns which

American Review, April, 1933. The articles on Lanier as a nationalist, growing out of A. Starke's *Sidney Lanier*, are cited in the bibliography. Edwin Mims, *The Advancing South*, 23–7, interestingly contrasts Walter Hines Page and Thomas Nelson Page. The first extended study of local color in the South, in life and in literature, is E. W. Parks, *Charles Egbert Craddock: A Study of Local Color in the South.*

[98] From an address delivered in 1891; quoted with great disapproval by Virginius Dabney, *op. cit.*, 225–6.

[99] J. D. Hicks, *The Populist Revolt.* See also Florence E. Smith's *The Populist Movement and Its Influence in North Carolina*, a doctoral thesis summarized in *Abstracts of Theses*, University of Chicago Humanistic Series, VIII, 215–22 (1929–30). For the continuing influence of populism, and the present state of political thought in the South, see G. F. Milton, "Also There is Politics," in *Culture in the South*, 115–25.

brought the poorer whites into power in several states and which, briefly, seemed on the point of re-establishing again agrarian control, lapsed back into desuetude as the cities and industries increased in size and wealth and influence.[100]

Today, the South remains a battlefield of two surviving philosophies of life. The exponents of industrialism, here as elsewhere, range from ultra-conservative individualists to communists; the advocates of agrarianism from those who favor localized industrialism to men who disbelieve completely in industrialism. Only through the efforts of agrarianism does the South retain a flavor of individuality, an intangible but real unity which yet differentiates it from other sections of the country.

II. POETIC THEORY

In the period which preceded the Revolutionary War, few men in the South concerned themselves with literary theories or criticism. In that, as in the verse which they wrote, there was a satisfactory tradition at hand: the tradition of English classical verse. Men with profound and philosophical minds studied political theory; they expressed their reflections through the medium of prose. Poetry was a graceful accomplishment. At times a writer like the anonymous Gentleman might attack in rhyme the corruption of the Virginia drama, and buttress with his support the position held by his contemporary in England, Alexander Pope. The drama, thought the Gentleman, should be in the tradition of Shakespeare; he deprecated the clowns and harlequins who infested the stage, and he concluded vigorously:

> "From foreign Trifling and unmanly Tone
>   We turn to downright nonsense of our own."[101]

In the main, such ideas were accepted so implicitly that men felt

[100] The best survey of the South as it exists today is *Culture in the South*, edited by W. T. Couch. The articles cover in detail all the points discussed here, and many others.

[101] *Poems on Several Occasions, by a Gentleman of Virginia* (Facsimile Text Society, 1930), 28–30.

no need for stating them. Only one observation, long a commonplace, need be made: the manner was more important than the matter of poetry.

This concentration upon form was in time to lead to extended consideration of theories and philosophies of poetry; in the early days this conventional acceptance was in striking contrast with the bold analysis of government made by leaders throughout the colonies. The first serious study of prosody was not by a practicing poet, but by that intensely curious and many-sided thinker, Thomas Jefferson.

Jefferson's taste in classical poetry was catholic yet impeccable; his taste in English poetry—save for his temporarily overpowering passion for the works of Ossian—sound. But the reader of his historically important and intrinsically interesting "Thoughts on English Prosody"[102] quickly realizes that Jefferson's analysis is the work of a gifted, untrained enthusiast who has reversed the customary attitude: instead of approaching Greek and Latin prosody from a background of English study, he considers native poetry from the point of view of a classicist. This essay, addressed to Monsieur F. J. de Chastellaux, was probably written while Jefferson was Secretary of State; in a preliminary letter the author explains his earlier adherence to the classical system of scansion by long and short syllables arranged into regular feet, which he had taken for granted as constituting the harmony of English verse. Although this system was employed by Samuel Johnson as the basis for his views on prosody, it is incorrect. English prosody, he has come to think, depends rather upon emphasis and accent.[103]

---

[102] Thomas Jefferson, "Thoughts on English Prosody," in *Writings* (ed. Lipscomb), XVIII, 414–51. Jefferson's ideas of classical pronunciation and scansion, which have value here only in illustrating the classical background from which he judged English poetry, are expressed in a letter to John Adams, March 21, 1819, *op. cit.*, XV, 181–6. See also J. W. Wayland, "The Poetical Tastes of Thomas Jefferson," *Sewanee Review*, XVIII, 283 ff. (1910).

[103] *Writings* (ed. Lipscomb), XVIII, 416–8.

If this discovery was new to Jefferson, it was by no means unknown to earlier English writers. On this foundation he erects certain rules which are somewhat startling in their rigidity:

That the accent shall never be displaced from the syllable whereon usage hath established it is the fundamental law of English verse.

There are but three arrangements into which these accents can be thrown in the English language which entitles the composition to be distinguished by the name of verse. That is, 1. Where the accent falls on all the odd syllables; 2. Where it falls on all the even syllables; 3. When it falls on every third syllable. If the reason of this be asked, no other can be assigned but that it results from the nature of the sounds which compose the English language and from the construction of the human ear.[104]

The author provides for no exceptions. Since he was no poet himself, this omission is not surprising. His scansion of lines was at times decidedly erratic; his statements sometimes far-fetched, as when he writes that "the language of Homer enabled him to compose in verse of six feet, the English language cannot bear this."[105] But his observations were made at first-hand, they represented his independent thoughts on the subject. For that reason there is distinctive value in his conclusions that the accentual basis of English verse leads to the same threefold distribution to which the hypothesis of *quantity* had led Dr. Johnson: trochaic, iambic, and anapestic. His metrical analyses of these measures have little intrinsic value.[106]

Jefferson was primarily interested in technique from the reader's standpoint. The writers of poetry were equally interested in a philosophical quality, which they felt vitiated much of their work. Richard Henry Wilde slowly evolved a theory as to his country's literary sterility: America was too young

[104] *Ibid.*, 418.   [105] *Ibid.*, 442.   [106] *Ibid.*, 421–51.

for poetry. With its great forests, mountains, rivers, and towns, it had "matter that the eye and mind, heart, fancy, memory could dwell upon," but for the poetic mind "without human passion, action, thought, Nature however beautiful is void."[107] In his dedication to *Hesperia* (1867), Wilde expressed his idea directly: "Few write well, except from personal experience—from what they have seen and felt—and modern life, in America especially, is utterly commonplace. It wants the objects and events which are essential to poetry." A realistic romantic, he believed that no American could write successfully a story about a foreign country; he recognized his own limitation in "want of invention"; but, since he was above all a romanticist, he could not rid himself of longing:

> Could we our country's scenery invest
> With history or legendary lore,
> Give to each valley an immortal guest
> Repeople with the past the desert shore,
> Pass out where Hampdens bled or Shakespeares rest,
> Exult o'er Memory's exhaustless store,
> As our descendants centuries hence may do—
> We should—and then shall have—our poets too![108]

This strikes deeper than the frequent complaints of lack of intellectual stimulation and companionship, of lack of encouragement from an appreciative audience. These things Wilde attributed to his country's immaturity. Rather, his statements antedate the romantic criticisms of such men as Van Wyck Brooks and Randolph Bourne. For that type of mind which draws sustenance from tradition and even more from books, these criticisms have definite validity, but they have only partial truth.

Southern magazines, rapidly increasing in number, were

---

[107] Richard Henry Wilde, *Hesperia*, 5–8. Wilde's feeling about himself and his country are stated in the dedication and early stanzas with a restraint which only increases its pathos.

[108] *Ibid.*, 8.

constantly publishing poetry and criticisms of poetry. These magazines were mainly English in spirit, in content, and in format.[109] The distinctively American magazine evolved under the guidance of Edgar Allan Poe, but before and after his period of editorship there were able and solid journals. A fine example of this type was the *Southern Review*, under the editorship of Hugh Swinton Legaré, but the *Review* had several distinguished rivals. Legaré was an erudite critic, and in particular his review of William Cullen Bryant's poems has elements of importance.[110] For Legaré was the Samuel Johnson of Charleston, and his words carried authority with the Carolinian poets. In this work he praised simple, natural, precise language—"the language of people of this world such as they use when they utter home-bred feelings in conversation with one another around the fireside or the festive board, not the fastidious, diluted, inexpressive jargon used nowhere but in second-rate books, and called elegant only by critics of the Della Cruscan school. . . . As to that more various elevated, powerful, and imaginative diction—itself a *creation*, and the most dazzling of poetic creations—such as we read in Pindar and the Greek tragedians, especially Aeschylus—such as we see in many parts of Shakespeare, and in almost every line of Milton —there is none of it here."[111] To these sane words on diction, Legaré adds a brief analysis of the sonnet; Bryant's sonnets he thought good, but far from masterpieces. He concludes with a

[109] Lyon Richardson, *Early American Magazines;* F. L. Mott, *History of American Magazines to 1850;* D. K. Jackson, *Poe and the Southern Literary Messenger.*

[110] H. S. Legaré, "Poems by W. C. Bryant," *Southern Review*, VIII, 443–62 (Feb., 1832). Valuable for interpretation of Charleston literature generally, as well as for Legaré's critical ideas, are Linda Rhea's *Hugh Swinton Legaré, A Charleston Intellectual* (especially chaps. V and VI, which treat the *Southern Review*), and E. H. Eby's *American Romantic Criticism, 1815–1860*, a dissertation available at the University of Washington Library (chap. III is devoted to a study of the culture of Charleston as reflected in an analysis of Legaré's critical essays).

[111] Legaré, *loc. cit.,* 444–5.

significant statement of the value of poetry: "Decided poetic merit is a great desideratum, in the social character of our country. A most exalted merit it is—precious in itself, still more precious as an index of what is felt and thought by a people, and as tending to foster and to warm into enthusiasm all the sentiments that do most honour to human nature."[112]

Poetry itself Legaré thought "but an abridged name for the sublime and beautiful, and for highly wrought pathos." In the middle of an essay which defended classical literature against the claims presented by an advocate of science, Legaré defines poetry in the terms of romanticism:

... It is spread over the whole face of nature—it is in the glories of the heavens and in the wonders of the great deep, in the voice of the cataract and of the coming storm, in Alpine precipices and solitudes, in the balmy gales and sweet bloom and freshness of spring. It is in every heroic achievement, in every lofty senti-ment, in every deep passion, in every bright vision of fancy, in every vehement affection of gladness or of grief, of pleasure or of pain. It is, in short, the feeling—the deep, the strictly *moral* feeling, which, when it is affected by chance or change in human life, as at a tragedy, we call sympathy—but as it appears in the still more mysterious connection between the heart of man and the forms and beauties of inanimate nature, as if they were instinct with a soul and a sensibility like our own, has no appro-priate appellation in our language, but is not the less real or the less familiar to our experience on that account. It is these feel-ings, whether utterance be given to them, or they be only nursed in the smitten bosom—whether they be couched in metre, or poured out with wild disorder and irrepressible rap-ture, that constitute the true spirit and essence of poetry, which is, therefore, necessarily connected with the grandest concep-tions and the most touching and intense emotions, with the fondest aspirations and the most awful concerns of mankind.[113]

[112] *Ibid.*, 462. As examples of Legaré's literary theories see also his essays on "Lord Byron's Character and Writings," and "Byron's Letters and Journals," in *Writings of Hugh S. Legaré*, II, 356–410, 411–48.

[113] Legaré, "Classical Literature," in *Writings*, II, 25.

These words were not without effect on able young poets in Charleston.

William Gilmore Simms succeeded to the literary dictatorship which Legaré had held. His influence extended throughout the section, as editor of several successive magazines,[114] as well as author of highly popular novels, biographies, and poems. A small number of his critical articles were collected in *Views and Reviews;* an even larger number are yet scattered in the files of magazines no longer easily procurable. The sweeping range of his interests led him to edit *A Supplement to the Plays of William Shakespeare*, to consider for other writers "The Epochs and Events of American History, as suited to the Purposes of Art in Fiction,"[115] and, at one time or another, to express his views on critics, poets, literature, economics, and other subjects. At least one distinguished critical essay came from his pen; "The Writings of James Fenimore Cooper" deserved Bryant's praise: "A critical essay of great depth and discrimination, to which I am not sure that anything hitherto written is fully equal."[116] In his remarks on poetry scattered through his essays and letters, Simms was on the side of common sense: although he admired Poe's genius, he judged Poe as "bizarre, rather than great or healthful." His advice to Thomas Holley Chivers is a good summary of his theory: "Rhyme is the mere decoration of thought . . . mannerism is a fatal weakness . . . seek for simplicity and wholeness—avoid yourself in your topics—write no more

[114] These magazines are listed in W. P. Trent's *William Gilmore Simms*, 340–1: *The Southern Literary Gazette* (1828–29); *The City Gazette* (1830–32); *The Cosmopolitan, an Occasional* (1833); *The Magnolia, or Southern Apalachian* (1842–43); *The Southern and Western Magazine and Review* (1845); *The Southern Quarterly Review* (1849–55); *The Columbia Phenix* (1865); *The Daily South Carolinian* (1865–66); *The Courier* (1870). Simms was also for many years correspondent and reviewer, perhaps literary editor, of the *Mercury*.

[115] Simms, *Views and Reviews*, I.

[116] Quoted in Trent, *op. cit.*, 137. Trent barely mentions Simms's criticism, but Trent's biography was, obviously, done with great haste and small research.

elegies, and discard all pet words, all phrases—discard all attempts at mysticism. Be manly, direct, simple, natural,—full, unaffected, and elaborate."[117] This was sensible advice to a man who infrequently transcended common sense, but whose brief flights into the sublime made any reasonable counsel seem out of place and superfluous.

Simms's poetic theories are not intrinsically important, although in later life he would state his views with a Johnsonian arrogance which at least once offended the discriminating Timrod.[118] More important than his dogmatic ideas, however, was his warm and friendly encouragement to such young poets as Timrod, Hayne, and James Mathewes Legaré. If his ideas were often rather simple and occasionally mistaken, his influence in its totality was quickening and remarkably fine.

His theory of the novel is highly important; as he saw it, "the modern Romance is the substitute which the people of the present day offer for the ancient epic."[119] For his definitions he went back of Sir Walter Scott to that neglected but important chronicler of chivalry, Froissart.[120] Although Simms applied his theory primarily to the romance, it helps to explain some of his longer poems. This theory was shared—independently, it

[117] See Simms's letter to Chivers, in Appendix, p. 321; it is typical of his general attitude.

[118] Trent, *op. cit.*, 233–4: "Although Hayne does not assign a cause for the breach between the two writers [Trent quotes from a letter of Hayne's, February 9, 1860, asking Simms to review Timrod's poetry], it is easy to infer what the true cause was. Timrod was critical by nature, and Simms was vulnerable in many places. Timrod knew that he could write real poetry, while Simms could not, and it probably vexed him to hear the elder man airing his often crude views upon poetical subjects in his positive Johnsonian manner."

[119] Simms, Preface to *The Yemassee* (1853 edition), where his theory of the novel is very fully developed.

[120] It is one of the anomalies of graduate study in this country that there is in print an American dissertation on *Froissart's Influence on the English Chronicle Play*, but no study that I have been able to find on Froissart's influence on American thought. H. M. Jones's *America and French Culture* is excellent in its treatment of social and cultural relationships; his promised volume on literary relationships will be exceedingly valuable, in a field which has received little attention.

seems—by the Virginian Philip Pendleton Cooke, who applied it both to tales and poetry. Cooke entitled his one volume, significantly, *Froissart Ballads;* in the preface he states that he has been "as faithful to the text of Froissart as the necessities of verse permitted."[121] Highest praise from Cooke goes to the old minstrels and bards, the makers of lays, whose high art leads back to the ancient days, and who vivify the legends of Arthur, Robin Hood, and other nobly picturesque figures of chivalry. Unfortunately, neither Cooke nor Simms wrote a good poem in this *genre:* the theory was better fitted for the prose romance.

This summary glance at the most significant critical thought reveals a keen interest in the way of writing, as regards both philosophy and technique. All of it is pertinent and interesting: here, in embryo, are major questions which remain as open to discussion as they were in the days of Wilde and Legaré. In politics the Southerner of the old school tended to be a theorist and philosopher; in literature he was similarly occupied, although his achievements were not comparable. In this form, however, can best be discerned the duality of Southern intellect, the intermingling (if not the perfect union) of classical and romantic tendencies and thought.[122] The literary influence of

---

[121] Cooke, Preface to *Froissart Ballads.* Of interest in this connection is the poem "The Power of the Bards," and also this quatrain of Cooke's:

> A certain freak has got into my head,
> Which I can't conquer for the life of me,
> Of taking up some history, little read,
> Or known, and writing it in poetry.

Of interest, also, is the first installment of his "English Poetry" (*Southern Literary Messenger*, I, 397–401, 557–64; II, 101–6), in which he discusses the minstrels and makers of lays. Scott may have been partially responsible: in the *Edinburgh Review*, Jan., 1815, he has an article on Froissart, in which he writes (347), "history has less the air of a narrative than of a dramatic representation."

[122] The complex nature of the influences on Southern thought has been indicated in the previous section. Remarkable, if not inexplainable by the implications of this study, however, is the duality which caused H. S. Legaré, in the middle of an essay on classical literature, to stop his discussion and give a thoroughly romantic definition of poetry; which led the accomplished Latinist J. M. Legaré to write, in the same volume, one poem

nineteenth-century England was direct and immediate and powerful, as the poetry of the writers clearly shows; but almost equally powerful were the living books of long-dead Greek and Latin poets.

For all this preoccupation with theory, no critic developed a system or a philosophy which radically changed the thought of his own and succeeding ages, until Edgar Allan Poe helped to evolve for a changing culture a philosophy which was suited for it. It is well to remember that these men, after Jefferson, were all contemporaries, and most of them friends and correspondents; the work of one man might well influence another. Only Legaré can justly be termed a learned man, by the standards of that day; by our looser requirements, which rate education in terms of degrees without differentiation as to subject matter, all were erudite. They wrote in a style no longer popular; perhaps their thinking, like their phraseology, is out of date. In the final analysis this may reflect not on their age but on our own.

The views—or perhaps the rationalizations—of Wilde and Simms and Cooke have a sensible quality which make them easily understandable. Their limitations are apparent. If their universe differed from our own, it was well-ordered and coherent. Their contemporaries—Chivers and Poe—can not so readily be tagged and placed in tight compartments: although masters of rationalization, these two poets elude the comprehension of rational men. One has received but slight attention; the other has been the subject of countless articles and biographies which have generated far more heat than light. The critical ideas of Chivers are curious and fascinating, but they help to explain, mainly, the poetry of Chivers; the ideas of Poe help to adumbrate his age.

in Latin and another in the manner of Leigh Hunt's "Abou Ben Adhem"; which led Poe to write a good essay on the classics (*Southern Literary Messenger*, II), but to pronounce of Tennyson, "In perfect sincerity I regard him as the noblest poet that ever lived." These contradictions are typical of the temper of Southern romanticists.

Chivers's critical theories are remarkable, in language as well
as in ideas. He envisioned poetry as "that crystal river of the
soul which runs through all the avenues of life, and after
purifying the affections of the heart, empties itself into the Sea
of God. . . . Poetry is the power given by God to man of
manifesting these relations. . . . Poetry is the soul of his nature,
whereby, from communing with the beauties of this earth, he
is capable of giving birth to other beings brighter than himself;
and of lifting up his spirit to the presence of those things which
he shall enjoy in another state; and which he manifests to *this*
through the instrumentality of certain words and sentences
melodiously concatenated; and such as correspond with the
definite and wise configurations of the mouth in the communication of thought through language."[123] He goes beyond Sir
Philip Sidney, who wrote that a poet was by the Romans
"called *Vates*, which is as much as a Diviner, Fore-seer, or
Prophet";[124] to Chivers the poets are the "Revelators of the
Divine Idea through the Beautiful."[125] But Chivers could not
be content with simple expression of these transcendental ideas.
He clothed them in metaphorical words; he quoted from many
languages the various definitions of a poet, and of poetry, and
he considered how these definitions supported his own belief
in the divine nature of art and artist. He agreed with, and perhaps antedated, Poe in the statement that Milton's *Paradise Lost*
is too long a poem to be entirely pleasing, and is poetic only in
passages, "the others being only the relatively connecting links
of the whole. It is, therefore, obvious that the idiosyncratic
merits of any poet depend entirely upon the manner in which
he has realized his dreams of the *crystalline revelation of the*

[123] Chivers, Preface to *Nacoochee*. Part of this Preface is reprinted in the
Appendix, p. 325.
[124] Philip Sidney, "An Apologie for Poetrie," in Smith and Parks, *The
Great Critics*, 148. It is interesting to contrast Chivers's definition, also,
with that of Emily Dickinson.
[125] Chivers, Preface to *Memoralia;* see Appendix, p. 327.

divine idea."[126] But Chivers did not believe, with Poe, that a poem must necessarily be brief; indeed, this preface is to a poem which is intended to be at once epical, lyrical and symbolic, and "an experiment upon the minds of the Chosen Few."[127]

This poem, *Atlanta*, is an elaborate glorification of poetry. Damon writes, "Its symbolism hardly needs explanation. Man's finer self is stolen from him by his baser passions; but eventually he tricks them into serving him. All night they cross the inner sea; and with the dawn appears the Island of Poetry, where his ideal lives, still unblemished. In the glorious cave (the ageless symbol of the body, made famous by Plato) he perfects himself in union with his higher self, through the medium of complete love."[128] Mentally Chivers had, long before this was written, taken refuge in that island of poetry, as compensation for the defeats which he felt in the practical world; he prefaced several volumes with his lyrical theories, and he wrote Simms in 1852 that he would soon publish a volume which would give "an analysis of Poetry from its Gothic up to its Greek manifestations."[129]

This analysis was to be "a new thing under the sun"—as original as his poems, which were "all original." In truth, Chivers was in all that he did an original, in the old sense of that word, with its kindred meaning of eccentric. His critical ideas, however, if we can judge from his prefaces, are not precisely new; they can be traced in varying form in the works of older and more normal critics. Essentially they are romantic, but they are not the nonsense which a careless reading of Chivers's

---

[126] Chivers, Preface to *Atlanta*. Although S. F. Damon (*Thomas Holley Chivers*, 243) suggests this priority about Milton because Chivers's preface was written in 1842 (although not printed until 1853), it seems unlikely; as early as 1831 Poe had written that "men do not like epics. . . . I dare say Milton preferred Comus to either [*Paradise Lost* or *Paradise Regained*]—if so, justly."

[127] *Ibid.*

[128] S. F. Damon, *op. cit.*, 246. Damon's biography is invaluable to students of Poe as well as of Chivers.

[129] See Chivers's letter to Simms, reprinted in the Appendix, pp. 322 ff.

luxuriant phrases might lead one to suspect. He believed that the *existere* of a poem must be coeternal with its *esse*, that in every poem there are two beauties—the outward beauty of art, the inward beauty of nature or passion—that a poem which unites perfectly this body and soul is a pure poem.[130] Few critics would dispute this, any more than they would dispute Pope's dictum that the sound should be an echo of the sense. More debatable is Chivers's theory of the refrain: he saw it not as an ornament, or a vital part, but as "an essence—a life—a vitality—an immortal soul."[131] As a general theory, in the way in which Chivers meant it, this statement is nonsense; only when applied to the specialized type of poetry which Chivers wrote does it have any validity. Poe's words probably express all that the over-exuberant Chivers meant: "In carefully thinking over all the usual artistic effects—or more properly *points*, in the theatrical sense—I did not fail to perceive immediately that no one had been so universally employed as that of the *refrain*. The universality of its employment sufficed to assure me of its intrinsic value, and spared me the necessity of submitting it to analysis. . . . As commonly used, the *refrain*, or burden, not only is limited to lyric verse, but depends for its impression upon the force of monotone—both in sound and thought. The pleasure is deduced solely from the sense of identity—of repetition. I resolved to diversify, and so heighten, the effect, by adhering in general to the monotone of sound, while I continually varied that of thought: that is to say, I determined to produce continuously novel effects, by the variation *of the application* of the *refrain*—the *refrain* itself remaining, for the most part, unvaried."[132]

When compared with those of Chivers, Poe's critical theories seem a model of rationality. They are also, in part, rationaliza-

---

[130] Of value here are his letter to Simms and his Preface to *Memoralia*.
[131] Chivers, Preface to *Virginalia*, p. 332 following.
[132] Poe, "The Philosophy of Composition."

tions of their author's own creative limitations. Even more, they are an attempt to develop a theory which would be applicable to the magazine age.[133]

His belief that a poem must be "the rhythmical creation of beauty," without didacticism and largely without passion, was adapted precisely to his type of writing. Yet it is difficult to agree wholeheartedly with Joseph Wood Krutch that Poe's psychological limitations are basic causes for his theories.[134] With at least equal justice this thesis can be reversed, since as early as 1831 Poe (following his chief master in criticism, Coleridge, and barely paraphrasing one of Coleridge's most famous definitions) declared that "a poem, in my opinion, is opposed to a work of science by having, for its *immediate* object, pleasure, not truth; to romance, by having for its object an *indefinite* instead of a *definite* pleasure, being a poem only so far as this object is attained."[135] In this essay the young poet stated in embryonic form his philosophy of literature: only the poet could be a critic of literature; only the indefinite poem, not concerned with direct moral issues, could be truly beautiful. (Yet critics, on the basis largely of his poetry and tales, continue to speak of Poe as un-American.) Even his theory of the necessity for a poem's brevity was implied, in his remarks upon Milton and the epic.

[133] One of the most sensible essays on Poe as a reviewer is J. B. Moore's introduction to his *Selections from Poe's Literary Criticism.* See also H. S. Canby's essay on Poe in *Classic Americans;* D. K. Jackson's *Poe and the Southern Literary Messenger;* and E. Marchand's valuable study, "Poe as a Social Critic," *American Literature,* VI, 28–43 (March, 1934).

[134] Easily the most valuable section of J. W. Krutch's *Edgar Allan Poe* is the final chapter, "The Philosophy of Composition." Krutch brilliantly restates the theory that Poe's theories, like his works, can be traced to limitations in Poe.

[135] Poe, Preface to *Poems,* 1831. On Poe's indebtedness to Coleridge, cf. F. Stovall, "Poe's Debt to Coleridge," University of Texas *Studies in English,* X, 70–127, and Killis Campbell, *The Mind of Poe.* A valuable work, if used with caution, is M. Alterton's *Origins of Poe's Critical Theory.* Extremely valuable is the documented and carefully worked out study by M. Alterton and Hardin Craig in *Edgar Allan Poe* (American Writers Series, 1935).

Norman Foerster has given an excellent summary of Poe's artistic creed:

> The end of art is pleasure, not truth. In order that pleasure may be intense, the work of art must have unity and brevity. In poetry, the proper means of arousing pleasure is the creation of beauty; not the beauty of concrete things alone, but also a higher beauty—supernal beauty. Music is an indispensable element in poetry, and is especially valuable in the poet's straining toward the supernal, since music comes nearer this goal than any other art. In the prose tale, on the other hand, the artist may seek to produce effects other than those of poetry,—effects of horror, terror, passion,—limiting himself in each case to a single effect.[136]

This summary, founded mainly upon "The Poetic Principle," gives Poe's rounded and integrated theory; he has developed consistently the rather scrappy suggestions in his early preface—which, naturally, is inferior to "The Poetic Principle"—but, since so much nonsense has been written about Poe, it has an unusual value. There was nothing wishy-washy about the man's thought: he formed a tenable if definitely limited theory early in life; he developed and expanded that theory (although always within the same limits) until it became a consistent aesthetic.

Thus he did not deny truth as part of a poem, but held that truth as such—that is, truth with a moral—could better be dealt with in prose.[137] Humor he thought "antagonistical to

---

[136] Foerster, *American Criticism*, 6–7. A fine essay (1–51) which points out many of the weaknesses of romanticism, as well as of Poe himself.

[137] In "The Philosophy of Composition," Poe wrote: "Now the object Truth, or the satisfaction of the intellect, and the object Passion, or the excitement of the heart, are, although attainable, to a certain extent, in poetry, far more readily attainable in prose. Truth, in fact, demands a precision, and Passion a *homeliness* (the truly passionate will comprehend me) which are absolutely antagonistic to that Beauty which, I maintain, is the excitement, or pleasurable elevation, of the soul. It by no means follows from any thing here said, that passion, or even truth, may not be introduced, and even profitably introduced, into a poem—for they may

that which is the soul of the muse proper"; sadness combined with beauty "invariably excites the sensitive soul to tears. Melancholy is thus the most legitimate of all the poetical tones."[138] Poe's failure to recognize in metaphysical poetry any element of what he considered the essence of poetry, his denial even that it was poetry, is not surprising, although, undeniably, it is narrow: poet-critics have, in the main, consistently believed that only the verse which they have written is *poetry*.[139] This does not mean that the author of "The Raven," then, can be utterly trusted when in "The Philosophy of Composition" he rationalizes for himself and for the world the method by which that poem came into being; what it does mean is that the student who is not overly obsessed with Freudianism can gain from poem and criticism a valuable knowledge of Poe's ratiocination.

From Poe's theories, also, he can gain a knowledge of the aesthetic which was beginning to rule in that time, and which largely dominates in our own. Poe's distrust and dislike of epics was not accidental; he may have taken suggestions from Schlegel or Kames or Blair[140] that a poem should, to be effective, be reasonably short, but such suggestions were valuable only

---

serve in elucidation, or aid the general effect, as do discords in music, by contrast—but the true artist will always contrive, first, to tone them into proper subservience to the predominant aim, and, secondly, to enveil them, as far as possible, in that Beauty which is the atmosphere and the essence of the poem." As Lewisohn has noted (*Expression in America*, 161), Poe uses the word truth "as though it meant proposition, scientific statement, maxim or saw." But he follows this observation with a sweeping misstatement of what Poe expressed. For an excellent interpretation, see F. Stovall's "Poe as a Poet of Ideas" (University of Texas *Studies in English*, XI, 56–62) and "An Interpretation of Poe's 'Al Aaraaf'" (*ibid.*, IX, 106–33).

[138] Poe, *loc. cit.*

[139] I have seen no wiser statement on this than Henry Timrod's observation ("A Theory of Poetry," *Atlantic Monthly*, XCVI, 325): "A very little examination will generally prove that they [poetic theories] have grown out of the idiosyncrasies of the poets themselves, and so, necessarily, seldom attain a greater breadth than suffices to shelter the theorist and the models from which he has drawn his arguments and his inspirations."

[140] Alterton, *op. cit.*, 73–5.

because as seeds they lodged in fallow ground. Poe was integrally a part of his environment; he was by profession a magazine editor. Assuredly he was expressing his sincerest beliefs when he wrote:

The increase, within a few years, of the magazine literature, is by no means to be regarded as indicating what some critics would suppose it to indicate—a downward tendency in American taste or in American letters. It is but a sign of the times— an indication of an era in which men are forced upon the curt, the condensed, the well-digested—in place of the voluminous —in a word, upon journalism in lieu of dissertation. We need now the light artillery rather than the Peace-makers of the intellect. I will not be sure that men at present think more profoundly than half a century ago, but beyond question they think with more rapidity, with more skill, with more tact, with more of method, and less of excrescence in the thought. Besides all this, they have a vast increase in the thinking material. They have more facts, more to think about. For this reason, they are disposed to put the greatest amount of thought in the smallest compass and disperse it with the utmost attainable rapidity. Hence the journalism of the age, hence, in especial, magazines. Too many we cannot have, as a general proposition; but we demand that they have sufficient merit to render them noticeable in the beginning, and that they continue in existence sufficiently long to permit us a fair estimation of their value.[141]

In addition, he belonged to the romantic, the lyric, period. Expression of mood, of heart, of subjectivity in general do not make for sustained expression: at base these moods are thin and tenuous. When portrayed at length this tenuous thinness becomes definitely apparent. In this general connection Ludwig Lewisohn wrote that "the literary sterility of the South ceases, like that of many other problems, to have any problematic

---

[141] Poe, "Marginalia." These ideas run through most of Poe's correspondence and criticism.

character so soon as we attain to the true conception of literature as, on its lowest terms, the expression of an experience that
is differentiated from the experience of the social or tribal
group."[142] As a definition of romanticism—that type of
romanticism, in particular, of which Lewisohn is a modern
master—this definition can hardly be excelled. The germ of it
can be traced back to the Renaissance, and to the rise of protestantism. But as a conception of literature it is exceedingly
narrow, with its basic untruth immediately obvious. Insert the
word *modern*, however, before either *conception* or *literature*.
Then all is clear: the lyric, the subjective, the romantic—that
which gave rise to the cult of the genius—come into being.
The aesthetic of romanticism can be found only dimly in
Young and Wordsworth; the exegesis of that aesthetic was the
work of Coleridge and, after him, of Poe. In addition, it was
Poe's function to restate this aesthetic in the terms which were
to be almost universally employed by men who wrote for what
may be denominated a magazine-literature.[143]

Poe's theories on prosody are relatively unimportant,[144]

[142] Lewisohn, *Expression in America*, 78. This definition should be
enough in itself to expose the absurdity of that critical point of view which
Lewisohn represents.

[143] Alterton, *op. cit.*, 7–45, discusses Poe's indebtedness to *Blackwood's
Edinburgh Magazine* and other British periodicals, but she fails to make
clear that Poe's indebtedness was mainly negative, that what he chiefly
learned from them was how *not* to edit a magazine or at least how to im-
prove upon the editing. Of some value in this connection are Kenneth
Leroy Daughrity's "Notes: Poe and Blackwood's," *American Literature*,
II, 289–92 (Nov., 1930), and D. K. Jackson's *Poe and the Southern Literary Messenger*, but I have found no thorough study of Poe's aesthetic from
this point of view. It seems, in the light of traditional criticism, the most
sensible method to use in considering Poe's theories.

[144] W. L. Werner, "Poe's Theories and Practises in Poetic Technique,"
American Literature, II, 157–65 (May, 1930), thinks just the opposite: his
theories have been discussed "in generalities with little mention of technical
details. The result has been a handing down of four conventional statements about his theories of verse: that all poems must be short; that poetry
is close to music; that beauty is the chief aim of poetry; and that 'The
Raven' was the result of a logical process. All these ideas can be found by
looking no farther than two of Poe's best known critical essays, 'The
Poetic Principle' and 'The Philosophy of Composition.' These conven-

when compared with his theories on poetry. Even so, they are not to be dismissed lightly. His method of using the refrain has been quoted above; his insistence upon melody, as well as harmony, in a poem naturally led to employment of such devices as repetition and alliteration. Although he never carried his experiments in sound to the extreme which Chivers did, he was so fascinated with the "tintinnabulation" of word-sounds that in "The Bells"—with its reiterative rhymes, its assonance and alliteration, its parallelisms and refrains—he deserved Emerson's judgment of "the jingle man," for this experiment in onomatopoeia—in spite of the symbolism which suggests youthful pleasure, marriage, disaster, and death—descends to mere echolalia. Yet it is consistent with his theories that harsh consonants should never disturb the music of a line, and that poetry, generally, is "an inferior or less capable music." He was less consistent in his practice with regard to certain exceedingly strict rules he laid down: that in diction the poet should avoid archaisms, contractions, inversions; that rhymes should not be inexact, identical, or light; and that contractions or elisions are not permissible. Undoubtedly Poe's liking for mathematical certainty, combined with a desire to avoid the metaphysical aspects which he deprecated in Wordsworth and Coleridge,

---

tional opinions may be correct, but they are merely repetitions of Poe's own generalizations. They treat no problems of meter or of rime and other repetitions; they say nothing of inversions, archaisms, contractions, stanza forms, or any other items in which a short, musical, beautiful poem by Poe differs from a short, musical, beautiful poem by Longfellow or Whitman or Edna Millay." This is to miss the point completely (without here taking into consideration the obvious falseness of Werner's statement about "The Raven," or his curious idea of generalizations). Poe's philosophical ideas remain a part of our thought: his theory on beauty forms an integral part of the cycle which culminated with "art for art's sake," and which, in another form, has been one of the chief bases of much modern criticism; his confusion of two art forms, music and poetry, is a confusion still made; his ideas on unity of effect and on brevity need no additional comment. But Poe's ideas on versification are of slight value even to technicians, and of value to biographers and readers only as they help to explain Poe and his poetry—and this consideration has rarely been overlooked.

caused him to make exact statements without appending the badly needed qualifications. This can easily be understood, and pardoned. But in the background of Poe's "Rationale of Verse" —a defect more obvious with Lanier, since he made it the foundation of his theory—there is a fundamental misconception: he was attempting to make a science of that which is, at most, a technique. When compared with this, his errors with regard to linguistic facts and to metrics and rhythm are decidedly minor.[145] True, his tendency to apply scientific principles to all things was as thoroughly in accord with the thought of his age as his philosophic theories were; factual misconceptions, however, can be lightly swept away in this case, at least, but the heritage of thought which the age of Poe bequeathed to us has become a part of that which we know.

The critical work of Henry Timrod—brief in quantity but excellent in quality—represented an attempt to controvert the statements (although not, basically, the romantic philosophy) of Poe. As a preliminary to this main task, he answered the essay of his older friend, William J. Grayson. A distinguished lawyer with intellectual tastes which led him to prefer Dryden and Pope to the overwhelmingly popular romantic poets, Grayson argued for a type of poetry which seemed to Timrod only a metrical prose.[146] "The poetry of the day is, for the most part,

[145] Poe, "The Rationale of Verse." G. W. Allen, *American Prosody*, 56–88, analyzes Poe's theories of prosody and his experiments. Unfortunately Allen does not consider Chivers—perhaps the most interesting American experimentalist in versification before Whitman.

[146] H. Timrod, in "A Theory of Poetry" (*Atlantic Monthly*, XCVI, 314, Sept., 1905), called it "that definition of poetry which represents it simply as the expression in verse of thought, sentiment, or passion, and which measures the difference between the poet and versifier only by the depth, power, and vivacity of their several productions." First delivered before the Methodist Female College, Columbia, S. C., 1863–64, this essay was not published until 1901, when it appeared in *The Independent* in abridged form, confusingly titled in the first installment "A Theory of Poetry"; in the second and third, "The Rationale of Poetry." It was reprinted in full in the *Atlantic Monthly*, XCVI, 313–26. The only consideration of Timrod's criticism is C. P. Voigt's slight "Timrod's Essays in Literary Criticism," *American Literature*, VI, 163–7 (May, 1934).

subtile and transcendental," Grayson wrote, yet "the school of Dryden and Pope is not entirely forgotten." Since even "the most fastidious appetite may tolerate an occasional change of diet, and exchange dainties now and then for plainer fare," he thought the heroic couplet offered, at least, "some variety to the poetic forms that are almost universally prevalent."[147] With excessive modesty Grayson advances these ideas, which are not without strong elements of truth but which were quite alien to nineteenth-century thought—even in the South, where the influence of the eighteenth century remained strongest. Perhaps wisely, Timrod dismissed Grayson's remarks as totally inadequate, to be easily refuted through the establishment "of a theory altogether opposed to it."[148]

Timrod's main intent was to refute Poe. He based his first attack—on the transiency of excitement which makes brevity essential to a poem—firmly upon the high seriousness of poetry[149] and upon the "thoughtful sublimity and the matured and almost inexhaustible strength of a healthy intellect."[150] Neither the writing nor the reading of poetry was a light matter, to be undertaken in a few moments of leisure; sustained writing requires not so much uninterrupted reading as sustained thought.[151]

[147] Grayson's essay, which first appeared in *Russell's Magazine*, July, 1857, was partially reproduced in his Preface to *The Hireling and the Slave*, xiv–xv.

[148] Timrod adds (*op. cit.*, 314): "I am the less inclined to give it a minute examination because though the idea is an old one and in strict accordance with the usage of the word poetry, it has never become popular, nor is it likely to become so, as it fails to satisfy even those who, displeased, they do not know why, and dimly conscious of the true faith, are yet unable to discover in their indefined emotions a logical refutation of the theory. The genuine lovers of poetry feel that its essential characteristics underlie the various forms which it assumes, however dim and shadowy those characteristics may seem to them."

[149] In passing, Timrod also noticed the absorption of "the young lady who pores over the metrical novels of Scott till midnight." When his influence on the South as a whole is considered, Scott's influence on Southern poets was remarkably small.

[150] *Ibid.*, 315.

[151] In his essay, "Literature in the South," *Russell's Magazine*, Aug., 1859, Timrod directly attacks the complacent conservatism of Southerners

The reader of *Paradise Lost*, "instead of sitting down to the study of the third book as to a new poem, brings with him all the impressions of his former reading to heighten the color and deepen the effect of that which is before him." This is far from saying, Timrod adds, that length makes a poem more valuable,[152] or even that *Paradise Lost* is uniformly excellent: "However noble the theme, there will be parts and aspects which do not admit of the presence of genuine poetry. Herein, however, I differ from Poe; inasmuch as I maintain that these parts may be raised so far above the ordinary level of prose by skillful verse as to preserve the general harmony of the poem and materially to insure its beauty as a work of art. And in the distinction between poetry and the poem, between the spirit and its body, which Poe recognizes when he comes to develop his theory, but which he blinks or ignores altogether in his remarks upon *Paradise Lost*, I shall look for the justification of my position. I hold that the confusion of these terms, of the subjective essence with the objective form, is the source of most of the errors and contradictions of opinion prevalent upon this theme."[153]

In some respects Timrod agreed with Poe. The author must regard each poem "strictly as a work of art." As such, it has "one purpose . . . the materials of which it is composed should be so selected as to enforce it." In another essay, where he defended the sonnet form, Timrod elaborated on this singleness of purpose: "The sonnet is designed, as it is peculiarly fitted, for

who regard literature as an "amusement, not as a study at least equal in importance, and certainly not inferior in difficulty, to law and medicine." He advocates systematic study of English in the schools.

[152] Timrod, "A Theory of Poetry," *loc. cit.*, 317: "If that ponderous production [the *Columbiad*] could be crushed into a space no larger than that occupied by an epigram, not a drop of genuine poetry could be forced from it."

[153] *Ibid.*, 318. Although Timrod speaks of Coleridge as the "profoundest poetical critic of any age," he is far more nearly allied with Wordsworth in his thought. See Annabel Newton's *Wordsworth in Early American Criticism.*

the development of a single thought, emotion, or picture. It is governed by another law not less imperative than that which determines its length . . . the law of unity."[154] Considerations both of art and of technique precluded a true poet from being an improvisator, from writing under the spur of inspiration: "A distinction must be made between the moment when the great thought strikes for the first time along the brain . . . and the hour of patient, elaborate execution." The hours of insight must be separated from the hours of labor.[155]

Poetry is not limited in subject matter, as Poe insists, for appropriate subjects can be found not only in the mysterious and the beautiful, but equally in the sublime and terrible, the commonplace and homely—in whatever subject the individual poet can transmute into poetry. These varied sources cannot be reduced until "the simple element of beauty" suffices for all: "Two other elements at least must be added; and these are power, when it is developed in some noble shape, and truth, whether abstract or not, when it affects the common heart of mankind."[156]

The indefinite must not be pushed too far; generalized imagery can not with advantage replace concrete imagery: "Poetry does not deal in abstractions. However abstract be his thought, the poet is compelled, by his passion-fused imagination, to give it life, form or color. Hence the necessity of

[154] Timrod, "The Character and Scope of the Sonnet," *Russell's Magazine*, May, 1857, reprinted in *The Outlook*, LXXVII, 706–9 (July 23, 1904). The sonnet, "a little harp of fourteen strings," he thought artificial only as all verse is artificial; its very restrictions are a challenge to the artist, requiring a condensation which can come only with thought and effort.

[155] In this connection Timrod quotes Wordsworth's "emotion recollected in tranquillity," and Matthew Arnold's

> "We cannot kindle when we will
> The fire that in the heart resides."

The last section of "A Theory of Poetry" (321–6) is chiefly an analysis of Wordsworth's poetry.

[156] *Ibid.*, 319–20. Timrod refers to Leigh Hunt's *Imagination and Fancy*, but adds that he had fixed upon this "trinity of elements" before he had read Hunt's book.

employing the *sensuous* or concrete words of the language, and hence the exclusion of long words which in English are nearly all purely and austerely abstract, from the poetic vocabulary."[157] To Timrod, and to his friends, these specific statements and general ideas seemed a complete refutation of Poe's principles, but when the critical essays of both men are examined from the vantage point which historical perspective gives, it is clear that, like Wordsworth and Coleridge before them, they complement rather than contradict each other, that they were describing the same shield from different points of view.

Lanier's critical theories, like Poe's, divide naturally in two categories: the philosophical and the prosodical. Unlike Poe's, the technical observations are not an integral part of his larger conceptions; although the two run along together harmoniously enough, they never fuse. While Lanier's ideas also help to explain his age and his section, they are, in the final analysis, a part of a submerging current, not a fountainhead. For that reason, Lanier's work can be more nearly valid, yet far less important.

His belief in the sacredness of art and of the religious rapport of the poet is akin to that of Chivers. At times his words take on something of the earlier poet's wild, mystical zeal, as when he admonished the young artist: "Unless you are suffused— soul and body, one might say—with that moral purpose which finds its largest expression in love—that is, the love of all things in their proper relation—unless you are suffused with this love do not dare to meddle with beauty, unless you are suffused with beauty, do not dare to meddle with love, unless you are suffused with truth, do not dare to meddle with goodness,—in a word, unless you are suffused with beauty, truth, wisdom, goodness *and* love, abandon the hope that the ages will accept you as an

---

[157] Timrod, "What Is Poetry," *Russell's Magazine*, Oct., 1857. The ideas in this essay are more fully developed in "A Theory of Poetry," where Timrod adds (318): "The poetry of words has never so strange a fascination as when it seems to suggest more than it utters."

artist."[158] That was his own creed, and he employed it, to the
detriment of his reputation as a critic, unsparingly. Whatever
justification can be made for some of the strangest judgments
on record can be found in Lanier's excessive enthusiasms and
his burningly intense belief in a narrow morality.[159]

In this study even a consideration of these flights from
reason would be unnecessary if Lanier's ideas could be justly
considered or explained without an attempt to understand
Lanier himself. Not only was he an abnormally spiritual man;
he was ill.[160] When D. C. Gilman described Lanier, he wrote
that "one said, 'He looks like Moses'; another, 'He looks like
Christ.' A German physiologist simply said 'Tuberculosis.' "[161]
The optimism which this disease is known to foster may well
be the basis for Lanier's desire to undertake everything, but to
be content with a haphazard mastery of each subject. Surely,
the specter of lack of time, the threatening nearness of death,
must have driven his acquisitive curiosity onward, while it left
him no time for working out the subjects which he touched.
In justice to Lanier, one must remember this constantly, and
must remember, also, that too many of his books are not
finished products, but publications edited and printed by others

---

[158] Lanier, *The English Novel*, 280. Similar statements run like a refrain
through the letters and criticisms of Lanier. By telescoping this quotation
without indicating any omissions, A. H. Starke (*Sidney Lanier*, 442) manages to make it sound fairly reasonable, removing many of its transcendental implications.

[159] Lanier, *Music and Poetry*, 20-1, where he writes: "The true artist
will never remain a bad man." An even better example is his verdict upon
the novels of Richardson, Fielding, Smollett, and Sterne, in *The English
Novel*, 168-80: "I protest that I can read none of these books without feeling as if my soul had been in the rain, draggled, muddy, miserable."
Lanier considers George Eliot the great culmination of the English novel.

[160] Recognition of Lanier's ill-health is more necessary when considering
his prose than his poetry. H. M. Jones, "Sidney Lanier," in *American
Poetry* (P. H. Boynton, ed.), 670-5, and G. Bradford, *American Portraits*,
59-83, consider his illness a motivating factor; E. Mims, *Sidney Lanier*,
4-7, emphasizes his buoyancy of spirit.

[161] D. C. Gilman, "Sidney Lanier: Reminiscences and Letters," *South
Atlantic Quarterly*, IV, 115-22 (April, 1905); quotation, 120.

after his death. This final item palliates the frequent errors in quotations and citations, and the superficial and dogmatic judgments which Lanier might well have revised.

An opportunity to reflect upon and to correct the manuscripts of these posthumous works would, beyond doubt, have greatly improved them. Time might have brought him a richer insight, health a broader and finer outlook. These were denied him. Remembrance of all this brings with it an overwhelming pity for the man, a poignant wish that all his prose except his letters could have been swept unknown into limbo, and only his poetry left. For there is no blinking the fact that Lanier's philosophies of life and of poetry are weak, and that occasional flashes of insight do not compensate for his fevered rhapsodies.

The precarious state of his health caused him to live "so exclusively in a world of artistic speculation and scientific questioning that things spiritual came to be more familiar to him than things material, and moral facts to be taken as much for granted as physical facts are."[162] Although his religious convictions prevented his really accepting Darwin's theories, his romantic faith in science caused him to admire Newton and Darwin intensely. By intuitive reasoning he convinced himself that no compromise, even, was needed, for science did not endanger—science, indeed, might strengthen—both religion and poetry.[163] He worked faithfully, if confusedly, to integrate the contradictory gods of religion and of science.

The artist was free to do as he willed with those tools which God had given him. Fine and true work could be accomplished

---

[162] Starke, *Sidney Lanier*, 444.

[163] Lanier, *The English Novel*, 135–6, 184. Equally indicative is Lanier's frequent attacking of Aristotle. In *Music and Poetry*, 71, he says, "these three phenomena—the modern scientist, the musician, and the landscape painter—are merely three developments, in different directions, of one mighty impulse which under-runs them all. This impulse is that direct sympathy with physical nature which the man of today possesses and which the man of old did not possess."

only by those who lived in accordance with God and nature. If he believed, as we are told, that great music is but the rhythm of a great personality,[164] he also paraphrases with entire approval Herbert Spencer's proposition that "where opposing forces act, rhythm appears, and [Spencer] has traced the rhythmic motions of nature to the antagonistic forces there found, such as the two motions which carry the earth towards and away from the sun and so result in the periodicity of the earth's progress, and others.

"Perhaps this view may be made, without strain, to bind together even facts so remote from each other as the physical and the moral. When we compare what one may call the literal rhythm which rules throughout physical nature with that metaphorical rhythm or proportion which governs good behavior as well as good art; when we find that opposition in the physical world results in rhythm, and that no opposition in the moral world—the fret, the sting, the thwart, the irreconcilable me as against all other me's, the awful struggle for existence, the desperate friction of individualities, the no of death to all requests—may also result in rhythm; when we perceive that through all those immeasurable agitations which constitute both moral and physical nature this beautiful and orderly principle of rhythm thus swings to and fro like the shuttle of a loom and weaves a definite and comprehensible pattern into the otherwise chaotic fabric of things: we may be able to see dimly into that old Orphic saying of the seer, 'The father of metre is rhythm, and the father of rhythm is God.' "[165] Here, truly, all is confusion. Religion and science and art were three powerful magnets, drawing his mind hither and yon. Lanier was powerless to separate them, and he lacked the power to fuse them into a complete philosophy, either for the world or for himself.

[164] H. S. McCowan, "Sidney Lanier," *Self-Culture*, X, 398–400 (Jan., 1900). See also Starke, *op. cit.*, 46, 439.
[165] Lanier, *The Science of English Verse*, 250.

This lack of philosophical integration carried over into his more direct theories of poetry. Lanier's demand for a heavy moral content seems as dated as Poe's demand for pure beauty. At least a partial reason for this is Lanier's phraseology: although he states his argument in chaotic and old-fashioned terms, he seems nearer the heart of creative expression than Poe. The most kindly critic can not say as much for his most elaborate treatise on versification, *The Science of English Verse*. The title alone reveals one fundamental misconception: there is an art of poetry, a technique of versification—but a *science of verse* is a contradiction of terms. The second fundamental error is Lanier's confusion of art-forms, his belief in the identity of music and poetry: "The art of sound must always be regarded the genus, and music and verse its two species. Prose, scientifically considered, is a wild variety of verse. . . . When we hear verse, we *hear* a set of relations between sounds; when we silently read verse, we *see* that which brings to us a set of relations between sounds; when we imagine verse, we *imagine* a set of relations between sounds."[166] From this definition Lanier develops the thesis that the laws which govern versification and musical composition are identical, for "there is absolutely no difference between the sound-relations used in music and those used in verse."[167]

With these and similar statements Lanier dismisses the vital element of intellectual content. That, one may say, he took for granted, although this supposition will, of itself, damage his theory considerably. His poems treat social and political topics, and he was greatly interested in contemporary ideas; but in his

[166] *Ibid.*, 23, 57. The reader interested in this subject will find the best treatment in Lessing's incompleted notes, printed in the Appendix to R. Phillimore's translation of Lessing's *Laocoön*. A similar confusion is frequently made between poetry and painting; the close and valid distinctions made in the *Laocoön*, in Sir Joshua Reynolds's *Discourses on Art*, and in Irving Babbitt's *The New Laocoön* have not deterred writers and critics from attempting to make one art perform the functions of another art.

[167] Lanier, *op. cit.*, 48.

theories he did not include these elements, and indeed leaves little room for them. Less obvious but equally important is another factor which weakens his theory: although words and music may, as Richard Wagner observed, complement each other, one can never replace the other. In attempting that replacement, which necessarily required an identity between the two forms, Lanier failed—as many another critic before him had failed in the attempt to make poetry and painting kindred forms.

In science, this misconception in the premise would at once establish the falseness of other observations. In a loose technique, like versification, the corollary does not inevitably follow. Men who employed the classical method of scansion have written very excellent verse in English; Sidney Lanier, who disdained the accentual method, wrote poems which can in most instances be scanned quite satisfactorily in that manner. It may be true that most poetry is normally read in ⅜ time, but that is no reason to say it was written in that time, or that it can not be read effectively with due regard to accent.[168] In brief, Lanier worked in a field where precise scientific statement is ineffective for the simple reason that one method may be as good, where the result is the basis of judgment, as another. For that reason Lanier's observations are of some value: if they never touch the whole of poetry, they do give a stimulating discussion of one important portion—sound. To other critics has gone the duty of fitting that part into the whole.

Lanier divides sound into four particulars: duration, inten-

---

[168] Allen (*American Prosody*, 277–306) gives a good discussion of Lanier's technical theories, with illustrations. He also cites various scientific experiments on versification, breath, language, etc.—but these are of dubious value as far as poetry is concerned. Russell (*An Hour of American Poetry*) adopts Lanier's theory as a basis for guidance, but his critical judgments reveal, sadly, that no system will prevent the human mind from being fallible, when judged by another equally fallible mind. For substantial studies, see Pearl E. Brown's *A Study of Sidney Lanier's Verse Technique* (1921) and Ruth Willcockson's *Rhythmical Principles and Practices of Sidney Lanier* (1928).

sity, pitch, and tone-color. Each of these he defines carefully; each sound "for the purpose of verse, is represented by one syllable." This comes eventually to mean that each foot, which may be composed of a varying number of syllables, is equal in temporal quality to every foot in the line; Lanier frequently substituted *bar* for foot, and he wrote that "In a strain of music any bar is exactly equal to any other bar in the time it occupies." Therefore, every poetic foot must be equal in time. And "rhythm of any sort is impossible, except through the co-ordination of time. Time is the essential basis of rhythm. 'Accent' can effect nothing except in arranging materials already rhythmical through some temporal recurrence."[169]

G. W. Allen has given a remarkably accurate summary of Lanier's conception of rhythm: "Briefly, the rhythms in Lanier's system are as follows: (1) The *temporal relation* is 'primary' rhythm, that is, the time covered by each separate sound ('verse-sound,' or syllable) and the pauses and silences. (2) *Accent*, which indicates the beginning of a new bar, forms a 'secondary' rhythm. (3) But English speech is not pronounced in syllable or sound groups but in 'phrases,' necessitated by the dependence of human speech upon respiration. Thus the *phrase* forms a 'tertiary' rhythm. Subheads of tertiary rhythm are alliteration, rhetorical emphasis (which includes both intensity and pitch accent), and logical accent. (4) The 'fourth order of rhythmic groups' is the *line*—meter is the number of verse-sounds in a line. Rime also has a rhythmic function because it marks the end of the line. (5) The 'fifth order of rhythmic groups' is the stanza. This rhythm, of course, is ordinarily marked by rime-schemes, but may be indicated by phrases and full stops."[170]

After extended analyses of many poems in the light of his theories, Lanier concluded his volume with a one-page chapter

[169] Lanier, *The Science of English Verse*, 24–65.
[170] Allen, *op. cit.*, 281.

which says that his science consists only of hints, not laws; that
"For the artist in verse there is no law: the perception and love
of beauty constitute the whole outfit; and what is herein set
forth is to be taken merely as enlarging that perception and
exalting that love. In all cases, the appeal is to the ear. . . ."[171]
Of what value, ultimately, is this platitude? Is the body of the
study as valueless as its hypothesis and its conclusion? When
all the false and worthless elements are stripped away, certain
other elements of value do remain, but they are suggestive hints
on the relation of melody and harmony to words, on the com-
plementary nature of music and words. This value itself is not
what Lanier intended, for he considered the laws of these arts
as identical.[172]

That Sidney Lanier was consciously aware of pictorial as
well as harmonic qualities in his verse is apparent from reading
the "Hymns of the Marshes," the "Song of the Chattahoochee," or half a dozen other of his poems. That he was in part
a local colorist can be discerned in his novel, *Tiger Lilies*,[173] in
Florida, with its gorgeous word pictures, and in his dialect
poems. In a manner almost underground, since the author's
name is rarely attached to it, one poem has circulated so exten-
sively that it has taken on the quality of a folk product. "Thar's
More in the Man Than Thar is in the Land" is not distinguished
poetry, but it warrants the title of Lanier's most popular poem,

---

[171] Lanier, *The Science of English Verse*, 315.

[172] I am considering here the value of his theories to poets and readers.
I doubt if Lanier stimulated the writing of scientific monographs on
prosody—he was a part of a century which desired to reduce all things to
scientific law. The value of treatises on prosody to poets is a debatable
subject; each poet develops his own method through study, imitation,
trial and error, etc., and rules suited to a Lanier may be worth nothing to
an Emerson or a Whitman. P. E. More (*Shelburne Essays*, First Series, 108)
has written the kindest possible judgment: "Lanier's brilliant work is un-
exceptionally able as a study of the *ideal or model* verse, but fails to consider the variance between the *ideal* and the actual rhythm."

[173] See especially chap. II, and the characters of Cain and Gorm
Smallin. Pictorial elements in the work of Southern poets generally are
discussed in the next section.

and it is a good example of local color poetry. Essentially, however, Lanier wanted to get away from a section where old values were rapidly disintegrating: "You are all so alive, up there, and we are all so dead, down here" he wrote in June, 1866, to a Northern friend.[174] This is not the mood of the local colorist, but of one who desires to be in the vanguard of change. It is not surprising that Sidney Lanier—who preferred burial in Baltimore to burial in Macon—never developed a theory of local color, never developed his beginnings in that field of writing.

The gifted Irwin Russell died young: he knew what he was about, but he never stated his ideas. Certain aspects of a life he cherished were disappearing from the world; something was happening to the Negroes in their freedom which recalled the vivid impressions of youth, when world and Negro alike had seemed more happily exuberant. Because it was a part of him, native to mind and almost a part of blood, he put on paper (with an artless artistry, equalled only by Joel Chandler Harris in his stories of Uncle Remus) his recollections of a Christmas night in the quarters.

When his theory was defined, poetically, it was the product of two young and sophisticated men, who had found a "tropically rich store of material, an unurbanized beauty, the possibility of legend, folk-song, romance, historical narrative, glorious land-scape, and an untired mood."[175] Southern poetry should be

---

[174] M. H. Northrup, "Sidney Lanier: Recollections and Letters," *Lippincott's Magazine*, LXXV, 302–15 (March, 1905). In 1860 Northrup, a graduate of Hamilton College, had come South to teach in Oglethorpe Academy; he and Lanier occupied adjoining rooms in the same boarding house. Northrup left the South in 1861, and went to Syracuse, where he became editor and owner of the Syracuse *Courier*.

[175] H. Allen and DuBose Heyward, "Poetry South," *Poetry*, XX, 47 (April, 1922). Parts of this essay are printed in the Appendix, pp. 360 ff. It is ironical that Hervey Allen, author of the plausibly smart local-color poem "Beyond Debate," should in this essay make such sweeping and unconvincing judgments. In this Southern issue Harriet Monroe gives a definition which even more obviously reveals the ideas so commonly held

regional, of and about places and persons; it should be distinctively sectional. Heyward and Allen, like many another poetaster, discovered that the surface qualities—picturesqueness of locale and speech, in particular—were easy. That easiness was deceptive, although the same elements which made it false in spirit also made many persons accept it as authentic. It is not easy to attain, but easy to handle. What few men seemed to realize was that local color when employed with discretion made an excellent background to give added reality, but a thin and quick-fading foreground.

The one tenable theory of this nature has been stated, and its difficulties analyzed, by a distinguished poet and critic: the craft of a poet must come "as part of a generally diffused tradition which has local roots and which he naturally appropriates as his own. . . . There ought to be something virile and positive in its art, as an art linked by devotion to a concrete place rather than animated by a loose enthusiasm for a 'national' culture which has no organic unity behind it."[176] Whether the poet is concerned with local or with universal subjects, this influence of a stable and vital tradition should have a deepening influence. Too often it does not have, since the tradition has either been discredited and discarded, by men like Grady and Page, or it has been falsified, by men like Heyward and Allen.

Allen Tate and John Crowe Ransom, equally, have joined in the contentions of Davidson, but they have gone beyond him in poetic theory and constructed a tight, logical philosophy which excellently explains what they are doing so well, but which leaves much to be desired in its failure to recognize other

that only the externalities and superficialities matter in the art of the local colorist. For an answer to this, see Donald Davidson's essay, in the Appendix, pp. 369 ff.

[176] D. Davidson, "The Southern Poet and His Tradition," *Poetry*, XL, 94–103 (May, 1932); reprinted in the Appendix, pp. 369 ff. See also Davidson's discussion of the problem of the artist in modern times: "A Mirror for Artists," in *I'll Take My Stand*, 28–60, and "The Trend of Literature," in *Culture in the South*, 183–210.

kinds of verse as poetry.[177] The three general attitudes possible in the modern world, in the order in which they have respectively dominated the minds of men, are the creative spirit, romantic irony, and the spirit of the practical will. Unquestionably, today, the scientific spirit, with its substitution of the will for the imagination, its "confidence in the limitless power of man to impose practical abstractions upon the world,"[178] is in the ascendant. But the true function of the creative spirit is "the quality of experience and not its control by the will." It is not concerned with propaganda or didacticism or melody or pure beauty, but only with totality of vision and of experience.[179]

[177] A distinction needs to be made between *kinds* of poetry and *degrees of excellence* in poetry. It would be foolish to attempt to evaluate the degrees of excellence in, say, Shakespeare and Jonson until one analyzed the difference in *kind*, and recognized that the two men were doing quite different things. Only then do degrees of excellence have much meaning. Only by this method, also, does the old statement of judging an author according to his intentions have much meaning; we can judge the excellence of his work within its kind (which is radically different). For brief but valuable discussions of this point, see Foerster, *American Criticism*, 50–1, and T. S. Eliot, *Selected Essays*, 136–9. The failure of Ransom and Tate to admit this distinction weakens, rather than strengthens, their dialectic: as when Tate writes (in "Three Types of Poetry," *New Republic*, March 14, 1934, 126) that "We must understand clearly that such lines as

'Life, like a dome of many-colored glass,
Stains the white radiance of Eternity'

are not poetry, but are the frustrated individual will trying to compete with science." That it is a weak kind of poetry, because of the defects which Tate brilliantly analyzes—the lack of wholeness of vision and of a sure grasp of the totality of experience—many persons, including the present writer, would agree; but to state as absolute and final that it is not poetry seems unnecessarily to narrow the meaning of *poetry*.

[178] Tate, *op. cit.*, 126–7. W. B. Yeats has called the rhetoric of romantic poets "the will trying to do the work of the imagination."

[179] These ideas, here stated baldly and without shading, have been developed into a rounded aesthetic by Tate, Ransom, Davidson, and Robert Penn Warren in many scattered essays, which need to be collected. Especially valuable are the essays of Davidson cited above; Allen Tate's "Three Types of Poetry," *New Republic*, March 14, 28, and April 11, 1934; "A Note on Milton," *New Republic*, November 20, 1931; John Crowe Ransom, "A Poem Nearly Anonymous," *American Review*, I, 179–203, 444–67 (May and Sept., 1933); "Poetry, A Note in Ontology," *ibid.*, III, 172–200 (May, 1934); Robert Penn Warren, "Sidney Lanier: The Blind Poet," *American Review*, I, 27–45 (Nov., 1933), and "A Note on Three

To convey this there is no substitute for sense, for what T. S. Eliot has called "tough reasonableness"; in the effort to make the impact of this greater, the modern poet is capable of going over his smooth metres and laboriously roughening them.[180] This point is relatively unimportant; the essential point is that the poet must work in the severe and subtle tradition of English verse, with a thorough comprehension of technique—a tradition and a technique to which Spenser, Shakespeare, and Milton *belonged*, as well as developed. Viewed in this light, the conventions of subject matter and of style which poets have adopted prevent only a weak "personal expression"; these conventions deepen its content, rather, by giving a formal, postponed, and reflective pleasure instead of an immediate and approximate pleasure.

Such theories do not make for great popularity, since the poetry which comes out of them has almost a classic quality with a certain necessary involvement which is alien to the romantic and scientific spirit. If these theories do not embrace all of poetry, they give a valid, tenable foundation on which one type of poetry—in at least some respects the best type of poetry—can be written. This quality John Peale Bishop emphasizes when he writes that "poetry must be traditional."[181]

Only because it diverges from the modern attitude does the theory of the Fugitive group of poets seem revolutionary. In general the conservative South has had little interest in radical experimentation. To speak of imagism, for example, as ever becoming a part of Southern poetic thought would be absurd; it deserves a brief notice here only because it was in part the product of a brilliant Southern poet, John Gould Fletcher.

Southern Poets" (Davidson, Ransom, Fletcher), *Poetry*, XL, 103–13 (May, 1932). Valuable also are the ideas of T. S. Eliot, in his *Selected Essays*.

[180] Ransom, "A Poem Nearly Anonymous," *loc. cit.*, 189. Ransom presents his reasons for thinking that Milton roughened the originally smooth structure of "Lycidas."

[181] "Speaking of Poetry," a prologue to *Now With His Love*.

Poetry, to his mind, was to render mood alone. Each mood could best be represented not only by sound but by color patterns conjoined. He aimed at "a presentation of daily life in terms of highly-orchestrated and coloured words." The form which he developed most highly, the Symphonies, are "examples of the use, or the abuse, of the *allusive* method (to borrow Garnett's phrase). My aim in them was to describe certain predominant moods in the terms of things happening. Thus one gets expectancy described as a traveller looking at blue mountains in the distance, and despair described in terms of a stoker on board a ship. Each mood was to be presented not as abstract sorrow or joy or rage, but as something seen, heard, felt, and actually happening. By these means, I approached close to that 'methodical confusion of all the senses' which was described as the visionary state by no less a poet than Arthur Rimbaud."[182]

In form these poems "seemed to be entirely shapeless," but Fletcher's defense is not easily overthrown: "I have always felt it more important for a poet to create his form according to the state of his feelings and the condition of his material, than to borrow one ready-made and to attempt to squeeze his feelings in it. Only a few metrical forms are really of universal applicability, perhaps the sonnet and blank verse are the only forms in English that can be used indiscriminately by all poets without loss of quality. I may have pushed metrical variation too far towards anarchy; for having employed it in preference to uniformity, I still feel I owe neither explanation nor apology."[183] These definite theories were influential on other poets, but it is perhaps well to note that the influence was on English

[182] Fletcher, Preface to *Preludes and Symphonies*, xii, reprinted in the Appendix, pp. 364 ff. Invaluable in this connection is Amy Lowell's *Tendencies in Modern American Poetry*. Glenn Hughes's favorable account, *Imagism and the Imagists*, is crammed with literary gossip which throws a revealing light on these persons and their beliefs; the book is extensive, well documented, and has an excellent bibliography.

[183] Fletcher, *op. cit.*, xiii.

and Northern rather than on Southern poets. They came early in his life, and his later poetry reveals that his statement, "since then I have tended increasingly to hold that poetry is also thought, and that thought and emotion play the part in poetry of counterpoint and melody in the works of musical composers,"[184] is the key to much of his finest work. The early poems were written by an expatriate, the later poems by a man reintegrated to his section. Although a knowledge of his ideas gives a richer quality to the reading of Fletcher's poems, it is important here only in that connection.

For theory and practice alike, in the South, tend among the better poets to be traditional. Of bad writing, of confused thinking, of radical experimentation, of local color writing and sentimental sweetmeats, no section and no country or age have a monopoly. What the intentions, implied or stated, back of this work may be does not greatly matter. Partisan defense would be foolish, as it would be useless. But it is never without value to consider carefully the theories of articulate poets of any time or place, for out of that consideration comes a better understanding of poetry. Since the Southern poets generally have been inclined to ponder and to discuss the *how* as well as the *why*, they have worked out a rich body of poetic theory, which, though uneven in quality and validity, sets an intelligible background for their work.

III. THE POETRY

If Richard Rich in 1610 carried his versified story of Virginia to London, it is equally true that the English colonists carried with them to Virginia their own songs, ballads, and poems. The early poetry was English poetry transplanted; the early ballads were English ballads twisted gradually to the pattern of a new environment.[185] Captain John Smith was, from a

---

[184] *Ibid.*, x.
[185] See the ballad, "The Brown Girl or Fair Ellender," selections following,

literary as well as general point of view, only a lesser Sir Walter Raleigh; George Sandys a temporary American counterpart of Michael Drayton[186] or George Chapman. To men like Smith or William Byrd or George Washington or St. George Tucker writing was the accomplishment, not the career, of a gentleman. The ability to write an appropriate poem, make a good speech or turn a neat phrase, and relate effectively a dramatic or useful anecdote were, one or all, likely to be a part of his equipment. But they were not necessarily important: no man was in likelihood of losing a lady for want of a sonnet.[187] Only Sandys, however, of these men had any professional pride in his poetry; the others were gentlemanly dabblers in the art of letters. Subjects for poetry were strictly occasional: the death of a great man, the winning of a victory, the song to a loved one. In his youth George Washington partially completed an acrostic to Frances Alexander,[188] but when inspiration failed him he abandoned the attempt as unimportant. This attitude was typical.

To attempt a complete description of the early poems produced in the South would be fruitless.[189] But several works deserve mention because they illustrate trends, and one poem

---

p. 4. There are many excellent collections of transplanted English ballads; two good examples are A. K. Davis's *Traditional Ballads of Virginia*, and Reed Smith's *South Carolina Ballads*.

[186] In his *Ode to the Virginian Voyage*, Drayton appeals to Sandys in particular to see that a literature will be produced in America. Sandys's translation of Ovid's *Metamorphoses*, published in 1623, was very popular. Dryden called him "the ingenious and learned Sandys, the best versifier of the former age."

[187] Philip Sidney, "An Apologie for Poetrie," in Smith and Parks's *The Great Critics*, 187. Moses, *op. cit.*, gives the general feeling, perhaps in exaggerated form: "It was a grace for any member of a well-founded family to do a sentiment to a rare turn; but to cultivate the talent seriously was a disgrace."

[188] Gordon, *Virginian Writers of Fugitive Verse*, 42–3. On p. 155 he gives a complete and very poor poem by Washington.

[189] The best account of colonial literature is M. C. Tyler's *History of American Literature, 1607–1765* (2 vols.). There are local histories and anthologies of almost every state.

deserves more attention because of its intrinsic merits than it generally receives.

That poem is "Bacon's Epitaph."[190] It is one of the very few poems written in America which merits the adjective *great*. Yet it is completely in the Southern tradition: it came out of conflict between frontier and seaboard; its author was so little a man of letters that today he is unknown;[191] it was strictly an occasional poem, in the best seventeenth-century manner, for a dead leader. The poem is richly allusive, classical in tone, sincere and dignified in emotion. Moses Coit Tyler wrote of it with justice as "this noble dirge, which has a stateliness, a compressed energy, and a mournful eloquence, reminding one of the commemorative verse of Ben Jonson";[192] even more, these nobly rhetorical couplets remind one of John Webster at his best. "Bacon's Epitaph" was the first and perhaps the greatest of the monopoems which make up so much of Southern poetry.

Of slighter caliber was the first volume of poems published in the South: *Poems on Several Occasions by a Gentleman of Virginia* (1736).[193] It is more impressive than such miscellaneous performances as appeared in the poet's corner of the *Virginia Gazette*[194] solely because one man had written a quantity of verse which he thought good enough to collect into a volume. In his preface the Gentleman warns the reader that "the following pieces are the casual productions of youth," but he desires only honest judgment, for "I am well assured that giving an undeserved Applause to bad Poems, is a much greater and more dangerous Piece of Injustice to the Author, than even discouraging those, which are good."[195] The poems deserved only

---

[190] For the historical incidents which caused the poem to be written, see the textual Notes, pp. 377 ff.

[191] Tyler, *op. cit.*, I, 79, suggests that it was by —— Cotton of Acquia Creek, but gives no reasons for the ascription.

[192] *Ibid.*, I, 78.   [193] The author remains unknown.

[194] Files of the *Virginia Gazette*, 1736–40, in Virginia Historical Society library.

[195] Preface to *Poems on Several Occasions*, in 1930 reprint.

moderate applause. Technically they reveal a limited command of blank verse, heroic couplets, and the simpler verse structures. The lyrics are pleasing, but slight in content: here are epistles after the manner of Horace, with a tendency toward moralizing; pastorals to Sylvia, with the faint licentiousness fashionable in that form; four imitations of Anacreon; and a satire, "On the Corruption of the Stage,"[196] which has interest only because the final line ("We turn to downright nonsense of our own") indicates that Virginia before 1736 had attempted sufficient dramatic efforts to earn the disapproval of the Gentleman's classical taste.

Although unimportant as literature, this easily available exhibit perfectly illustrates certain important features of Southern poetry. To attempt to compare it, favorably or unfavorably, with the works of Michael Wigglesworth or Anne Bradstreet would indeed be an attempt to measure the veriest of pigmies. But this difference is important: the Virginian's poetry is less indigenous and more graceful. If he never reached the goal of authentic poetry (as Anne Bradstreet did once in the poignant "Before the Birth of One of My Children"), he never stooped to the philosophical banalities of her "Contemplations," or to the pathological horrors of Wigglesworth's *Day of Doom*. The manner and attitude of the Virginian are highly civilized; he is more interested in a girdle than in a prayer, for poetical purposes; but he has back of him no content of thought shaped either from a personal philosophy or from a fund of common ideas which needed expression. Wigglesworth wrote directly out of a Puritan's conscience: he was a *choragus* for one section of Puritan thought; he had something in hand which he felt needed to be said, and he said it in wretched verse. The Gentleman had only a graceful attitude.

This attitude can be traced to the Southern view of poetry as a genteel accomplishment. There was no lack of serious thought

[196] *Ibid.*, 28–30.

in the South, but when Byrd or Wythe or Jefferson or Washington had something of importance to communicate, he put
it into prose. Poetry was limited almost to *vers de société*.
When Eben Cook in 1708 wrote his vigorous Hudibrastic
satire on Maryland,[197] he used verse to vent his spleen—but he
was exceptional in this. Satire was usually light and pleasant,
more nearly related to the polite thrusts of Matthew Prior than
to the stiletto shafts of Alexander Pope. Occasionally it was
robust and Rabelaisian, as in the jingle about the establishment
of a paper mill:

> Nice Delia's smock, which, neat and whole,
> No man durst finger for his soul;
> Turned to *Gazette*, now all the town
> May take it up, or smooth it down.[198]

Mainly, poetry was polite and decorous. Only with the coming of the Revolution did it acquire a sharp edge, and even then
the poets produced nothing memorable. There was no dearth
of writing, but mostly these poems were modeled after older
works, and rarely is an authentic note struck. The pretty
picture of "Virginia Banishing Tea"[199] had counterparts equally
good, or bad, in other sections; the elegies, martial calls, and
ballads were all feeble and derivative. The South, and the
nation, had no poetic Jefferson—only a Freneau. Out of the
frontier came one or two homely songs whose apt images are
yet memorable: no line expresses better the ideas of combatants
than "'Twas on a pleasant mountain/The Tory heathens lay."[200]
But such sharp aptness of phrase is rare.

[197] The complete title describes the book: "The Sot-weed Factor; or, A
voyage to Maryland. A Satyr. In which is describ'd The Laws, Government, Courts, and Constitutions of the Country, and also the Buildings,
Feasts, Frolicks, Entertainments and Drunken Humours of the Inhabitants of that Part of America. In Burlesque Verse. By Eben. Cook, Gent."

[198] Gordon, *op. cit.*, 45, 158–9. It was printed in the *Virginia Gazette*
in July, 1744, and signed J. Dumbleton.

[199] Gordon, *op. cit.*, 54–5, 168.

[200] See Selections following, p. 7, and Notes, p. 378.

During the days of war there appeared in the *Virginia Gazette* a rhymed catalogue which celebrated "The Belles of Williamsburg," and it was popular enough to bring forth a sequel. The authors were Dr. James McClurg, author of a medical treatise upon the human bile, and St. George Tucker, the annotator of Blackstone.[201] This was the stuff of which poetry was made, by gentlemen-versifiers who had more important work to do in the world, but who would, occasionally, turn to verse for the expression of social ideas or of personal emotions. The lawyer wrote, shortly before his death, the best of the early Southern lyrics, "Resignation," with its plaintively haunting note of melancholy, but even his reflections on the transiency of life and the approach of death lack finality.

After the Revolution several volumes of versified trivialities appeared,[202] which might on occasion (as in the case of John Shaw's dainty lyric) gain wide approval because of sentimentality and singing rhyme rather than intrinsic value. For a few months or years Baltimore, Richmond, and Charleston had each its magazine, before 1800,[203] but nothing memorable came out of them. Poems and magazines were pale imitations of English models, and it seemed in no way strange that Washington Allston, poet and sculptor, should go from Charleston to live permanently in England.[204]

Allston did what most men wanted to do. Among those who remained in Charleston the foremost poet of early days was

---

[201] Gordon, *op. cit.*, 59–61, 174–7. See also the textual notes on Tucker.

[202] The best known of these books were: *Poems*, by Arouet (Joseph Ladd Brown, of Rhode Island and Charleston, 1786); William Mumford, *Poems and Compositions in Prose* (1798); *Poems of the Late John Shaw* (1810).

[203] F. L. Mott, *History of American Magazines*, 204–5, 790–1.

[204] J. B. Flagg, *Life and Letters of Washington Allston* (1892). After graduation from Harvard in 1800, Allston went to London, where he lived most of the time until 1818; from that time until his death in 1843 he resided in Boston and Cambridge. R. H. Dana edited Allston's *Poems* in 1850; Southey ranked his verse "among the first productions of modern times."

William Crafts,[205] a Harvard-educated wit who modeled his conversation after Robert Treat Paine, and his poetry after Alexander Pope. His *Sullivan's Island* follows slavishly Pope's *Windsor Forest;* his longer, more important work, *The Raciad,* recounts in couplets not often sprightly the great social and sporting event of the Southern city. Crafts gathered round himself a group of kindred spirits, who met together and talked and on rare occasions read poems: if they were not greatly interested in producing literature, they were at least interested in all things literary. An abler poet and a better man was Samuel Henry Dickson, but with him, in typically Southern fashion, poetry was only a hobby. His profession was the practice and teaching of medicine, and he left as monument not deathless verses but a flourishing medical school.[206]

Neither Crafts nor Dickson was intensely interested in the writing of poetry. On the basis of surface appearances the same statement can be made of Richard Henry Wilde, lawyer and congressman, but the statement would be utterly false. Wilde in his own opinion failed in life when he failed to write poetry which would endure. This was in part due to the vitiating nature of his belief that a great literary work could be written only in a land rich with legend and tradition and culture; in part to external circumstance, for his finest poem, "My Life Is Like the Summer Rose," brought not fame but charges of plagiarism, from men who should have known better.[207] Consciousness of literary sterility combined with a driving ardor for poetry caused him to take up scholarly research, but this substitute for creative expression never fully satisfied him.

[205] *A Selection in Prose and Poetry, from the Miscellaneous Writings of the Late William Crafts* (he died September, 1826, at the age of thirty-five), with a memoir of his life, was published in 1828. An excellent contemporary review is H. S. Legaré's "Crafts' Fugitive Writings," in Legaré's *Works,* II, 142–65; for a brief modern appraisal, see V. L. Parrington, *op. cit.,* II, 112–4.
[206] Dickson's poems have never been collected.
[207] See Anthony Barclay's pamphlet, *Wilde's Summer Rose.*

For all his misgivings, Wilde had a spark of genuine poetry within him. That he could have been a great poet in any time or place seems doubtful; in addition to theories and circumstances, he would have had to overcome a defect within himself. His poems do not develop in idea, theme, or story. Although he imitated Byron, he failed where the Englishman best succeeded: in communicable movement. Ironically, even in Wilde's sonnet, "To Lord Byron," this defect appears, for the lines seem to stop on a single idea, the words pile up without developing the thought. In his long unfinished poem, *Hesperia*, this static diffuseness nullifies the total value of a work which, in short sequences, is often powerful and arresting. The man reveals himself in the poem, although unintentionally, and the man revealed is worth knowing: a reflective philosopher, a satirist who attacks abstractions like gold rather than persons, a traveler with an eye for scenery, which he describes without quite fusing the objects into a word-portrait; above all, a man who could speak with justice of "my inexpressible weariness of life and spirit."[208]

As a poet he depended too much on eye and soul, upon that thin romantic atmosphere which, he felt, was thin because of lack of richness in his environment, and too little upon intellectual content. He had a knack mainly for writing melodious and impressive single lines (his best line, perhaps, was "On that lone shore loud moans the sea," with its graphic imagery accented by monotonous alliteration and rich vowel-color). On a few occasions, however, his inclination toward rhetorical oratory seems a natural part of the poem, as in the poignantly memorable "Farewell to America," or in the depth of feeling which strikes sharply through the deceptively light surface of "To the Mocking-Bird." The scanty records of Wilde's life

---

[208] R. H. Wilde, dedication of *Hesperia* (to the Marchioness Manfredina di Coenza). On the influence of Byron in America, see W. E. Leonard's *Byron and Byronism in America*.

do not show a man of infinite sadness, but the poems do; a congenial and successful person, to the world, but to himself a fit companion for the Lord Byron whom he admired so greatly. From this troubled and frustrated poet who judged himself and his work so stringently came one almost perfect lyric and a body of work which has been unjustly neglected.

If Wilde has with justice been relegated to the position of author of one poem, Edward Coote Pinkney has for no reason at all been accorded the same fate. In five years of writing, before his death at twenty-six, he produced half a dozen excellent lyrics and at least one stirring ode.[209] In personal character Pinkney represented a wide and influential strain in the Southern

[209] T. O. Mabbott and F. L. Pleadwell (*The Life and Works of Edward Coote Pinkney*, v–vi) have written a paragraph of such excellence as a summary that it well deserves inclusion here: "The importance historically of the first of the Southern lyrists, Poe's most immediate forerunner, and of the most noted poet of the United States Navy is evident enough. But Pinkney's verses have more claim to attention than their historical interest alone would entitle them to hold; they are in themselves poetry 'of the first water,' at their best 'perfect chrysolites,' as Willis has called them, at their worst never what any poet need blush to own. True, like every young poet, Pinkney had masters, though unlike many a young man he was of catholic taste, and numbered among his models poets ancient and modern, not only Tom Moore, but also the Cavalier lyrists; not only Byron, but Wordsworth as well. If some poems are imitative, others are strikingly original, and all have more or less a markedly individual flavor, unlike that of any other verse, distinctive, and in itself the sign of the true poetic gift. One of the fragments, *Cornelius Agrippa*, a palpable imitation of *Don Juan*, will illustrate this point. Compare it, in subject and treatment, with *Don Juan* and any other imitation of Byron, and the poet's innate originality is at once revealed. Then read one of the finest of the lyrics, 'Look out upon the stars, my love,' or the tremendous closing quatrain of *The Voyager's Song*, or the gallant *Health*, and the poet's power rings out clear. Distinguished particularly for enthusiasm, warm and vivid imagery, and what Hubner terms 'classic elegance of diction' Pinkney may be considered a worthy predecessor of the three other great Southern poets, Poe, Timrod, and Lanier; while his absolute preëminence in his own special field of English literature is perhaps as notable as that of Poe himself in his. Yet, except for the selections in the Anthologies, few have read Pinkney's poems; the slight bulk of his work, published before his early death, militated against his reputation; and of late years copies of the early editions of his *Poems* have become so scarce that many a student who desired to read other poems by the author of *A Health* has found it impossible to procure them outside of the very largest libraries."

group: he was a moral cavalier, who was touchy as to his honor and quick to challenge any man who impinged on it, who wrote gallant love songs to one fair lady at a time, and who was affected by classical, neoclassical, and romantic thought and poetry.[210] If his lyrics can be best compared with those of Thomas Carew, his indebtedness to Wordsworth's songs to Lucy cannot be overlooked; if in his longer work he took as models chiefly Lord Byron and Thomas Moore, he drew also upon Milton and Donne and the Elizabethan dramatists, upon Catullus and other Roman poets. For Pinkney was studious and learned, gay and moral, a young man who was gradually shaping and refining his thought and his poetry.

There is clear evidence in his poetry that he was working out a personal philosophy which would have deepened and enriched his individual lyric gift; out of his experimentation with more ambitious poems might have come a poem that was derivative only in the good sense of the word, that was distinctly his own while it remained securely in the tradition of English poetry.

This consideration gives to his career, inevitably, a sense of brilliant promise rather than a complete fulfillment. Yet his incompleteness is far from failure: Pinkney, like his section, was cut off at the period of greatest achievement, and, again like his section, his real values have been strangely neglected. In his thin sheaf of poems can be found some trash and much immature and incomplete work, but in at least a dozen poems, also, can be found the singing note of the true lyric poet.

The year that Pinkney died in Baltimore (1828) William Gilmore Simms of Charleston was editing his first magazine. Three years before he had published his first volume of verse: a monody in heroic couplets on the death in 1825 of General Charles Cotesworth Pinckney.[211] At the time Simms was a

[210] *Ibid.*, 24–9. There is no evidence that Pinkney ever fought a duel.
[211] Trent, *William Gilmore Simms*, 44–5.

young law student who watched from outside the group of wits presided over by William Crafts; in the years that followed he knocked almost vainly at the door of the literary group which, under the leadership of Hugh Swinton Legaré, founded *The Southern Review* and made Charleston a center of literary effort.[212] Not only was Simms a poor man of an undistinguished family, but he was also arrogantly free with his opinions. His vigorous opposition to Nullification, for one example, prejudiced many people against him.[213] Also, the leaders of the community thought better of the learned essays of Legaré than of any poems and stories; as for creative literature, in particular, they had a marked preference for English over American books.

Simms continued to write and to publish poetry, but he soon abandoned the heroic couplet for the looser Byronic forms. Only by accident did he turn romancer, and he never abandoned poetry—he valued his poems, in fact, more highly than his novels. His enormous energy, mental and physical, needed many outlets. The range of his poetry was astonishingly wide. He wrote long romantic narratives in verse, after the manner of Byron and Scott, sonnets after the manner of Wordsworth, and occasional poems of many types. In this final respect, Simms as poet was typically Southern. He preferred the occasional subject, preferred to write at white heat while men were stirred mightily by some immediate event.

In that was his fatal flaw, poetically. Brief and subjective lyric poems can be dashed off, in spite of all that critics may say, and some of them are surprisingly good; long poems even of the romantic type require a sustained thought—an effort which the Southerner grounded in the tenets of inspirational romanticism was unwilling to give to fiction or verse, but which he gave unsparingly to political theory. Simms shared this

---

[212] Linda Rhea (*Hugh Swinton Legaré*, 91-130) gives the best description of *The Southern Review* and of Legaré's work as editor.
[213] Trent, *op. cit.*, 58–62.

attitude, with the result that his long poems contain vivid and stirring passages, but mainly they contain a facile correctness which rarely attains distinction. Although his poetic masters were Byron and Wordsworth, his mind was more like Dryden's. But he lacked Dryden's severe genius; he could expand an idea much more easily than he could prune back the luxuriant growth of his fancy.

By 1860 Simms had published eighteen volumes of poetry. If Pinkney wrote too little, quantitatively, to gain him the critical consideration he deserved, Simms managed to smother some really excellent work under the weight of too much mediocrity. This bulky inequality is enough to explain why casual readers have passed him by, but it does not explain why the anthologists or, even more, his biographer, have paid so little attention to separating the good from the bad. For Simms could write powerfully, if not perfectly: in the rank undergrowth of words in "The Edge of the Swamp" there is caught a miasmic atmosphere redolent with local color; in many short poems the man's mental vitality more than compensates for his lack of artistry. That he lacked utterly the faculty of self-criticism was best revealed when he expanded and sadly vitiated his finest poem, until it lost the grandeur and finality of the first version:[214] "The Lost Pleiad" is an orchestrated expression of the transiency of the most stable objects, a poem which cuts through the conventionalities of that over-used subject and gives to it a lasting freshness and significance.

Simms was a man of positive defects and flaws. These are obvious enough, but their obviousness has for too long obscured his equally positive merits and achievements. From his entire poetic work only a small volume of excellent poems could be selected, but that volume would entitle Simms to rank with the better American poets.

Equally drastic principles of selectivity must be exercised on

[214] See notes on "The Lost Pleiad," p. 382.

the work of Thomas Holley Chivers, of Georgia. Damon has appropriately written that Chivers "straddled the famous fence between the sublime and the ridiculous, and quite as often fell on the one side as on the other. . . . He knew nothing about correctness. He made up words; his grammar was shaky; his rhymes were often common; he repeated his metaphors over and over; he padded his stanzas; he borrowed the best lines of other poets; he mixed his mythologies; he said silly, inconsequential things; he lacked restraint of every kind. He was morbid—worse yet, fashionably morbid; he believed in angels and was always writing about them; he was appallingly sincere; he printed far too much, under the impression that everything versified at the proper heat of enthusiasm was sacred. Nevertheless, through all his work, good and bad, runs the curious undercurrent of power which is the peculiar manifestation of genius."[215]

All this is true. It can be discerned by a careful reading of any typical Chivers poem, such as "Lily Adair." He was an eccentric, an *original*. On the surface his poetry is more easily identified with persons and places, with his background and his immediate life, than Poe's. To a large degree all that Chivers wrote was autobiographical. Poetry was a cathartic by which he partially purged his system. When marriage failed, he pitied in verse his broken life; when he beheld the Mississippi, he demanded with "mystical ardor" that it speak to him; when one of his children died, he wrote agonized yet liquid elegies. He gave to autobiographical facts a tinge of metaphysical idea, which transmuted the best of these poems into a borderland between this world and the next. It was not, exactly, a matter of all being grist that came to his mill; it was rather the absolute faith which Chivers had in the poet being the revelator of the divine will. While he dramatized himself and his sufferings, at first in

[215] S. F. Damon, *Thomas Holley Chivers*, xvi–xvii; Damon's entire introduction is a masterly piece of criticism.

Byronic fashion and later in his own original manner, even his most absurd dramatizations seem an integral part of his morbid subjectivity.

He was much possessed by death. Over one-third of his poems deal with that subject.[216] But he tended to escape quickly from the here to the hereafter, and his faith in immortality was unshakable. Moreover, he trusted implicitly the power of his musical words to sweep the reader into transcendental ecstasy at any moment. For Chivers had seen visions, which colored most of everything he wrote; he was a Swedenborgian, an associationist, a mystic without a sense of balance.

Let it be said here, also, that he was a poet. When all the qualifications—and they are numerous—have been listed which must be made, there remains an intrinsic value to his best poems which cannot be denied. "Inspiration and technique are the twin wings on which every poet soars; and both of Chivers' lacked many feathers. But occasionally in his eccentric flight, he shot high,"[217] wrote Damon, putting his finger upon the fundamental weakness of Thomas Holley Chivers. These things the Georgia poet had, although unevenly; what he lacked was the intellectual power to discipline them to his purpose. Inspiration and technique are not enough: at best, they result in the straitly limited poetry of a Coleridge or a Shelley. Chivers was not, in his kind, comparable in ability to the two Englishmen, who in their turn are not comparable to Webster and Jonson and Donne, much less to Shakespeare or Dante or Homer. But the field of poetry is wide, and capable of including diverse types and wide ranges of excellence. Only a prejudiced person would claim for Chivers a high place: all of his poetry is extraordinary, a great part of it is incredibly bad, but a residue of lyrical poetry (comparable, Damon suggests, to Beddoes' work rather than to Blake's)[218] is purely melodious and thinly authentic.

[216] *Ibid.*, 47–9, 164.   [217] *Ibid.*, 281.   [218] *Ibid.*, 275–8.

To this writer, at least, it seems impossible that we should ever again attempt an evaluation of the life and work of Edgar Allan Poe without a consideration also of Chivers. This distinction may be tentatively suggested: that Poe had a wild genius disciplined by artistry, Chivers a wayward talent which occasionally became genius. The two were literary brothers. Each man in his youth followed Byron, each in his early maturity Coleridge; each evolved strikingly individual theories and types of poetry which have obvious similarities. Each borrowed freely from the other and from any other poet whose work seemed attractive. Each was an unusual product of his time and of his peculiar environment (Poe by adoption the son of a Virginia gentleman, Chivers by birth a wealthy Georgian), yet each escaped from that environment into a cloudy, haunted other-world.[219]

This is important because later critics have evolved strange theories to explain the "mystery" of Poe. That he was at times a drunkard, and possibly an opium addict, is true enough, but these explain strange vagaries in his conduct without explaining his creative achievement in the least; that he was sexually impotent may have been true, but there seem few reasons to believe it, and many reasons not to believe it;[220] that he was a literary "man without a country," unique and unlocalized, is unadulterated nonsense.[221] Much misinterpretation might have been avoided if only slight attention had been paid to Chivers.

[219] It is interesting to compare Poe's critical works with the prefaces of Chivers in this respect, and Damon's analysis of Chivers's mind with K. Campbell's *The Mind of Poe*. Campbell has collected a vast amount of valuable material.

[220] J. W. Krutch (*Edgar Allan Poe*) and Ludwig Lewisohn (*Expression in America*, 154–68) present Freudian psychoanalyses of Poe with much sincerity but with very slight proof. Krutch paid no attention to similar persons of Poe's time.

[221] Allen (*Israfel—The Life and Times of Edgar Allan Poe*) has set the poet against the background of his environment. See also P. E. More, *Shelburne Essays*, First Series, 51–71: "The unearthly visions of Poe and Hawthorne are in no wise the result of literary whim or of unbridled individualism, but are deep-rooted in American history."

For he took no drugs, he preached abstinence from tobacco and alcohol, he fathered seven children, and he was, quite plainly, a citizen of Georgia.[222] Yet his critical theories parallel Poe's; his metaphysical speculations go far beyond Poe's; his poems have the same ghost-haunted atmosphere, and his visions are just as far removed from everyday reality.

To understand these men requires an understanding also of their age—a subject far too involved for analysis here, and one rarely treated. They were part of the romantic movement which had so many facets, but which, in the main, can be said to have completed the work of protestantism in making the individual all-important. It was a heady doctrine, which in the form of transcendentalism almost swept the cool Emerson from his moorings; in the form of German philosophy, it unseated Coleridge.[223] Men were affected in different ways: Poe detested transcendentalism as such, while every philosophical thought he uttered revealed a similar source; Chivers was attracted by it, and went beyond it into spiritualism. Both men, in that period of rootless intellects, explored the mental frontier: Poe pseudorationally, in *Eureka;* Chivers mystically, in *Search after Truth.* These wild books have numerous parallels by American writers of that day; they are in no sense unique; they are American variants of a widely scattered development of thought.

Poe's mind[224] had more of balance than did the mind of

[222] Damon, *op. cit.*, 122–24, 136, 151; J. A. Harrison, "Poe and Chivers," in *Complete Works of Edgar Allan Poe* (1902), VII, 266–88.

[223] See particularly J. L. Lowes, *The Road to Xanadu.* Poe and Chivers pillaged royally from the domain of Coleridge, the strangest and most significant Romantic in the English tradition. See Floyd Stovall's study, "Poe's Debt to Coleridge," University of Texas *Studies in English*, X, 70–127.

[224] His own statement is of value: "Men have called me mad but the question is not yet settled whether madness is or is not the loftiest intelligence, whether much that is glorious, whether all that is profound, does not spring from disease of thought—from *moods* of mind exalted at the expense of the general intellect." (Quoted by R. B. Johnson, "Memoir," *The Complete Works of Edgar Allan Poe*, Oxford Edition, xxxix.) See also W. F. Taylor's "Israfel in Motley: A Study of Poe's Humor," *Sewanee Review*, XLII, 330–40 (July–Sept., 1934).

Chivers or, for another example, of Bronson Alcott; his mind, indeed, seems that of an inferior, and American, Coleridge. That is, Poe could rationalize rather than philosophize about his beliefs; but in each case, if the reader will allow the first premises, the dialectic and the logic hold together with surprising tightness. Poe's theories of poetry require certain elements, previously discussed; his practice may have caused the theories, or the process may have been reversed. In all probability theory and practice developed together, the one as a normal part of the other.

At its best his poetry represents mood exalted at the expense of intellect. His aim was a dark beauty, secured in part by indefinite imagery and melodic, almost hypnotic, rhythm. That Poe could recognize and state poetically an intellectual truth he demonstrated in the "Sonnet—To Science": the destruction of age-old myth by science is his theme, and it is a worthy one. (The fascination which science held for Poe is more readily seen in his stories.) If he could realize such facts, he could not as poet remain greatly interested in them; he infinitely preferred his "ghoul-haunted woodland of Weir." Only a few poems deal with a specific locale. They catch instead an atmosphere, a somber mood, a haunted spirit.[225] His range was exceedingly narrow, his productivity small. His theme is slightly varied, yet basically constant: the death of a beautiful woman, the realm of the spirit, the psychological state of the poet when his mind is partially in another world. Combinations or variations of these themes are at the heart of nearly all of his finest lyrics.

The plot that Poe tilled was strait and infertile. From it, however, he wrung a few exquisite plants. With infinite pains he reworked his poems, elaborating here and pruning there, re-

[225] This is only partially true of his earlier poems, when he was largely imitating Byron and drawing upon Shelley and Moore as well as Coleridge; it does not include the versified trivialities to such ladies as Mrs. Osgood and Mrs. Shew. These poems reveal Poe at his worst, when he is reveling in romantic phrases and tender sentiments.

publishing his revised poem, and then subjecting it to additional revision. Perhaps it would be more appropriate to compare Poe with a lapidary, for he was constantly polishing his small and finely-cut gems. Even the best are likely to have one flaw: Poe's phraseology was lush as well as liquid.[226] His greater defect can be summarized in Poe's own judgment of Bryant, whom he denied a place with "the spiritual Shelleys" because "the objects in the moral or physical universe coming within the periphery of his vision" are exceedingly limited; "The relative extent of these peripheries of poetical vision must ever be a primary consideration in our classification of poets."[227] Where Poe's periphery ended it is most important that a great poet's shall begin: in completeness of vision. He saw only one phase of those realities which are of the human spirit. His "shuddering harmonies of the murky subconscious, and roseate harmonies of sensuous longing posing as spirituality"[228] are complete in themselves—but they are not extensive in scope or sympathy. Within his narrowed range Poe's achievement is remarkably high. It is this quality which gives him a certain pre-eminence

---

[226] For an example, see lines 3–4 of the first stanza of "Lenore," one of his best poems. Aldous Huxley ("Vulgarity in Literature," *Saturday Review of Literature*, VII, 158–9, Sept. 27, 1930) has objected to Poe's selection of proper names: "These proper-name rhyme-jewels are particularly flashy in Poe's case because they are mostly dissyllabic. Now, the dissyllabic rhyme in English is poetically so precious and so conspicuous by its richness that, if it is not perfect in itself and perfectly used, it emphatically ruins what it was meant emphatically to adorn." It is easy to agree with R. C. Pettigrew ("Poe's Rime," *American Literature*, IV, 151–9, Jan., 1933) that we may "grant that necessity was the mother of Poe's inventiveness in the names of *Auber, Weir, Yaanek, Ulalume*—are not these words of the very essence of the weird, and is not this sufficient compensation for their questionable parentage?" But this choice of unusual names was very common with nineteenth-century poets: for example, the names of women in Tennyson's "May Queen" (1832), in Keats, etc. A. G. Newcomer ("The Poe-Chivers Tradition Re-examined," *Sewanee Review*, XII, 28–30, Jan., 1904) discusses this phase of romantic poetry slightly.

[227] Foerster, *American Criticism*, 50. Foerster's conclusions seem excellent and accurate.

[228] *Ibid.*, 50.

over Emerson or Whitman, whose vast peripheries of vision are rarely clarified or expressed in words of finality. What Poe had to say is communicated poetically and with finality. But there is more to be said—and failure in this regard makes Edgar Allan Poe a limited poet.

Deliberate experiments in prosody began with Poe and Chivers. Each desired to write in original forms.[229] Poe stated his ideas clearly in "The Philosophy of Composition," in "The Rationale of Verse," and in other essays; all his efforts were directed toward "the creation of novel moods of beauty, in form, in color, in sound, in sentiment."[230] As G. W. Allen has observed, "All of Poe's experimentation with rime, alliteration, 'indefinite' imagery, and even meter, progresses toward the attainment of this one ideal, and is realized most successfully in such poems as *Ulalume*, *Lenore*, and *The Raven*. Here we have the 'essential' Poe (at any rate in versification); here his theory and practice most unmistakably converge."[231]

Only in "The Bells" did Poe carry this experimentation with onomatopoeia to an extreme, with his attempts to represent four moods through jolly sleigh bells, mellow wedding bells, loud alarum bells, and solemn tolling bells. Generally he attempted to fit meter and stanza form to the precise mood of the poem, to make every poetic device accentuate the sense by fusing sound and sense (or atmosphere) into a whole.[232]

Chivers was bolder and less successful in his experimentation.

[229] Cf. Chivers's letter to Simms (Appendix, p. 322) and Poe's "The Philosophy of Composition" (Appendix, pp. 338 ff).

[230] Poe, review of Longfellow's *Ballads and Other Poems*.

[231] *American Prosody*, 85; pages 56–88 contain an excellent discussion of Poe's experiments in technique.

[232] Poe describes the purpose of the versification and devices used in "The Raven" in "The Philosophy of Composition." Although some critics have dismissed the essay as a hoax, I see no reason why it should not be regarded as extremely valuable in explaining Poe's general method and his intent. Naturally it must be used with caution, since it was rationalization of how the poem had been written *after* the actual writing—but Poe's constant revisions and experimentations are proof that his mind was often engrossed with such problems.

In his first volume he calmly invented a stanza of nine lines, rhyming *ababcdcdd*, in an attempt to round out with an extra rhyme the tonal qualities of a common form; in a late and revised version of "Georgia Waters" he returned to this stanza form with a slight variation in the rhyme—*ababcbcbb*. Usually his experiments were directed toward the cult of sound.[233] Melody, musical overtones, hypnotic sound, meant more to him than idea or thought. This was responsible for his belief that the refrain was not an ornament, but an essence, of a poem. For the sake of euphony he did not hesitate to invent new words, or to twist the meaning of strange and archaic words until he secured the liquid melody that he thought vital. Certain words and refrains do yeoman service many times. He was attempting to build songs "out of pure sound and a rich stream of apparently unrelated images."[234] The richness of open vowels, of luxuriant alliteration and repetitive devices were not enough to satisfy him: "He was interested in the songs of birds, the metallic diapason of bells, the weird thin music of the Chinese, the puffing of a railroad."[235] In one poem he imitated with great success the rhythm of the negro songs, using negro dialect. In several poems he wrote in the cadence that Whitman used most often. Only one of these experimental poems need be quoted here, his "Railroad Song":

> Clitta, clatta, clatta, clatter,
> Like the devil beating batter
> Down below in iron platter—
> Which subsides into a clanky,

[233] Chivers, *The Path of Sorrow*. See also Damon, *op. cit.*, 208, 227. Of less interest are his poems in blank verse, although they have definite elements of originality. Damon thinks that the poet counted ten syllables to the line, and let the accent fall as it might. Whatever the cause, the result is sometimes chaotic, sometimes powerful.

[234] Damon, *op. cit.*, 234.

[235] *Ibid.*, 235. Damon reprints excerpts from these poems (230–41) and discusses the indebtedness of Swinburne, Rossetti, Kipling, Poe, and other poets (265,273). I have followed his account closely.

And a clinky, and a clanky,
And a clinky, clanky, clanky,
And a clanky, clinky, clanky;
And the song that I now offer
For Apollo's Golden Coffer—
With the friendship that I proffer—
Is for Riding on a Rail.[236]

Like his other experiments with sound it was intended to be recitative, and it antedated the similar experiments of Vachel Lindsay. However, these poems were buried in almost forgotten magazines; although interesting in themselves, they had little effect upon Southern poets.

Poe and Chivers belong to that class loosely denominated by the word *genius*. Simms did not. But he valued their friendship, and they in turn valued his; they kept in touch through correspondence. Simms submitted his work to Poe, who gladly published it; and he preached to both men from afar the unwelcome doctrine of his prejudiced common sense. More nearly akin to Simms in mind and work was Philip Pendleton Cooke, who attempted with little success to recapture the old bardic ardor in his ballads on historical subjects. Cooke also wrote with great rapidity. Only once did he attain a marked popular esteem, with the delicately pleasing "Florence Vane." A better poem, possibly because it expressed spontaneously Cooke's ideal of the way of living, was his "Life in the Autumn Woods." Cooke did not have Simms's vitality, however; his character, his work, and even his promise all are pleasant, but all seem definitely slight.[237] By 1850 Poe and Cooke were dead;

[236] Here quoted from Damon. Chivers was evidently well pleased with this poem: he printed it in *The Georgia Citizen*, June 21, 1851; *Graham's Magazine*, Feb., 1852; *Waverley Magazine*, Oct. 8, 1853.

[237] No study of Cooke has been made. A few of his letters on literary conditions in the South and on his own work are reprinted in a short article, "Philip Pendleton Cooke," *Southern Literary Messenger*, XVII, 669–73 (Oct., 1851; reprinted from *International Magazine*).

after 1853 (when he published three volumes of poetry) Chivers practically passed from the literary scene.

Simms continued. And the group which gathered around him in Charleston was no mean one. To its leadership he came late, after the death of Hugh Swinton Legaré—but to leadership he had come, until in the 1850's he was the "Nestor" of Southern letters, the master of "Woodlands" and the friend of literary aspirants.[238] This group had a convenient meeting place in Russell's Bookstore, for "Lord John" Russell was more interested in good conversation than in sales. In the afternoon, when work was done, certain men would drop in to browse and talk: Simms, William J. Grayson, James L. Petigru, Samuel Henry Dickson and his namesake and son-in-law J. Dickson Bruns, James Mathewes Legaré, and other distinguished persons. Younger men were coming to the shop to take the place of those who died, like Legaré, or of those who moved away, like Dickson. To this coterie belonged Basil Gildersleeve, Henry Timrod, and Paul Hamilton Hayne. Here books were discussed, poems read, and theories debated. A smaller club of nine men met frequently at Simms's town house—the "Wigwam"—and facetious neighbors who lived blocks away would comment next morning on the poet's thunderous declamations.

Even the names of some of these Charleston intellectuals have been forgotten; in a few instances, justly. One gifted poet has dropped from sight, with a resultant loss to our poetry: James Mathewes Legaré's one small book, with the unpromising title *Orta-Undis*, contains five poems which have, beneath the gentle moralizing and simple verse structure, a graceful and individual statement of old truths in pleasingly new combinations. His book is uneven, his poetry often derivative but some-

[238] P. H. Hayne, "Ante-Bellum Charleston," *Southern Bivouac*, I, 193–202, 257–68, 327–36, gives a picturesque and sympathetic account of life in Charleston. His first article deals chiefly with H. S. Legaré and R. Y. Hayne; his second with Simms; his third with Russell's Bookshop and *Russell's Magazine*—which Hayne edited. See also Trent, *op. cit.*, 226–37.

times authentic. Legaré remained strictly within the Southern
tradition: a classicist, his title poem is in Latin; an occasional
poet, he wrote an excellent and memorable tribute to his kinsman, Hugh Swinton Legaré; a lover of nature, he wrote well on
that popular and difficult subject. In these poems his romanticism, his indebtedness to Wordsworth, Schiller, and Tennyson,
can be found, but playing over this romanticism is the precision
of mind natural to a classicist. Ironically enough, his most
widely reprinted poem was an oriental legend, "Ahab-Mohammed," in the manner of Leigh Hunt's "Abou Ben Adhem."
For Legaré wrote better poems—slight enough, it is true, yet
poems which reveal a fresh, observant eye for nature and for
earth, and a rhythm and style which ideally fitted his gentle
muse.[239]

Legaré was a minor figure. By some odd trick of fate, Timrod has been relegated to a role which Legaré deserved. In his
early days Timrod was the conventional poet, following closely
in the footsteps of Wordsworth. That he understood the meaning and purpose of poetry he clearly revealed in his critical
articles; in the youthful *Vision of Poesy* he wrote:

> My task hath been, beneath a mightier power,
> To keep the world forever fresh and young ...
>
> I turn life's tasteless waters into wine,
> And flash them through and through with purple tints.

But the vision, though high and noble, is the work of youth,
and as poetry it is weak and uneven. One feels beneath the lines
desire, not conviction; dreams, not philosophy or reflection. In
the assertion that "the poet to the whole wide world belongs"
there is a wealth of meaning: all the rootlessness of one who had
learned the technique, had mastered the art of poetic reference
and communication, but had never really had anything to say.

[239] L. Lewisohn, "James Mathewes Legaré," in *Library of Southern Literature*, VII, 3191 ff.

He wrote pleasing tributes to ladies and graceful poems about nature, but he suffered much from his inability to loose the feelings that stirred within him.

The war awakened all his dormant emotions. The whole wide world was forgotten in his absorption with something which lay nearer his hand and his heart. His technique and intellectual turn of mind now served him well: although sincerity and throbbing emotion beat through his words in passionate undertones, the passion never carries the verse into formlessness of thought or reference. Instead an almost classic coolness and restraint appears, from first to last, in his war poems. This quality more than any other marks Timrod's undoubted superiority over his comrade Hayne—over, for that matter, every Southern poet except Edgar Allan Poe. The friendly Northern critic, Thomas Wentworth Higginson, thought that South Carolina was somewhat to blame for Hayne's poetic shortcomings: it denied him "a nation," and thus made a handicap of his love for the state.[240] But the geographical sweep of a man's affections has nothing to do with his poetic intensity; in Timrod's case the state was enough and nation or world would not have made Hayne a greater poet: the diffuseness of his writing thinned out the content. Not that Hayne felt less deeply than Timrod—it was not that; Hayne failed in the attempt to communicate that feeling. He had certain natural advantages: "the passion for the poet's calling, the thirst for natural beauty, the spirit of brooding peace, the reminiscent note, the mystic strain."[241] But the thirst for natural beauty was a sensuous and surface thirst; although he lived for twenty years at Copse Hill, Hayne never seems to have acquired a feeling of the richness and fertility of earth, or of man's dependence upon it.

Possibly Hayne had felt too deeply the tragedy of war and

[240] T. W. Higginson, "Paul Hamilton Hayne," in *Chautauquan*, VII, (Jan., 1887).
[241] *Ibid.*

defeat, of poverty and reconstruction. In his poetry there is a certain negative quality, a turning away from what was immediately about him, which shows more glaringly in his complete works than it possibly can in a selection. A kindly man, he had no desire to cherish animus, and his letters and poems to various Northern poets ring plaintively with a desire for fellowship and friendly feeling. But the ugly, stubborn facts were all about him, obtruding even into the quietude of Copse Hill—and he could neither bear nor deny them. True, he never, as Lanier did, spoke directly the messages which a progressive nation desired to hear; he retired within himself, although his correspondence with American and European poets was surprisingly large. But his retirement was real enough, in the sense that he preferred not to think of what had happened, or what, under an industrialistic regime, was happening to the South. Literature meant escape; poetry meant beauty. And he could find beauty in the pines, in the clouds, in the birds, in the lush vegetation that grew so plentifully around him. Beauty was not much in men, and when he thought of nobility it brought him back too swiftly to older days which wrung a man's heart to think upon.

The escape was involuntary, perhaps, and surely from the standpoint of one individual's happiness it was far better than any amount of, most likely, unavailing thought. Hayne never shirked a direct task. He edited the poems of Timrod, before his own poems were collected, and he wrote for that volume a preface which is just and generous, which deserves, indeed, more adjectives of praise than captious men in our day would ever permit to be given it without a cynical sneer. For back of it, and hovering close to the surface, are the unshed tears of men who could not weep, and who rarely, very rarely, yielded to the hysteria which every man at that time must, in part, have felt. Hayne told the pathetic story of Timrod's life with tenderness, with ungrudging admiration, yet with a certain calmness of phrase which tears the heart. The man was infinitely gentle, and great.

Yet it is as poets that we must, finally, be concerned with Hayne and Timrod. That Hayne was a minor poet is certain: his reputation must rest upon a few competent and noble sonnets, and upon a few truly fine lyrics. He wrote narrative poems which can be read as easily as the similar works of Tennyson or William Morris can be read. Although the average level of craftsmanship which he attained in all his work is amazingly high, his finest achievements are never far above that standard. Lanier noted his obvious faults: "First, we observe a frequently recurring *lapsus* of thought, in which Mr. Hayne falls into trite similes, worn collocations of words, and common-place sentiments. ... The second fault ... is diffuseness, principally originating in a lavishness and looseness of adjectives."[242] These faults suggest a diffuseness of thought as well as of words, a lack of that predestinate iron which is the heritage of great poets. He could write poignant monodies for his friends after their deaths, kindly tributes to fellow poets and to his son—but he was at his best when he sang of the pines or when he considered the fleeting transiency of his own days.

Timrod's frail body lacked strength, but his mind possessed the clarity of thought and the iron which Hayne's mind somehow lacked. He saw a poem as a whole, yet as composed of lines, and his best poems combine a clear distinction of line with a sense of rounded completeness. His early nature poems are Wordsworthian in tone and character; even his excellent sonnets owe something to that earlier poet. In the best of this work—particularly in "I Know Not Why" and "Most Men Know Love"—he began to speak in his own tongue. When war came he spoke boldly: in long odes like "Ethnogenesis" and "The Cotton Boll," in spirited lyrics like "Carolina" and "Charleston"—all first-rate poems. "The Cotton Boll" belongs

[242] Lanier, *Music and Poetry*, 206–7.

definitely to the land, rather than to nature as such; "it is the voice of the agricultural, commercial, and militant South."[243] Timrod could express this quality, but he could express even better the sadness and horror of war. In "Spring" he achieved a perfect balance with his idyllic yet half-sad picture of a world breaking into bloom thrown abruptly in contrast with "the call of death":

> Yet not more surely shall the Spring awake
> The voice of wood and brake,
> Than she shall rouse, for all her tranquil charms,
> A million men to arms.

Not only was it Timrod who sang of war; it was Timrod who wrote for the dead a memorial poem "that approximates perfection."[244] His "Ode" has the supreme artistic merit of throbbing with vibrant emotion in its effect upon a reader, yet of possessing a classic coolness of phrase which might have been carved from stone. The poet indulges in no histrionic exhibitionism, but this controlled and inevitable verse leaves nothing to be said:

> In seeds of laurel in the earth
> The blossom of your fame is blown,
> And somewhere, waiting for its birth,
> The shaft is in the stone!

Before 1860 the stimulus of war produced few notable lyrics in the South; from the War of 1812, perhaps the greatest occasional song ever produced in America, "The Star-Spangled Banner"; from the Mexican War, Theodore O'Hara's "The Bivouac of the Dead." Key wrote nothing else of importance; O'Hara, at most, wrote only two other poems. One of these has close kinship with "The Bivouac": it honors Daniel Boone, it

243 G. A. Wauchope, *Henry Timrod*, 27.
244 Trent, *op. cit.*, 235.

follows the same form, and it too is elegiac. Each man succeeded in expressing with finality the emotions of a people.
These poems have almost an anonymous value, seeming to stem
out of the general consciousness rather than from one man's
mind; it is that happy quality which gives to them enduring worth.

No single poem written during the Civil War quite attains
this height; two works, however, almost achieved it. The near-
est approach is Randall's "Maryland, My Maryland." Written
at white heat one night, read to his students next day, and published in the New Orleans *Delta* within a week, it spread over
the entire South when it was set to the music of the German college tune "Lauriger Horatius" (itself founded on "Tannenbaum,
O Tannenbaum"). Something of universality and of anonymity "My Maryland" does possess; it has been spoken of as
"the Marseillaise of the Confederacy," but this statement is
over-strong. The concentrated lines suggest the passion of
a people proclaiming liberty, but the song falls a little short
of finality—a lack easily explained in the fact that men were
too widespread, no longer homogeneous enough to feel great
passion as a tribal possession. Loyalty too was divided and
uncertain, for North and South were still one nation; the foe
was not quite foreign. The song which permeated even more
widely through the South, which indeed as to music answered
every requirement, was "Dixie," written by Dan D. Emmett
for Bryant's minstrels in 1859. The older version has the homely
picturesqueness of a folk ballad: it was stirring, not dignified.
After the manner of folk ballads the text underwent many sea
changes—in some instances improvements, in others, detri-
ments. But as a song it quickly became the possession of a
people, gaining in time the unofficial rank of a national (after the
Confederacy was defeated, a sectional) anthem. This came
about almost in spite of the words, for the text was altered
and changed many times,[245] while men and women sought

[245] See the notes on "Dixie," pp. 387 ff.

vainly to write words for the music which would be both dignified and popular. The effort was vain. Most attempts were
silly or sentimental or bombastic; the best version is Albert
Pike's somewhat pompous "Southrons, hear your country call
you!" Pike's version is literary, made for the printed page instead of the camp or singing group. "Dixie" as usually sung at
present may well be described as the finest ballad which America
has produced.

Other songs attained a tremendous popularity with the soldiers: "The Bonnie Blue Flag," "Lorena," and "Listen to the
Mocking-Bird" are probably the best examples. Even more
interesting are the verses improvised for the occasion by the
soldiers themselves. A writer in the *Southern Bivouac* (July,
1885) has described this making of homemade epics:

As the long contest dragged on, and war, losing much of its
earlier illusions, became a stern, bitter, and exceedingly monotonous reality, these "high-toned" lyrics were tacitly voted
rather too romantic and poetical for the actual field, and were
remitted to the parlor and the piano stool. The soldiers chanted
in quite other fashion on the march or seated at the campfire.
In these crude rhymes, some of them improvised for the moment, there was less of flourish but more of meaning, not so
much bravado but a good deal more point. They were sappy
with the homely satire of the camps, which stings friend and
foe alike. Innumerable verses were composed and sung to popular refrains. The Army of Virginia and the Army of Tennessee
had each its history rudely chronicled as fast as made in this
rough minstrelsy. Every corps and command contributed some
commemorative stanza. The current events of campaigns were
told in improvised verse as rapidly as they occurred and were
thereafter skillfully recited by the rhapsodist who professed to
know the whole fragmentary epic.[246]

These improvisations have chiefly folk values. The poets

[246] *Cambridge History of American Literature*, II, 297. This chapter (III,
Book III) gives a detailed account of the "Poets of the Civil War."

were not idle. Every person who could write patriotic verse, it seems, did so, North and South: the result on both sides is an amazing mélange of excellent, fair, bad, and terrible poetry. The course of the war can be traced in the poetry, can be traced, indeed, in the work of the best Southern poet, Timrod. He anticipated the war with his hopefully prophetic "The Cotton Boll"; hailed the birth of the Confederacy with a stately ode, "Ethnogenesis"; rallied the South in general with the passionate "A Cry to Arms," and South Carolina in particular, somewhat later, with the ringing lyric, "Carolina"; wrote nobly an elegy to "The Unknown Dead"; cried pathetically for the end of bloodshed and the return of peace in a bitter pastoral, "Spring"; mourned the destruction of his native city with "Charleston"; and at last, when war's fever was over, Timrod wrote the noblest of his poems (the finest that came out of the war), the "Ode" to the Confederate dead. Yet Timrod's war poetry was but a part—although the finest part—of his poetic achievement. If the same continuity cannot be found in the work of another individual, it can be found in the sweep of poetry which tended to submerge individual personalities under stress of emotion, and to give most of the poems a distinct kinship with related poems by other men. However sharply defined each elegy may be, for instance, it relates to other elegies in attitude and often in phraseology, until the conclusion seems inescapable that these grew out of a folk consciousness as much as they did out of an individual's brain.

If the war brought forth no poem which assumed universality, defeat did. (This question is not one of literary values alone, by any means; none of these poems considered from this angle—"The Star-Spangled Banner," "The Bivouac of the Dead," "Dixie," or "The Conquered Banner"—compare with the best work of Poe or Timrod, to stick to Southern poets; it has to do with the acceptance almost as a heritage of a poem by a people.) Father Ryan had served as soldier and chaplain through the war, and to the Confederacy he had given his whole allegiance. At white heat he dashed off "The Conquered Banner," and it was accepted immediately as the poem of defeat. Ryan had many of the qualities of the scōp, the bard of the people;[247] he almost improvised his poems, he felt a little more deeply what all were feeling, and gave adequate expression to that common emotion. Ryan left no memorable poem of the war, but immediately afterward he wrote three of the finest poems that we have: the other two, "The Sword of Robert Lee" and "A Land without Ruins," are of the same general type, but they failed to strike quite the same note.

The tragic histories of Edgar Allan Poe and of Thomas Holley Chivers might well have been the subjects for Greek dramatists: each man possessed a fatal flaw within himself, although that flaw is partially indefinable. Neither man had balance; neither acted, in literature or in life, with moderation. Timrod's was a modern tragedy: he was crushed and beaten by outside forces—grinding poverty which led to sickness and to death—over which he could have no possible control. Timrod in early days had too much balance; he could not turn himself loose and write. The result is that he left no bad poems in the sense that certain poems of Poe and particularly of Chivers are bad; but in that early work no magnificent passages sweep the reader away. The war released him, and the war in turn ruined him.

To a lesser degree the war also ruined many another Southern poet. In Hayne's case health was spared; he lived on in a poverty which was not quite a matter of starvation, but which forced him away from the social life he had known and loved. How plaintively he cherished the autographs of Simms and Timrod, written on the bare walls of his hut; how faithfully he corresponded with men whom he could not visit—these tokens show a mental starvation which is only a little less pathetic than

[247] See the notes on "The Conquered Banner," p. 395.

the bodily starvation of Timrod. And Hayne needed the stimulus of conversation, the wit of verbal battle, more than most poets. Left alone, he mellowed rather than ripened.

The war which set abstraction free did more than cut off men in their prime. It changed an entire way of life, it uprooted an old, sound culture and substituted for it a new civilization. The result of that uprooting can best be traced in the life and poetry of Sidney Lanier. In Lanier's failure there are elements both of modern and of Greek tragedy; after the war he struggled manfully if unavailingly against the relentless forces of poverty and of disease. But his failure as a poet must also be sought within himself; he attempted to substitute a vague emotional sensibility for philosophy and thought.

This is easily illustrated. A contemporary critic wrote that "Mr. Lanier's poetic sensibility and poetic purpose cannot make up for a lack of clear expression in his writing. This lack is the evidence not so much of want of practice in composition as of discipline of thought."[248] Set against this criticism the poet's reply, in a letter to this brother: ". . . It has naturally caused me to make a merciless arraignment and trial of my artistic purposes; and an unspeakable content arises out of the revelation that they come from the ordeal confirmed in innocence and clearly defined in their relations with all things. I do not hate the people who have so cruelly maltreated me; they knew not what they did. . . ."

This characteristic evasion of the real problem is at the heart of one's difficulty in judging the work of Lanier. To evaluate the work of Poe it is necessary only to understand the strict limitations which he, or nature, imposed, then to place Poe's performance within that limit and to set that narrow but precise art in the tradition. Artistic evaluations are never exact, but a reasonably just approximation is not difficult. Timrod likewise thought and wrote with precision. But the voice of Lanier is a

[248] See Starke, *op. cit.*, 245–6, where the criticism and reply are quoted.

large voice with a sweep and breadth which has caused Edwin
Mims to write that "there are moods when the imperfection of
Lanier pleases more than the perfection of Poe—even from the
artistic standpoint."[249] This dimensional power requires examination in the light of Lanier's confident intention to be a great
poet: "I *know*, through the fiercest tests of life, that I am in
soul, and shall be in life and utterance, a great poet."[250]

As always, qualifications must be made. Many poems are
sadly in need of revision; those poems which Lanier did revise
are greatly improved over the earlier versions. He had little
time for revision. On that score many imperfections can be
forgiven him. Also, his theories that music and poetry were
governed by identical laws may have hampered his work. This
point is doubtful: what Lanier succeeded in doing was in pre-
senting musical effects (which is far different from using musical
methods).[251] These are incidental; they can be allowed to one
who speaks out of a large and wise philosophy.

But this largeness is in part confusion founded upon abstraction. This appears in the first lines of "The Symphony":

> "O Trade! O Trade! would thou wert dead!
> The time needs heart—'tis tired of head:
> We're all for love," the violins said.

---

[249] E. Mims, *Sidney Lanier*, 342.

[250] *Ibid.*, 361 (quoted). See also Lanier's letter to his father, written from
Baltimore, November 29, 1873, and quoted, *ibid.*, 124–6.

[251] T. S. Eliot (*Selected Essays*, 282) in writing on Swinburne makes
a point which is equally applicable to Lanier: "The beauty or effect of
sound is neither that of music nor that of poetry which can be set to
music. There is no reason why verse intended to be sung should not
present a sharp visual image or convey an important intellectual meaning,
for it supplements the music by another means of affecting the feelings.
What we get in Swinburne is an expression by sound, which could not
possibly associate itself with music. For what he gives is not images and
ideas and music, it is one thing with a curious mixture of suggestions of all
three." However, W. L. Schramm, a careful metrical student who has
specialized on the subject for years, thinks (*American Literature*, March,
1935) that the latest and most scientific investigations have supported the
"supreme importance" of Lanier's stress on time.

The trade which he attacks in rhapsodic fashion is embodied in the nationalism which he praised so highly in "Psalm of the West"—a problem which Lanier never considered. He would solve the evils which trade had brought with a single phrase, *Love thy neighbor*, and he added, explicitly, the corollary that *All men are neighbors*,[252] thus reducing love to a humanitarian abstraction which, in the attempt to embrace equally those who live in New York and Shanghai with those who live next door, inevitably makes personal affection approximate close to zero. This is perhaps best illustrated in the chaotic "Psalm of the West":

> And Science be known as the sense making love to the All,
> And Art be known as the soul making love to the All,
> And Love be known as the marriage of man with the All—
> Till Science to knowing the Highest shall lovingly turn,
> Till Art to loving the Highest shall consciously burn,
> Till Science to Art as a man to a woman shall yearn,
> —Then Morn!

Even the capitals are indicative. It is, as Warren has observed, "probably, a defect of taste to prefer 'darling Tennyson' to Milton; it is a defect of another order to confound science with art, the abstract with the concrete, the practical with the contemplative."[253] This defect is plain: to Lanier, the world was governed by Platonic abstractions. His mind was soft and sentimental, capable even, in that same poem, of depicting the Civil War as a joust between Head (the North) and Heart (the South), with a remarkable power for reversing what little imagery he put into this queer poem. Once again he had evaded the central problem while he talked in honeyed abstractions.

To my mind this goes beyond a statement that Lanier did not

[252]The italics are Lanier's; the phrases from "The Symphony."
[253]R. P. Warren, "Sidney Lanier: The Blind Poet," *American Review*, II, 27–45 (Nov., 1933). This is the best critical appraisal of Lanier's poetry; of less extent, but valuable, is Allen Tate's "A Southern Romantic," *New Republic*, LXXVI, 67–70 (Aug. 30, 1933).

understand the function of ideas in art. It explains the man—a man confused, muddled in his philosophy, and with no love for thought. "Metaphors come of love rather than of thought,"[254] he wrote, and if by love is understood a vague emotional sensitivity, what he called an "etherialization," then Lanier's failure as a philosophical poet is explained.

When as poet he attempted only to feel and to see, Lanier approached greatness. He beheld more than conventional landscapes: he saw details of nature in sharp objectivity. "In 'Corn' for once an American poet strode into our splendid native golden fields and sang what his eyes saw, and deeper, what the harvest of the fields can be for man." The poem only partially deserves this high praise, for in it are more than traces of the vague, cloudy rhetoric and tortured fancy which Edmund Gosse detected as substitutes for passion and imagination:[255]

> Old hill! Old hill! thou gashed and hairy Lear
> Whom the divine Cordelia of the year,
> E'en pitying spring, will vainly try to cheer—

This straining for effect at any cost mars a fine poem; it was a fault which Lanier could never eradicate. At least, however, he recognized it: "I have frequently noticed in myself a tendency to a diffuse style; a disposition to push my metaphors too far, employing a multitude of words to heighten the patness of the image and so making of it a *conceit*."[256] What he failed to recognize is perhaps even more important, that too often his metaphors and conceits—as above, and in the poem "Clover"—

[254] Lanier, "Nature-Metaphors," in *Music and Poetry*, 95. Lanier defines love as "a term here used to signify the general underlying principle of all emotion."

[255] E. Gosse, "Has America Produced a Poet?" in *Questions at Issue*, 78–81. On Lanier's philosophic and artistic attitude toward nature see N. Foerster's essay in *Nature in American Literature;* and see S. T. Williams's essay on Lanier in *American Writers on American Literature*, ed. by John Macy.

[256] Cf. Warren's discussion of this letter, written by Lanier to his father, January 18, 1864; quoted in Mims, *op. cit.*, 56.

do not represent anything. They have only a blurred relation to the subject.[257]

His fondness for secondhand metaphors drawn from books gives a faint, unconvincing literary odor to many of his poems. When he sees nature through a Shakespearean play, as in "Marsh Song—At Sunset," he invariably keeps the idea abstract; it never achieves the status of experience. Fortunately he sometimes forgets his unassimilated reading, forgets his belief that the artist must be "afire with moral beauty just as with physical beauty," forgets his philosophy, and writes. Then he becomes the poet. Then he writes such valid and impressive poems as the artless and spontaneously spiritual "Ballad of Trees and the Master" and the quick-moving, brutal, uncharacteristic "Revenge of Hamish."

When one forgets the message intended for the brain and concentrates on the pictorial harmonies intended for eye and ear, one can find a definite beauty in "Sunrise" and "Song of the Chattahoochee." In this he excelled. With good reason have critics acclaimed "The Marshes of Glynn" his finest poem; the philosophical moral is bedded so deeply that the reader is hardly conscious of it, while the gorgeous sweep of scene is carried by an uneven melodious effect which weaves and twists through forest patterns, through the live-oaks and the marsh-grass, the marsh and the sea. The effect is hypnotic:

> How still the plains of the waters be!
> The tide is in his ecstasy.
> The tide is at his highest height:
>   And it is night.

Entire sections of it are magnificently sensuous, and only those sections have much value. But they comprise most of the poem.

In his spontaneous lyrics and his sensuous descriptive verse Lanier achieves striking and original effects. I do not refer to

[257] Cf. Allen Tate, *op. cit.*, 68.

his virtuosity in such a poem as "The Symphony," with its simulation of each instrument in an orchestra. That is only a clever experiment in technique by a dexterous artificer, which concentrates attention on the superficial form. In better and less obvious poems he skillfully used alliteration, tone color, vowel sounds, and mixed rhythms to give musical effects and pictorial values: the ultimate effect is that of a richly embroidered sensuosity, which, unlike Swinburne's, never shades into sensuality. Only when he neglects his philosophy does he write authentic poetry. For that reason it is impossible to agree with John Macy that only "three volumes of unimpeachable poetry have been written in America, 'Leaves of Grass,' the thin volume of Poe, and the poetry of Sidney Lanier"[258]—(there are, also, Emerson and Timrod and Emily Dickinson). In Lanier's case the elimination of bad poems must be too drastic. Yet, in the six or eight which remain, there is the distinctive mark of a poet who wrote far better than he knew, who achieved a limited but fine body of work which in the main is unlike that which greater poets have done.

Father Ryan and Father Tabb, the two Catholic poets of the South, indicate two divergent attitudes. Each had served in the war, but to Ryan, for all his piety, the war and the South were consuming and passionate subjects of tragedy. He was not a great poet, but he was handling with dignity a great theme. Tabb was a younger man; after the war he studied and taught in Baltimore; in his poetry the influence of the war can hardly be traced. The one was a mystic who could never rid himself of reality; the younger a realist who could not quite achieve mysticism. Possibly that is why Ryan's poetry, for all its limitations, remains so attractive, while Tabb's polished epigrams are quickly read and rarely remembered.

---

[258] J. Macy, *The Spirit of American Literature*, 309–23. Russell (*An Hour of American Literature*, 112–16) concludes his enthusiastic appreciation with "Behold the advantages of a poet that is also a musician!"

Lanier hymned a new nation; Ryan eulogized a dead nation; Tabb withdrew into a cloistered school. An able poet different from any of these men devoted his brief and troubled life to the effort of recapturing tranquillity in a period of emotional stress. He caught the difficult spirit which gives an inner reality to the superficial aspects of local color; with reason Joel Chandler Harris wrote that "Irwin Russell was among the very first of Southern writers to appreciate the literary possibilities of the negro character."[259] His dialect poems are slightly sentimentalized, and his work is incomplete: before his death Russell was planning a series of poems and novels which might have placed him with Harris and his stories of Uncle Remus. As it is, only one poem raises him above the rank of an erratic, wandering, yet richly gifted minstrel. That poem is "Christmas-Night in the Quarters"—a masterpiece which has been inexplicably neglected, but which is not surpassed by a more famous poem in the same *genre:* Whittier's "Snow-Bound." For his ideas of poetry Russell owed much to Robert Burns, but any direct indebtedness is hardly discernible. Yet, like Burns, he attempted to portray—never to exploit or to degrade in making out a case —characters whom he knew and loved. He never portrayed a single character who captivated the imagination of a people, but in "Christmas-Night" he wrote an operetta of the Negro in convincing dialect, and with a skillful fusion of the religious, humorous, pathetic, and noble elements of life which his friends in the quarters possessed.

In the South, as in the country generally, the years from 1880 to 1910 were relatively barren. A few people yet living spanned these years, but they wrote no intrinsically great poetry. William Hamilton Hayne continued to write in the tradition of his father; if as poet he was of smaller caliber, he yet produced a volume of respectable worth. In Tennessee John Trotwood

[259] J. C. Harris, Preface to *Christmas-Night in the Quarters and Other Poems,* by Irwin Russell.

Moore painted glowing landscapes in prose and verse, and wrote at least one ballad of a Confederate soldier which transcends verse and becomes poetry. Similarly, Walter Malone concentrated primarily on the surface aspects of nature, won fame with a poem which said well what many persons wanted to hear, and wrote an epic poem, *De Soto*, which almost attains greatness but which few people have cared to read.

Only Madison Cawein received much critical attention or acclaim. His poems of nature had more deftness, evoked more distinctly an atmosphere of a person who writes of a land that he knows. This impression is largely due to Cawein's greater skill and craftsmanship; in lesser degree, possibly, to a greater body of sustained work over a score of years. Edmund Gosse thought that his early work suffered from a lack of criticism in the South,[260] but a more reasonable estimate is that Cawein lacked the faculty of self-criticism. Even Gosse preferred Cawein's pantheistic poems and gentle lyrics. A few of these have distinctive beauty, but mostly they are rather commonplace restatements of old and well-worn subjects. Cawein's work, however, has at times a drive and bite for which he is not given credit; he mixed these poems, together with his best poems of nature, with such a profuse welter of mediocre verses of the same general type that great selectivity is required before one realizes that he is, at intervals, an able poet.

These writers belong definitely to the past. Such poets as Lizette Woodworth Reese, Olive Tilford Dargan, and Cale Young Rice have elements of kinship with them, but they have significant differences. They continue to write and to publish volumes—a fact which makes consideration of their work tentative and incomplete. Miss Reese has, unfortunately, become known as the author of one poignant sonnet, "Tears," while the remainder of her work is neglected. Yet she has an individual way of observing small things in life and in nature,

[260] Gosse, preface to Madison Cawein's *Kentucky Poems*.

and of transmuting her observation into gentle, precise poetry. Rice has written with facility of the surface aspects of many nations; his range of subject matter has been astonishingly varied. It is picturesque, and at times bitter, but there is no fusion of artist and subject, of matter and manner—a fusion which Miss Reese, in her slight lyrics of the countryside she knows, has achieved.

When they have noticed his work at all, critics have placed William Alexander Percy with the other poets who apparently antedated the "poetic renascence."[261] Although his first verses were not published until 1911, this classification has some reason: Percy has written in traditional forms of ancient and medieval subjects; he was brusque and outspoken only in statements against metropolitan life and people:

> Too much is said too loudly; I am dazed.
> The silken sound of whirled infinity
> Is lost in voices shouting to be heard.
> I once knew men as earnest and less shrill.

This quality of withdrawal was not likely to attract the shrill voices; neither was the deceptively quiet poetry which he wrote.[262] Possibly the underlying philosophy, also, will not again be popular: that man, although foredoomed to failure and conscious that in this world faith is ever likely to be defeated by fact, wins a victorious acceptance over defeat since the entire human person is greater than his physical self or the inevitable accident of circumstance. This conquest of athos over pathos has been the source of high tragedy in such diverse writers as Shakespeare and Schiller; in Percy's hands the theme never becomes quite overpowering, but it is given adequate and moving statement.

What has been called the "renascence" of American poetry,

---

[261] Cf. Donald Davidson, "The Trend of Literature," in *Culture in the South*, 182–210.

[262] Llewellyn Powys, Introduction to W. A. Percy's *Selected Poems*.

about 1912,[263] had little immediate effect upon the South. It was not without effect upon gifted persons—such as Conrad Aiken and John Gould Fletcher—but it permeated through the consciousness of the section slowly. Both Aiken and Fletcher became cosmopolitans and experimentalists: only by the accident of birth could Aiken be considered a Southern poet. Fletcher has, since 1930, returned definitely to his region, and has advocated regionalism, which he has interpreted through the medium of imagist poetry. He expressed with exactness his intent: "To describe an incident or a scene along with its connotation of emotion, the connotation being *implicit in some part of the scene itself.*"[264] Through impressionism and imagism he developed a highly allusive method, which brings out overtones and connotations primarily from things *seen;* at the same time he developed his own forms: pictorial in detail, symphonic in movement—an orchestration of highly colored words. His poetry, wrote Conrad Aiken in 1919, "contains little of the emotion which relates to the daily life of men and women. . . . It is a sort of absolute poetry, a poetry of detached waves and brilliance, a beautiful flowering of language alone."[265] This was extreme criticism, then; since that time Fletcher's poetry has caught the impact of past upon present, of fallowness upon barrenness (as in "Earth"), but this content has often gone unnoticed because he wrote in untraditional forms. Although the value of his experiments need not be discounted, the attention given to his technique has obscured somewhat the conservative religious and philosophical voice which speaks through his later poems.

[263] A good journalistic discussion is given in the Introduction to Louis Untermeyer's *Modern American Poetry.* See also Amy Lowell's *Tendencies in Modern American Poetry.*

[264] Fletcher, "The Modern Southern Poets," *Westminster Magazine,* XXIII, 240 (Jan., 1935).

[265] Conrad Aiken, *Scepticisms;* a brilliant but somewhat biased analysis of Fletcher's early work. See also Amy Lowell, *op. cit.,* and Glenn Hughes, *Imagism and the Imagists.*

It is significant that in 1912 Fletcher thought it necessary to leave the United States, like Ezra Pound and T. S. Eliot; their influence was felt from abroad, but it was tenuous and indirect. More immediate was the recognition about the same time of Edwin Arlington Robinson, the emergence of Edna St. Vincent Millay, Robert Frost, Carl Sandburg, Edgar Lee Masters, and other poets who revivified an art which had seemed almost dead. Not until 1920 was the Southern poet stirred to action. Diverse groups began to write poetry and to publish little magazines.[266]

With a single exception these groups may be divided in two categories. One was up-to-date, smart, and sophisticated; the other interested in the realistic-romantic possibilities of local color. Two examples of each type may be cited: in New Orleans Julius Friend and John McClure edited *The Double Dealer;*[267] in Richmond Emily Clark (with some assistance from James Branch Cabell, Ellen Glasgow, and other established writers) edited *The Reviewer.*[268] These magazines were smart and sophisticated, but rootless. In a letter written, significantly, to the editor of *The Reviewer*, H. L. Mencken summarized their inadequacy: "Friend is failing in New Orleans because he is trying to print an imitation of *The Dial* and *The Smart Set.*"[269] The attempt to write and to publish works of literary merit was an exciting game, but none of the editors had a clear idea of what literature was. When the first enthusiasm had faded, neither the magazines nor their chief contributors seemed very important. They gained more attention than several groups which concentrated on local subjects, like the Virginia group which published *The Lyric* at Norfolk.[270] Most promising of

[266] D. Davidson, *op. cit.*, and J. B. Hubbell, "Southern Magazines," in *Culture in the South*, 159–82.

[267] Hubbell, *op. cit.*, 174–7. Hubbell quotes liberally from the bellicose editorials in *The Double Dealer*.

[268] *Ibid.*, 176–9; Emily Clark, *Innocence Abroad*.

[269] Quoted in Hubbell, *op. cit.*, 176.

[270] *The Lyric* migrated from Norfolk to Roanoke; cf. Davidson, *op. cit.*, 189.

the local colorist schools was that at Charleston, which published a yearbook instead of a magazine, and which, under Hervey Allen, DuBose Heyward, and Josephine Pinckney, evolved definite theories of how such poetry should be written.[271] This promise never materialized; Allen and Heyward sought picturesque values only, and soon abandoned poetry for fiction. Of all their verses, only Heyward's "The Prodigal" has the stamp of durability. Miss Pinckney's verse has a more authentic quality: to observation she added sympathetic insight—and she has continued to write poetry.

For some reason these groups have dissolved and the poets who composed them have failed to develop. The "Fugitives" of Nashville began modestly in 1922 to publish a small magazine of verse, *The Fugitive*, which was voluntarily abandoned four years later; the authors cloaked their identities under absurd pseudonyms, sponsored no cause, and issued no manifesto.[272] At first glance they represented only another symptom of the intellectual ferment which promised so much, in widely scattered sections of the South—and of the nation. But the discontinuance of the magazine and gradual disintegration of the group was not, in this case, a sign of decay. Some of these poets continued to write and to develop, along individual rather than communal lines, but with a basis of intellectual kinship. Three men—John Crowe Ransom, Donald Davidson, Allen Tate—are definitely among the leading poets of our time; two others—Robert Penn Warren and Alec B. Stevenson—have quite as definitely contributed valid poems, and may in no remote tomorrow attain the same recognition. In addition there is Merrill Moore, a gifted *improvisator* who cast his ironic comments on life into an irregular sonnet form, with lines which depended upon stress rather than scansion, and with a break

---

[271] See the Southern number of *Poetry*, edited by Hervey Allen and DuBose Heyward, April, 1922.
[272] See the Introduction to *Fugitives, an Anthology of Verse*.

in the unit at any point where the thought required it; these skillful "American" sonnets covered a wide range, with a unity imposed only by the poet's personal and, seemingly, almost intuitive philosophy.[273] With good reason John Gould Fletcher has stated that the doctrine of the "Nashville school" and of its affiliates "has become now the central tradition of Southern poetry."[274] Ransom, Davidson, Tate, and Warren have also been critics of literature, and of life.

Roughly they belong to the modern metaphysical school. Poetry is not simply an expression of an emotion or the evocation of an object; it is closely akin to the ideas which are at base religious, and which make a philosophy. Poetry represents the transmutation of "an intensely felt ordinary experience, an intense moral situation, into an intensely realized art."[275] Such work is not romantic, or ornamental; it is a part of life, as seen through the completed experience of an individual poet. Normally it would be a personal expression of an integrated person in a defined society. Under a scientific civilization, however, the artist "is *against* or *away from* society, and the disturbed relationship becomes his essential theme, no matter whether he evades or accepts the treatment of the theme itself."[276] Dislocation of the artist has resulted in that "dissociation of sensibility"[277] which T. S. Eliot has focused as the center of the poet's problem in modern times.

This is the center of Ransom's poetry. He has written of

---

[273] For an appraisal, see Louis Untermeyer, "Merrill Moore," *Sewanee Review*, XLIII, 58–61 (Jan., 1935).

[274] Fletcher, "The Modern Southern Poets," *Westminster Magazine*, XXIII, 249 (Jan., 1935). Fletcher's essay is acute, and outspokenly honest.

[275] Allen Tate, "Poetry and the Absolute," *Sewanee Review*, XXXV, 41–52 (Jan., 1927).

[276] Donald Davidson, "A Mirror for Artists," in *I'll Take My Stand*. See also the critical articles by Davidson, Tate, Ransom, and Warren previously cited, or listed in the bibliography, and an excellent essay by W. S. Knickerbocker, "The Fugitives of Nashville," *Sewanee Review*, XXXVI, 211–24 (April, 1928).

[277] T. S. Eliot, *Selected Essays*.

"intricate psychological cruxes,"[278] frequently casting his poem into the minor dramatic fable which Thomas Hardy used, but he has made the protagonists of his poems sufferers "from that complaint of 'dissociation of sensibility.'" [279] The poem itself is a commentary on the situation, its irony deriving from the "fact that these perhaps otherwise admirable people 'cannot fathom nor perform their nature.'" It is a poetry in which wit is employed not as ornament but as part of the texture, in which at times the images are stated precisely but are telescoped in such a way that the intellectualized cross references are difficult to comprehend. Essentially Ransom's poetry is ironical, with an exact precision of thought and imagery; his standard is remarkably high, so that a certain evenness of quality, combined with his preference for short dramatic episodes, prevents generally one poem from standing out: his apparently unconnected poems fit together naturally and build up to an integrated structure which expresses Ransom's philosophy largely by exposing the insufficiency of people in a world devoid of grace and myth.

Donald Davidson's first volume, *An Outland Piper*, has a strong resemblance to Ransom's work, with an added mystical element which was possibly derived, in manner, from William Blake. Poetically, however, Ransom has worked through negation; in *The Tall Men* and in later poems, Davidson has been affirmative. A major voice speaks: "It surely is clear, to anyone who has read American poetry carefully, that the blank verse here [in *The Tall Men*] is entirely *sui generis:* no other American poet, unless it be Hart Crane in the rare moments when the flame in him broke through his own inflated rhetoric, has so authentically sounded the heroic note."[280] Here is

[278] Knickerbocker, *op. cit.*, 222.
[279] R. P. Warren, "John Crowe Ransom: A Study in Irony," *Virginia Quarterly Review*, XI, 93–112 (Jan., 1935). A keen, perceptive essay, far more illuminating than the analysis of Ransom's work in G. Williamson's *John Donne and the Poetry of Today*.
[280] Fletcher, *op. cit.*, 236.

largeness and sweep of vision, but without confusion; only in the attempts at emphasis and minute analysis—too often reminiscent of Eliot—and in the lack of a defined climax, can defects be pointed out; in the later, more closely integrated "Lee in the Mountains," there is a complete resolution. In his criticism Davidson has made frontal attacks on a scientific and industrial civilization with its abstract literature; in his poetry he has stated his own philosophy in a manner paralleled only, in our time, by Robert Frost.

The poems of Allen Tate, like those of Ransom, can be classified as metaphysical. Where Ransom is most concerned with God, Tate is most possessed by death. This differentiation in subject matter is suggestive rather than final: in many ways the poetry and the philosophy of the two are akin. Tate's poetry is even more exact, with a stringent distillation which telescopes much matter into a few closely packed lines. He revises and refines his work until the fusion of idea and technique achieves a finality of statement which is absolute. Most of his poetry is involved with the question of self-definition, which involves also the metaphysical questions of the bases of life. His approach is oblique, his method consisting of "gradually circling round the subject, threatening it and filling it with suspense, and finally accomplishing its demise without ever quite using the ultimate violence on it."[281] This is a difficult art, perhaps best achieved when the poem is most objectified—as in "Ode to the Confederate Dead"—or when personal intensity is combined with his closely-knit interrelation of thought and emotion—as in "Sonnets of the Blood." In these works Tate achieves the status of a major poet.

Closely allied in spirit to the work of Ransom and Tate is that of Robert Penn Warren. It has a broader sweep and it is more directly rooted in earth. Also, Warren's language is

[281] Quoted from Tate in Untermeyer's *Modern American Poetry*, 778.

Saxon, in contrast to the Latinity of phrase employed by Ransom and Tate. But his bold imagery, his compressed, elliptical play of wit are closely related. Inevitably, since his verses have not been collected, he seems a poet of magnificent promise rather than of positive achievement. The same judgment must be applied to Alec B. Stevenson—whose sinuously powerful lines and strict form are well revealed in "Icarus in November." His work also is uncollected, but the quality of a few poems raises it beyond the plane of tentative acceptance.

This group includes other poets whose work has not, as yet, become defined; an appraisal of their work would savor more of prophecy than of achievement.[282] It has drawn other poets, as well: John Peale Bishop (whose early work was derivative, if not directly imitative, of Rimbaud, Eliot, and other poets and whose thought was vitiated by an obsession with Freudian psychologies) has emerged in his later poems as a religious poet, with a tonic attitude of skeptical disillusionment as to the nature of the ritual, but with a firm belief that the world must be saved through the Christian myth, and that the ritual must, somehow, be found. Allied to the group on agrarian rather than on metaphysical grounds is Jesse Stuart, prolific and uneven, but with a capacity for writing in brief sequences a direct, highly personal poetry with an intense drive and emotion. In the seven hundred and three sonnets which comprise *Man with the Bull-Tongue Plow*, there are many positive defects, but there are also the positive merits of keen, unstudied observation of mountain people and of nature, of the elemental questions of life and love and death.

The type of poetry has changed. There is no lack of romantic

---

[282] A considerable number of younger poets who have been directly or indirectly connected with this group and influenced by it include: William Davidson, Marshall Morgan, Richmond Croom Beatty, Edwin Richardson Frost, W. R. Moses, Manson Radford, George Marion O'Donnell, and Randall Jarrell. Only Frost has collected his poems into a volume (*Daemon from the Rock*).

and occasional poetry and poets, but the ablest of the modern writers have voiced through their poetry a philosophy of living. Although it has presented ideas as well as emotions, this poetry has retained a warmth and grace which is traditional—and it has, above all, remained distinctively Southern.

SELECTED BIBLIOGRAPHY

Only the most useful books and articles are, for reasons of space, listed here, since even a fairly complete bibliography would fill a large volume. One apparent disparity needs explanation: where adequate biographies are available, I have not tried to give any except the most important magazine articles; where no single standard work exists, the list of smaller items is increased.

I. ANTHOLOGIES

Alderman, E. A., Harris, J. C., Kent, C. W., and others. *The Library of Southern Literature*. Atlanta: 1908–23. 17 vols. (Inclusive rather than critical, with good and bad works hopelessly mixed together, this huge collection is indispensable, in spite of its faults, to the student of Southern literature. A good bibliography of books and articles on Southern literature is given in Vol. XIV, pp. 6549–6560.)

American Review, The (Poetry Supplement, edited by Allen Tate), Vol. III, May, 1934. (Similar to Tate's edition of *Poetry*, with more recent poetry, and with more general critical essays by John Crowe Ransom, Cleanth Brooks, and Robert Penn Warren.)

Browne, Francis F., ed. *Bugle-Echoes, a Collection of the Poetry of the Civil War, Northern and Southern.* New and revised ed. New York: 1886. (Valuable for the quotations from personal letters of various authors to the editor.)

Gordon, Armistead C., Jr. *Virginian Writers of Fugitive Verse.* With an introduction by Thomas Nelson Page. New York: 1923. (Excellent extended critical essay and good selection of poems, excluding all poems that had appeared in volume form where volume was written exclusively by author.)

Griswold, Rufus W. *The Poets and Poetry of America.* Philadelphia: 1842. Seventh edition, revised: 1846. (Useful for reference, but notoriously unreliable as regards texts and information about authors.)

Best all. of recent poetry [handwritten annotation]

Hibbard, Addison, ed. *The Lyric South*. New York: 1928. (An anthology of Southern poetry after 1915, including only poets who had published a volume of verse. Uncritical; apparently the editor was more interested in local color in poetry than in good work.)

Holliday, Carl. *Three Centuries of Southern Poetry (1607–1907)*. Nashville: 1908. (Brief biographical notes, and selections from Southern poetry.)

Kent, Charles W., comp. *Southern Poems*. Boston: 1913. (A brief selection of poems, in pamphlet form.)

Otis, William Bradley. *American Verse, 1625–1807*. New York: 1909. (Extensive rather than critical; contains brief passages about many titles otherwise unknown, however, and a good bibliography.)

Painter, F. V. N. *Poets of the South*. New York: 1903. (A series of biographical and critical studies with typical poems, annotated.)

Painter, F. V. N. *Poets of Virginia*. Richmond: 1907. (Useful for reference purposes, as Painter is usually meticulous about facts.)

Poetry (Southern Number, edited by DuBose Heyward and Hervey Allen), Vol. XX, April, 1922. (Modern poetry, mostly of the local color type, by Southeastern poets. A valuable essay by Heyward and Allen on the value of local color as subject matter for poetry is included—parts of the essay are given in the Appendix to this book.)

Poetry (Southern Number, edited by Allen Tate), Vol. XL, May, 1932. (Good representation of modern Southern poets, particularly of the Fugitives, with excellent critical essays by Allen Tate, Donald Davidson, and Robert Penn Warren. Parts of the essays by Tate and Davidson will be found in the Appendix.)

Simms, William Gilmore. *War Poetry of the South*. New York: 1867. (Although hastily edited, it is the best of the Southern war anthologies. At least twenty similar books were edited by Southerners; most of them are listed in *Cambridge History of American Literature*, II, 585.)

really good minor anthology

Trent, William P. *Southern Writers: Selections in Prose and Verse*. New York: 1905. (Brief biographical notes and brief selections from Southern authors from John Smith through Madison Cawein.)

Wegelin, Oscar. *Early American Poetry*. (Vol. I, 1650–1799; Vol. II, 1800–1820.) Second ed., revised and enlarged. New York: 1930. (The full title pages of some fourteen hundred volumes and pamphlets of verse, arranged alphabetically by authors, with a special list of anonymous writings, and with an index of titles.)

II. GENERAL

Allen, G. W. *American Prosody*. New York: 1935. (Detailed and excellent analyses of the prosody of major American poets.)

Baskervill, W. M. *Southern Writers*. Nashville: 1897–1903. 2 vols. (Vol. I by Baskervill, Vol. II by other men.) (Readable articles, not very detailed or critical, on leading Southern writers. The poets treated are Irwin Russell, Sidney Lanier, Margaret Junkin Preston, and Madison Cawein.)

Clark, Emily. *Innocence Abroad*. New York: 1931. (Casual reflections on Southern literature and authors by the editor of *The Reviewer*. Contains a chapter on DuBose Heyward, and one on James Branch Cabell.)

Couch, W. T., editor, and others. *Culture in the South*. Chapel Hill: 1933. (A symposium by thirty-one authors on many phases of modern Southern life. Easily the best book on the subject.)

Davidson, James Wood. *The Living Writers of the South*. New York: 1869. (Inclusive rather than critical, and not always accurate, but valuable in preserving the works of men who might otherwise have been entirely lost.)

Hayne, Paul H. "Ante-Bellum Charleston," *Southern Bivouac*, Vol. I. (The first section deals with H. S. Legaré, R. Y. Hayne, and early Charleston; the second gives a remarkable picture of W. G. Simms; and the third paper deals with John Russell's bookshop and the literary coterie that frequented it.)

Henneman, John Bell, and others. *The South in the Building of a Nation*. Richmond: 1909. 12 vols. (Subtitled "A history of the Southern States designed to record the South's part in the making of the American nation; to portray the character and genius, to chronicle the achievements and progress, and to illustrate the life and traditions of the Southern people." Vol. VII, *History of the Literary and Intellectual Life of the South*, is particularly useful.)

Holliday, Carl. *A History of Southern Literature*. New York: 1906. (Appreciative and readable textbook on Southern literature. Far from reliable in critical judgments, and rather scanty in factual information.)

Hubner, Charles W. *Representative Southern Poets*. New York: 1906. (Appreciative, semi-critical essays on Lanier, Paul H. Hayne, Timrod, Ryan, Hope, Ticknor, Preston, Pinkney, Chivers, and Poe.)

Lewisohn, Ludwig. "Books We Have Made," Charleston *News and Courier*, July 5–September 20, 1903. (Valuable and almost inaccessible papers on the writers of South Carolina.)

Link, S. A. *Pioneers of Southern Literature*. Nashville: 1899–1900. 2 vols. (Fairly slight, readable essays on various Southern writers. Includes chapters on Paul Hamilton Hayne, F. O. Ticknor, Henry Timrod, William Gilmore Simms, Edgar Allan Poe, War Poets of the South, and Singers in Various Keys.)

Mabie, Hamilton Wright. "The Poetry of the South," *International Monthly*, Vol. V, February, 1902. (Interesting but unimportant essay, praising the moralists.)

Mims, Edwin. *The Advancing South*. Garden City, N. Y.: 1926. (Excellent contrast of new forces in Southern life with older forces. Especially good on literature.)

Moses, Montrose J. *The Literature of the South*. New York: 1910. (Full-bodied and thorough piece of work, mainly excellent. Some rather surprising omissions and some rather strange judgments. Although not completely reliable, it is probably the best textbook available at this time.)

Parrington, Vernon Louis. *Main Currents in American Thought*,

Vol. II. New York: 1927. (Parrington's consideration [pp. 3–180] is invaluable as background for any study of Southern literature.)

Phillips, Ulrich B. *Life and Labor in the Old South*. Boston: 1929. (One of the most valuable general books on life in the old South.)

Rittenhouse, Jessie B. *The Younger American Poets*. Boston: 1904. (Contains appreciative essays on Lizette Reese and Madison Cawein.)

Rutherford, Mildred Lewis. *The South in History and Literature*. Atlanta: 1907. (Old-fashioned and sentimental, partly handbook and partly anthology.)

Stribling, T. S. "Southern Verse," *Poet Lore*, Vol. XVII, Winter Number, 1906. (Southern literature is homogeneous and indigenous: "Tear one southern writer away from his beloved Southland . . . and lo! his inspiration dies; his song has fled.")

Trent, William P. "Poetry of the American Plantation," *Sewanee Review*, Vols. VII, VIII, October, 1899, and January, 1900. (An excellent article on a specialized topic, although marred by Trent's liberal bias, which could see little good in the agrarian way of life.)

Trent, William P., and others. *The Cambridge History of American Literature*. New York: 1917–1921. 4 vols. (Chaotic and uneven mass of information by distinguished scholars, with excellent bibliographies. Especially weak in its treatment of Southern literature, the only adequate part being a good chapter on "Poets of the Civil War: The South.")

Twelve Southerners. *I'll Take My Stand: The South and the Agrarian Tradition*. New York: 1930. (Indispensable in any serious study of the South.)

Tyler, Moses Coit. *A History of American Literature During the Colonial Time*. (Vol. I, 1607–1676; Vol. II, 1677–1765.) New York: 1878. (The standard work on the period.)

Tyler, Moses Coit. *The Literary History of the American Revolution*. (Vol. I, 1763–1776; Vol. II, 1776–1783.) New York: 1897. (The standard work on the period.)

Untermeyer, Louis. *The New Era in American Poetry*. New York: 1919.

Untermeyer, Louis. *American Poetry Since 1900*. New York: 1923. (Provocative but unusually good surveys of American poetry, with casual glances at the Southern scene.)

Wertenbaker, Thomas J. *Patrician and Plebeian in Virginia*. Charlottesville: 1910. (More specialized than Phillips's *Life and Labor*, it is extremely valuable in interpreting the rise of classes in the South.)

Woodberry, George E. "The South in American Letters," *Harper's Magazine*, Vol. CVII, October, 1903. (A fair and stimulating, but of necessity a superficial, article.)

R.B. Varel — Human Geo. of South

III. AUTHORS

Anonymous. *Poems on Several Occasions, by a Gentleman of Virginia*. Williamsburg: 1736. Reproduced from the edition of 1736 with a bibliographical note by Ralph L. Rusk. Facsimile Text Society. New York: 1930.

Bishop, John Peale. *Now with His Love*. New York: 1933.

Cabell, James Branch. *From the Hidden Way*. New York: 1916.
  McNeill, Warren A. *Cabellian Harmonics*. New York: 1928. (Considers chiefly the symbolism and prose.)

Cawein, Madison. *Collected Poems*. Indianapolis: 1907. 5 vols.
  Rothert, Otto A. *The Story of a Poet: Madison Cawein*. Louisville: 1921. (Filson Club Publication, No. 30.) (A storehouse of valuable but unassimilated information, with many illustrations, excerpts from many letters, seven prose articles in full, estimates and reminiscences of Cawein by friends and friendly critics. The bibliography is unusually extensive.)

Chivers, Thomas Holley. *The Path of Sorrow, or, The Lament of Youth*. Franklin, Tennessee: 1832.

Chivers, Thomas Holley. *Nacoochee; or, The Beautiful Star, with Other Poems*. New York: 1837.

Chivers, Thomas Holley. *The Lost Pleiad; and Other Poems*. New York: 1845.

Bowers — the Tragic Era

Odum — negro — + negro folk songs

Chivers, Thomas Holley. *Eonchs of Ruby*. New York: 1851.

Chivers, Thomas Holley. *Memoralia; or, Phials of Amber Full of the Tears of Love*. Philadelphia: 1853.

Chivers, Thomas Holley. *Virginalia; or, Songs of My Summer Nights*. Philadelphia: 1853.

Chivers, Thomas Holley. *Atlanta; or, The True Blessed Island of Poesy*. Macon, Georgia: 1853.

Chivers, Thomas Holley. *Birthday Song of Liberty*. Atlanta: 1856.

    Benton, Joel. *In the Poe Circle*. New York: 1889. (First, second, and fourth chapters are given to the Poe-Chivers affair. Benton writes very sensibly on the matter, but apparently had little information at hand.)

    Damon, S. Foster. *Thomas Holley Chivers, Friend of Poe*. New York: 1930. (Excellent criticism of Chivers as poet; weak on biographical details, which was probably unavoidable, but inexcusably weak on the background of Chivers's life. Contains a good bibliography. Damon and Lewis Chase have in preparation an edition of the complete works of Chivers—a work which will be invaluable to the student of American poetry.)

    Woodberry, George E. "The Poe-Chivers Papers," *Century Magazine*, LXV (N. S. XLIII), January, February, 1903.

    Woodberry, George E. *Life of Edgar Allan Poe*. Boston: 1909. II, 376–90. (A valuable selection of letters by Poe and Chivers. Woodberry does not accept the internal evidence of the poem "To My Mother," and gives date of birth as 1807. Gives Chivers's reminiscences of Poe.)

Cooke, John Esten.

    Beaty, John O. *John Esten Cooke, Virginian*. New York: 1922. (Scholarly but rather weak in style.)

Cooke, Philip Pendleton. *Froissart Ballads and Other Poems*. Philadelphia: 1847.

    Anonymous (probably J. R. Thompson). "Poems by P. P. Cooke [Froissart Ballads]," *Southern Literary*

Messenger, Vol. XV, July, 1847. (" . . . Charming little volume.")

Anonymous. "Philip Pendleton Cooke," *Southern Literary Messenger* (reprinted from *International Magazine*), Vol. XVII, October-November, 1851. (Useful short article, including several letters on Southern literary conditions by Cooke.)

Anonymous. "Recollections of Philip Pendleton Cooke," *Southern Literary Messenger*, Vol. XXVI, June, 1858. (An excellent personal sketch of the life of Cooke.)

Dargan, Olive Tilford. *Lute and Furrow*. New York: 1922.

Davidson, Donald. *An Outland Piper*. Boston: 1924.

Davidson, Donald. *The Tall Men*. Boston: 1927.

Emmett, Dan D.

Galbreath, Charles Burleigh. *Daniel Decatur Emmett*. Columbus, Ohio: 1904. (A fairly good biography of the author of "Dixie.")

Flash, Henry Lyndon. *Poems*. New York: 1906.

Fletcher, John Gould. *Preludes and Symphonies*. Boston: 1922; New York: 1930. (Includes *Irradiations—Sand and Spray* [1914] and *Goblins and Pagodas* [1916].)

Fletcher, John Gould. *The Tree of Life*. New York: 1918.

Fletcher, John Gould. *Breakers and Granite*. New York: 1921.

Fletcher, John Gould. *The Black Rock*. New York: 1928.

Aiken, Conrad. *Scepticisms: Notes on Contemporary Poetry*. New York: 1919. (Gives a brilliant analysis of Fletcher's use of the "allusive method," and a very good discussion of imagistic poetry.)

Lowell, Amy. *Tendencies in Modern American Poetry*. New York: 1917. (Brilliant but biased criticism of one famous imagist poet by an equally famous imagist. Contains biographical as well as critical material.)

Hayne, Paul Hamilton. *Poems* (edited by Margaret Junkin Preston). Boston: 1882.

Hayne, William Hamilton. "Paul H. Hayne's Methods of Composition," *Lippincott's Magazine*, Vol. L, December, 1892.

Higginson, Thomas Wentworth. "Paul Hamilton Hayne," *Chautauquan*, Vol. VII, January, 1887. (A generous, discriminating, and analytical essay, which praises Hayne perhaps too highly. Higginson thought, however, that South Carolina denied him "a nation," and this handicapped him as a poet.)

Preston, Margaret Junkin. "Paul Hamilton Hayne," *Southern Bivouac*, Vol. II, September, 1886. (Sympathetic, personal essay on a Southern poet by a Southern poet.)

Hayne, William Hamilton. *Sylvan Lyrics*. New York: 1893.

Heyward, DuBose. *Carolina Chansons* (with Hervey Allen). New York: 1922.

Heyward, DuBose. *Skylines and Horizons*. New York: 1924.

Key, Francis Scott. *Poems of the Late Francis Scott Key*. With an introductory letter by Chief Justice Taney. New York: 1857.

Lanier, Sidney. *Poems of Sidney Lanier* (edited by Mrs. Sidney Lanier). New York: 1916.

Lanier, Sidney. *The Science of English Verse*. New York: 1880. (A selection from this volume, which explains Lanier's theories of the relationship of poetry and music, is given in the Appendix, p. 355 ff.)

Lanier, Sidney. *Music and Poetry*. New York: 1899. (More general statement, in reviews and essays, of Lanier's philosophy of poetry. Also contains a good essay on Paul Hamilton Hayne.)

Graham, P. E. "Lanier and Science," *American Literature*, IV, 288–92 (November, 1932); "Lanier's Reading," University of Texas *Studies in English*, XI, 63–89 (1931). (Valuable studies on Lanier's intellectual interests.)

Lanier, Clifford. "Reminiscences of Sidney Lanier," *Chautauquan*, Vol. XXI, July, 1895. (Rather pathetic personal reminiscences of early life and of war days by a brother and early collaborator who is determined not to obtrude his own personality.)

Mims, Edwin. *Sidney Lanier*. Boston: 1905. (Sympathetic and well-written study of Lanier against a Southern and nationalist background. Still the best work on the poet.)

Ransom, John Crowe. "Hearts and Heads," *American Review*, Vol. II, March, 1934. (A reply to Starke's reply to the strictures of Tate and Warren. Considerable attention is given to Lanier's philosophy.)

Starke, Aubrey H. *Sidney Lanier*. Chapel Hill: 1933. (Extremely detailed study, containing some previously unpublished poems, and a thorough bibliography.)

Starke, Aubrey H. "The Agrarians Deny a Leader," *American Review*, Vol. II, March, 1934. (A reply to Messrs. Warren and Tate, and a rather unsuccessful attempt to make Lanier an agrarian philosopher.)

Tate, Allen. "Sidney Lanier" (review of Starke's biography), *New Republic*, August 30, 1933. (Unfavorable analysis of Lanier's theories of poetry, of his imagery, and of his philosophy.)

Thayer, William R., editor. "Letters of Sidney Lanier," *Atlantic Monthly*, Vol. LXXIV, July, 1894. (Letters to Gilbert Peacock, editor of the Philadelphia *Evening Bulletin*, from 1875 to 1880. Valuable biographical material, especially with regard to Lanier's work for the exposition of 1876.)

Warren, Robert Penn. "Sidney Lanier: The Blind Poet" (a review of Starke's biography), *American Review*, Vol. II, November, 1933. (Similar to Tate's review, but with fuller examples of Lanier's defects as a poet.)

Lee, Lawrence. *Summer Goes On*. New York: 1933.

Legaré, James Mathewes. *Orta-Undis and Other Poems*. Boston: 1848.

Lucas, Daniel Bedinger. *The Land Where We Were Dreaming and Other Poems* (edited by Virginia Lucas and Charles W. Kent). Charlottesville: 1913.

Lucas, Daniel Bedinger. *The Wreath of Eglantine and Other Poems*. Baltimore: 1869.

McClure, John. *Airs and Ballads*. New York: 1918.

Malone, Walter. *Poems*. Memphis: 1904.

Moore, Merrill. *The Noise That Time Makes*. New York: 1929.

O'Hara, Theodore.

> Ranck, George W. *The Bivouac of the Dead and Its Author*. Baltimore: 1875; reissued, Cincinnati: 1898. (Although the author overpraises O'Hara, his 41-page book contains valuable information, and the best texts of "The Bivouac of the Dead" and "The Old Pioneer.")
>
> O'Sullivan, Daniel E. "Theodore O'Hara," *Southern Bivouac*, Vol. V, January, 1887. (A valuable article defending Ranck's edition of "The Bivouac of the Dead," and giving a possible third poem, "Second Love," by O'Hara.)
>
> Wilson, Robert Burns. "Theodore O'Hara," *Century Magazine*, Vol. XVIII, May, 1890. (Brief but useful biographical sketch, with photograph.)

Palmer, John Williamson. *For Charlie's Sake and Other Ballads and Lyrics*. New York: 1901.

Percy, William Alexander. *Selected Poems*. New Haven: 1930. (Contains selections from *Sappho in Levkas and Other Poems* [1915], *In April Once* [1920], and *Enzio's Kingdom and Other Poems* [1924].)

Pike, Albert. *General Albert Pike's Poems* (edited by Fred W. Allsopp). Little Rock: 1900.

Pinckney, Josephine. *Sea-Drinking Cities*. New York: 1927.

Pinkney, Edward Coote. *Poems*. Baltimore: 1838.

> Mabbott, Thomas Ollive, and Pleadwell, Frank Lester. *Life and Works of Edward Coote Pinkney*. New York: 1926. (Exceedingly thorough but unexciting volume on a romantic figure, with a good bibliography and reliable text of all of Pinkney's poems. Unfortunately the poems are reprinted in such a poor arrangement that they are unpleasant to read.)
>
> Anonymous. "Pinkney's Poems" (review), *North American Review*, Vol. XXI, October, 1825. (Praises the poetry as exquisite, but adds that it has the fault of often being obscure.)

Poe, Edgar Allan. *Poems* (newly collected and edited by E. C. Stedman and G. E. Woodberry). Chicago: 1895.

Poe, Edgar Allan. *Complete Works of Edgar Allan Poe* (edited by James C. Harrison). New York: 1902. 16 vols., with biography.

Poe, Edgar Allan. *Poems* (edited by Killis Campbell with an extensive introduction and exceptionally thorough notes). Boston: 1917.

Poe, Edgar Allan. *Representative Selections* (edited by M. Alterton and H. Craig). New York: 1935. (Contains selections from Poe's poems, stories, criticism, and philosophy, with an annotated bibliography, notes, and an introduction which traces the growth of Poe's philosophic, political, social, and literary theories.)

 Allen, Hervey. *Israfel: The Life and Times of Edgar Allan Poe*. New York: 1926. 2 vols. Rev. ed., in 1 vol., New York: 1934. (Meticulous and scholarly attempt to give all the facts of Poe's life. In spite of a few inaccuracies, it is probably the best biography of Poe, and is particularly valuable in setting Poe against the background of his life and environment.)

 Campbell, Killis. *The Mind of Poe*. Cambridge, Mass.: 1933. (A collection of scholarly essays. Professor Campbell, in discussing the "Origins of Poe," pays no attention to Pinkney or Chivers, and but slight attention to Coleridge. Many of his line by line comparisons are unconvincing. But he has given valuable support to the idea that Poe was integrally related to Southern society, in what is easily the best essay in the book, "The Backgrounds of Poe." Of value, also, is the chapter on "Poe's Reading.")

 Krutch, Joseph Wood. *Edgar Allan Poe: A Study in Genius*. New York: 1926. (A brilliant but mainly unreliable attempt to explain Poe's life and works by means of Freudian psychology. Another defect is the large number of slight but irritating inaccuracies.)

Preston, Mrs. Margaret Junkin. *Beechenbrook*. Richmond: 1865.

Preston, Mrs. Margaret Junkin. *Old Songs and New*. New York: 1870.

Preston, Mrs. Margaret Junkin. *Cartoons*. Boston: 1875.

Preston, Mrs. Margaret Junkin. *Colonial Ballads, Sonnets and Other Verse*. New York: 1887.

Allan, Elizabeth Preston. *The Life and Letters of Margaret Junkin Preston*. Boston: 1930. (Especially valuable for the correspondence with other Southern poets. A good picture of Civil War and Reconstruction days. The biographer greatly overrates Mrs. Preston's poems.)

Randall, James Ryder. *The Poems of James Ryder Randall* (edited by Matthew Page Andrews). New York: 1910.

Randolph, Innis. *Poems* (compiled by his son from the original manuscript). Baltimore: 1898.

Ransom, John Crowe. *Poems About God*. New York: 1919.

Ransom, John Crowe. *Chills and Fever*. New York: 1924.

Ransom, John Crowe. *Two Gentlemen in Bonds*. New York: 1927.

Reese, Lizette Woodworth. *Selected Poems*. New York: 1926.

Reese, Lizette Woodworth. *White April*. New York: 1930.

Reese, Lizette Woodworth. *A Victorian Village*. New York: 1929. (An autobiography which tells more about her poetry than any criticism could.)

Harris, R. P. "April Weather: The Poetry of Lizette Woodworth Reese," *South Atlantic Quarterly*, Vol. XXIX, April, 1930. (Very appreciative article; places Reese as forerunner, with Dickinson, of modern female poets. Very little information.)

Rice, Cale Young. *Selected Plays and Poems*. New York: 1926.

Rice, Cale Young. *Stygian Freight*. New York: 1927.

Rice, Cale Young. *Seed of the Moon*. New York: 1929.

Rice, Cale Young. *High Perils*. New York: 1933.

Russell, Irwin. *Poems*. New York: 1888; second edition, New York: 1917. (The first edition contains a laudatory preface by Joel Chandler Harris; the 1917 edition is more inclusive, and has an excellent biographical sketch of Russell by Maurice Garland Fulton.)

Kern, Alfred Allen. "Biographical Notes on Irwin Russell," *Texas Review*, Vol. II, October, 1916. (Useful personal facts and anecdotes about the life of an almost unknown poet.)

Ryan, Abram Joseph. *Poems: Patriotic, Religious, Miscellaneous*. Baltimore: 1888.

Hewlett, James Howell. "An Unknown Poem by Father Ryan," *Modern Language Notes*, Vol. XLIV, April, 1929. (Relates incidents of a visit of Father Ryan in Danville, Ky., and gives a poem written to a friend there.)

White, Kate. "Father Ryan—The Poet-Priest of the South," *South Atlantic Quarterly*, Vol. XVIII, January, 1919. (An appreciative essay, of little value.)

Shaw, John. *Poems by the late John Shaw*, to which is prefaced a biographical sketch of the author by Edward Earle. Philadelphia: 1810.

Simms, William Gilmore. *Areytos, or Songs of the South*. Charleston: 1846; revised and enlarged in 1860.

Simms, William Gilmore. *Poems: Descriptive, Dramatic, Legendary, and Contemplative*. (2 vols. of miscellaneous poems culled from earlier volumes with fresh additions.) New York and Charleston: 1853.

Trent, William P. *William Gilmore Simms*. Boston: 1892. (Of little value on Simms's poetry; not of very much value in any way, as Trent continually over-simplifies Southern life and problems. Contains a fairly good bibliography of Simms's writing.)

Stuart, Jesse. *Man with the Bull-Tongue Plow*. New York: 1934.

Tabb, John Banister. *The Poetry of Father Tabb* (edited by Francis A. Litz). New York: 1928. (Contains all of Tabb's poetry except *The Rosary in Rhyme* [1904] and *Quips and Quidities* [1904].)

Finn, Mary Paulina (pseud. M. S. Pine). *John Bannister Tabb*. Washington: 1915. (Slight, hero-worshiping biography by a devoted reader. Not always accurate:

the correct spelling of Tabb's middle name, for example, is *Banister*.)

Hale, M. Gordon. "Rev. John B. Tabb, A.M.," *Bachelor of Arts*, Vol. II, May, 1896. (Brief article by a personal friend, biographical and appreciative; includes some personal poems written to family of writer.)

Litz, Francis A. *Father Tabb: A Study of His Life and Works*. Baltimore: 1923. (Careful, scholarly biography of Tabb, with a somewhat cautious tendency to overrate his poems. Contains many previously unpublished poems—all of which were republished in Litz's *The Poetry of Father Tabb*.)

Meynell, Alice. "Father Tabb," *Catholic World*, Vol. XC, February, 1910. (Enthusiastic essay, comparing Tabb with George Herbert.)

Tabb, Jennie Masters. *Father Tabb: His Life and Work* (with an introduction by Charles Alphonso Smith). Boston: 1921. (Pleasant, unimportant, highly appreciative biography, with many quotations of poems. Written by Tabb's niece.)

Tate, Allen. *Mr. Pope and Other Poems*. New York: 1928.

Tate, Allen. *Poems (1928–1931)*. New York: 1932.

Thompson, John Reuben. *Poems of John R. Thompson* (edited by John S. Patton). New York: 1920.

Ticknor, Francis Orray. *Poems* (with an introductory note by Paul Hamilton Hayne). Philadelphia: 1879. Enlarged edition, edited by Michelle Cutliffe Ticknor. New York: 1911.

Timrod, Henry. *Poems of Henry Timrod*. New York: 1873. (Edited by Paul Hamilton Hayne with an excellent biographical sketch.)

Timrod, Henry. *Poems of Henry Timrod* (edited by Timrod Memorial Association of South Carolina). Boston: 1899. (Contains all poems in earlier edition with some previously uncollected poems.)

Timrod, Henry. "The Character and Scope of the Sonnet," *Russell's Magazine*, May, 1857; reprinted in *The Outlook*, Vol. LXXVII, July, 1904.

Timrod, Henry. "A Theory of Poetry," *Atlantic Monthly*, XCVI, 313–26 (Sept., 1905). First delivered before the Methodist Female College, Columbia, S. C., in 1863–64, this essay was not published until 1901, when it was printed in *The Independent*, in abridged form; the first installment entitled "A Theory of Poetry," (LIII, 712–716, March 28, 1901); the second and third installments entitled "The Rationale of Poetry," (LIII, 760–64, April 4, 1901, and 830–33, April 11, 1901).

Timrod, Henry. "What Is Poetry," *Russell's Magazine*, October, 1857.

   Rivers, William James. *A Little Book: To Obtain Means for Placing a Memorial Stone on the Grave of the Poet Henry Timrod*. Charleston: no date. (Contains poems by Professor Rivers, who once taught Timrod, and a brief essay on "The Characteristics of Henry Timrod's Poetry, and his Rank as a Poet.")

   Thompson, Henry T. *Henry Timrod: Laureate of the Confederacy*. Columbia, South Carolina: 1928. (Useful piece of straight biography by an admirer of Timrod. Includes a liberal selection from his poetry.)

   Voigt, C. P. "Timrod's Essays in Literary Criticism," *American Literature*, Vol. VI, May, 1934. (Slight but keen article. Useful bibliographical material.)

   Wauchope, George Armstrong. *Henry Timrod: Man and Poet. University of South Carolina Bulletin*, April, 1915. (Fair biographical sketch by a later admirer.)

Wilde, Richard Henry. *Hesperia, a Poem* (edited by his son, William Cummins Wilde). Boston: 1867.

   Anonymous. "Richard Henry Wilde and Dante," *International Miscellany*, Vol. I, July, 1850. (Defense of Wilde's unpublished work on Dante and of his discovery of the fresco of Giotto.)

   Barclay, Anthony. *Wilde's Summer Rose, an authentic account of the origin, mystery, and explanation of Hon. R. H. Wilde's alleged plagiarism*. Published by the Georgia Historical Society, Savannah: 1871.

Jones, Charles C. *The Life, Literary Labors and Neglected Grave of Richard Henry Wilde*. Augusta: 1885. (Pamphlet.)

Miller, Stephen F. *Bench and Bar of Georgia*. Philadelphia: 1858. 2 vols. (An article dealing mainly with the legal and political career of Wilde, but valuable because it includes a brief sketch of Wilde's life by his son, John P. Wilde. The sketch draws heavily on Griswold's *Poets and Poetry of America*.)

Starke, Aubrey H. "Richard Henry Wilde: Some Notes and a Check-List," *American Book Collector*, Vols. IV, V, November, December, 1933, January, 1934. (A preliminary checklist of twenty-four items by or about Wilde; Mr. Starke plans a complete bibliography. The notes are valuable in helping to straighten out Wilde's life; Starke avoids any criticism of Wilde's work.)

IV. NEGRO SONGS AND SPIRITUALS

Only a few standard items could, for reasons of space, be listed here. Excellent reproductions of the songs can be found in the Hampton Series, *Negro Folk-Songs*, four volumes, recorded by Natalie Curtis Burlin and published by G. Schirmer, New York.

Jackson, George Pullen. *White Spirituals in the Southern Uplands*. Chapel Hill: 1933. (A brilliant study of folk singers and their songs; the two chapters on negro spirituals, pp. 243–302, are the best yet written on the origin of the spirituals, and their growth out of the white fasola songs.)

Johnson, James Weldon. *The Book of American Negro Spirituals* (with musical arrangements by J. Rosamond Johnson). New York: 1925.

Johnson, James Weldon. *The Second Book of Negro Spirituals* (with musical arrangements by J. Rosamond Johnson). New York: 1926. (Two excellent books of spirituals, with excellent texts and music. J. W. Johnson contributed to the first volume a brilliant but not entirely sound essay on the spirituals.)

Krehbiel, Henry E. *Afro-American Folk-Songs*. New York: 1914. (A thorough piece of work which asserted that the songs were original with the negro. ". . . The white inhabitants of the continent have never been in the state of cultural ingenuousness which prompts spontaneous emotional utterance." But Carl E. Seashore and Guy B. Johnson made psychological tests of the native musical ability of white and black, and Johnson concluded that they "revealed no significant differences in the basic sensory musical capacities between whites and negroes."—*The American Negro*, Vol. CXXXX of *The Annals*, Philadelphia: 1928, p. 188 [published by American Academy of Political and Social Sciences].)

Odum, Howard W., and Johnson, Guy B. *The Negro and His Songs*. Chapel Hill: 1925.

Odum, Howard W., and Johnson, Guy B. *Negro Workaday Songs*. Chapel Hill: 1926. (Good studies of the origins and texts of the folk songs.)

Sandburg, Carl. *The American Songbag*. New York: 1927. (Some valuable material is given, pp. 225–254 and pp. 469–488.)

White, Newman I. *American Negro Folk-Songs*. Cambridge, Mass.: 1928. (Although the author neglects the tune elements, he does cite many instances when the negro folk songs borrowed from the white. A valuable piece of work. Includes a very extensive and useful bibliography.)

*

Selections from
SOUTHERN POETS

*

EARLY BALLADS, SONGS, AND POEMS

THE SEA MARK[1]

Aloof, aloof, and come no near,
The dangers do appear
Which, if my ruin had not been,
You had not seen:
I only lie upon this shelf
   To be a mark to all
   Which on the same might fall,
That none may perish but myself.

If in or outward you be bound
Do not forget to sound;   10
Neglect of that was caused of this
To steer amiss.
The seas were calm, the wind was fair,
   That made me so secure,
   That now I must endure
All weathers, be they foul or fair.

The winter's cold, the summer's heat
Alternatively beat
Upon my bruised sides, that rue,
Because too true,   20
That no relief can ever come:
   But why should I despair
   Being promised so fair,
That there shall be a day of Doom.

CAPTAIN JOHN SMITH

[1] Superior figures throughout the text refer to correspondingly numbered notes in pp. 377 ff.

THE BROWN GIRL OR FAIR ELLENDER[2]

1. "Mother, dear mother, come riddle to me,
    Come riddle all as one;
  It's must I marry fair Ellender,
    Or bring the Brown girl home?"

2. "The Brown girl she has a house and home,
    Fair Ellender has none;
  Therefore I'd seek you with my own blessing
    The Brown girl you bring home."

3. "Mother, dear mother, come riddle to me,
    Come riddle all as one;   10
  It's must I go to Low Thomas's wedding,
    Or tarry with you at home?"

4. "You know you have a-many a friend,
    You know you have a foe;
  Therefore I'd seek you with my own blessing
    To Low Thomas's wedding don't go."

5. She dressed herself in pearl of gold,
    She dressed herself in green;
  And every town that she rode through
    She was taken to be some queen.   20

6. "Low Thomas, Low Thomas, is this your bride?
    I pray she looks very brown;
  You could have gotten as fair a lady
    As ever the sun shone on."

7. The Brown girl she had a little penny-knife,
    It was both keen and sharp;
  Between the long ribs and the short ones
    She pressed fair Ellender's heart.

8. "Fair Ellender, fair Ellender,
    What makes you look so pale? 30
  I thought you bore as high a color
    As any other female?"

9. "Low Thomas, Low Thomas, are you blind,
    Or can't you very well see?
  For don't you see my own heart blood
    Come streaming down my knees?"

10. He took the Brown girl by the hand,
    And led her through the hall;
  He drew his sword, cut off her head,
    And kicked it against the wall. 40

11. He pointed the handle toward the sun,
    The point toward his breast.
  Here is the going to three true loves,
    God send our souls to rest.

ANONYMOUS

BACON'S EPITAPH, MADE BY HIS MAN[3]

Death, why so cruel? What! No other way
To manifest thy spleen, but thus to slay
Our hopes of safety, liberty, our all,
Which, through thy tyranny, with him must fall
To its late chaos? Had thy rigid force
Been dealt by retail, and not thus in gross,
Grief had been silent. Now we must complain,
Since thou, in him, hast more than thousand slain,
Whose lives and safeties did so much depend
On him their life, with him their lives must end. 10
  If 't be a sin to think Death bribed can be
We must be guilty; say 't was bribery
Guided the fatal shaft. Virginia's foes,
To whom for secret crimes just vengeance owes

Deserved plagues, dreading their just desert,
Corrupted Death by Paracelsian art
Him to destroy, whose well tried courage such,
Their heartless hearts, nor arms nor strength could touch.
    Who now must heal those wounds or stop that blood
The Heathen made, and drew into a flood?   20
Who is it must plead our cause? Nor trump nor drum
Nor Deputations; these, alas! are dumb
And cannot speak. Our arms (though ne'er so strong)
Will want the aid of his commanding tongue,
Which conquered more than Caesar. He o'erthrew
Only the outward frame; this could subdue
The rugged works of nature. Souls replete
With dull chill cold, he'd animate with heat
Drawn forth of reason's limbec. In a word,
Mars and Minerva both in him concurred   30
For arts, for arms, whose pen and sword alike
As Cato's did, may admiration strike
Into his foes; while they confess withal
It was their guilt styled him a criminal.
Only this difference does from truth proceed:
They in the guilt, he in the name must bleed.
While none shall dare his obsequies to sing
In deserved measures; until time shall bring
Truth crowned with freedom, and from danger free
To sound his praises to posterity.   40
    Here let him rest; while we this truth report
He's gone from hence unto a higher Court
To plead his cause, where he by this doth know
Whether to Caesar he was friend, or foe.

Anonymous

LONG HAS THE FURIOUS PRIEST[4]

    Long has the furious priest assay'd in vain
    With sword and fagot infidels to gain;
    But now the milder soldier wisely tries,

By gentler methods, to unveil their eyes.
Wonders apart, he knew 'twere vain t'engage
The fixed perversions of misguided age:
With fairer hopes, he forms the Indian youth
To early manners, probity, and truth.
The lion's whelp, thus, on the Libyan shore,
Is tamed and gentled by the artful Moor,   10
Not the grim sire inured to blood before.

WILLIAM BYRD

EPIGRAM[5]

Scaurus hates *Greek*, and is become
    Mere *Trojan* in his Spight;
But why so fierce against the Men,
    So learned and polite?

The *Trojans* stole, and kept by Force
    A Dame, elop'd from Duty;
But you can't plead e'en this Pretence
    Of having stole one BEAUTY.

A GENTLEMAN OF VIRGINIA

THE BATTLE OF KING'S MOUNTAIN[6] *Ballad*

'Twas on a pleasant mountain
    The Tory heathens lay,
With a doughty major at their head,
    One Ferguson, they say.

Cornwallis had detach'd him
    A-thieving for to go,
And catch the Carolina men,
    Or bring the rebels low.

The scamp had rang'd the country
    In search of royal aid,   10

And with his owls, perch'd on high,
  He taught them all his trade.

But ah! that fatal morning,
  When Shelby brave drew near!
'Tis certainly a warning
  That ministers should hear.

And Campbell, and Cleveland,
  And Colonel Sevier,
Each with a band of gallant men,
  To Ferguson appear.   20

Just as the sun was setting
  Behind the western hills,
Just then our trusty rifles sent
  A dose of leaden pills.

Up, up the steep together
  Brave Williams led his troop,
And join'd by Winston, bold and true,
  Disturb'd the Tory coop.

The royal slaves, the royal owls,
  Flew high on every hand;   30
But soon they settled—gave a howl,
  And quarter'd to Cleveland.

I would not tell the number
  Of Tories slain that day,
But surely it is certain
  That none did run away.

For all that were a-living,
  Were happy to give up;
So let us make thanksgiving,
  And pass the bright tin-cup.   40

To all the brave regiments,
    Let's toast 'em for their health,
And may our good country
    Have quietude and wealth.

ANONYMOUS

SONG[7]

Who has robbed the ocean cave,
    To tinge thy lips with coral hue?
Who from India's distant wave,
    For thee those pearly treasures drew?
        Who, from yonder orient sky,
        Stole the morning of thine eye?

Thousand charms, thy form to deck,
    From sea, and earth, and air are torn;
Roses bloom upon thy cheek,
    On thy breath their fragrance borne.   10
        Guard thy bosom from the day,
        Lest thy snows should melt away.

But one charm remains behind,
    Which mute earth can ne'er impart;
Nor in ocean wilt thou find,
    Nor in the circling air a heart.
        Fairest! would'st thou perfect be,
        Take, oh take that heart from me.

JOHN SHAW

RESIGNATION[8]

Days of my youth,
    Ye have glided away;
Hairs of my youth,
    Ye are frosted and gray;

Eyes of my youth,
  Your keen sight is no more;
Cheeks of my youth,
  Ye are furrowed all o'er;
Strength of my youth,
  All your vigor is gone;   10
Thoughts of my youth,
  Your gay visions are flown.

Days of my youth,
  I wish not your recall;
Hairs of my youth,
  I'm content ye should fall;
Eyes of my youth,
  You much evil have seen;
Cheeks of my youth,
  Bathed in tears have you been;   20
Thoughts of my youth,
  You have led me astray;
Strength of my youth,
  Why lament your decay?

Days of my age,
  Ye will shortly be past;
Pains of my age,
  Yet awhile can ye last;
Joys of my age,
  In true wisdom delight;   30
Eyes of my age,
  Be religion your light;
Thoughts of my age,
  Dread ye not the cold sod;
Hopes of my age,
  Be ye fixed on your God.
                          ST. GEORGE TUCKER

THE STAR-SPANGLED BANNER[9]

O! say, can you see, by the dawn's early light,
  What so proudly we hailed at the twilight's last gleaming—
Whose broad stripes and bright stars, through the clouds of the
    fight,
  O'er the ramparts we watched were so gallantly streaming!
And the rocket's red glare, the bombs bursting in air,
Gave proof through the night that our flag was still there;
O! say, does that star-spangled banner yet wave
O'er the land of the free, and the home of the brave?

On that shore dimly seen through the mists of the deep,
  Where the foe's haughty host in dread silence reposes,   10
What is that which the breeze, o'er the towering steep,
  As it fitfully blows, half conceals, half discloses?
Now it catches the gleam of the morning's first beam,
In full glory reflected now shines on the stream;
'Tis the star-spangled banner; O! long may it wave
O'er the land of the free, and the home of the brave.

And where is that band who so vauntingly swore
  That the havoc of war and the battle's confusion,
A home and a country should leave us no more?
  Their blood has washed out their foul footsteps' pollution. 20
No refuge could save the hireling and slave
From the terror of flight, or the gloom of the grave;
And the star-spangled banner in triumph doth wave
O'er the land of the free and the home of the brave.

O! thus be it ever, when freemen shall stand
  Between their loved homes and the war's desolation!
Blest with victory and peace, may the heav'n-rescued land
  Praise the power which hath made and preserved us a nation.
Then conquer we must, when our cause it is just,
And this be our motto: "In God is our trust."   30

And the star-spangled banner in triumph shall wave
O'er the land of the free, and the home of the brave.

FRANCIS SCOTT KEY

RICHARD HENRY WILDE

Richard Henry Wilde was born in Dublin, Ireland, September 24, 1789. His father, Richard Wilde, was a wholesale hardware merchant and Irish patriot often in disfavor with the authorities; his mother, Mary Newitt Wilde, was descended from a prominent Tory family which had abandoned American soil at the outbreak of the Revolution. The Wildes landed in Baltimore in 1797, in a ship partly owned by Mr. Wilde. At the outbreak of the Irish Revolution the following year, Wilde's business was confiscated, he was accused of treason, and for that reason he remained in America. Young Richard was a sickly child, later described by his son as of "quiet, retiring, solitary, and studious habits." He was educated by his mother and by a tutor. When he was thirteen, his father died, and his mother soon moved to Augusta, Georgia, where Wilde clerked in her drygoods store by day, and read law without tutelage by night, since he could not pay the usual fee for instruction. He was admitted to the bar in March, 1809, before he was of legal age—going to another county to be examined, in order that his mother might not know of his rejection if he failed. At the time he was "pale and emaciated, feeble, and with a consumptive cough," but from this time on his health gradually improved. At twenty-one he was elected solicitor-general of the Superior Court of Richmond County, and by virtue of this office Attorney-General of Georgia; in 1818, barely over the required age, he was elected to Congress, where he served intermittently until 1835. Although he won a considerable reputation for statesmanship and oratory, Wilde apparently thought of himself as a lawyer by necessity, a politician by accident: he wrote that he "found no party which did not require of its followers what no honest man should, and no gentleman would do."

In the meantime, Wilde's poetical experiences had been most unfortunate. His brother James had been a lieutenant in the

Seminole War, and had interested Richard in Florida to the extent that he began an epic—one lyric of which, "The Lament of the Captive," was published without his knowledge about 1815, and became widely popular. It was soon reported in the *North American Review* that the poem was a translation from Alcaeus—an absurd and easily disproved charge, but one which troubled Wilde greatly. Claimants also appeared in behalf of an Irish poet named Daniel O'Kelly. Mr. Anthony Barclay of Savannah, who had first translated the poem into Greek, subsequently published an *Authentic Account of Wilde's Alleged Plagiarism* (Savannah, 1871), stating that he had translated the poem to amuse and confound a coterie of friends, but the unpleasant notoriety apparently made Wilde afraid of writing other poetry for some years. (This was not an unusual piece of literary pleasantry in the South; the same sort of joke, without the tragic consequences, was played on Timrod.) Another possible reason for his leaving the epic unfinished was that his brother James, for whom the poem was being written, was killed in a duel.

After his political defeat in 1835, Wilde went to Italy where he spent the next five years of his life. The true reasons are not altogether clear, but from his poem *Hesperia* it seems that he had fallen in love with an Italian lady who was already married —his wife had died in 1827. Other poems indicate his discontent with this country. While in Italy he wrote his *Conjectures Concerning the Love, Madness, and Imprisonment of Torquato Tasso* (2 vols., New York, 1842) and worked on, but never completed, a biography of Dante and translations from the Italian lyric poets. Neither volume has been published. Perhaps Wilde's greatest fame in Italy was due to his discovery —with the later help of several Italians and Englishmen—of a portrait of Dante by Giotto which had long been concealed by whitewash on the walls of the Podesta in Florence.

After his return to Georgia in 1840, Wilde practiced law for a year before accepting the professorship of constitutional law in the University of Louisiana, then at New Orleans. He died there in 1847, a victim of the yellow fever epidemic of that year. His long poem *Hesperia*—in four cantos, titled successively "Florida," "Virginia," "Hesperia," "Louisiana"—was edited by his son and published in 1867.

STANZAS[10]

My life is like the summer rose,
    That opens to the morning sky,
But, ere the shades of evening close,
    Is scattered on the ground—to die!
Yet on the rose's humble bed
The sweetest dews of night are shed,
As if she wept the waste to see—
But none shall weep a tear for me!

My life is like the autumn leaf
    That trembles in the moon's pale ray: 10
Its hold is frail—its date is brief,
    Restless—and soon to pass away!
Yet, ere that leaf shall fall and fade,
The parent tree will mourn its shade,
The winds bewail the leafless tree—
But none shall breathe a sigh for me!

My life is like the prints which feet
    Have left on Tampa's desert strand;
Soon as the rising tide shall beat,
    All trace will vanish from the sand;   20
Yet, as if grieving to efface
All vestige of the human race,
On that lone shore loud moans the sea—
But none, alas! shall mourn for me!

TO THE MOCKING-BIRD[11]

Winged mimic of the woods! thou motley fool!
    Who shall thy gay buffoonery describe?
Thine ever-ready notes of ridicule
    Pursue thy fellows still with jest and gibe.
    Wit, sophist, songster, Yorick of thy tribe,

Thou sportive satirist of Nature's school,
    To thee the palm of scoffing we ascribe.
Arch-mocker and mad Abbot of Misrule!
    For such thou art by day—but all night long
Thou pourest a soft, sweet, pensive, solemn strain,   10
    As if thou didst in this thy moonlight song
Like to the melancholy Jacques complain,
    Musing on falsehood, folly, vice, and wrong,
And sighing for thy motley coat again.

TO LORD BYRON[12]

Byron! 'tis thine alone on eagles' pinions,
    In solitary strength and grandeur soaring,
    To dazzle and delight all eyes; outpouring
The electric blaze on tyrants and their minions;
Earth, sea, and air, and powers and dominions,
    Nature, man, time, the universe exploring;
And from the wreck of worlds, thrones, creeds, opinions,
    Thought, beauty, eloquence, and wisdom storing:
O! how I love and envy thee thy glory,
    To every age and clime alike belonging;   10
Link'd by all tongues with every nation's glory,
    Thou Tacitus of song! whose echoes, thronging
O'er the Atlantic, fill the mountains hoary
    And forests with the name my verse is wronging.

A FAREWELL TO AMERICA[13]

Farewell, my more than fatherland!
    Home of my heart and friends, adieu!
Lingering beside some foreign strand,
    How oft shall I remember you!
    How often, o'er the waters blue,
Send back a sigh to those I leave,
    The loving and beloved few,
Who grieve for me—for whom I grieve!

We part!—no matter how we part,
    There are some thoughts we utter not,   10
Deep treasured in our inmost heart,
    Never revealed, and ne'er forgot!
    Why murmur at the common lot?
We part!—I speak not of the pain—
    But when shall I each lovely spot
And each loved face behold again?

It must be months, it may be years,
    It may—but no!—I will not fill
Fond hearts with gloom, fond eyes with tears,
    "Curious to shape uncertain ill."   20
    Though humble—few and far—yet, still
Those hearts and eyes are ever dear;
    Theirs is the love no time can chill,
The truth no chance or change can sear!

All I have seen, and all I see,
    Only endears them more and more;
Friends cool, hopes fade, and hours flee,
    Affection lives when all is o'er!
    Farewell, my more than native shore!
I do not seek or hope to find,   30
    Roam where I will, what I deplore
To leave with them and thee behind!

SAMUEL HENRY DICKSON

Samuel Henry Dickson, the second son of Samuel and Mary
Neilson Dickson, was born in Charleston, South Carolina,
September 20, 1798. His parents were Scottish Presbyterians,
his father a schoolmaster, and Samuel studied under him until
he entered, at thirteen, the sophomore class at Yale. He received his A.B. in 1814, his M.D. from the University of Pennsylvania in 1819, although he had practiced medicine during
the yellow fever epidemic in Charleston in 1817. At twenty-one

he was in charge of the Marine and Yellow Fever Hospitals in Charleston; in 1824 he helped to found a medical college there. In 1833 he founded the Medical College of South Carolina, remaining as professor there until 1847, when he went to the University of the City of New York for three years, before returning to his former position. In 1858 he left Charleston permanently to teach at the Jefferson Medical College in Philadelphia, where he died March 31, 1872.

Dickson was purely an occasional poet. He wrote several important books on medicine and medical studies, and was recognized as an authority on fevers, pathology, and therapeutics. He never collected his fugitive poems, and his literary fame (in the gifted coterie of Charleston writers that included Simms, Timrod, and Hayne) rests only upon the haunting, nostalgic lyric, "I Sigh for the Land of the Cypress and Pine."

I SIGH FOR THE LAND OF THE CYPRESS AND PINE

I sigh for the land of the cypress and pine,
Where the jessamine blooms, and the gay woodbine;
Where the moss droops low from the green oak tree,—
Oh, that sun-bright land is the land for me!

The snowy flower of the orange there
Sheds its sweet fragrance through the air;
And the Indian rose delights to twine
Its branches with the laughing vine.

There the deer leaps light through the open glade,
Or hides him far in the forest shade,
When the woods resound in the dewy morn
With the clang of the merry hunter's horn.

10

There the hummingbird, of rainbow plume,
Hangs over the scarlet creeper's bloom;
While 'midst the leaves his varying dyes
Sparkle like half-seen fairy eyes.

There the echoes ring through the livelong day
With the mock-bird's changeful roundelay;
And at night, when the scene is calm and still,
With the moan of the plaintive whip-poor-will.   20

Oh! I sigh for the land of the cypress and pine,
Of the laurel, the rose, and the gay woodbine,
Where the long, gray moss decks the rugged oak tree,—
That sun-bright land is the land for me.

EDWARD COOTE PINKNEY

Edward Coote Pinkney, the seventh child of William and
Maria Rodgers Pinkney, was born in London on October 1,
1802. He lived in London almost continuously for eight years,
while his father served as commissioner to settle claims under
the Jay Treaty and as Minister Plenipotentiary (1807–1810).
After the family returned to Baltimore Edward studied at St.
Mary's College and Baltimore College until in 1815 he was
appointed midshipman in the United States Navy. His term
of service included duty in the Mediterranean—where he was
commended for bravery in a skirmish with pirates and repri-
manded for "disrespect to a superior officer"—and in the West
Indies. Shortly before his father's death in 1822 Edward returned to Baltimore, remaining inactive in the service until he
resigned in October, 1824. He fell in love with Miss Mary
Hawkins, and to her he wrote "Serenade," and other poems, but
to no avail. In 1823 he challenged John Neal, eccentric man
of letters, for calumniation of William Pinkney in Neal's novel,
Randolph, and when satisfaction was refused he placarded Neal
as a coward. That same year he published in book form a long
poem, *Rodolph*. In 1824 he was admitted to the bar, and was
married to Georgiana McCausland on October 12. Early
in 1826 he was appointed professor of belles-lettres in the University of Maryland, a position which carried with it no pay,
and he made an abortive attempt to join the Mexican navy.
When supporters of John Quincy Adams started a newspaper,
The Marylander, in Baltimore (December, 1827), Pinkney was
appointed editor and served until his death on April 11, 1828.

SONG[14]

We break the glass, whose sacred wine
  To some beloved health we drain,
Lest future pledges, less divine,
  Should e'er the hallowed toy profane;
And thus I broke a heart, that poured
  Its tide of feelings out to thee,
In draughts, by after-times deplored,
  Yet dear to memory.

But still the old empassioned ways
  And habits of my mind remain,   10
And still unhappy light displays
  Thine image chambered in my brain,
And still it looks as when the hours
  Went by like flights of singing birds,
Or that soft chain of spoken flowers,
  And airy gems, thy words.

THE VOYAGER'S SONG[15]

"A tradition prevailed among the natives of Puerto Rico, that in the Isle of Bimini, one of the Lucayos, there was a fountain of such wonderful virtue, as to renew the youth and recall the vigor of every person who bathed in its salutary waters. In hopes of finding this grand restorative, Ponce de Leon and his followers, ranged through the islands, searching with fruitless solicitude for the fountain, which was the chief object of the expedition."—ROBERTSON'S *America*.

I

Sound trumpets, ho!—weigh anchor—loosen sail—
The seaward flying banners chide delay;
As if 'twere heaven that breathes the kindly gale,
Our life-like bark beneath it speeds away.
Flit we, a gliding dream, with troublous motion,
Across the slumbers of uneasy ocean;

And furl our canvas by a happier land,
So fraught with emanations from the sun,
That potable gold streams through the sand
        Where element should run.   10

II

Onward, my friends, to that bright, florid isle,
The jewel of a smooth and silver sea,
With springs on which perennial summers smile
A power of causing immortality.
For Bimini;—in its enchanted ground,
The hallowed fountains we would seek, are found;
Bathed in the waters of those mystic wells,
The frame starts up in renovated truth,
And, freed from Time's deforming spells,
        Resumes its proper youth.   20

III

Hail, better birth!—once more my feelings all
A graven image to themselves shall make,
And, placed upon my heart for pedestal,
That glorious idol long will keep awake
Their natural religion, nor be cast
To earth by Age, the great Iconoclast,
As from Gadara's founts they once could come,
Charm-called, from these, Love's genii shall arise,
And build their perdurable home,
        Miranda, in thine eyes.   30

IV

By Nature wisely gifted, not destroyed
With golden presents, like the Roman maid,
A sublunary paradise enjoyed,
Shall teach thee bliss incapable of shade;—
An Eden ours, nor angry gods, nor men,
Nor star-clad Fates, can take from us again.

Superior to animal decay,
Sun of that perfect heaven, thou'lt calmly see
Stag, raven, phenix, drop away
      With human transiency. 40

V

Thus, rich in being,—beautiful,—adored,
Fear not exhausting pleasure's precious mine;
The wondrous waters we approach, when poured
On passion's lees, supply the wasted wine:
Then be thy bosom's tenant prodigal,
And confident of termless carnival.
Like idle yellow leaves afloat on time,
Let others lapse to death's pacific sea,
We'll fade nor fall, but sport sublime
      In green eternity. 50

VI

The envious years, which steal our pleasures, thou
May'st call at once, like magic memory, back,
And, as they pass o'er thine unwithering brow,
Efface their footsteps ere they form a track.
Thy bloom with wilful weeping never stain,
Perpetual life must not belong to pain.
For me,—this world hath not yet been a place
Conscious of joys so great as will be mine,
Because the light has kissed no face
      Forever fair as thine. 60

SERENADE[16]

Look out upon the stars, my love,
  And shame them with thine eyes,
On which, than on the lights above,
  There hang more destinies.
Night's beauty is the harmony
  Of blending shades and light;

Then, Lady, up,—look out, and be
   A sister to the night!—

Sleep not!—thine image wakes for aye,
   Within my watching breast: 10
Sleep not!—from her soft sleep should fly,
   Who robs all hearts of rest.
Nay, Lady, from thy slumbers break,
   And make this darkness gay,
With looks whose brightness well might make
   Of darker nights a day.

A HEALTH[17]

I fill this cup to one made up of loveliness alone,
A woman, of her gentle sex the seeming paragon;
To whom the better elements and kindly stars have given
A form so fair, that, like the air, 'tis less of earth than heaven.

Her every tone is music's own, like those of morning birds,
And something more than melody dwells ever in her words;
The coinage of her heart are they, and from her lips each flows
As one may see the burthened bee forth issue from the rose.

Affections are as thoughts to her, the measures of her hours;
Her feelings have the fragrancy, the freshness, of young
    flowers;   10
And lovely passions, changing oft, so fill her, she appears
The image of themselves by turns,—the idol of past years!

Of her bright face one glance will trace a picture on the brain,
And of her voice in echoing hearts a sound must long remain,
But memory such as mine of her so very much endears,
When death is nigh my latest sigh will not be life's but hers.

I fill this cup to one made up of loveliness alone,
A woman, of her gentle sex the seeming paragon—

Her health! and would on earth there stood some more of such
    a frame,
That life might be all poetry, and weariness a name.   20

SONG[18]

Day departs this upper air,
   My lively, lovely lady;
And the eve-star sparkles fair,
   And our good steeds are ready.
Leave, leave these loveless halls,
   So lordly though they be;—
Come, come—affection calls—
   Away at once with me!

Sweet thy words in sense as sound,
   And gladly do I hear them;   10
Though thy kinsmen are around,
   And tamer bosoms fear them.
Mount, mount,—I'll keep thee, dear,
   In safety as we ride;—
On, on—my heart is here,
   My sword is at my side!

THE WIDOW'S SONG[19]

I burn no incense, hang no wreath,
   On this, thine early tomb;
Such cannot cheer the place of death,
   But only mock its gloom.
Here odorous smoke and breathing flower
   No grateful influence shed;
They lose their perfume and their power,
   When offered to the dead.

And if, as is the Afghaun's creed,
   The spirit may return,   10

A disembodied sense to feed,
    On fragrance, near its urn—
It is enough, that she, whom thou
    Did'st love in living years,
Sits desolate beside it now,
    And falls these heavy tears.

SELF-ESTEEM[20]

I know that perfect self-esteem
Is boyhood's most seductive dream:
Like others, when my course began,
I revelled in it,—but the man
To whom experience betrays
The sordor of life's miry ways,
Feels that the hope is—Oh! how vain,
To tread them through without a stain.

ON PARTING[21]

Alas! our pleasant moments fly
    On rapid wings away,
While those recorded with a sigh,
    Mock us by long delay.

Time,—envious time,—loves not to be
    In company with mirth,
But makes malignant pause to see
    The work of pain on earth.

MELANCHOLY'S CURSE OF FEASTS[22]

Pale, funeral flowers
    His drinking garlands twine;
The star, named "Wormwood," fall
    On the grape's tears, his wine!

A lacrymary glass
  To him the goblet be;
Along the lighted board,
  No gladness let him see!

Hang shadowy skeletons
  In his Egyptian halls;   10
Be dark handwritings traced
  On his Assyrian walls!

Let each vase semble well
  A cinerary urn;
Its fruit, to ashes like
  The dead sea apples, turn!

Thus into wretched mirth
  Of hours, his life compress,—
A miserable mass
  Of grief and drunkenness.   20

WILLIAM GILMORE SIMMS

William Gilmore Simms was born on April 17, 1806, in
Charleston, South Carolina. His father, also William Gilmore
Simms, was a merchant; his mother, Harriet Singleton Simms,
died on January 29, 1808, shortly after the deaths of two of
her sons. To the broken husband and father Charleston seemed
a "place of tombs." In one week his hair turned white; soon
he mounted his horse and turned toward Tennessee, leaving
his surviving son practically an orphan, in the care of his
grandmother. The older Simms had taken the bankrupt law
only a few months before, and the household he left behind
was constantly faced with poverty. Although free schools were
in disrepute and were wretchedly taught, to a free school young
William had to go for two years; his entire schooling consisted
of less than six years in all. Lack of formal education was in
part remedied by omnivorous reading. Early he turned to the
writing of poetry: when eight years old, he celebrated in verse

the American victories over Great Britain. Other verses followed in profusion, but school and verse-making alike could not withstand poverty, and young Simms was apprenticed to a druggist. Since his grandmother did not approve of wasting candles, he was forced to read at night—after working all day— by a candle put into a large box. Book and head followed the candle; his grandmother would see no light, and he could read undisturbed.

Two elements seem to have influenced Simms greatly, in addition to his reading: the stories of the Revolutionary War and of witchcraft told him by his grandmother, and the stories of Indian and partisan warfare his father related while on a visit to Charleston about 1817 (he had served under Andrew Jackson at New Orleans and in the Indian campaigns in Florida).

When his druggist apprenticeship ended, Simms began to read law, and to write more poems. In 1824 he visited his father in Mississippi, and felt tempted to remain; the experiences of frontier life made a deep impression upon him, but he preferred Charleston and a literary life. At nineteen he published his first volume of poems; at twenty he married Anna Malcolm Gibbs; at twenty-one he was admitted to the bar, was the father of a daughter, and was publishing a second volume of poetry. The life of Simms was active and varied, from this time on: he practiced law with fair success for a few years; edited a magazine, *The Tablet*, which lasted for one year; bought and edited a newspaper, which failed when Simms with his usual vehemence opposed Nullification. Only his personal bravery prevented a mob from destroying his printing office. The failure of *The Charleston City Gazette* took all of Simms's money, but other losses crowded upon him: his father died in 1830, his grandmother soon afterward, and his wife in 1832. Leaving his daughter in the care of her mother's family, Simms left the state where he was personally unpopular, and went north. While there he published a long poem, *Atalantis*, the story of a sea fairy persecuted by the love of a sea demon. The poem was immediately successful. Then, almost by accident, he became a romancer, with the story of a crime, *Martin Faber*, which succeeded so well that he worked incessantly upon a longer and more original story of border life. This novel, *Guy Rivers* (1834), and *The Yemassee* (1835) established Simms as one of the most popular novelists in the country.

In 1836 Simms married Chevillette Roach, daughter of a well-to-do planter, and from that time on he lived at her country house, "Woodlands," entertaining lavishly his Northern and Southern friends: William Cullen Bryant, G. P. R. James, John R. Thompson, Paul Hamilton Hayne, and countless others. Sometimes he longed for political fame, and he served in the state legislature for one term (1844–46), and failed by only one vote to be elected lieutenant governor. But mainly he was busy with writing, with unbelievable industry: he wrote over seventy books, edited, or helped to edit, not less than ten Southern magazines, and contributed freely to any Southern journal that asked for a story, an article, or a poem. The variety of his work is almost as amazing as its quantity: in addition to eighteen volumes of poetry and over thirty novels, he wrote three plays, four biographies (*Francis Marion, Chevalier Bayard, John Smith, Nathanael Greene*), a history and a geography of South Carolina, miscellaneous works on slavery, American history, literary criticism—and even edited *A Supplement to the Plays of William Shakespeare*. It is not surprising that his later work was hurried and slipshod; it is rather amazing that he should have written, in the main, interestingly, and in the best of his novels and poems, excellently.

In the decade before the Civil War Simms expounded valiantly the Southern ideal of agrarian life—defending it, as regarded slavery, with considerable ingenuity and no little truth, and as regarded the general ideals of a cultured and gracious way of life, with an intelligence and justice that is only today coming to be recognized at its true worth. He was indisputably the Dr. Johnson, the Father Abbot of the Charleston group—as distinguished a coterie, for all the lack of recognition that a later history has accorded them, as America has had—and he talked constantly with them. Open-handed and open-hearted, he handed out whiskey punches and praise to all whom he thought deserving, until he roused in such young men as Paul Hamilton Hayne a feeling of hero worship.

When war came, Simms wanted to fight, but he was too old and feeble for any fighting save with the pen. He could plan military actions that later were adopted by the Southern authorities; he could write spirited poems and voluminous letters and occasional editorials; and all of these he did, but he was mainly a spectator in a drama where he desired an active part. Misfortunes crowded round him: his wife and several of his children died, his house was partially burned by accident and then completely destroyed by federal troops, his city was captured, and his friends were suffering grievously. And the final defeat of the South brought little peace to Simms. Although old and broken in health, he had to write countless potboilers to make a meager living, and his leonine spirit forced him on to looking after, as best he could, friends who were even more destitute than he. Heartbreaking days went to securing money and work for Timrod and other men; even more agonized labor went into his editing of *War Poetry of the South* (1867), a final tribute to his section and to his friends. But he continued to write cheering and hearty letters, spirited if uneven romances, and, with tragic frequency, noble obituaries for his rapidly decreasing multitude of friends, until he too died, June 11, 1870. He prepared his own epitaph, so truly worded that, after it, nothing can be said: "Here lies one who after a reasonably long life, distinguished chiefly by unceasing labors, has left all his better works undone."

THE SWAMP FOX[23]

We follow where the Swamp Fox guides,
    His friends and merry men are we;
And when the troop of Tarleton rides,
    We burrow in the cypress tree.
The turfy hammock is our bed,
    Our home is in the red deer's den,
Our roof, the tree-top overhead,
    For we are wild and hunted men.

We fly by day and shun its light,
    But prompt to strike the sudden blow,   10
We mount and start with early night,
    And through the forest track our foe,
And soon he hears our chargers leap,
    The flashing saber blinds his eyes,
And ere he drives away his sleep,
    And rushes from his camp, he dies.

Free bridle-bit, good gallant steed,
　　That will not ask a kind caress
To swim the Santee at our need,
　　When on his heels the foemen press—　　20
The true heart and the ready hand,
　　The spirit stubborn to be free,
The twisted bore, the smiting brand—
　　And we are Marion's men, you see.

Now light the fire and cook the meal,
　　The last, perhaps, that we shall taste;
I hear the Swamp Fox round us steal,
　　And that's a sign we move in haste.
He whistles to the scouts, and hark!
　　You hear his order calm and low.　　30
Come, wave your torch across the dark,
　　And let us see the boys that go.

We may not see their forms again,
　　God help 'em, should they find the strife!
For they are strong and fearless men,
　　And make no coward terms for life;
They'll fight as long as Marion bids,
　　And when he speaks the word to shy,
Then, not till then, they turn their steeds,
　　Through thickening shade and swamp to fly.　　40

Now stir the fire and lie at ease—
　　The scouts are gone, and on the brush
I see the Colonel bend his knees,
　　To take his slumbers too. But hush!
He's praying, comrades; 'tis not strange;
　　The man that's fighting day by day
May well, when night comes, take a change,
　　And down upon his knees to pray.

Break up that hoecake, boys, and hand
　　The sly and silent jug that's there;　　50

I love not it should idly stand
    When Marion's men have need of cheer.
'Tis seldom that our luck affords
    A stuff like this we just have quaffed,
And dry potatoes on our boards
    May always call for such a draught.

Now pile the brush and roll the log;
    Hard pillow, but a soldier's head
That's half the time in brake and bog
    Must never think of softer bed.   60
The owl is hooting to the night,
    The cooter crawling o'er the bank,
And in that pond the flashing light
    Tells where the alligator sank.

What! 'tis the signal! start so soon,
    And through the Santee swamp so deep,
Without the aid of friendly moon,
    And we, Heaven help us! half asleep!
But courage, comrades! Marion leads;
    The Swamp Fox takes us out tonight;   70
So clear your swords and spur your steeds,
    There's goodly chance, I think, of fight.

We follow where the Swamp Fox guides,
    We leave the swamp and cypress tree,
Our spurs are in our coursers' sides,
    And ready for the strife are we.
The Tory camp is now in sight,
    And there he cowers within his den;
He hears our shouts, he dreads the fight,
    He fears, and flies from Marion's men.   80

THE EDGE OF THE SWAMP[24]

'Tis a wild spot, and even in summer hours,
With wondrous wealth of beauty and a charm
For the sad fancy, hath the gloomiest look,
That awes with strange repulsion. There, the bird
Sings never merrily in the sombre trees,
That seem to have never known a term of youth,
Their young leaves all being blighted. A rank growth
Spreads venomously round, with power to taint;
And blistering dews await the thoughtless hand
That rudely parts the thicket. Cypresses,   10
Each a great ghastly giant, eld and gray,
Stride o'er the dusk, dank tract,—with buttresses
Spread round, apart, not seeming to sustain,
Yet link'd by secret twines, that underneath,
Blend with each arching trunk. Fantastic vines,
That swing like monstrous serpents in the sun,
Bind top to top, until the encircling trees
Group all in close embrace. Vast skeletons
Of forests, that have perish'd ages gone,
Moulder, in mighty masses, on the plain;   20
Now buried in some dark and mystic tarn,
Or sprawl'd above it, resting on great arms,
And making, for the opossum and the fox,
Bridges, that help them as they roam by night.
Alternate stream and lake, between the banks,
Glimmer in doubtful light: smooth, silent, dark,
They tell not what they harbor; but, beware!
Lest, rising to the tree on which you stand,
You sudden see the moccasin snake heave up
His yellow shining belly and flat head   30
Of burnish'd copper. Stretch'd at length, behold
Where yonder Cayman, in his natural home,
The mammoth lizard, all his armor on,
Slumbers half-buried in the sedgy grass,

Beside the green ooze where he shelters him.
The place, so like the gloomiest realm of death,
Is yet the abode of thousand forms of life,—
The terrible, the beautiful, the strange,—
Wingéd and creeping creatures, such as make
The instinctive flesh with apprehension crawl,   40
When sudden we behold. Hark! at our voice
The whooping crane, gaunt fisher in these realms,
Erects his skeleton form and shrieks in flight,
On great white wings. A pair of summer ducks,
Most princely in their plumage, as they hear
His cry, with senses quickening all to fear,
Dash up from the lagoon with marvellous haste,
Following his guidance. See! aroused by these,
And startled by our progress o'er the stream,
The steel-jaw'd Cayman, from his grassy slope,   50
Slides silent to the slimy green abode,
Which is his province. You behold him now,
His bristling back uprising as he speeds
To safety, in the centre of the lake,
Whence his head peers alone,—a shapeless knot,
That shows no sign of life; the hooded eye,
Nathless, being ever vigilant and sharp,
Measuring the victim. See! a butterfly,
That, travelling all the day, has counted climes
Only by flowers, to rest himself a while,   60
And, as a wanderer in a foreign land,
To pause and look around him ere he goes,
Lights on the monster's brow. The surly mute
Straightway goes down; so suddenly, that he,
The dandy of the summer flowers and woods,
Dips his light wings, and soils his golden coat,
With the rank waters of the turbid lake.
Wondering and vex'd, the pluméd citizen
Flies with an eager terror to the banks,
Seeking more genial natures,—but in vain.   70
Here are no gardens such as he desires,

No innocent flowers of beauty, no delights
Of sweetness free from taint. The genial growth
He loves, finds here no harbor. Fetid shrubs,
That scent the gloomy atmosphere, offend
His pure patrician fancies. On the trees,
That look like felon spectres, he beholds
No blossoming beauties; and for smiling heavens,
That flutter his wings with breezes of pure balm,
He nothing sees but sadness—aspects dread,   80
That gather frowning, cloud and fiend in one,
As if in combat, fiercely to defend
Their empire from the intrusive wing and beam.
The example of the butterfly be ours.
He spreads his lacquer'd wings above the trees,
And speeds with free flight, warning us to seek
For a more genial home, and couch more sweet
Than these drear borders offer us tonight.

THE LOST PLEIAD[25]

I

18th cent. style

Not in the sky,
Where it was seen
So long in eminence of light serene,—
Nor on the white tops of the glistering wave,
Nor down, in mansions of the hidden deep,
Though beautiful in green
And crystal, its great caves of mystery,—
Shall the bright watcher have
Her place, and, as of old, high station keep!

II

Gone! gone!   10
Oh! never more, to cheer
The mariner, who holds his course alone
On the Atlantic, through the weary night,

When the stars turn to watchers, and do sleep,
Shall it again appear,
With the sweet-loving certainty of light,
Down shining on the shut eyes of the deep!

III

The upward-looking shepherd on the hills
Of Chaldea, night-returning, with his flocks,
He wonders why his beauty doth not blaze,   20
Gladdening his gaze,—
And, from his dreary watch along the rocks,
Guiding him homeward o'er the perilous ways!
How stands he waiting still, in a sad maze,
Much wondering, while the drowsy silence fills
The sorrowful vault!—how lingers, in the hope that night
May yet renew the expected and sweet light,
So natural to his sight!

IV

And lone,
Where, at the first, in smiling love she shone,   30
Brood the once happy circle of bright stars:
How should they dream, until her fate was known,
That they were ever confiscate to death?
That dark oblivion the pure beauty mars,
And, like the earth, its common bloom and breath,
That they should fall from high;
Their lights grow blasted by a touch, and die,—
All their concerted springs of harmony
Snapt rudely, and the generous music gone!

V

Ah! still the strain   40
Of wailing sweetness fills the saddening sky;
The sister stars, lamenting in their pain
That one of the selectest ones must die,—
Must vanish, when most lovely, from the rest!

Alas! 'tis ever thus the destiny.
Even Rapture's song hath evermore a tone
Of wailing, as for bliss too quickly gone.
The hope most precious is the soonest lost,
The flower most sweet is first to feel the frost.
Are not all short-lived things the loveliest?   50
And, like the pale star, shooting down the sky,
Look they not ever brightest, as they fly
From the lone sphere they blest!

'TIS TRUE THAT LAST NIGHT I ADORED THEE

'Tis true that last night I adored thee,
    But 'twas moonlight, the song, and the wine;
The cool morning air has restored me,
    And no longer I deem thee divine;
I confess thou art pretty and tender,
    And when thou canst catch me again,
As last night, on a desperate *bender*,*
    Once more I'll submit to thy chain.

The fact is, dear Fanny, I'm human,
    Very weak, I may say, on a *spree*;**   10
And no matter of what sort the woman,
    I'm her slave if she *cottons**** to me.
But this cursèd sobriety ever
    Undoes every chain of delight,
And my memory, by daylight, has never
    Any sense of what takes place by night.

---

* Our Collegiate naturally uses what is supposed to be flash dialect. But, in truth, flash language, not to be guilty of a pun, is very often the language of the fancy. Here, the word *bender* is simply figurative; signifying the rather circuitous progress, snake fashion, which a young blood is apt to take, after the professors have all retired for the night. [*Simms's note.*]

** *Spree*, is simply an American contraction of the French word *esprit*, which, freely rendered in our idiom, means "on the wing." [*Simms's note.*]

*** *Cottons*—clings closely; a figure drawn from the now general use of cotton wool in the manufacture of chemise and shirt. [*Simms's note.*]

I'm a man of most regular habit
    When daylight comes round, on my word;
And though loving, by night, as a rabbit,
    With the sunrise I'm cool as a curd;   20
I'm quite willing in moonlight for capture,
    But she's a bright woman whose skill,
Having spell'd the short hours with rapture,
    With the daylight can fetter me still.

THE GRAPE-VINE SWING[26]

Lithe and long as the serpent train,
    Springing and clinging from tree to tree,
Now darting upward, now down again,
    With a twist, and a twirl that are strange to see:
Never took serpent a deadlier hold,
    Never the cougar a wilder spring,
Strangling the oak with the boa's fold,
    Spanning the beech with the condor's wing.

Yet no foe that we fear to seek—
    The boy leaps wild to thy rude embrace;   10
Thy bulging arms bear as soft a cheek
    As ever on lover's breast found place:
On thy waving train is a playful hold
    Thou shalt never to lighter grasp persuade;
While a maiden sits in thy drooping fold,
    And swings and sings in the noonday shade!

Oh! giant strange of our southern woods,
    I dream of thee still in the well-known spot,
Though our vessel strains o'er the ocean floods,
    And the northern forest beholds thee not;   20
I think of thee still with a sweet regret,
    As the cordage yields to my playful grasp—
Dost thou spring and cling in our woodlands yet?
    Does the maiden still swing in thy giant clasp?

THE DECAY OF A PEOPLE

This the true sign of ruin to a race—
   It undertakes no march, and, day by day
Drowses in camp, or, with the laggard's pace,
   Walks sentry o'er possessions that decay;
   Destined, with sensible waste, to fleet away;—
For the first secret of continued power
   Is the continued conquest;—all our sway
Hath surety in the uses of the hour;
If that we waste, in vain wall'd town and lofty tower!

SONG IN MARCH

I

Now are the winds about us in their glee,
Tossing the slender tree;
Whirling the sands about his furious car,
March cometh from afar;
Breaks the seal'd magic of old winter's dreams,
And rends his glassy streams;
Chafing with potent airs, he fiercely takes
Their fetters from the lakes,
And, with a power by queenly Spring supplied,
Wakens the slumbering tide.   10

II

With a wild love he seeks young Summer's charms
And clasps her to his arms;
Lifting his shield between, he drives away
Old Winter from his prey;—
The ancient tyrant whom he boldly braves,
Goes howling to his caves;
And, to his northern realm compell'd to fly,
Yields up the victory;
Melted are all his bands, o'erthrown his towers,
And March comes bringing flowers.   20

SONNET[27]

We are a part of all things that we see,
   Share in a common nature, and are taught
   By what they suffer; with their feelings fraught,
Are bound by their captivity; or free,
   When they are wanton. Earth and sea and air
   Master us through our sympathies. We share
The elements around us, till we flee
   From our own nature to a converse strange
With other natures; find in rock and tree
Mute friends that teach, and never disagree,   10
   Rebuke not, yet exhort; and so we range
Capricious as the winds that stir the sea,
   Constant in nothing save the love of change.

THOMAS HOLLEY CHIVERS

Thomas Holley Chivers, "the lost poet of Georgia," is an elusive figure factually and poetically. Even the date of his birth is uncertain: from a poem in *Conrad and Eudora*, written October 18, 1834, and titled "On the Anniversary of my Twenty-Fifth Year," his biographer, S. Foster Damon, believes that he was born October 18, 1809; but Chivers himself claimed 1807 as the year of his birth, and on his tombstone his age is given as "*aetat*, 52" (he died December 18, 1858). Damon also thinks that Chivers may have "antedated his birth, so that he would appear older than his rival Poe, who was actually his senior by nine months." In spite of Damon's strong faith in the poem, the weight of evidence seems to favor October 18, 1807, as the date of Chivers's birth. He was born near Washington, Georgia, the oldest of the seven children of Col. Robert Chivers. After graduating from a Georgia preparatory school, he studied medicine at Transylvania College, writing his thesis on "Intermittent and Remittent Fevers" and receiving his M.D. with distinction in 1830. But his father was a wealthy cotton planter, and Chivers soon abandoned medicine for poetry.

In 1831 he visited the Cherokee Indians, with whom he seems to have sympathized, had a vision of harp-playing angels, and prepared to publish his first book of poems, *The Path of Sorrow* (privately printed at Franklin, Tennessee, 1832). Most of the poems deal with his unhappy marriage, contracted before he was twenty and before he went to Transylvania, but of which little is definitely known. From the poems, the marriage seems to have been broken off when friends of the bride slandered Chivers's character (unjustly, he protests) and he was not permitted to see her. This tragic episode rankled, and was never forgotten or forgiven: in his will Chivers left this first wife and her daughter one dollar each.

In 1837, while living temporarily in the North, Chivers married Harriet Hunt of Springfield, Massachusetts. The same year he went to New York, where he published *Nacoochee*, with a preface which contains his theory as to the transcendental nature of poetry. His acquaintance with Edgar Allan Poe began in 1840, when Poe sent him a prospectus of the *Penn Magazine*. Shortly after, Poe described Chivers as "one of the best and one of the worst poets in America"; when Chivers protested, Poe soothed his feelings, and continued from that time to praise especially the strength and originality of the Georgian. Although Chivers seems never to have backed Poe's magazines with financial support, he did write Poe to come South and live with him at his expense, and after Poe's death Chivers prepared a biography of his friend, intended to be frank but to point out the merits of Poe's poems; unfortunately it was never published. Chivers's own poetry continued to appear regularly in magazines; two of the most famous of his poems ("The Lost Pleiad" and "To Allegra Florence in Heaven") were elegies for his daughter who died October 18, 1842. Not long after, he lost his three other children, and he began more intensive studies in Swedenborgianism, Spiritualism, and Mesmerism—publishing in 1848 the result of his investigation, *Search After Truth; or, A New Revelation of the Psycho-Physiological Nature of Man.*

In 1851 he published *Eonchs of Ruby* (the first word apparently meaning *Conchs*). Immediately Chivers was charged with plagiarism by followers of Poe—a charge which Poe himself never made—and he retaliated by charging that Poe had borrowed from him. Undoubtedly each man's work had greatly influenced the other; in some cases the priority rested with Chivers, in some with Poe, but the actual amount of plagiarism is probably negligible and unimportant; certainly it is impossible to straighten out in a brief space. Chivers continued to publish poetry, three volumes appearing in 1853, and his last book, a dramatization of the Deirdre legend (*The Sons of Usna*), in 1858. He died at Decatur, Georgia, December 18, 1858.

FAITH[28]

Faith is the flower that blooms unseen
By mountains of immortal green—
A hoped-for harvest in the skies,
In which the reaper never dies—
A tree to which the power is given
To lift its branches into heaven;
And from whose boughs of gorgeous fruit
A loftier tree shall take its root.

Lord! we are grafted into thine,
When broken off from Adam's vine;   10
And so, from that degenerate tree,
We grow into the life of thee!
For, by the prunings of thy word,
Are we then purged into the Lord;
And like Mount Zion we shall stand
The Temples of our native land.

Lord! if the stars should take their flight,
And vanish from the halls of night;
And if the morning should appear,
And vanish from the evening near;   20
And if the rivers should run dry,
And every flower that decks them die;
And if the world should cease to be—
I would not lose my trust in thee.

[handwritten annotations: "Repetition, use of refrain" / "about Southern theme" / "Too metaphorical, hyperbolical" / "Hopkins lacke story will told of any will events till to make rythm classical"]

GEORGIA WATERS[29]

On thy waters, thy sweet valley-waters,
    Oh! Georgia! how happy were we!
When thy daughters, thy sweet smiling daughters,
    First gathered sweet-william for me,
Then thy wildwood, thy dark, shady wildwood
    Had many bright visions for me!
For my childhood, my bright rosy childhood
    Was cradled, dear Georgia! in thee—
    Bright land of my childhood, in thee!

On thy mountains, thy green purple mountains
    The seasons were waiting on thee,
When thy fountains, thy clear crystal fountains
    Flowed sporting in gladness for me.
Now thy waters, thy sweet valley-waters
    Rush laughing in song to the Sea;
While thy daughters, thy sweet smiling daughters
    Still gather sweet-william for me—
    Dear land of my childhood, for me!

SONG OF ADORATION TO GOD[30]

In that day shall this song be sung in the land.—Isaiah 26:1.

    Lord! in the Temple of thy love,
    Bowed in thy radiance from above,
    Mantled with thy redeeming light,
    And ordered in thy steps aright;
    Let the soft wooings of thy wings
    Shadow the music of my strings.

    Lord! like the desert fount that flowed
    Fast by the feet of Hagar bowed,
    Thirsting amid the desert wild
    She wandered with her outcast child—

Oh! pour upon me thy soft beams,
And circle me with heavenly streams.

If, in the whirlwinds of the sea,
A prayer is offered up to thee;
If thou art on the page of night,
Written in syllables of light;
And if thy hands have made the sun,
Lord! tell me what thou hast not done!

If thou hast ceiled the heavens with blue,
And laced them with the morning dew;   20
If thou hast placed the stars of light
Upon the curtains of the night;
And if thy hands have made them ways,
Lord! let me offer up my praise!

If, from the chaos of old Night,
The stars were whispered into flight!
If, when another word was given,
The sun stood on the hills of heaven!
And if these things were made for me,
Lord, tell me what to do for thee!   30

Lo! if the universe hath words,
And they are spoken by the birds!
And if the rivers roll along
In the deep eloquence of song;
If these have been since time began,
Lord! what should be the praise of man!

If night doth prophesy to night
The language of the morning light;
And if the morning doth appear
To whisper to the evening near;   40
And if these things pour forth to thee,
Lord! what should not be said by me!

Are not the songsters of the grove
Vocal with thy redeeming love?
Are not the burning stars of even
The members of thy church in heaven?
And if they are but lamps to me,
Lord! teach me how to worship thee!

THE CRUCIFIXION[31]

From the Temple torn asunder
    Of his God-Humanity,
Lofty piles of echoing thunder
    Rolled in groans of agony!

From his heart, the blood down-spilling,
    Incense-smoke of pain was sent,
Blotting out the Sun, while filling
    Heaven and Earth with wonderment!

SONNET: GRIEF[32]

"Sorrow is better than laughter; for by the sadness of the countenance the
heart is made better."—BIBLE.

As the uncertain twittering of the birds,
    Striving with Winter, which has been so long,
Dies inarticulate—ending not in song—
    So did my voice, with many plaintive words,
Strive, in the winter of my grief, to sing,
    But died in silence—they could not be spoken—
Because, within my heart, there was no spring
    Of joy to call them forth—*my heart was broken!*
For Disappointment's frost had withered up
    Affection's flowers!—Youth's Garden now was bare!   10
I have drunk poison from Death's empty cup,
    Whose bottom now contains the dregs of care,
Which mock my lips with bitterness, to think
    That of Youth's wine there is not more to drink!

ISADORE[33]

"I approach thee—I look dauntless into thine eyes. The soul that loves can dare all things. Shadow, I defy thee, and compel."—ZANONI.

I

While the world lay round me sleeping,
    I, alone, for ISADORE,
Patient Vigils lonely keeping—
Some one said to me while weeping,
    "Why this grief forever more?"
And I answered, "I am weeping
    For my blessed ISADORE!"

II

Then the Voice again said, "Never
    Shall thy soul see ISADORE!
God from thee thy love did sever—   10
He has damned thy soul forever!
    Wherefore then her loss deplore?
Thou shalt live in Hell forever!
    Heaven now holds thine ISADORE!

III

"She is dead—the world benighted—
    Dark for want of ISADORE!
Have not all your hopes been blighted?
How can you be reunited?
    Can mere words the dead restore?
Have not all your hopes been blighted?   20
    Why then hope for ISADORE?"

IV

"Back to Hell, thou ghostly Horror!"
    Thus I cried, dear ISADORE!
"Phantom of remorseless Sorrow!
Death might from thee pallor borrow—
    Borrow leanness ever more!

Back to Hell again!—tomorrow
   I will go to ISADORE!"

V

"When my soul to Heaven is taken,"
   Were thy words, dear ISADORE!   30
"Let no other one awaken
In thy heart, because forsaken,
   What was felt for me before!
When my soul to Heaven is taken,
   Oh! forget not ISADORE!

VI

"Oh! remember this, Politian!"
   Said my dying ISADORE!
"Till from out this clayey prison
In the flowery FIELDS ELYSIAN
   We unite forever more!   40
Oh! remember this, Politian!
   And forget not ISADORE!"

VII

Then before my raptured vision
   Came sweet HOPE, dear ISADORE!
From the flowery FIELDS ELYSIAN
Crying out to me, "Politian!
   Rise—rejoice forever more!
Angels wait for thee, Politian!
   Up to Heaven to ISADORE!"

VIII

Then from out my soul departed
   Deepest grief, dear ISADORE!   50
Bliss, that never me deserted,
Entered in the broken-hearted—
   Giving life forever more—
Bliss that never me deserted,
   Like thy love, dear ISADORE!

IX

Myriad VOICES still are crying,
    Day and night, dear ISADORE!
"Come, come to the PURE LAND* lying
Far up in the sky undying—   60
    There to rest forever more!
Purified, redeemed, undying—
    Come to Heaven to ISADORE!

X

"Blest Companion of th' Eternal!
    Come away to ISADORE!
From the griefs that are diurnal
To the joys that are supernal—
    Sempiternal on Heaven's shore!
Bliss supernal, joys eternal
    Up in Heaven with ISADORE.   70

XI

"Cast away thy garb of mourning,
    Worn so long for ISADORE!
For those glory-garments burning
In the BRIGHT ISLES OF THE MORNING,
    Like the stars forever more.
Golden Days are now returning—
    Up to Heaven to ISADORE!

* Plato speaks of the "PURE EARTH" above, (την γην χαθαραν εν χαθαρω χεισθαι ουρανο,) the abode of Divinity, of innocence, and life. It is an immemorial tradition. It was a revelation to the Hebrews. This "PURE EARTH" above, is, no doubt, the primeval Paradise of Love—the antetype of that which Adam lost. Aristotle in his Hymn to Virtue, speaks of the "BLESSED ISLES" above. The Νησοι Μακάρων, or ISLES OF THE BLEST, were the ELYSIUM of the departed Heroes who were considered immortal —the same as the MANITOLINE of the Indians, where they say the souls of the deathless Chieftains of the world dance in hormonian choirs around the throne of Ataensic to the most delightful music. They believe that the future felicity of the departed of this world consists in rejoining, in the flower-gemmed Savannahs of the Fields of Immortality, the long, lost objects of their affections in the joyful festivities of the Chase. [*Chivers's note.*]

XII

"Lay aside thy load of sorrow,
　　Borne so long for ISADORE!
Pilgrim, pierced by Death's cold arrow,　　　80
Thou shalt see thy love tomorrow
　　Up in Heaven forever more!
Lay aside thy load of sorrow—
　　Come to Heaven to ISADORE!

XIII

"Come away, Oh! mournful mortal!
　　Come to Heaven to ISADORE!
Through Death's ebon, iron Portal
To the joys that are immortal
　　On Helusion's happy shore!
Come away, Oh! mournful mortal!　　　90
　　Into Heaven to ISADORE!

XIV

"Up to God who will befriend you!
　　Up to Heaven to ISADORE!
Angels waiting to attend you—
Every aid you wish to lend you—
　　Singing, shouting on Heaven's shore!
Angels waiting to attend you
　　To your blessed ISADORE!"

XV

From the griefs that are diurnal—
　　Bitter griefs, dear ISADORE!　　　100
To the joys that are eternal—
To the bliss that is supernal—
　　Sempiternal on Heaven's shore—
Thou art gone through years eternal
　　There to rest, dear ISADORE!

XVI

There thy comates shall be Angels—
    White-robed Angels, ISADORE!
Singing Heaven's DIVINE EVANGELS
Through the Eternal Years, all change else,
    Changeless there forever more!   110
Thou, ASTARTE of the Angels!
    Knowest this so, dear ISADORE!

XVII

From the Paradise now wasted
    Of thy form, dear ISADORE!
Lilly-bell that Death has blasted!
Purest Pleasures have I tasted
    In the Edenic days of Yore.
Joys celestial have I tasted
    From thy flower, dear ISADORE!

XVIII

Like two spirits in one being,   120
    Were our souls, dear ISADORE!
Every object singly seeing—
In all things, like one, agreeing
    In those HALCYON DAYS of Yore.
We shall live so in our being
    Up in Heaven, dear ISADORE!

XIX

Myriad Voices still are crying
    Day and night, dear ISADORE!
"Come, come to the PURE LAND lying
Far up in the sky undying—   130
    There to rest forever more!
Purified, redeemed, undying—
    Come to Heaven to ISADORE!"

XX

ADON-AI! GOD OF GLORY!
  Who dost love mine ISADORE!
Who didst hear her prayerful story
In this world when she was sorry—
  Gone to Heaven forever more!
ADON-AI! GOD OF GLORY!
  Take me home to ISADORE!   140

TO ALLEGRA FLORENCE IN HEAVEN[34]

When thy soft round form was lying
On the bed where thou wert sighing,
I could not believe thee dying,
  Till thy angel-soul had fled;
For no sickness gave me warning,
Rosy health thy cheeks adorning—
Till that hope-destroying morning,
  When my precious child lay dead!

Now, thy white shroud covers slightly
Thy pale limbs, which were so sprightly,   10
While thy snow-white arms lie lightly
  On thy soul-abandoned breast;
As the dark blood faintly lingers
In thy pale, cold, lily fingers,
Thou, the sweetest of Heaven's singers!
  Just above thy heart at rest!

Yes, thy sprightly form is crowded
In thy coffin, all enshrouded,
Like the young Moon, half enclouded,
  On the first night of her birth;   20
And, as down she sinks when westing,
Of her smiles the Night divesting—
In my fond arms gently resting,
  Shall thy beauty to the earth!

Like some snow-white cloud just under
Heaven, some breeze has torn asunder,
Which discloses, to our wonder,
    Far beyond, the tranquil skies;
Lay thy pale, cold lids, half closing,
(While in death's cold arms reposing,   30
Thy dear seraph form seemed dozing—)
    On thy violet-colored eyes.

For thy soft blue eyes were tender
As an angel's, full of splendor,
And, like skies to earth, did render
    Unto me divine delight;
Like two violets in the morning
Bathed in sunny dews, adorning
One white lily-bed, while scorning
    All the rest, however bright.   40

Some fair Flower, which loves to flourish
As the Earth desires to nourish
On her breast, while it doth perish,
    And will barren look when gone;
So, my soul did joy in giving
Thee what thine was glad receiving
From me, ever more left grieving
    In this dark, cold world alone!

Holy angels now are bending
To receive thy soul ascending   50
Up to Heaven to joys unending,
    And to bliss which is divine;
While thy pale, cold form is fading
Under death's dark wings now shading
Thee with gloom which is pervading
    This poor, broken heart of mine!

For, as birds of the same feather
On the earth will flock together,

So, around thy Heavenly Father,
   They now gather there with thee— 60
Ever joyful to behold thee—
In their soft arms to enfold thee,
And to whisper words oft told thee,
   In this trying world by me!

With my bowed head thus reclining
On my hand, my heart repining,
Shall my salt tears, ever shining,
   On my pale cheeks, flow for thee—
Bitter soul-drops ever stealing
From the fount of holy feeling, 70
Deepest anguish now revealing,
   For thy loss, dear child! to me!

As an egg, when broken, never
Can be mended, but must ever
Be the same crushed egg forever—
   So shall this dark heart of mine!
Which, though broken, is still breaking,
And shall never more cease aching
For the sleep which has no waking—
   For the sleep which now is thine! 80

And as God doth lift thy spirit
Up to Heaven, there to inherit
Those rewards which it doth merit
   Such as none have reaped before;
Thy dear father will, tomorrow,
Lay thy body with deep sorrow,
In the grave which is so narrow—
   There to rest forevermore!

BURDENS OF UNREST

MARY'S LAMENT FOR SHELLEY LOST AT SEA [35]

"Stay for me there! I will not fail
To meet thee in that hollow vale!"
                                        BISHOP HENRY KING.

"Thou wilt not be consoled—I wonder not!"
                                        SHELLEY.

I

I hear thy spirit calling unto me
    From out the deep,
Like Archytas* from old Venetia's sea,
    While I here weep!
Saying, Come, strew my body with the sand,
And bury me upon the land, the land—
Out of this sea, dear Mary! on the land, the land!

II

Oh! never, never more! no, never more!
    Lost in the deep!
Will thy sweet beauty visit this dark shore,   10
    Where I now weep!
For thou art gone forevermore from me,
Sweet Mariner! lost, murdered by the sea!
Ulysses of my soul's deep love lost in the sea!

III

Ever—forevermore, bright, glorious one,
    Drowned in the deep!
In Spring-time—Summer—Winter—all alone—
    Must I here weep!
Thou spirit of my soul! thou light of life!
While thou art absent, Shelley, from thy wife!   20
Absent, dear Swan of Albion, from thy weeping wife!

*"Horace represents the spirit of Archytas addressing itself, from the
Gulf of Venice, to a Mariner, earnestly requesting him to strew light sand
over his body, which lay unburied on the beach."—BUCK's *Beauties and
Sublimities of Nature.* [*Chivers's note.*]

IV

Celestial pleasure once to contemplate
    Thy power, great Deep!
Possesst my soul! but evermore shall hate
    While I here weep!
Crowd out thy memory from my soul, oh! Sea!
For killing him who was so dear to me!
More dear than Heaven's high Lord to Mary unto me!

V

He was the incarnation of pure Truth,
    Oh! mighty Deep!   30
And thou didst murder him in prime of youth,
    For whom I weep!
And, murdering him, didst *more* than murder me!
Who was my Heaven on earth, oh! treacherous Sea!
My *more* than Heaven on earth, oh! *more* than murderous Sea!

VI

My spirit wearied not to succor his,
    Oh! mighty Deep!
The oftener done the greater was the bliss;
    But now I weep!
And where his beauty lay, unceasing pain   40
Now dwells—my heart can know no joy again!
Poor Doveless Ark! can know no joy on earth again!

VII

God of my fathers! God of that bright One
    Drowned in the Deep!
Shall we not meet again beyond the sun—
    No more to weep?
Yes, I shall meet him there—the lost—the bright—
The glorious Shelley! Spring of my delight!
Fountain of all my pleasure! life of my delight!

VIII

Now, like Orion on some cloudless night   50
  Above the Deep,
I see his soul look down from Heaven—*how bright!*
  While I here weep!
And there, like Hesperus the stars of even,
Beckon my soul away to him in Heaven—
Sitting, star-crowned, upon the highest sill in Heaven!

SONG TO ISA[36]

I

Upon thy lips now lies
  The music-dew of love;
And in thy deep blue eyes,
  More mild than heaven above,
  The meekness of the dove.

II

More sweet than the perfume
  Of snow-white jessamine,
When it is first in bloom,
  Is that sweet breath of thine,
  Which mingles now with mine.   10

III

Like an Æolian sound,
  Out of an ocean shell,
Which fills the air around
  With music, such as fell
  From lips of ISRAFEL;*

IV

Over thy lips now flow,
  Out of thy heart for me,

* "The angel Israfel, who has the most melodious voice of all God's creatures."—SALE. [*Chivers's note.*]

Sweet songs, which none can know
But him who hopes to be
Forevermore with thee.   20

V

And like the snow-white Dove
Frightened from earth at even
On tempests borne above,—
My swift-winged soul is driven
Upon thy voice to heaven!

THE CHAPLET OF CYPRESS[37]

AN ELEGY ON THE DEATH OF MY SISTER

"The Good die first."

I

Up through the hyaline ether-sea,
Star-diademed, in chariot of pure pain,
Through th' empyreal star-fires radiantly,
Triumphant over Death in Heaven to reign
Thy soul is gone, seeking its BLEST ABODE,
Where break the songs of stars against the feet of God.

II

At Heaven's high portals thou dost stand,
Bands of attendant Angels by thy side—
Gazing with rapture on the PROMISED LAND—
Pale—meek—with thy last sickness, purified,   10
By suffering, from the sins of earth, to be
A white-robed Angel round God's throne eternally.

III

Like stars at midnight in the sky,
Were all the dark things in this world to thee;
The joys of earth, when thou wert called to die,
Were ringing in thine ears most audibly,
When Angel-voices from the far-off skies,
Poured on thy soul rivers of rapturous melodies.

IV

Upon thy pale, cold, silent face,
Still speaking of the death that thou didst die—   20
   A living light, which Death could not efface,
Was shed, crowning thy young mortality—
   As if the power had unto thee been given
   To show us here on earth what thou art now in Heaven.

V

For when thy coffin-lid was moved,
Fast flowing tears of endless pity fell
   Upon thy pale, cold brow, so much beloved,
From our torn hearts, as we then cried, FAREWELL!
   Like dews upon some withered lily-leaf—
   Rivers of sorrow from deep seas of bitter grief!   30

VI

At thine, the newest grave dug here,
Beside our parents' graves, we humbly bow,
   Offering our hearts to God in silent prayer—
Asking ourselves who of us next must go
   Where thou art gone, to see what thou hast seen—
   To be what thou art now, if now what thou hast been!

VII

I recollect the last long night
We played together—brothers—sisters—all—
   Took notice of the infinite delight
That filled thy soul, till laughter's waterfall   40
   Gushed, gurgling from thy lips in joyful flow—
   And this, dear ONE! was only three short months ago!

VIII

Then thou wert gayer than the gay,
And full of pleasure to the very brim—
   Whiling, with gladness, all thy time away—

Not thinking thou wert soon to go to HIM—
    Thy Father's father, there, in Heaven, to shine
    With thy dear mother—brother—sister Adaline!

IX

    Thou wilt behold my Florence there,
And she will know thee in that world above,   50
    By that, which, wanting, makes us strangers here!
And she will love thee with the same deep love
    She loved me in this world, if thou wilt tell
    Her thou art my dear sister—Angel, fare-thee-well!

APOLLO[38]

What are stars, but hieroglyphics of God's glory writ in light-
    ning
    On the wide-unfolded pages of the azure scroll above?
But the quenchless apotheoses of thoughts forever brightening
    In the mighty Mind immortal of the God, whose name is
    Love?
Diamond letters sculptured, rising, on the azure ether pages,
    That now sing to one another—unto one another shine—
God's eternal Scripture talking, through the midnight, to the
    Ages,
    Of the life that is immortal, of the life that is divine—
    Life that *cannot* be immortal, but the life that is divine.

Like some deep, impetuous river from the fountains everlasting,
    Down the serpentine soft valley of the vistas of all Time,   11
Over cataracts of adamant uplifted into mountains,
    Soared his soul to God in thunder on the wings of thought
    sublime.
With the rising golden glory of the sun in ministrations,
    Making oceans metropolitan of splendor for the dawn—
Piling pyramid on pyramid of music for the nations—
    Sings the Angel who sits shining everlasting in the sun,
    For the stars, which are the echoes of the shining of the sun.

Like the lightnings piled on lightnings, ever rising, never
    reaching,
  In one monument of glory towards the golden gates of God—
Voicing out themselves in thunder upon thunder in their
    preaching,   21
  Piled this Cyclop up his Epic where the Angels never trod.
Like the fountains everlasting that forever more are flowing
  From the throne within the centre of the City built on high,
With their genial irrigation life forever more bestowing—
  Flows his lucid, liquid river through the gardens of the sky,
  For the stars forever blooming in the gardens of the sky.

THE VOICE OF THOUGHT[39]

Faint as the far-down tone
  Beneath the sounding sea,
Muffled, by its own moan,
  To silent melody;
So faint we cannot tell
  But that the sound we hear
Is some sweet roses' smell
  That falls upon our ear;
(As if the Butterfly
  Shaking the Lily-bell,   10
While drinking joyfully,
  Should toll its own death-knell!)
Sweeter than Hope's sweet lute
  Singing of joys to be,
When Pain's harsh voice is mute,
  Is the Soul's sweet song to me.

LILY ADAIR[40]

On the beryl-rimmed rebecs of Ruby,
  Brought fresh from the hyaline streams,
She played, on the banks of the Yuba,
  Such songs as she heard in her dreams.

Like the heavens, when the stars from their eyries
    Look down through the ebon night air,
Were the groves by the Ouphantic Fairies
    Lit up for my Lily Adair—
    For my child-like Lily Adair—
    For my heaven-born Lily Adair—   10
For my beautiful, dutiful Lily Adair.

Like two rose-leaves in sunshine when blowing,
    Just curled softly, gently apart,
Were her lips by her passion, while growing
    In perfume on the stalk of her heart.
As mild as the sweet influences
    Of the Pleiades 'pregning the air—
More mild than the throned Excellencies
    Up in heaven, was my Lily Adair—
    Was my Christ-like Lily Adair—   20
    Was my lamb-like Lily Adair—
Was my beautiful, dutiful Lily Adair.

At the birth of this fair virgin Vestal,
    She was taken for Venus' child;
And her voice, though like diamond in crystal,
    Was not more melodious than mild.
Like the moon in her soft silver splendor,
    She was shrined in her own, past compare,
For no Angel in heaven was more tender
    Than my beautiful Lily Adair—   30
    Than my dove-like Lily Adair—
    Than my saint-like Lily Adair—
Than my beautiful, dutiful Lily Adair.

There she stood on the arabesque borders
    Of the beautiful blossoms that blew
On the banks of the crystalline waters,
    Every morn, in the diaphane dew.

The flowers, they were radiant with glory,
    And shed such perfume on the air,
That my soul, now to want them, feels sorry,   40
    And bleeds for my Lily Adair—
    For my much-loved Lily Adair—
    For my long-lost Lily Adair—
For my beautiful, dutiful Lily Adair.

TO IDEALON

Soul of the sunny South! thy voice is heard
    In the deep stillness of the virgin heart!
Thy name is coupled with that heavenly word,
    And never from her chambers shall depart!
For thou shalt whisper unto those that sigh
A soothing voice—whose tones shall never die!

Soul of the sunny South! let not thy lays,
    Flung on the waters, perish in the sea!
No! let them come back after many days,
    To feed the heart that once was life to thee!   10
Go—like the turtle that has left her grove,
And pour thy spirit upon those that love.

EDGAR ALLAN POE

Edgar Allan Poe, the second child of David and Elizabeth
Arnold Poe, was born in Boston, January 19, 1809, where his
parents were acting in a stock company. Edgar's grandfather,
also David Poe, was an assistant quartermaster general in the
Revolutionary War; at the age of seventy-two he fought in
the War of 1812. But he was too prosaic a man to appreciate
an actor son, unthrifty and addicted to drink, and he allowed
that son to shift for himself. On December 8, 1811, Edgar's
mother died in Richmond, and he was taken, although never
legally adopted, into the family of John Allan, a tobacco merchant. Poe's older brother William was cared for by his grandfather. John Allan was not at that time the prosperous man

who is often portrayed as ruining Poe by overindulgence; he lived above his tobacco shop, and gradually expanded his business. This expansion led in 1815 to a visit to England, for the purpose of starting a branch business there, and in London the Allans remained for five years.

During this period Poe attended the Manor House School at Stoke Newington, near London; after his return to Richmond he studied at the schools of Masters Clarke and Burke until he entered the University of Virginia, where he remained from February 14 to December 15, 1826. In the study of ancient and modern languages Poe won some favorable commendation, but his excessive gambling debts caused Mr. Allan to withdraw him from school. For a few months he clerked in Allan's counting room, but soon he left without notice, going in the spring of 1827 to Boston. There he published *Tamerlane and Other Poems, by a Bostonian;* there in May he enlisted as Edgar A. Perry in the United States Army. He served for almost two years, gaining the rank of sergeant-major, and serving at least part of the time in Charleston, South Carolina. On April 15, 1829, he was honorably discharged, and the following year he entered West Point. He was soon dismissed—apparently through deliberate infractions of the rules because he could not get Allan's consent to resign—but he dedicated his third volume of poems (1831) to the students of West Point.

For two years he lived in complete obscurity in Baltimore, writing with little success until in October, 1833, his story, "Ms. Found in a Bottle," won the first prize of fifty dollars in a contest held by the *Baltimore Saturday Visiter*. His poem, "The Coliseum," would have been awarded the poetry prize if his story had not won the larger prize. John Pendleton Kennedy, the author of *Swallow Barn* and a judge in the contest, became his lifelong friend; he helped Poe to place his manuscripts, and in 1835 helped secure for him the assistant editorship of the *Southern Literary Messenger* (December, 1835–January, 1837). Once settled in Richmond, Poe secretly married (September 22, 1835) his thirteen year old cousin Virginia Clemm; on May 16, 1836, he remarried her publicly. As an editor Poe was highly successful (every magazine that he edited increased greatly in circulation), but he was at this time drinking heavily, and he was discharged. In New York he worked as free-lance writer, as editor of *Burton's Gentleman's Magazine*

(July, 1839–June, 1840) and of *Graham's Magazine* (February, 1841–April, 1842), and he became nationally famous for his criticisms and stories. Not until the appearance of *The Raven and Other Poems* in 1845 was he widely known as a poet; his contemporaries valued more highly his stories and his honest, slashing criticisms.

It is probable that Poe used opium in these days, when his output of work was so great, and after the death of his wife (January 30, 1847) Poe went to pieces. He dallied with the idea of marrying various other women, and proposed to several of them; he wrote pathetic letters to his friends—yet he found time also to write some of his best poems and stories, and to plan a new magazine. In 1849 he returned to Richmond, apparently to arrange a marriage with Sarah Elmira Shelton, but for some reason started north, and disappeared for five days. With a weak heart he had been warned by physicians against drinking, but in Baltimore he seems to have been plied with liquor by politicians who desired his vote, and this indulgence proved fatal. He died in Baltimore, October 7, 1849.

His literary executor, Rufus W. Griswold, hastily wrote a biography partly malicious and partly false (some of the errors being due to Poe's own romanticizations of his career), and the true facts of his life are still in some doubt. Unfortunately Chivers's biography was not published, and Poe was vilified on many sides. But his peccadillos were small enough, and relatively unimportant; they could not for long obscure the large amount of excellent work that he had done in fiction, in criticism, and above all in poetry.

TO SCIENCE[41]

A PROLOGUE TO "AL AARAAF"

Science! true daughter of Old Time thou art,
    Who alterest all things with thy peering eyes.
Why preyest thou thus upon the poet's heart,
    Vulture, whose wings are dull realities?
How should he love thee? or how deem thee wise,
    Who wouldst not leave him in his wandering
To seek for treasure in the jewelled skies,
    Albeit he soared with an undaunted wing?

Hast thou not dragged Diana from her car,
  And driven the Hamadryad from the wood
To seek a shelter in some happier star?
  Hast thou not torn the Naiad from her flood,
The Elfin from the green grass, and from me
The summer dream beneath the tamarind-tree?

ROMANCE[42]

Romance, who loves to nod and sing
With drowsy head and folded wing
Among the green leaves as they shake
Far down within some shadowy lake,
To me a painted paroquet
Hath been—a most familiar bird—
Taught me my alphabet to say,
To lisp my very earliest word
While in the wild wood I did lie,
A child—with a most knowing eye.

Of late, eternal condor years
So shake the very Heaven on high
With tumult as they thunder by,
I have no time for idle cares
Through gazing on the unquiet sky;
And when an hour with calmer wings
Its down upon my spirit flings,
That little time with lyre and rhyme
To while away—forbidden things—
My heart would feel to be a crime
Unless it trembled with the strings.

TO HELEN[43]

Helen, thy beauty is to me
  Like those Nicæan barks of yore,
That gently, o'er a perfumed sea,
  The weary, wayworn wanderer bore
  To his own native shore.

On desperate seas long wont to roam,
  Thy hyacinth hair, thy classic face,
Thy Naiad airs, have brought me home
  To the glory that was Greece
And the grandeur that was Rome.   10

Lo! in yon brilliant window-niche
  How statue-like I see thee stand,
  The agate lamp within thy hand!
Ah, Psyche, from the regions which
  Are Holy Land!

THE CITY IN THE SEA[44]

Lo! Death has reared himself a throne
In a strange city lying alone
Far down within the dim West,
Where the good and the bad and the worst and the best
Have gone to their eternal rest.
There shrines and palaces and towers
(Time-eaten towers that tremble not)
Resemble nothing that is ours.
Around, by lifting winds forgot,
Resignedly beneath the sky   10
The melancholy waters lie.

No rays from the holy heaven come down
On the long night-time of that town;
But light from out the lurid sea
Streams up the turrets silently,
Gleams up the pinnacles far and free:
Up domes, up spires, up kingly halls,
Up fanes, up Babylon-like walls,
Up shadowy long-forgotten bowers
Of sculptured ivy and stone flowers,   20
Up many and many a marvellous shrine
Whose wreathèd friezes intertwine
The viol, the violet, and the vine.

Resignedly beneath the sky
The melancholy waters lie.
So blend the turrets and shadows there
That all seem pendulous in air,
While from a proud tower in the town
Death looks gigantically down.

There open fanes and gaping graves   30
Yawn level with the luminous waves;
But not the riches there that lie
In each idol's diamond eye,—
Not the gayly-jewelled dead,
Tempt the waters from their bed;
For no ripples curl, alas,
Along that wilderness of glass;
No swelling tell that winds may be
Upon some far-off happier sea;
No heavings hint that winds have been   40
On seas less hideously serene!

But lo, a stir is in the air!
The wave—there is a movement there!
As if the towers had thrust aside,
In slightly sinking, the dull tide;
As if their tops had feebly given
A void within the filmy Heaven!
The waves have now a redder glow,
The hours are breathing faint and low;
And when, amid no earthly moans,   50
Down, down that town shall settle hence,
Hell, rising from a thousand thrones,
Shall do it reverence.

ISRAFEL[45]

And the angel Israfel, whose heart-strings are a lute, and who has the sweetest voice of all God's creatures.—KORAN.

In Heaven a spirit doth dwell
    Whose heart-strings are a lute;
None sing so wildly well
As the angel Israfel,
And the giddy stars (so legends tell),
Ceasing their hymns, attend the spell
    Of his voice, all mute.

Tottering above
    In her highest noon,
    The enamoured moon   10
Blushes with love,
    While, to listen, the red levin
    (With the rapid Pleiads, even,
    Which were seven)
    Pauses in Heaven.

And they say (the starry choir
    And the other listening things)
That Israfeli's fire
Is owing to that lyre
    By which he sits and sings,   20
The trembling living wire
    Of those unusual strings.

But the skies that angel trod,
    Where deep thoughts are a duty,
Where Love's a grown-up God,
    Where the Houri glances are
Imbued with all the beauty
    Which we worship in a star.

[handwritten marginal note: Protest / Cry against fate / + man made conditions]

Therefore thou art not wrong,
  Israfeli, who despisest   30
An unimpassioned song;
To thee the laurels belong,
  Best bard, because the wisest:
Merrily live, and long!

The ecstasies above
  With thy burning measures suit:
Thy grief, thy joy, thy hate, thy love,
  With the fervor of thy lute:
  Well may the stars be mute!

Yes, Heaven is thine; but this   40
  Is a world of sweets and sours;
  Our flowers are merely—flowers,
And the shadow of thy perfect bliss
  Is the sunshine of ours.

If I could dwell
Where Israfel
  Hath dwelt, and he where I,
He might not sing so wildly well
  A mortal melody,
While a bolder note than this might swell   50
  From my lyre within the sky.

TO ONE IN PARADISE[46]

Thou wast all that to me, love,
  For which my soul did pine:
A green isle in the sea, love,
  A fountain and a shrine
All wreathed with fairy fruits and flowers,
  And all the flowers were mine.

Ah, dream too bright to last!
  Ah, starry Hope, that didst arise

[handwritten margin notes: "Compare Heaven to earth & its sorrow till" and "Love for Elmira + Death of mrs allan"]

But to be overcast!
　　A voice from out the Future cries,   10
"On! on!"—but o'er the Past
　　(Dim gulf!) my spirit hovering lies
Mute, motionless, aghast.

For, alas! alas! with me
　　The light of Life is o'er!
No more—no more—no more—
　　(Such language holds the solemn sea
　　To the sands upon the shore)
Shall bloom the thunder-blasted tree,
　　Or the stricken eagle soar.   20

And all my days are trances,
　　And all my nightly dreams
Are where thy gray eye glances,
　　And where thy footstep gleams—
In what ethereal dances,
　　By what eternal streams.

THE COLISEUM[47]

Type of the antique Rome! Rich reliquary
Of lofty contemplation left to Time
By buried centuries of pomp and power!
At length—at length—after so many days
Of weary pilgrimage and burning thirst
(Thirst for the springs of lore that in thee lie),
I kneel, an altered and an humble man,
Amid thy shadows, and so drink within
My very soul thy grandeur, gloom, and glory.

Vastness, and Age, and Memories of Eld!   10
Silence, and Desolation, and dim Night!
I feel ye now, I feel ye in your strength,

O spells more sure than e'er Judæan King
Taught in the gardens of Gethsemane!
O charms more potent than the rapt Chaldee
Ever drew down from out the quiet stars!

Here, where a hero fell, a column falls;
Here, where the mimic eagle glared in gold,
A midnight vigil holds the swarthy bat;
Here, where the dames of Rome their gilded hair   20
Waved to the wind, now wave the reed and thistle;
Here, where on golden throne the monarch lolled,
Glides, spectre-like, unto his marble home,
Lit by the wan light of the hornèd moon,
The swift and silent lizard of the stones.

But stay! these walls, these ivy-clad arcades,
These mouldering plinths, these sad and blackened shafts,
These vague entablatures, this crumbling frieze,
These shattered cornices, this wreck, this ruin,
These stones—alas! these gray stones—are they all,   30
All of the famed and the colossal left
By the corrosive Hours to Fate and me?

"Not all"—the Echoes answer me—"not all!
Prophetic sounds and loud arise forever
From us, and from all Ruin, unto the wise,
As melody from Memnon to the Sun.
We rule the hearts of mightiest men—we rule
With a despotic sway all giant minds.
We are not impotent, we pallid stones:
Not all our power is gone, not all our fame,   40
Not all the magic of our high renown,
Not all the wonder that encircles us,
Not all the mysteries that in us lie,
Not all the memories that hang upon
And cling around about us as a garment,
Clothing us in a robe of more than glory."

THE HAUNTED PALACE[48]

In the greenest of our valleys
   By good angels tenanted,
Once a fair and stately palace—
   Radiant palace—reared its head.
In the monarch Thought's dominion,
   It stood there;
Never seraph spread a pinion
   Over fabric half so fair.

Banners yellow, glorious, golden,
   On its roof did float and flow   10
(This—all this—was in the olden
   Time long ago),
And every gentle air that dallied,
   In that sweet day,
Along the ramparts plumed and pallid,
   A wingèd odor went away.

Wanderers in that happy valley
   Through two luminous windows saw
Spirits moving musically,
   To a lute's well-tunèd law,   20
Round about a throne where, sitting,
   Porphyrogene,
In state his glory well befitting,
   The ruler of the realm was seen.

And all with pearl and ruby glowing
   Was the fair palace door,
Through which came flowing, flowing, flowing,
   And sparkling evermore,
A troop of Echoes, whose sweet duty
   Was but to sing,   30
In voices of surpassing beauty,
   The wit and wisdom of their king.

But evil things, in robes of sorrow,
   Assailed the monarch's high estate;
(Ah, let us mourn, for never morrow
   Shall dawn upon him desolate!)
And round about his home the glory
   That blushed and bloomed,
Is but a dim-remembered story
   Of the old time entombed.   40

And travellers now within that valley
   Through the red-litten windows see
Vast forms that move fantastically
   To a discordant melody;
While, like a ghastly rapid river,
   Through the pale door
A hideous throng rush out forever,
   And laugh—but smile no more.

THE CONQUEROR WORM[49]

arabesque
horror
dismal

Lo! 'tis a gala night
   Within the lonesome latter years.
An angel throng, bewinged, bedight
   In veils, and drowned in tears,
Sit in a theatre to see
   A play of hopes and fears,
While the orchestra breathes fitfully
   The music of the spheres.

Mimes, in the form of God on high,
   Mutter and mumble low,
And hither and thither fly;   10
   Mere puppets they, who come and go
At bidding of vast formless things
   That shift the scenery to and fro,
Flapping from out their condor wings
   Invisible Woe.

That motley drama—oh, be sure
   It shall not be forgot!
With its Phantom chased for evermore
   By a crowd that seize it not,   20
Through a circle that ever returneth in
   To the self-same spot;
And much of Madness, and more of Sin,
   And Horror the soul of the plot.

But see amid the mimic rout
   A crawling shape intrude:
A blood-red thing that writhes from out
   The scenic solitude!
It writhes—it writhes!—with mortal pangs
   The mimes become its food,   30
And seraphs sob at vermin fangs
   In human gore imbued.

Out—out are the lights—out all!
   And over each quivering form
The curtain, a funeral pall,
   Comes down with the rush of a storm,
While the angels, all pallid and wan,
   Uprising, unveiling, affirm
That the play is the tragedy, "Man,"
   And its hero, the Conqueror Worm.   40

THE RAVEN[50]

Once upon a midnight dreary, while I pondered, weak and
    weary,
Over many a quaint and curious volume of forgotten lore,—
While I nodded, nearly napping, suddenly there came a tapping,
As of some one gently rapping, rapping at my chamber door.
"'Tis some visitor," I muttered, "tapping at my chamber door:
         Only this and nothing more."

Ah, distinctly I remember it was in the bleak December,
And each separate dying ember wrought its ghost upon the
  floor.
Eagerly I wished the morrow;—vainly I had sought to borrow
From my books surcease of sorrow—sorrow for the lost Lenore,
For the rare and radiant maiden whom the angels name Lenore:
    Nameless here for evermore.   12

And the silken sad uncertain rustling of each purple curtain
Thrilled me—filled me with fantastic terrors never felt before;
So that now, to still the beating of my heart, I stood repeating
" 'Tis some visitor entreating entrance at my chamber door,
Some late visitor entreating entrance at my chamber door:
    This it is and nothing more."

Presently my soul grew stronger; hesitating then no longer,
"Sir," said I, "or Madam, truly your forgiveness I implore; 20
But the fact is I was napping, and so gently you came rapping,
And so faintly you came tapping, tapping at my chamber door,
That I scarce was sure I heard you"—here I opened wide the
  door:—
    Darkness there and nothing more.

Deep into that darkness peering, long I stood there wondering,
  fearing,
Doubting, dreaming dreams no mortals ever dared to dream
  before;
But the silence was unbroken, and the stillness gave no token,
And the only word there spoken was the whispered word,
  "Lenore?"
This I whispered, and an echo murmured back the word,
  "Lenore":
    Merely this and nothing more.   30

Back into the chamber turning, all my soul within me burning,
Soon again I heard a tapping somewhat louder than before.
"Surely," said I, "surely that is something at my window
  lattice;

Let me see, then, what thereat is, and this mystery explore;
Let my heart be still a moment and this mystery explore:
                              'Tis the wind and nothing more."

Open here I flung the shutter, when, with many a flirt and
      flutter,
In there stepped a stately Raven of the saintly days of yore.
Not the least obeisance made he; not a minute stopped or
      stayed he;
But, with mien of lord or lady, perched above my chamber
      door,   40
Perched upon a bust of Pallas just above my chamber door:
                              Perched, and sat, and nothing more.

Then this ebony bird beguiling my sad fancy into smiling
By the grave and stern decorum of the countenance it wore,—
"Though thy crest be shorn and shaven, thou," I said, "art
      sure no craven,
Ghastly grim and ancient Raven wandering from the nightly
      shore:
Tell me what thy lordly name is on the Night's Plutonian
      shore!"
                              Quoth the Raven, "Nevermore."

Much I marvelled this ungainly fowl to hear discourse so
      plainly,
Though its answer little meaning—little relevancy bore;   50
For we cannot help agreeing that no living human being
Ever yet was blessed with seeing bird above his chamber door,
Bird or beast upon the sculptured bust above his chamber door,
                              With such name as "Nevermore."

But the Raven, sitting lonely on the placid bust, spoke only
That one word, as if his soul in that one word he did outpour.
Nothing further then he uttered, not a feather then he fluttered,
Till I scarcely more than muttered,—"Other friends have flown
      before;

On the morrow *he* will leave me, as my Hopes have flown
    before."
                 Then the bird said, "Nevermore." 60

Startled at the stillness broken by reply so aptly spoken,
"Doubtless," said I, "what it utters is its only stock and store,
Caught from some unhappy master whom unmerciful Disaster
Followed fast and followed faster till his songs one burden
    bore:
Till the dirges of his Hope that melancholy burden bore
                 Of 'Never—nevermore.' "

But the Raven still beguiling all my fancy into smiling,
Straight I wheeled a cushioned seat in front of bird and bust
    and door;
Then, upon the velvet sinking, I betook myself to linking
Fancy unto fancy, thinking what this ominous bird of yore, 70
What this grim, ungainly, ghastly, gaunt, and ominous bird of
      yore
                 Meant in croaking "Nevermore."

Thus I sat engaged in guessing, but no syllable expressing
To the fowl whose fiery eyes now burned into my bosom's
    core;
This and more I sat divining, with my head at ease reclining
On the cushion's velvet lining that the lamp-light gloated o'er,
But whose velvet violet lining with the lamp-light gloating o'er
                 She shall press, ah, nevermore!

Then, methought, the air grew denser, perfumed from an un-
    seen censer
Swung by seraphim whose foot-falls tinkled on the tufted
    floor. 80
"Wretch," I cried, "thy God hath lent thee—by these angels
    he hath sent thee
Respite—respite and nepenthe from thy memories of Lenore!
Quaff, oh quaff this kind nepenthe, and forget this lost Lenore!"
                 Quoth the Raven, "Nevermore."

"Prophet!" said I, "thing of evil! prophet still, if bird or devil!
Whether Tempter sent, or whether tempest tossed thee here
    ashore,
Desolate yet all undaunted, on this desert land enchanted—
On this home by Horror haunted—tell me truly, I implore:
Is there—*is* there balm in Gilead?—tell me—tell me, I implore!"
              Quoth the Raven, "Nevermore." 90

"Prophet!" said I, "thing of evil—prophet still, if bird or devil!
By that Heaven that bends above us, by that God we both
    adore,
Tell this soul with sorrow laden if, within the distant Aidenn,
It shall clasp a sainted maiden whom the angels name Lenore:
Clasp a rare and radiant maiden whom the angels name Lenore!"
              Quoth the Raven, "Nevermore."

"Be that word our sign of parting, bird or fiend!" I shrieked,
    upstarting:
"Get thee back into the tempest and the Night's Plutonian
    shore!
Leave no black plume as a token of that lie thy soul hath spoken!
Leave my loneliness unbroken! quit the bust above my door! 100
Take thy beak from out my heart, and take thy form from off
    my door!"
              Quoth the Raven, "Nevermore."

And the Raven, never flitting, still is sitting, still is sitting
On the pallid bust of Pallas just above my chamber door;
And his eyes have all the seeming of a demon's that is dreaming,
And the lamp-light o'er him streaming throws his shadow on
    the floor:
And my soul from out that shadow that lies floating on the
    floor
              Shall be lifted—nevermore!

LENORE[51]

Ah, broken is the golden bowl! the spirit flown forever!
Let the bell toll!—a saintly soul floats on the Stygian river;
And, Guy De Vere, hast *thou* no tear?—weep now or never-
    more!
See, on yon drear and rigid bier low lies thy love, Lenore!
Come, let the burial rite be read—the funeral song be sung:
An anthem for the queenliest dead that ever died so young,
A dirge for her the doubly dead in that she died so young.

"Wretches, ye loved her for her wealth and hated her for her
    pride,
And when she fell in feeble health, ye blessed her—that she
    died!
How *shall* the ritual, then, be read? the requiem how be sung 10
By you—by yours, the evil eye,—by yours, the slanderous
    tongue
That did to death the innocence that died, and died so young?"

Peccavimus; but rave not thus! and let a Sabbath song
Go up to God so solemnly the dead may feel no wrong.
The sweet Lenore hath gone before, with Hope that flew
    beside,
Leaving thee wild for the dear child that should have been thy
    bride:
For her, the fair and debonair, that now so lowly lies,
The life upon her yellow hair but not within her eyes;
The life still there, upon her hair—the death upon her eyes.

"Avaunt! avaunt! from fiends below, the indignant ghost is
    riven—   20
From Hell unto a high estate far up within the Heaven—
From grief and groan, to a golden throne, beside the King of
    Heaven!
Let no bell toll, then,—lest her soul, amid its hallowed mirth,

Should catch the note as it doth float up from the damnèd
    Earth!
And I!—to-night my heart is light!—no dirge will I upraise,
But waft the angel on her flight with a Pæan of old days!"

ULALUME[52]

The skies they were ashen and sober;
    The leaves they were crispèd and sere,
    The leaves they were withering and sere;
It was night in the lonesome October
    Of my most immemorial year;
It was hard by the dim lake of Auber,
    In the misty mid region of Weir:
It was down by the dank tarn of Auber,
    In the ghoul-haunted woodland of Weir.

Here once, through an alley Titanic   10
    Of cypress, I roamed with my Soul—
    Of cypress, with Psyche, my Soul.
These were days when my heart was volcanic
    As the scoriac rivers that roll,
    As the lavas that restlessly roll
Their sulphurous currents down Yaanek
    In the ultimate climes of the pole,
That groan as they roll down Mount Yaanek
    In the realms of the boreal pole.

Our talk had been serious and sober,   20
    But our thoughts they were palsied and sere,
    Our memories were treacherous and sere,
For we knew not the month was October,
    And we marked not the night of the year,
    (Ah, night of all nights in the year!)
We noted not the dim lake of Auber
    (Though once we had journeyed down here),
Remembered not the dank tarn of Auber
    Nor the ghoul-haunted woodland of Weir.

1847 after va, 's death

And now, as the night was senescent   30
   And star-dials pointed to morn,
   As the star-dials hinted of morn,
At the end of our path a liquescent
   And nebulous lustre was born,
Out of which a miraculous crescent
   Arose with a duplicate horn,
Astarte's bediamonded crescent
   Distinct with its duplicate horn.

And I said—"She is warmer than Dian:
   She rolls through an ether of sighs,   40
   She revels in a region of sighs:
She has seen that the tears are not dry on
   These cheeks, where the worm never dies,
And has come past the stars of the Lion
   To point us the path to the skies,
   To the Lethean peace of the skies:
Come up, in despite of the Lion,
   To shine on us with her bright eyes:
Come up through the lair of the Lion,
   With love in her luminous eyes."   50

But Psyche, uplifting her finger,
   Said,—"Sadly this star I mistrust,
   Her pallor I strangely mistrust:
Oh, hasten!—oh, let us not linger!
   Oh, fly!—let us fly!—for we must."
In terror she spoke, letting sink her
   Wings until they trailed in the dust;
In agony sobbed, letting sink her
   Plumes till they trailed in the dust,
   Till they sorrowfully trailed in the dust.   60

I replied—"This is nothing but dreaming:
   Let us on by this tremulous light!
   Let us bathe in this crystalline light!

Its sibyllic splendor is beaming
    With hope and in beauty tonight:
    See, it flickers up the sky through the night!
Ah, we safely may trust to its gleaming,
    And be sure it will lead us aright:
We safely may trust to a gleaming
    That cannot but guide us aright,   70
    Since it flickers up to Heaven through the night."

Thus I pacified Psyche and kissed her,
    And tempted her out of her gloom,
    And conquered her scruples and gloom;
And we passed to the end of the vista,
    But were stopped by the door of a tomb,
    By the door of a legended tomb;
And I said—"What is written, sweet sister,
    On the door of this legended tomb?"
    She replied—"Ulalume—Ulalume—   80
    'Tis the vault of thy lost Ulalume!"

Then my heart it grew ashen and sober
    As the leaves that were crispèd and sere,
    As the leaves that were withering and sere,
And I cried—"It was surely October
    On *this* very night of last year
    That I journeyed—I journeyed down here,
    That I brought a dread burden down here:
    On this night of all nights in the year,
    Ah, what demon has tempted me here?   90
Well I know, now, this dim lake of Auber,
    This misty mid region of Weir:
Well I know, now, this dark tarn of Auber
    This ghoul-haunted woodland of Weir."

ANNABEL LEE[53] *wife*

It was many and many a year ago,
    In a kingdom by the sea,
That a maiden there lived whom you may know
    By the name of Annabel Lee;
And this maiden she lived with no other thought
    Than to love and be loved by me.

I was a child and she was a child,
    In this kingdom by the sea,
But we loved with a love that was more than love,
    I and my Annabel Lee;   10
With a love that the wingèd seraphs of heaven
    Coveted her and me.

And this was the reason that, long ago,
    In this kingdom by the sea,
A wind blew out of a cloud, chilling
    My beautiful Annabel Lee;
So that her highborn kinsmen came
    And bore her away from me,
To shut her up in a sepulchre
    In this kingdom by the sea.   20

The angels, not half so happy in heaven,
    Went envying her and me;
Yes! that was the reason (as all men know,
    In this kingdom by the sea)
That the wind came out of the cloud by night,
    Chilling and killing my Annabel Lee.

But our love it was stronger by far than the love
    Of those who were older than we,
    Of many far wiser than we;

And neither the angels in heaven above,   30
   Nor the demons down under the sea,
Can ever dissever my soul from the soul
   Of the beautiful Annabel Lee:

For the moon never beams, without bringing me dreams
   Of the beautiful Annabel Lee;
And the stars never rise, but I feel the bright eyes
   Of the beautiful Annabel Lee;
And so, all the night-tide, I lie down by the side
Of my darling—my darling—my life and my bride,
   In her sepulchre there by the sea,   40
   In her tomb by the sounding sea.

ELDORADO

    Gayly bedight,
    A gallant knight,
In sunshine and in shadow,
    Had journeyed long,
    Singing a song,
In search of Eldorado.

    But he grew old,
    This knight so bold,
And o'er his heart a shadow
    Fell as he found   10
    No spot of ground
That looked like Eldorado.

    And, as his strength
    Failed him at length,
He met a pilgrim shadow:
    "Shadow," said he,
    "Where can it be,
This land of Eldorado?"

> "Over the Mountains
> Of the Moon, 20
> Down the Valley of the Shadow,
> Ride, boldly ride,"
> The shade replied,
> "If you seek for Eldorado!"

PHILIP PENDLETON COOKE

Philip Pendleton Cooke, the oldest child of John Rogers and Maria Pendleton Cooke and older brother of John Esten Cooke, was born on October 26, 1816, at the "Stone House" in Martinsburg, Virginia (now West Virginia). Of distinguished lineage on both sides of the family, he was educated by a tutor until he entered Princeton at the age of fifteen. After some difficulties with the faculty about youthful escapades, he graduated in 1834. By that time his earliest poems were appearing in the *Knickerbocker Magazine*. He returned to Charles Town, Virginia, to read law in his father's office, and before he was twenty-one he was practicing law and was married to Anne Tayloe Burwell. After his marriage Cooke lived at "The Vineyard," in Clarke County, where he divided his time between law, literature, and sports. He contributed a series of articles on Early English Poetry to the first volume of the *Southern Literary Messenger*, but his first wide recognition came with the publication of "Florence Vane" in *Burton's Gentleman's Magazine* for March, 1840. His one volume of poems, *Froissart Ballads and Other Poems*, was published in 1847, at the suggestion of his cousin, John Pendleton Kennedy. He called the ballads "versified transcripts from Froissart"; the three which stem from Froissart were, he wrote, "as faithful to the text as the necessities of the verse permitted me to make them." He also contributed several prose romances—*The Crime of Andrew Blair, John Carper, The Hunter of Lost River*, and the unfinished *Chevalier Merlin*—to the *Southern Literary Messenger*, but just as he was attaining the full maturity of his literary power, he died at thirty-three (January 20, 1850) from pneumonia brought on by swimming the icy waters of the Shenandoah while in pursuit of wild game.

FLORENCE VANE[54]

I loved thee long and dearly
   Florence Vane;
My life's bright dream and early
   Hath come again;
I renew, in my fond vision,
   My heart's dear pain,
My hopes, and thy derision,
   Florence Vane.

The ruin lone and hoary,
   The ruin old,   10
Where thou didst hark my story,
   At even told,—
That spot—the hues Elysian
   Of sky and plain—
I treasure in my vision,
   Florence Vane.

Thou wast lovelier than the roses
   In their prime;
Thy voice excelled the closes
   Of sweetest rhyme;   20
Thy heart was as a river
   Without a main;
Would I had loved thee never,
   Florence Vane.

But fairest, coldest wonder!
   Thy glorious clay
Lieth the green sod under—
   Alas the day!
And it boots not to remember
   Thy disdain—   30
To quicken love's pale ember,
   Florence Vane.

  The lilies of the valley
   By young graves weep,
  The pansies love to dally
   Where maidens sleep;
  May their bloom, in beauty vieing,
   Never wane
  Where thine earthly part is lying,
   Florence Vane!   40

LIFE IN THE AUTUMN WOODS[55]

Summer has gone,
And fruitful Autumn has advanced so far
That there is warmth, not heat, in the broad sun,
And you may look, with naked eye, upon
  The ardors of his car;
The stealthy frosts, whom his spent looks embolden,
  Are making the green leaves golden.

What a brave splendor
Is in the October air! how rich, and clear,
And bracing, and all-joyous! We must render 10
Love to the Spring-time, with its sproutings tender,
  As to a child quite dear;
But Autumn is a thing of perfect glory,
  A manhood not yet hoary.

I love the woods,
In this good season of the liberal year;
I love to seek their leafy solitudes,
And give myself to melancholy moods,
  With no intruder near,
And find strange lessons, as I sit and ponder, 20
  In every natural wonder.

But not alone,
As Shakespeare's melancholy courtier loved Ardennes,

Love I the browning forest; and I own
I would not oft have mused, as he, but flown
    To hunt with Amiens—
And little thought, as up the bold deer bounded,
    Of the sad creature wounded.

    A brave and good,
But world-worn knight—soul-wearied with his part   30
In this vexed life—gave man for solitude,
And built a lodge, and lived in Wantley wood,
    To hear the belling hart.
It was a gentle taste, but its sweet sadness
    Yields to the hunter's madness.

    What passionate
And keen delight is in the proud swift chase!
Go out what time the lark at heaven's red gate
Soars joyously singing—quite infuriate
    With the high pride of his place;   40
What time the unrisen sun arrays the morning
    In its first bright adorning.

    Hark! the quick horn—
As sweet to hear as any clarion—
Piercing with silver call the ear of morn;
And mark the steeds, stout Curtal and Topthorne,
    And Greysteil and the Don—
Each one of them his fiery mood displaying
    With pawing and with neighing.

    Urge your swift horse   50
After the crying hounds in this fresh hour;
Vanquish high hills, stem perilous streams perforce,
On the free plain give free wings to your course,
    And you will know the power
Of the brave chase,—and how of griefs the sorest
    A cure is in the forest.

Or stalk the deer;
The same red lip of dawn has kissed the hills,
The gladdest sounds are crowding on your ear,
There is a life in all the atmosphere:— 60
    Your very nature fills
With the fresh hour, as up the hills aspiring
    You climb with limbs untiring.

    It is a fair
And goodly sight to see the antlered stag
With the long sweep of his swift walk repair
To join his brothers; of the plethoric bear
    Lying in some high crag,
With pinky eyes half closed, but broad head shaking,
    As gadflies keep him waking. 70

    And these you see,
And, seeing them, you travel to their death
With a slow, stealthy step, from tree to tree,
Noting the wind, however faint it be.
    The hunter draws a breath
In times like these, which, he will say, repays him
    For all care that waylays him.

    A strong joy fills
(A joy beyond the tongue's expressive power)
My heart in Autumn weather—fills and thrills! 80
And I would rather stalk the breezy hills
    Descending to my bower
Nightly, by the sweet spirit of Peace attended,
    Than pine where life is splendid.

From THE POWER OF THE BARDS[56]
. . . .

And owe we not these visions
    Fresh to the natural eye—
This presence in old story—
    To the good art and high?

The high art of the poet,
   The maker of the lays?
Doth not his magic lead us
   Back to the ancient days?

For evermore be honored
   The voices sweet, and bold,   10
That thus can charm the shadows
   From the true life of old.

THEODORE O'HARA

Theodore O'Hara, the son of Kane (or Kean) and Helen Hardy O'Hara, was born in Danville, Kentucky, February 11, 1820. His father, a political exile from Ireland, conducted an academy there and later at Frankfort, and personally taught Theodore until he entered the senior class of St. Joseph's Academy at Bardstown. In his last year he served as professor of Greek, while he continued his studies for a degree. After graduation, he studied law in the office of Judge William Owsley, with John C. Breckinridge as a fellow student. For a time, in 1845, he worked in the Treasury Department at Washington. When war with Mexico broke out O'Hara was appointed a captain in the United States Army, serving with distinction and being breveted major for gallantry in action. A varied career followed: he practiced law in Washington, fought with the Cubans in their rebellion against Spain (being severely wounded at Cardenas), and edited the Mobile *Register* for John Forsythe (at the time Minister to Mexico). Afterward he edited the Louisville *Times* and the Frankfort *Yeoman*, and served the government diplomatically in the Tehuantepec grant negotiations. During the Civil War O'Hara commanded the 12th Alabama regiment, then served on the staff of General Albert Sidney Johnston, and helped that officer from his horse at Shiloh when Johnston was mortally wounded. O'Hara also served as Chief of Staff under John C. Breckinridge—once his fellow student. After the war he went into the cotton business at Columbus, Georgia, but lost all his possessions in a fire. He retired to a plantation near Guerrytown, Alabama, where

he died of bilious fever on June 6, 1867. In 1874 his remains were moved to Frankfort, Kentucky.

Although his political and literary addresses would fill a
goodly volume, O'Hara's poetry consists of only two or three
poems. "Second Love" is doubtfully ascribed to him by Daniel
O'Sullivan; "The Old Pioneer" and "The Bivouac of the
Dead," both occasional pieces, represent all his known work.
The latter poem was written in August, 1847, for the dedication of a monument in Frankfort to the Kentuckians who died
in the Mexican War.

THE BIVOUAC OF THE DEAD[57]

The muffled drum's sad roll has beat
    The soldier's last tattoo;
No more on Life's parade shall meet
    The brave and daring few.
On Fame's eternal camping-ground
    Their silent tents are spread,
And Glory guards with solemn round
    The bivouac of the dead.

No answer of the foe's advance
    Now swells upon the wind;   10
No troubled thought at midnight haunts
    Of loved ones left behind;
No vision of the morrow's strife
    The warrior's dream alarms;
No braying horn nor screaming fife
    At dawn shall call to arms.

Their shivered swords are red with rust;
    Their plumèd heads are bowed;
Their haughty banner, trailed in dust,
    Is now their martial shroud;   20
And plenteous funeral-tears have washed
    The red stains from each brow,
And their proud forms, in battle gashed,
    Are free from anguish now.

The neighing steed, the flashing blade,
    The trumpet's stirring blast,
The charge, the dreadful cannonade,
    The din and shout, are past;
No war's wild note, nor glory's peal,
    Shall thrill with fierce delight   30
Those breasts that nevermore shall feel
    The rapture of the fight.

Like the dread northern hurricane
    That sweeps his broad plateau,
Flushed with the triumph yet to gain,
    Came down the serried foe.
Our heroes felt the shock, and leapt
    To meet them on the plain;
And long the pitying sky hath wept
    Above our gallant slain.   40

Sons of our consecrated ground,
    Ye must not slumber there,
Where stranger steps and tongues resound
    Along the heedless air.
Your own proud land's heroic soil
    Shall be your fitter grave:
She claims from war his richest spoil—
    The ashes of her brave.

So 'neath their parent turf they rest,
    Far from the gory field;   50
Borne to a Spartan mother's breast
    On many a bloody shield.
The sunshine of their native sky
    Smiles sadly on them here,
And kindred hearts and eyes watch by
    The heroes' sepulcher.

Rest on, embalmed and sainted dead!
    Dear as the blood you gave,

No impious footsteps here shall tread
    The herbage of your grave;   60
Nor shall your glory be forgot
    While fame her record keeps,
Or honor points the hallowed spot
    Where valor proudly sleeps.

Yon marble minstrel's voiceless tone
    In deathless songs shall tell,
When many a vanquished age hath flown,
    The story how ye fell.
Nor wreck, nor change, nor winter's blight,
    Nor time's remorseless doom,   70
Shall dim one ray of holy light
    That gilds your glorious tomb.

THE OLD PIONEER

A dirge for the brave old pioneer!
    Knight-errant of the wood!
Calmly beneath the green sod here
    He rests from field and flood;
The war-whoop and the panther's screams
    No more his soul shall rouse,
For well the aged hunter dreams
    Beside his good old spouse.

A dirge for the brave old pioneer!
    Hushed now his rifle's peal;   10
The dews of many a vanished year
    Are on his rusted steel;
His horn and pouch lie moldering
    Upon the cabin-door;
The elk rests by the salted spring,
    Nor flees the fierce wild boar.

A dirge for the brave old pioneer!
    Old Druid of the West!

His offering was the fleet wild deer,
   His shrine the mountain's crest.   20
Within his wildwood temple's space
   An empire's towers nod,
Where erst, alone of all his race,
   He knelt to Nature's God.

A dirge for the brave old pioneer!
   Columbus of the land!
Who guided freedom's proud career
   Beyond the conquered strand;
And gave her pilgrim sons a home
   No monarch's step profanes,   30
Free as the changeless winds that roam
   Upon its boundless plains.

A dirge for the brave old pioneer!
   The muffled drum resound!
A warrior is slumbering here
   Beneath his battle-ground.
For not alone with beast of prey
   The bloody strife he waged,
Foremost where'er the deadly fray
   Of savage combat raged.   40

A dirge for the brave old pioneer!
   A dirge for his old spouse!
For her who blest his forest cheer
   And kept his birchen house.
Now soundly by her chieftain may
   The brave old dame sleep on,
The red man's step is far away,
   The wolf's dread howl is gone.

A dirge for the brave old pioneer!
   His pilgrimage is done;   50
He hunts no more the grizzly bear
   About the setting sun.

Weary at last of chase and life
   He laid him here to rest,
Nor recks he now what sport or strife
   Would tempt him further west.

A dirge for the brave old pioneer!
   The patriarch of his tribe!
He sleeps—no pompous pile marks where,
   Nor lines his deeds describe.   60
They raised no stone above him here,
   Nor carved his deathless name—
An empire is his sepulchre,
   His epitaph is Fame.

JAMES MATHEWES LEGARÉ

Of James Mathewes Legaré, very little is known today. He was born in Charleston in 1823, of Huguenot ancestry, and was a distant cousin of Hugh Swinton Legaré. He studied law, but followed that profession with indifferent success; patented several inventions, but apparently made no money from them. At twenty-five he published his one book, *Orta-Undis and Other Poems* (the title poem is written in Latin), and he contributed occasionally to the Southern magazines which appeared intermittently in Charleston. He died in 1859.

This complete neglect is all the more remarkable when the quality of his work is considered. Only Ludwig Lewisohn has given him the critical praise he deserves: "It is the surprising merit of Legaré to have used these simple lyric meters with firmness and distinction, to have developed an occasional originality of form, and to have made those forms, old and new, carry adequately an observation and a spiritual interpretation of nature, alert, painstaking, and true. . . . He had the poet's eye: he turned an imaginative sight upon the simple appearances that attracted him and was then able to present in brief compass pictures of nature that take the mind at once with their delicacy and truth."

ON THE DEATH OF A KINSMAN[58]

I see an Eagle winging to the sun—
Who sayeth him nay?
He glanceth down from where his wing hath won.
His heart is stout, his flight is scarce begun,—
Oh hopes of clay!

Saw he not how upon the cord was lain
A keen swift shaft;
How Death wrought out in every throbbing vein,
In every after agony of pain,
His bitter craft!   10

Like old Demetrius, the sun had he
Beheld so long,
Now things of earth no longer could he see,
And in his ear sang Immortality
A pleasant song.

Icarus like, he fell when warm and near
The sunshine smiled:
He rose strong-pinioned in his high career—
—*Thy dust remains, thy glorious spirit where,*
Minerva's child?   20

Therefore him Fame had written fair and high
Upon her scroll,
Who fell like sudden meteor from the sky,
Who strenuous to win at last did die
E'en at the goal.

16 47 78th century style

TO A LILY

Go bow thy head in gentle spite,
Thou lily white.
For she who spies thee waving here,
With thee in beauty can compare
As day with night.

Soft are thy leaves and white: Her arms
Boast whiter charms.
Thy stem prone bent with loveliness
Of maiden grace possesseth less:
Therein she charms.   10

Thou in thy lake dost see
Thyself: So she
Beholds her image in her eyes
Reflected. Thus did Venus rise
From out the sea.

Inconsolate, bloom not again
Thou rival vain
Of her whose charms have thine outdone:
Whose purity might spot the sun,
And make thy leaf a stain.   20

HAW-BLOSSOMS

While yesterevening, through the vale
Descending from my cottage door
I strayed, how cool and fresh a look
All nature wore.

The calmïas and golden-rods,
And tender blossoms of the haw,
Like maidens seated in the wood,
Demure, I saw.

The recent drops upon their leaves
Shone brighter than the bluest eyes   10
And filled the little sheltered dell
Their fragrant sighs.

Their pliant arms they interlaced,
As pleasant canopies they were:
Their blossoms swung against my cheek
Like braids of hair.

And when I put their boughs aside
And stooped to pass, from overhead
The little agitated things
A shower shed   20

Of tears. Then thoughtfully I spoke;
Well represent ye maidenhood,
Sweet flowers. Life is to the young
A shady wood.

And therein some like golden-rods,
For grosser purposes designed,
A gay existence lead, but leave
No germ behind.

And others like the calmïas,
On cliff-sides inaccessible,   30
Bloom paramount, the vale with sweets
Yet never fill.

But underneath the glossy leaves,
When, working out the perfect law,
The blossoms white and fragrant still
Drop from the haw;

Like worthy deeds in silence wrought
And secret, through the lapse of years,

In clusters pale and delicate
The fruit appears.   40

In clusters pale and delicate
But waxing heavier each day,
Until the many-colored leaves
Drift from the spray.

Then pendulous, like amethysts
And rubies, purple ripe and red,
Wherewith God's feathered pensioners
In flocks are fed.

Therefore, sweet reader of this rhyme,
Be unto thee examples high   50
Not calmïas and golden-rods
That scentless die:

But the meek blossoms of the haw,
That fragrant are wherever wind
The forest paths, and perishing
Leave fruits behind.

FLOWERS IN ASHES[59]

Where, with unruffled surface wide,
The waters of the river glide
Between the arches dimly in the early dawn descried;

While musing, Sweet, of thee,—once more
I crossed the bridge as oft of yore,
I saw a shallop issue from the shadow of the shore.

With practised ease the boatman stood,
And dipped his paddle in the flood:
And so the open space was gained, and left behind the wood.

The dripping blade, with measured stroke,   10
In ripples soft the surface broke;
As once Apollo, kissing oft, the nymph Cyrene woke.

And, fast pursuing in his wake,
I heard the dimpling eddies break
In murmurs faint, as if they said—Herefrom example take.

Unruffled as this river, lies
The stream of life to youthful eyes;
On either bank a wood and mart, and overhead God's skies.

Behind thee slopes the pleasant shore,
The tumult of the town before,   20
And thou, who standest in the stern, hast in thy hand an oar.

Oh son of toil, whose poet's heart
Grieves from thy quiet woods to part,
And yet whose birthright high it is, to labor in the mart,

To thee, a child, the bloom was sweet;
But manhood loves the crowded street,
And where in closes, loud and clear, the forging hammers beat.

But even there may bloom for thee
The blossoms childhood loved to see;
And in the cinders of thy toil, God's fairest flowers be.   30

THE REAPER

How still Earth lies!—behind the pines
The summer clouds sink slowly down.
The sunset gilds the higher hills
And distant steeples of the town.

Refreshed and moist the meadow spreads,
Birds sing from out the dripping leaves,

And standing in the breast-high corn
I see the farmer bind his sheaves.

It was when on the fallow fields
The heavy frosts of winter lay,   10
A rustic with unsparing hand
Strewed seed along the furrowed way.

And I too, walking through the waste
And wintry hours of the past,
Have in the furrows made by griefs
The seeds of future harvests cast.

Rewarded well, if when the world
Grows dimmer in the ebbing light,
And all the valley lies in shade,
But sunset glimmers on the height.   20

Down in the meadows of the heart
The birds sing out a last refrain,
And ready garnered for the mart
I see the ripe and golden grain.

HENRY TIMROD

Henry Timrod was born in Charleston, South Carolina,
December 8, 1829. He was of German parentage; his grandfather, a merchant tailor, had served in the Revolutionary War,
and his father, William Henry Timrod, was a bookbinder and
bookseller; his mother was Thyrza Prince Timrod. The father
was something more than a bookseller, he was also a poet of
more than local renown: Washington Irving said of his "To
Time—the Old Traveller" that "Tom Moore has written no
finer lyric"—a compliment which today seems far weaker than
in the 1820's. William Timrod also earned distinction as a soldier
in the Seminole War, where he served as captain of the German
Fusiliers; as a result of the hardships and exposure suffered at
that time, he died in 1838. Henry Timrod attended the Coates

private school, where he occupied the desk next to Paul Hamilton Hayne, one not far from Basil L. Gildersleeve; it was to Hayne that he showed his first verse—a display of exhibitionism which won for the young poets a bushing from the "down east" schoolmaster. In 1847 Timrod entered the University of Georgia, but ill health forced him to leave without taking a degree. For a short time he read law in the office of James L. Petigru, but he soon abandoned law for poetry and the hope of a professorship—a hope never realized. He worked as private tutor in several families, but all his leisure time he devoted to reading and to poetry. Some of his earliest work was to translate the poetry of Catullus, and his classical training is apparent in his poetry. In the decade 1850–60, he wrote a thin sheaf of nature poems, which were collected and published in book form in 1860, and he contributed to *Russell's Magazine* four critical articles on poetry which do not deserve the neglect they have received.

Timrod's greatest poems are his war poems. He was stirred emotionally no more than other poets of his day, but his classical turn of mind gave a form, a certain cool severity, to even his most impassioned utterances. In 1862 a plan was formed to issue his poems in an English edition, but was abandoned under the stress of war. Too frail for military service, Timrod worked as war correspondent, and was present at the battle of Shiloh; in 1864 he became editor of the Columbia *South Carolinian*, and soon after married Kate S. Goodwin—the "Katie" of several of his poems. But this period of happiness was short-lived: Columbia was captured, sacked, and burned by the Federal Army on February 17, 1865. Timrod was completely ruined. Suffering from tuberculosis and often from malnutrition, he went from one small job to another; even his devoted friends, Simms and Hayne, could do little to help him. He wrote to Hayne (March 30, 1866): "You ask me to tell you my story for the last year. I can embody it all in a few words: *beggary, starvation, death* (of his son, his sister, and his brother-in-law), *bitter grief, utter want of hope!* . . . To confess the truth, my dear Paul, I not only feel that I can write no more verse, but I am perfectly indifferent to the fate of what I have already composed. I would consign every line of it to eternal oblivion, for—*one hundred dollars in hand!*" Temporary work as a clerk in the governor's office gave him a brief respite. Late in 1866

Mr. C. B. Richardson, the publisher, invited Timrod to visit him in New York, but not all the efforts of Timrod and his friends could raise the money. He received some help from General Wade Hampton, and in April of 1867 he visited Hayne at "Copse Hill." But he was far gone: in September he suffered hemorrhages in rapid succession. He died on October 6, 1867. His poetry was collected and published by Paul Hamilton Hayne in 1873.

WHY SILENT

Why am I silent from year to year?
　Needs must I sing on these blue March days?
What will you say, when I tell you here,
　That already, I think, for a little praise,
　　I have paid too dear?

For, I know not why, when I tell my thought,
　It seems as though I fling it away;
And the charm wherewith a fancy is fraught,
　When secret, dies with the fleeting lay
　　Into which it is wrought.　　　　　10

So my butterfly-dreams their golden wings
　But seldom unfurl from their chrysalis;
And thus I retain my loveliest things,
　While the world, in its worldliness, does not miss
　　What a poet sings.

SONNET: I KNOW NOT WHY[60]

I know not why, but all this weary day,
Suggested by no definite grief or pain,
Sad fancies have been flitting through my brain;
Now it has been a vessel losing way,
Rounding a stormy headland; now a gray
Dull waste of clouds above a wintry main;
And then, a banner, drooping in the rain,
And meadows beaten into bloody clay.

Strolling at random with this shadowy woe
At heart, I chanced to wander hither! Lo!   10
A league of desolate marsh-land, with its lush,
Hot grasses in a noisome, tide-left bed,
And faint, warm airs, that rustle in the hush,
Like whispers round the body of the dead!

SONNET: MOST MEN KNOW LOVE

Most men know love but as a part of life;
They hide it in some corner of the breast,
Even from themselves; and only when they rest
In the brief pauses of that daily strife,
Wherewith the world might else be not so rife,
They draw it forth (as one draws forth a toy
To soothe some ardent, kiss-exacting boy)
And hold it up to sister, child, or wife.
Ah me! why may not love and life be one?
Why walk we thus alone, when by our side,   10
Love, like a visible God, might be our guide?
How would the marts grow noble! and the street,
Worn like a dungeon-floor by weary feet,
Seem then a golden court-way of the Sun!

ETHNOGENESIS[61]

I

Hath not the morning dawned with added light?
And shall not evening call another star
Out of the infinite regions of the night,
To mark this day in Heaven? At last, we are
A nation among nations; and the world
Shall soon behold in many a distant port
        Another flag unfurled!
Now, come what may, whose favor need we court?
And, under God, whose thunder need we fear?
        Thank Him who placed us here   10

Beneath so kind a sky—the very sun
Takes part with us; and on our errands run
All breezes of the ocean; dew and rain
Do noiseless battle for us; and the Year,
And all the gentle daughters in her train,
March in our ranks, and in our service wield
     Long spears of golden grain!
A yellow blossom as her fairy shield,
June flings her azure banner to the wind,
     While in the order of their birth   20
Her sisters pass, and many an ample field
Grows white beneath their steps, till now, behold,
     Its endless sheets unfold
THE SNOW OF SOUTHERN SUMMERS! Let the earth
Rejoice! beneath those fleeces soft and warm
     Our happy land shall sleep
     In a repose as deep
     As if we lay intrenched behind
Whole leagues of Russian ice and Arctic storm!   29

II

And what if, mad with wrongs themselves have wrought,
     In their own treachery caught,
     By their own fears made bold,
     And leagued with him of old,
Who long since in the limits of the North
Set up his evil throne, and warred with God—
What if, both mad and blinded in their rage,
Our foes should fling us down their mortal gage,
And with a hostile step profane our sod!
We shall not shrink, my brothers, but go forth
To meet them, marshaled by the Lord of Hosts,   40
And overshadowed by the mighty ghosts
Of Moultrie and of Eutaw—who shall foil
Auxiliars such as these? Nor these alone,
     But every stock and stone
     Shall help us; but the very soil,

And all the generous wealth it gives to toil,
And all for which we love our noble land,
Shall fight beside, and through us; sea and strand,
    The heart of woman, and her hand,
Tree, fruit, and flower, and every influence,   50
        Gentle, or grave, or grand;
        The winds in our defence
Shall seem to blow; to us the hills shall lend
        Their firmness and their calm;
And in our stiffened sinews we shall blend
        The strength of pine and palm!

III

Nor would we shun the battle-ground,
        Though weak as we are strong;
Call up the clashing elements around,
        And test the right and wrong!   60
On one side, creeds that dare to teach
What Christ and Paul refrained to preach;
Codes built upon a broken pledge,
And Charity that whets a poniard's edge;
Fair schemes that leave the neighboring poor
To starve and shiver at the schemer's door,
While in the world's most liberal ranks enrolled,
He turns some vast philanthropy to gold;
Religion, taking every mortal form
But that a pure and Christian faith makes warm,   70
Where not to vile fanatic passion urged,
Or not in vague philosophies submerged,
Repulsive with all Pharisaic leaven,
And making laws to stay the laws of Heaven!
And on the other, scorn of sordid gain,
Unblemished honor, truth without a stain,
Faith, justice, reverence, charitable wealth,
And, for the poor and humble, laws which give,
Not the mean right to buy the right to live,
        But life, and home, and health!   80

To doubt the end were want of trust in God,
    Who, if he has decreed
  That we must pass a redder sea
Than that which rang to Miriam's holy glee,
    Will surely raise at need
    A Moses with his rod!

IV

But let our fears—if fears we have—be still,
And turn us to the future! Could we climb
Some mighty Alp, and view the coming time,
The rapturous sight would fill   90
    Our eyes with happy tears!
Not only for the glories which the years
Shall bring us; not for lands from sea to sea,
And wealth, and power, and peace, though these shall be;
But for the distant peoples we shall bless,
And the hushed murmurs of a world's distress:
For, to give labor to the poor,
    The whole sad planet o'er,
And save from want and crime the humblest door,
Is one among the many ends for which   100
    God makes us great and rich!
The hour perchance is not yet wholly ripe
When all shall own it, but the type
Whereby we shall be known in every land
Is that vast gulf which lips our Southern strand,
And through the cold, untempered ocean pours
Its genial streams, that far off Arctic shores
May sometimes catch upon the softened breeze
Strange tropic warmth and hints of summer seas.

nature + patriotic

THE COTTON BOLL [62]

While I recline
At ease beneath
This immemorial pine,
Small sphere!
(By dusky fingers brought this morning here
And shown with boastful smiles),
I turn thy cloven sheath,
Through which the soft white fibres peer,
That, with their gossamer bands,
Unite, like love, the sea-divided lands,   10
And slowly, thread by thread,
Draw forth the folded strands,
Than which the trembling line,
By whose frail help yon startled spider fled
Down the tall spear-grass from his swinging bed,
Is scarce more fine;
And as the tangled skein
Unravels in my hands,
Betwixt me and the noonday light,
A veil seems lifted, and for miles and miles   20
The landscape broadens on my sight,
As, in the little boll, there lurked a spell
Like that which, in the ocean shell,
With mystic sound,
Breaks down the narrow walls that hem us round,
And turns some city lane
Into the restless main,
With all his capes and isles!

Yonder bird,
Which floats, as if at rest,   30
In those blue tracts above the thunder, where
No vapors cloud the stainless air,
And never sound is heard,

Unless at such rare time
When, from the City of the Blest,
Rings down some golden chime,
Sees not from his high place
So vast a cirque of summer space
As widens round me in one mighty field,
Which, rimmed by seas and sands,   40
Doth hail its earliest daylight in the beams
Of gray Atlantic dawns;
And, broad as realms made up of many lands,
Is lost afar
Behind the crimson hills and purple lawns
Of sunset, among plains which roll their streams
Against the Evening Star!
And lo!
To the remotest point of sight,
Although I gaze upon no waste of snow,   50
The endless field is white;
And the whole landscape glows,
For many a shining league away,
With such accumulated light
As Polar lands would flash beneath a tropic day!
Nor lack there (for the vision grows,
And the small charm within my hands—
More potent even than the fabled one,
Which oped whatever golden mystery
Lay hid in fairy wood or magic vale,   60
The curious ointment of the Arabian tale—
Beyond all mortal sense
Doth stretch my sight's horizon, and I see,
Beneath its simple influence,
As if with Uriel's crown,
I stood in some great temple of the Sun,
And looked, as Uriel, down!)
Nor lack there pastures rich and fields all green
With all the common gifts of God,
For temperate airs and torrid sheen   70

Weave Edens of the sod;
Through lands which look one sea of billowy gold
Broad rivers wind their devious ways;
A hundred isles in their embraces fold
A hundred luminous bays;
And through yon purple haze
Vast mountains lift their plumed peaks cloud-crowned;
And, save where up their sides the ploughman creeps,
An unhewn forest girds them grandly round,
In whose dark shades a future navy sleeps!   80
Ye Stars, which, though unseen, yet with me gaze
Upon this loveliest fragment of the earth!
Thou Sun, that kindlest all thy gentlest rays
Above it, as to light a favorite hearth!
Ye Clouds, that in your temples in the West
See nothing brighter than its humblest flowers!
And you, ye Winds, that on the ocean's breast
Are kissed to coolness ere ye reach its bowers!
Bear witness with me in my song of praise,
And tell the world that, since the world began,   90
No fairer land hath fired a poet's lays,
Or given a home to man!

But these are charms already widely blown!
His be the meed whose pencil's trace
Hath touched our very swamps with grace,
And round whose tuneful way
All Southern laurels bloom;
The Poet of "The Woodlands," unto whom
Alike are known
The flute's low breathing and the trumpet's tone,   100
And the soft west wind's sighs;
But who shall utter all the debt,
O Land wherein all powers are met
That bind a people's heart,
The world doth owe thee at this day,
And which it never can repay,

Yet scarcely deigns to own!
Where sleeps the poet who shall fitly sing
The source wherefrom doth spring
That mighty commerce which, confined 110
To the mean channels of no selfish mart,
Goes out to every shore
Of this broad earth, and throngs the sea with ships
That bear no thunders; hushes hungry lips
In alien lands;
Joins with a delicate web remotest strands;
And gladdening rich and poor,
Doth gild Parisian domes,
Or feed the cottage-smoke of English homes,
And only bounds its blessings by mankind! 120
In offices like these, thy mission lies,
My Country! and it shall not end
As long as rain shall fall and Heaven bend
In blue above thee; though thy foes be hard
And cruel as their weapons, it shall guard
Thy hearth-stones as a bulwark; make thee great
In white and bloodless state;
And haply, as the years increase—
Still working through its humbler reach
With that large wisdom which the ages teach— 130
Revive the half-dead dream of universal peace!
As men who labor in that mine
Of Cornwall, hollowed out beneath the bed
Of ocean, when a storm rolls overhead,
Hear the dull booming of the world of brine
Above them, and a mighty muffled roar
Of winds and waters, yet toil calmly on,
And split the rock, and pile the massive ore,
Or carve a niche, or shape the archèd roof;
So I, as calmly, weave my woof 140
Of song, chanting the days to come,
Unsilenced, though the quiet summer air
Stirs with the bruit of battles, and each dawn

Wakes from its starry silence to the hum
Of many gathering armies. Still,
In that we sometimes hear,
Upon the Northern winds, the voice of woe
Not wholly drowned in triumph, though I know
The end must crown us, and a few brief years
Dry all our tears,   150
I may not sing too gladly. To Thy will
Resigned, O Lord! we cannot all forget
That there is much even Victory must regret.
And, therefore, not too long
From the great burthen of our country's wrong
Delay our just release!
And, if it may be, save
These sacred fields of peace
From stain of patriot or of hostile blood!
Oh, help us, Lord! to roll the crimson flood   160
Back on its course, and, while our banners wing
Northward, strike with us! till the Goth shall cling
To his own blasted altar-stones, and crave
Mercy; and we shall grant it, and dictate
The lenient future of his fate
There, where some rotting ships and crumbling quays
Shall one day mark the Port which ruled the Western seas.

A CRY TO ARMS[63]

Ho! woodsmen of the mountain side!
    Ho! dwellers in the vales!
Ho! ye who by the chafing tide
    Have roughened in the gales!
Leave barn and byre, leave kin and cot,
    Lay by the bloodless spade;
Let desk, and case, and counter rot,
    And burn your books of trade.

The despot roves your fairest lands;
    And till he flies or fears,   10

Your fields must grow but armèd bands,
    Your sheaves be sheaves of spears!
Give up to mildew and to rust
    The useless tools of gain;
And feed your country's sacred dust
    With floods of crimson rain!

Come, with the weapons at your call—
    With musket, pike, or knife;
He wields the deadliest blade of all
    Who lightly holds his life.   20
The arm that drives its unbought blows
    With all a patriot's scorn,
Might brain a tyrant with a rose,
    Or stab him with a thorn.

Does any falter? let him turn
    To some brave maiden's eyes,
And catch the holy fires that burn
    In those sublunar skies.
Oh! could you like your women feel,
    And in their spirit march,   30
A day might see your lines of steel
    Beneath the victor's arch.

What hope, O God! would not grow warm
    When thoughts like these give cheer?
The Lily calmly braves the storm,
    And shall the Palm-tree fear?
No! rather let its branches court
    The rack that sweeps the plain;
And from the Lily's regal port
    Learn how to breast the strain!   40

Ho! woodsmen of the mountain side!
    Ho! dwellers in the vales!

Ho! ye who by the roaring tide
　　Have roughened in the gales!
Come! flocking gayly to the fight,
　　From forest, hill, and lake;
We battle for our Country's right,
　　And for the Lily's sake!

CAROLINA[64]

I

The despot treads thy sacred sands,
Thy pines give shelter to his bands,
Thy sons stand by with idle hands,
　　　　Carolina!
He breathes at ease thy airs of balm,
He scorns the lances of thy palm;
Oh! who shall break thy craven calm,
　　　　Carolina!
Thy ancient fame is growing dim,
A spot is on thy garment's rim;   10
Give to the winds thy battle hymn,
　　　　Carolina!

II

Call on thy children of the hill,
Wake swamp and river, coast and rill,
Rouse all thy strength and all thy skill,
　　　　Carolina!
Cite wealth and science, trade and art,
Touch with thy fire the cautious mart,
And pour thee through the people's heart,
　　　　Carolina!   20
Till even the coward spurns his fears,
And all thy fields and fens and meres
Shall bristle like thy palm with spears,
　　　　Carolina!

III

Hold up the glories of thy dead;
Say how thy elder children bled,
And point to Eutaw's battle-bed,
        Carolina!
Tell how the patriot's soul was tried,
And what his dauntless breast defied;   30
How Rutledge ruled and Laurens died,
        Carolina!
Cry! till thy summons, heard at last,
Shall fall like Marion's bugle-blast
Re-echoed from the haunted Past,
        Carolina!

IV

I hear a murmur as of waves
That grope their way through sunless caves,
Like bodies struggling in their graves,
        Carolina!   40
And now it deepens; slow and grand
It swells, as, rolling to the land,
An ocean broke upon thy strand,
        Carolina!
Shout! let it reach the startled Huns!
And roar with all thy festal guns!
It is the answer of thy sons,
        Carolina!

V

They will not wait to hear thee call;
From Sachem's Head to Sumter's wall   50
Resounds the voice of hut and hall,
        Carolina!
No! thou hast not a stain, they say,
Or none save what the battle-day

Shall wash in seas of blood away,
                    Carolina!
Thy skirts indeed the foe may part,
Thy robe be pierced with sword and dart,
They shall not touch thy noble heart,
                    Carolina!   60

VI

Ere thou shalt own the tyrant's thrall
Ten times ten thousand men must fall;
Thy corpse may hearken to his call,
                    Carolina!
When, by thy bier, in mournful throngs
The women chant thy mortal wrongs,
'Twill be their own funereal songs,
                    Carolina!
From thy dead breast by ruffians trod
No helpless child shall look to God;   70
All shall be safe beneath thy sod,
                    Carolina!

VII

Girt with such wills to do and bear,
Assured in right, and mailed in prayer,
Thou wilt not bow thee to despair,
                    Carolina!
Throw thy bold banner to the breeze!
Front with thy ranks the threatening seas
Like thine own proud armorial trees,
                    Carolina!   80
Fling down thy gauntlet to the Huns,
And roar the challenge from thy guns;
Then leave the future to thy sons,
                    Carolina!

SPRING

Spring, with that nameless pathos in the air
Which dwells with all things fair,
Spring, with her golden suns and silver rain,
Is with us once again.

Out in the lonely woods the jasmine burns
Its fragrant lamps, and turns
Into a royal court with green festoons
The banks of dark lagoons.

In the deep heart of every forest tree
The blood is all aglee,   10
And there's a look about the leafless bowers
As if they dreamed of flowers.

Yet still on every side we trace the hand
Of Winter in the land,
Save where the maple reddens on the lawn,
Flushed by the season's dawn;

Or where, like those strange semblances we find
That age to childhood bind,
The elm puts on, as if in Nature's scorn,
The brown of Autumn corn.   20

As yet the turf is dark, although you know
That, not a span below,
A thousand germs are groping through the gloom,
And soon will burst their tomb.

Already, here and there, on frailest stems
Appear some azure gems,
Small as might deck, upon a gala day,
The forehead of a fay.

In gardens you may note amid the dearth
The crocus breaking earth;   30
And near the snowdrop's tender white and green,
The violet in its screen.

But many gleams and shadows need must pass
Along the budding grass,
And weeks go by, before the enamored South
Shall kiss the rose's mouth.

Still there's a sense of blossoms yet unborn
In the sweet airs of morn;
One almost looks to see the very street
Grow purple at his feet.   40

At times a fragrant breeze comes floating by,
And brings, you know not why,
A feeling as when eager crowds await
Before a palace gate

Some wondrous pageant; and you scarce would start,
If from a beech's heart,
A blue-eyed Dryad, stepping forth, should say,
"Behold me! I am May!"

Ah! who would couple thoughts of war and crime
With such a blessed time!   50
Who in the west wind's aromatic breath
Could hear the call of Death!

Yet not more surely shall the Spring awake
The voice of wood and brake,
Than she shall rouse, for all her tranquil charms,
A million men to arms.

There shall be deeper hues upon her plains
Than all her sunlit rains,

And every gladdening influence around,
Can summon from the ground.   60

Oh! standing on this desecrated mould,
Methinks that I behold,
Lifting her bloody daisies up to God,
Spring kneeling on the sod,

And calling, with the voice of all her rills,
Upon the ancient hills
To fall and crush the tyrants and the slaves
Who turn her meads to graves.

CHARLESTON[65]

Calm as that second summer which precedes
    The first fall of the snow,
In the broad sunlight of heroic deeds,
    The City bides the foe.

As yet, behind their ramparts stern and proud,
    Her bolted thunders sleep—
Dark Sumter, like a battlemented cloud,
    Looms o'er the solemn deep.

No Calpe frowns from lofty cliff or scar
    To guard the holy strand;   10
But Moultrie holds in leash her dogs of war
    Above the level sand.

And down the dunes a thousand guns lie couched,
    Unseen, beside the flood—
Like tigers in some Orient jungle crouched
    That wait and watch for blood.

Meanwhile, through streets still echoing with trade,
    Walk grave and thoughtful men,

Whose hands may one day wield the patriot's blade
    As lightly as the pen.   20

And maidens, with such eyes as would grow dim
    Over a bleeding hound,
Seem each one to have caught the strength of him
    Whose sword she sadly bound.

Thus girt without and garrisoned at home,
    Day patient following day,
Old Charleston looks from roof, and spire, and dome,
    Across her tranquil bay.

Ships, through a hundred foes, from Saxon lands
    And spicy Indian ports,   30
Bring Saxon steel and iron to her hands,
    And Summer to her courts.

But still, along yon dim Atlantic line,
    The only hostile smoke
Creeps like a harmless mist above the brine,
    From some frail, floating oak.

Shall the Spring dawn, and she still clad in smiles,
    And with an unscathed brow,
Rest in the strong arms of her palm-crowned isles,
    As fair and free as now?   40

We know not; in the temple of the Fates
    God has inscribed her doom;
And, all untroubled in her faith, she waits
    The triumph or the tomb.

CHRISTMAS[66]

How grace this hallowed day?
Shall happy bells, from yonder ancient spire,
Send their glad greetings to each Christmas fire
    Round which the children play?

Alas! for many a moon,
That tongueless tower hath cleaved the Sabbath air,
Mute as an obelisk of ice, aglare
    Beneath an Arctic noon.

Shame to the foes that drown
Our psalms of worship with their impious drum,   10
The sweetest chimes in all the land lie dumb
    In some far rustic town.

There, let us think, they keep,
Of the dead Yules which here beside the sea
They've ushered in with old-world, English glee,
    Some echoes in their sleep.

How shall we grace the day?
With feast, and song, and dance, and antique sports,
And shout of happy children in the courts,
    And tales of ghost and fay?   20

Is there indeed a door,
Where the old pastimes, with their lawful noise,
And all the merry round of Christmas joys,
    Could enter as of yore?

Would not some pallid face
Look in upon the banquet, calling up
Dread shapes of battles in the wassail cup,
    And trouble all the place?

How could we bear the mirth,
While some loved reveler of a year ago   30
Keeps his mute Christmas now beneath the snow,
    In cold Virginian earth?

How shall we grace the day?
Ah! let the thought that on this holy morn
The Prince of Peace—the Prince of Peace was born,
    Employ us, while we pray!

Pray for the peace which long
Hath left this tortured land, and haply now
Holds its white court on some far mountain's brow,
    There hardly safe from wrong!   40

Let every sacred fane
Call its sad votaries to the shrine of God,
And, with the cloister and the tented sod,
    Join in one solemn strain!

With pomp of Roman form,
With the grave ritual brought from England's shore,
And with the simple faith which asks no more
    Than that the heart be warm!

He, who, till time shall cease,
Will watch that earth, where once, not all in vain,   50
He died to give us peace, may not disdain
    A prayer whose theme is—peace.

Perhaps ere yet the Spring
Hath died into the Summer, over all
The land, the peace of His vast love shall fall,
    Like some protecting wing.

Oh, ponder what it means!
Oh, turn the rapturous thought in every way!

Oh, give the vision and the fancy play,
    And shape the coming scenes!   60

    Peace in the quiet dales,
Made rankly fertile by the blood of men,
Peace in the woodland, and the lonely glen,
    Peace in the peopled vales!

    Peace in the crowded town,
Peace in a thousand fields of waving grain,
Peace in the highway and the flowery lane,
    Peace on the wind-swept down!

    Peace on the farthest seas,
Peace in our sheltered bays and ample streams,   70
Peace wheresoe'er our starry garland gleams,
    And peace in every breeze!

    Peace on the whirring marts,
Peace where the scholar thinks, the hunter roams,
Peace, God of Peace! peace, peace, in all our homes,
    And peace in all our hearts!

THE UNKNOWN DEAD

The rain is plashing on my sill,
But all the winds of Heaven are still;
And so it falls with that dull sound
Which thrills us in the church-yard ground,
When the first spadeful drops like lead
Upon the coffin of the dead.
Beyond my streaming window-pane,
I cannot see the neighboring vane,
Yet from its old familiar tower
The bell comes, muffled, through the shower.   10
What strange and unsuspected link
Of feeling touched, has made me think—

While with a vacant soul and eye
I watch the gray and stony sky—
Of nameless graves on battle-plains
Washed by a single winter's rains,
Where, some beneath Virginian hills,
And some by green Atlantic rills,
Some by the waters of the West,
A myriad unknown heroes rest.   20
Ah! not the chiefs, who, dying, see
Their flags in front of victory,
Or, at their life-blood's noble cost
Pay for a battle nobly lost,
Claim from their monumental beds
The bitterest tears a nation sheds.
Beneath yon lonely mound—the spot
By all save some fond few forgot—
Lie the true martyrs of the fight
Which strikes for freedom and for right.   30
Of them, their patriot zeal and pride,
The lofty faith that with them died,
No grateful page shall farther tell
Than that so many bravely fell;
And we can only dimly guess
What worlds of all this world's distress,
What utter woe, despair, and dearth,
Their fate has brought to many a hearth.
Just such a sky as this should weep
Above them, always, where they sleep;   40
Yet, haply, at this very hour,
Their graves are like a lover's bower;
And Nature's self, with eyes unwet,
Oblivious of the crimson debt
To which she owes her April grace,
Laughs gayly o'er their burial-place.

ODE[67]

I

Sleep sweetly in your humble graves,
    Sleep, martyrs of a fallen cause;
Though yet no marble column craves
    The pilgrim here to pause.

II

In seeds of laurel in the earth
    The blossom of your fame is blown,
And somewhere, waiting for its birth,
    The shaft is in the stone!

III

Meanwhile, behalf the tardy years
    Which keep in trust your storied tombs,   10
Behold! your sisters bring their tears,
    And these memorial blooms.

IV

Small tributes! but your shades will smile
    More proudly on these wreaths today,
Than when some cannon-moulded pile
    Shall overlook this bay.

V

Stoop, angels, hither from the skies!
    There is no holier spot of ground
Than where defeated valor lies,
    By mourning beauty crowned!   20

SONNET: AT LAST, BELOVED NATURE

At last, beloved Nature! I have met
Thee face to face upon thy breezy hills,
And boldly, where thy inmost bowers are set,
Gazed on thee naked in thy mountain rills.
When first I felt thy breath upon my brow,
Tears of strange ecstasy gushed out like rain,
And with a longing, passionate as vain,
I strove to clasp thee. But, I know not how,
Always before me didst thou seem to glide;
And often from one sunny mountain-side,   10
Upon the next bright peak I saw thee kneel,
And heard thy voice upon the billowy blast;
But, climbing, only reached to feel
The shadow of a Presence which had passed.

PAUL HAMILTON HAYNE

Paul Hamilton Hayne was born in Charleston, South Carolina, January 1, 1830. He was an only child. His father, Lieut. Paul Hamilton Hayne, died soon after Paul's birth, and the boy was brought up by his mother, Emily McElhenny Hayne, and his distinguished uncle, Robert Young Hayne. He attended Coates's School, where he formed a lifelong friendship with Henry Timrod, and Charleston College. At twenty-one he was admitted to the bar; in 1852 he married Mary Middleton Michel, the daughter of a French surgeon who had served Bonaparte with distinction before emigrating to Charleston. His poems of nature soon became popular and before the Civil War he published three volumes of verse: *Poems* (1855), *Sonnets and Other Poems* (1857), and *Avolio* (1860). For three years he edited *Russell's Magazine* (1857–1860; the name came from John Russell, at whose bookstore the magazine was planned), but the magazine could not survive the trying days that preceded the Civil War.

Too frail for army life, Hayne served as aide on the staff of

Governor Pickens, and wrote martial lyrics. During the bombardment of Charleston his house and library were burned; after the capture of the city his family silver and all his possessions were stolen or destroyed. After the war Hayne, without money and in poor health, moved with his family to Copse Hill, near Augusta, Georgia, where he owned a few acres of pine land. Here he erected "a poor apology for a dwelling," made furniture out of packing boxes, and settled himself to the task of making a living by his writing. Although the living was meager, Hayne invited Timrod and other poverty-stricken friends to visit with him; after Timrod's death he edited his poems, and wrote for the volume one of the noblest and most pathetic essays ever published, penetrating in its criticism yet unhesitatingly proclaiming Timrod the greatest of the South Carolina poets—a gesture that takes on additional nobility when one remembers that Hayne's best volume of poetry, *Legends and Lyrics* (1872), had been published the year before. He also wrote *Lives of Robert Young Hayne and Hugh Swinton Legaré* (1878), and a life of Simms that unfortunately has never been published. Hayne's friendships, though made and carried on chiefly by correspondence, were wide and varied, including Longfellow, Bryant, Holmes, William Morris and other men whom he hoped (in most cases vainly) some day to see. Many of his later poems were written to them, and to his son William Hamilton Hayne—who became in turn a capable and not undistinguished poet. In 1882 Hayne's *Collected Poems* were published. He died at Copse Hill on July 6, 1886.

SHELLEY

Because they thought his doctrines were not just,
Mankind assumed for him the chastening rod,
And tyrants reared in pride, and strong in lust,
Wounded the noblest of the sons of God;
The heart's most cherished benefactions riven,
Basely they strove to humble and malign
A soul whose charities were wide as heaven,
Whose *deeds*, if not his *doctrines*, were divine;
And in the name of Him, whose sunshine warms
The evil as the righteous, deemed it good   10

To wreak their bigotry's relentless storms
On one whose nature was not understood.
Ah, well! God's ways are wondrous; it may be
His seal hath not been set to man's decree.

MY STUDY[68]

This is my world! within these narrow walls,
I own a princely service. The hot care
And tumult of our frenzied life are here
But as a ghost and echo; what befalls
In the far mart to me is less than naught;
I walk the fields of quiet Arcadies,
And wander by the brink of hoary seas,
Calmed to the tendance of untroubled thought;
Or if a livelier humor should enhance
The slow-time pulse, 'tis not for present strife,   10
The sordid zeal with which our age is rife,
Its mammon conflicts crowned by fraud or chance,
But gleamings of the lost, heroic life,
Flashed through the gorgeous vistas of romance.

THE PINE'S MYSTERY

Listen! the somber foliage of the Pine
    A swart Gitana of the woodland trees,
Is answering what we may but half divine,
    To those soft whispers of the twilight breeze!

Passion and mystery murmur through the leaves,
    Passion and mystery, touched by deathless pain,
Whose monotone of long, low anguish grieves
    For something lost that shall not live again!

VICKSBURG[69]

A BALLAD

For sixty days and upwards,
  A storm of shell and shot
Rained round us in a flaming shower,
  But still we faltered not.
"If the noble city perish,"
  Our grand young leader said,
"Let the only walls the foe shall scale
  Be ramparts of the dead!"

For sixty days and upwards,
  The eye of heaven waxed dim;   10
And e'en throughout God's holy morn,
  O'er Christian prayer and hymn,
Arose a hissing tumult,
  As if the fiends in air
Strove to engulf the voice of faith
  In the shrieks of their despair.

There was wailing in the houses,
  There was trembling on the marts,
While the tempest raged and thundered,
  'Mid the silent thrill of hearts;   20
But the Lord, our shield, was with us,
  And ere a month had sped,
Our very women walked the streets
  With scarce one throb of dread.

And the little children gambolled,
  Their faces purely raised,
Just for a wondering moment,
  As the huge bombs whirled and blazed,
Then turned with silvery laughter
  To the sports which children love,   30

Thrice-mailed in the sweet, instinctive thought
      That the good God watched above.

Yet the hailing bolts fell faster,
      From scores of flame-clad ships,
And about us, denser, darker,
      Grew the conflict's wild eclipse,
Till a solid cloud closed o'er us,
      Like a type of doom and ire,
Whence shot a thousand quivering tongues
      Of forked and vengeful fire.   40

But the unseen hands of angels
      Those death-shafts warned aside,
And the dove of heavenly mercy
      Ruled o'er the battle tide;
In the houses ceased the wailing,
      And through the war-scarred marts
The people strode, with step of hope,
      To the music in their hearts.

ASPECTS OF THE PINES

Tall, sombre, grim, against the morning sky
      They rise, scarce touched by melancholy airs,
Which stir the fadeless foliage dreamfully,
      As if from realms of mystical despairs.

Tall, sombre, grim, they stand with dusky gleams
      Brightening to gold within the woodland's core,
Beneath the gracious noontide's tranquil beams—
      But the weird winds of morning sigh no more.

A stillness, strange, divine, ineffable,
      Broods round and o'er them in the wind's surcease,   10
And on each tinted copse and shimmering dell
      Rests the mute rapture of deep hearted peace.

Last, sunset comes—the solemn joy and might
  Borne from the West when cloudless day declines—
Low, flutelike breezes sweep the waves of light,
  And lifting dark green tresses of the pines,

Till every lock is luminous—gently float,
  Fraught with hale odors up the heavens afar
To faint when twilight on her virginal throat
  Wears for a gem the tremulous vesper star.   20

THE SNOW-MESSENGERS

DEDICATED TO JOHN GREENLEAF WHITTIER AND HENRY WADSWORTH
LONGFELLOW, WITH PEN PORTRAITS OF BOTH

The pine-trees lift their dark bewildered eyes—
Or so I deem—up to the clouded skies;
No breeze, no faintest breeze, is heard to blow:
In wizard silence falls the windless snow.

It falls in breezeless quiet, strangely still;
'Scapes the dulled pane, but loads the sheltering sill.
With curious hand the fleecy flakes I mould,
And draw them inward, rounded, from the cold.

The glittering ball that chills my fingertips
I hold a moment's space to loving lips;   10
For from the northward these pure snow-flakes came,
And to *my* touch their coldness thrills like flame.

Outbreathed from luminous memories nursed apart,
Deep in the veiled *adytum* of the heart,
The type of Norland dearth such snows may be:
They bring the soul of summer's warmth to me.

Beholding them, in magical light expands
The changeful charm that crowns the northern lands,
And a fair past I deemed a glory fled
Comes back, with happy sunshine round its head.   20

For Ariel fancy takes her airiest flights
To pass once more o'er Hampshire's mountain heights,
To view the flower-bright pastures bloom in grace
By many a lowering hill-side's swarthy base;

The fruitful farms, the enchanted vales, to view,
And the coy mountain lakes' transcendent blue,
Or flash of sea-waves up the thunderous dune,
With wan sails whitening in the midnight moon;

The cataract front of storm, malignly rife
With deathless instincts of demoniac strife,   30
Or, in shy contrast, down a shaded dell,
The rivulet tinkling like an Alpine bell;

And many a cool, calm stretch of cultured lawn,
Touched by the freshness of the crystal dawn,
Sloped to the sea, whose laughing waters meet
About the unrobed virgin's rosy feet.

But, tireless fancy, stay the wing that roams,
And fold it last near northern hearts and homes.

These tropic veins still own their kindred heat,
And thoughts of thee, my cherished South, are sweet—   40
Mournfully sweet—and wed to memories vast,
High-hovering still o'er thy majestic past.

But a new epoch greets us; with it blends
The voice of ancient foes now changed to friends.
Ah! who would friendship's outstretched hand despise,
Or mock the kindling light in generous eyes?

So, 'neath the Quaker-poet's tranquil roof,
From all dull discords of the world aloof,
I sit once more, and measured converse hold
With him whose nobler thoughts are rhythmic gold;   50

See his deep brows half puckered in a knot
O'er some hard problem of our mortal lot,
Or a dream soft as May winds of the south
Waft a girl's sweetness round his firm-set mouth.

Or should he deem wrong threats the public weal,
Lo! the whole man seems girt with flashing steel;
His glance a sword thrust, and his words of ire
Like thunder-tones from some old prophet's lyre.

Or by the hearth-stone when the day is done,
Mark, swiftly launched, a sudden shaft of fun;   60
The short quick laugh, the smartly smitten knees,
And all sure tokens of a mind at ease.

Discerning which, by some mysterious law,
Near to his seat two household favorites draw,
Till on her master's shoulders, sly and sleek,
Grimalkin, mounting, rubs his furrowed cheek;

While terrier Dick, denied all words to rail,
Snarls as he shakes a short protesting tail,
But with shrewd eyes says, plain as plain can be,
"Drop that sly cat. I'm worthier far than she."   70

And he who loves all lowliest lives to please,
Conciliates soon his dumb Diogenes,
Who in return his garment nips with care,
And drags the poet out, to take the air.

God's innocent pensioners in the woodlands dim,
The fields and pastures, know and trust in him;
And in *their* love his lonely heart is blessed,
Our pure, hale-minded Cowper of the West!

*   *   *

The scene is changed; and now I stand again
By one, the cordial prince of kindly men,   80

Courtly yet natural, comrade meet for kings,
But fond of homeliest thoughts and homeliest things.

A poet too, in whose warm brain and breast
What birds of song have filled a golden nest,
Till in song's summer prime their wings unfurled,
Have made Arcadian half the listening world,

Around whose eve some radiant grace of morn
Smiles like the dew-light on a mountain thorn.
Blithely he bears Time's envious load today:
Ah! the green heart o'ertops the head of gray.   90

Alert as youth, with vivid, various talk
He wiles the way through grove and garden walk,
Fair flowers untrained, trees fraught with wedded doves,
Past the cool copse and willowy glade he loves.

Here gleams innocuous of a mirthful mood
Pulse like mild fire-flies down a dusky wood,
Or keener speech (his leonine head unbowed)
Speeds lightning-clear from thought's o'ershadowing cloud.

O deep blue eyes! O voice as woman's low!
O firm white hand, with kindliest warmth aglow!   100
O manly form, and frank, sweet, courteous mien,
Reflex of museful days and nights serene!

Still are ye near me, vivid, actual still,
Here in my lonely fastness on the hill;
Nor can ye wane till cold my life-blood flows,
And fancy fades in feeling's last repose.

What! snowing yet? The landscape waxes pale;
Round the mute heaven there hangs a quivering veil,
Through whose frail woof like silent shuttles go
The glancing glamours of the glittering snow.   110

Yes, falling still, while fond remembrance stirs
In these wan-faced, unwonted messengers.
Dumb storm! outpour your arctic heart's desire!
Your flakes to me seem flushed with fairy fire!

TO LONGFELLOW

(ON HEARING HE WAS ILL)

O thou, whose potent genius (like the sun
     Tenderly mellowed by a rippling haze)
  Hast gained thee all men's homage, love and praise,
Surely thy web of life is not outspun,
Thy glory rounded, thy last guerdon won!
    Nay, poet, nay!—from thought's calm sunset ways
May new-born notes of undegenerate lays
Charm back the twilight gloom ere day be done!

But past the poet crowned I see the friend—
    Frank, courteous, true—about whose locks of gray,   10
Like golden bees, some glints of summer stray;
     Clear-eyed, with lips half poised 'twixt smile and sigh;
A brow in whose soul-mirroring manhood blend
    Grace, sweetness, power and magnanimity!

TO W. H. H.

How like a mighty picture, tint by tint,
This marvellous world is opening to thy view!
Wonders of earth and heaven; shapes bright and new,
Strength, radiance, beauty, and all things that hint
Most of the primal glory, and the print
Of angel footsteps; from the globe of dew
Tiny, but luminous, to the encircling blue,
Unbounded, thou drink'st knowledge without stint;
Like a pure blossom nursed by genial winds,
Thy innocent life, expanding day by day,   10

Upsprings, spontaneous, to the perfect flower;
Lost Eden-splendors round thy pathway play,
While o'er it rise and burn the starry signs
Which herald hope and joy to souls of power.

I pray the angel in whose hands the sum
Of mortal fates in mystic darkness lies,
That to the soul which fills these deepening eyes,
Sun-crowned and clear, the spirit of Song may come;
That strong-winged fancies, with melodious hum
Of plumèd vans, may touch to sweet surprise   20
His poet nature, born to glow and rise,
And thrill to worship though the world be dumb;
That love, and will, and genius, all may blend
To make his soul a guiding star of time,
True to the purest thought, the noblest end,
Full of all richness, gentle, wise, complete,
In whose still heights and most ethereal clime,
Beauty, and faith, and plastic passion meet.

A LITTLE WHILE I FAIN WOULD LINGER YET

A little while (my life is almost set!)
    I fain would pause along the downward way,
    Musing an hour in this sad sunset-ray,
While, Sweet! our eyes with tender tears are wet;
A little hour I fain would linger yet.

A little while I fain would linger yet,
    All for love's sake, for love that cannot tire;
    Though fervid youth be dead, with youth's desire,
And hope has faded to a vague regret,
A little while I fain would linger yet.   10

A little while I fain would linger here:
    Behold! who knows what strange mysterious bars
    'Twixt souls that love, may rise in other stars?

Nor can love deem the face of death is fair;
A little while I still would linger here.

A little while I yearn to hold thee fast,
   Hand locked in hand, and loyal heart to heart;
   (O pitying Christ! those woeful words, "*We part!*")
So ere the darkness fall, the light be past,
A little while I fain would hold thee fast.   20

A little while, when night and twilight meet;
   Behind, our broken years; before, the deep
   Weird wonder of the last unfathomed sleep.
A little while I still would clasp thee, Sweet;
A little while, when night and twilight meet.

A little while I fain would linger here;
   Behold! who knows what soul-dividing bars
   Earth's faithful loves may part in other stars?
Nor can love deem the face of death is fair:
A little while I still would linger here.   30

IN HARBOR

I think it is over, over,
   I think it is over at last,
Voices of foeman and lover,
The sweet and the bitter have passed:—
Life, like a tempest of ocean
Hath outblown its ultimate blast:
There's but a faint sobbing sea-ward
While the calm of the tide deepens lee-ward,
And behold! like the welcoming quiver
Of heart-pulses throbbed thro' the river,   10
   Those lights in the harbor at last,
   The heavenly harbor at last!

I feel it is over! over!
   For the winds and the waters surcease;

Ah!—few were the days of the rover
   That smiled in the beauty of peace!
And distant and dim was the omen
That hinted redress or release:—
From the ravage of life, and its riot,
What marvel I yearn for the quiet   20
   Which bides in the harbor at last?
For the lights with their welcoming quiver
That throb through the sanctified river
   Which girdles the harbor at last,
   This heavenly harbor at last?

I *know* it is over, over,
   I know it is over at last!
Down sail! the sheathed anchor uncover,
For the stress of the voyage has passed:
Life, like a tempest of ocean   30
   Hath outbreathed its ultimate blast:
There's but a faint sobbing sea-ward,
While the calm of the tide deepens lee-ward;
And behold! like the welcoming quiver
Of heart-pulses throbbed thro' the river,
   Those lights in the harbor at last,
   The heavenly harbor at last!

CIVIL WAR BALLADS, SONGS, AND POEMS

DIXIE[70]

I wish I was in de land ob cotton,
Old times dar am not forgotten;
   Look away! Look away! Look away! Dixie Land!
In Dixie Land whar I was born in,
Early on one frosty mornin',
   Look away! Look away! Look away! Dixie Land!

Chorus:

Den I wish I was in Dixie! Hooray! Hooray!
In Dixie's Land we'll take our stand, to lib an' die in Dixie.
Away! away! away down South in Dixie.
Away! away! away down South in Dixie.   10

Ole missus marry "Will-de-weaber";
Willum was a gay deceaber;
    Look away, look away, look away, Dixie Land!
But when he put his arm around her,
He smiled as fierce as a forty-pounder;
    Look away, look away, look away, Dixie Land!

His face was sharp as a butcher's cleaber;
But dat did not seem to greab her;
    Look away, look away, look away, Dixie Land!
Ole missus acted de foolish part,   20
And died for a man dat broke her heart;
    Look away, look away, look away, Dixie Land!

Now here's a health to de next ole missus,
An' all the gals dat want to kiss us;
    Look away, look away, look away, Dixie Land!
But if you want to drive 'way sorrow,
Come hear dis song tomorrow;
    Look away, look away, look away, Dixie Land!

Dar's buckwheat cakes and Injin batter,
Makes you fat or a little fatter;   30
    Look away, look away, look away, Dixie Land!
Den hoe it down an' scratch your grabble,
To Dixie's land I'm bound to trabble;
    Look away, look away, look away, Dixie Land!
                                    DAN D. EMMETT

Literary Ballad
1. Repetition
2. false Patriotism

DIXIE[71]

I

Southrons, hear your country call you!
Up! lest worse than death befall you!
　　To arms! to arms! to arms! in Dixie!
Lo! all beacon fires are lighted,
Let our hearts be now united!
　　To arms! to arms! to arms! in Dixie!
　　　Advance the flag of Dixie!
　　　　Hurrah! Hurrah!
　　For Dixie's land we'll take our stand,
　　　To live or die for Dixie!　　　　　　　10
　　To arms!　To arms!
　　　And conquer peace for Dixie!
　　To arms!　To arms!
　　　And conquer peace for Dixie!

II

Hear the Northern thunders mutter!
Northern flags in South winds flutter!
　　To arms! to arms! to arms! in Dixie!
Send them back your fierce defiance!
Stamp upon the cursed alliance!
　　To arms! to arms! to arms! in Dixie!　　20
　　　Advance the flag of Dixie!　[Chorus]

Refrain
Rythm

III

Fear no danger! shun no labor!
Lift up rifle, pike and sabre!
　　To arms! to arms! to arms! in Dixie!
Shoulder pressing close to shoulder,
Let the odds make each heart bolder!
　　To arms! to arms! to arms! in Dixie!
　　　Advance the flag of Dixie!　[Chorus]

IV

How the South's great heart rejoices,
At your cannon's ringing voices;   30
   To arms! to arms! to arms! in Dixie!
For faith betrayed and pledges broken,
Wrongs inflicted, insults spoken!
   To arms! to arms! to arms! in Dixie!
      Advance the flag of Dixie!   [Chorus]

V

Strong as lions, swift as eagles,
Back to their kennels hunt these beagles!
   To arms! to arms! to arms! in Dixie!
Cut the unequal bonds asunder!
Let them hence each other plunder!   40
   To arms! to arms! to arms! in Dixie!
      Advance the flag of Dixie!   [Chorus]

VI

Swear upon your country's altar,
Never to give up or falter;
   To arms! to arms! to arms! in Dixie!
Till the spoilers are defeated,
Till the Lord's work is completed.
   To arms! to arms! to arms! in Dixie!
      Advance the flag of Dixie!   [Chorus]

VII

Halt not till our Federation,   50
Secures among earth's Powers its station!
   To arms! to arms! to arms! in Dixie!
Then at peace and crowned with glory,
Hear your children tell the story!
   To arms! to arms! to arms! in Dixie!
      Advance the flag of Dixie!   [Chorus]

VIII

If the loved ones weep in sadness,
Victory soon shall bring them gladness.
   To arms! to arms! to arms! in Dixie!
Exultant pride soon banish sorrow;   60
Smiles chase tears away tomorrow,
   To arms! to arms! to arms! in Dixie!
     Advance the flag of Dixie!
       Hurrah! Hurrah!
For Dixie's land we'll take our stand,
     To live or die for Dixie!
To arms! To arms!
     And conquer peace for Dixie!
To arms! To arms!
     And conquer peace for Dixie!   70
                  ALBERT PIKE

MARYLAND, MY MARYLAND[72]

The despot's heel is on thy shore,
     Maryland!
His torch is at thy temple door,
     Maryland!
Avenge the patriotic gore
That flecked the streets of Baltimore,
And be the battle queen of yore,
     Maryland, my Maryland!

Hark to an exiled son's appeal,
     Maryland!   10
My Mother State, to thee I kneel,
     Maryland!
For life and death, for woe and weal,
Thy peerless chivalry reveal,
And gird thy beauteous limbs with steel,
     Maryland, my Maryland!

Thou wilt not cower in the dust,
   Maryland!
Thy beaming sword shall never rust,
   Maryland!   20
Remember Carroll's sacred trust,
Remember Howard's warlike thrust,
And all thy slumberers with the just,
   Maryland, my Maryland!

Come! 'tis the red dawn of the day,
   Maryland!
Come with thy panoplied array,
   Maryland!
With Ringgold's spirit for the fray,
With Watson's blood at Monterey, 30
With fearless Lowe and dashing May,
   Maryland, my Maryland!

Dear Mother! burst the tyrant's chain,
   Maryland!
Virginia should not call in vain,
   Maryland!
She meets her sisters on the plain—
"*Sic semper!*" 'tis the proud refrain
That baffles minions back amain,
   Maryland!   40
Arise in majesty again,
   Maryland, my Maryland!

Come! for thy shield is bright and strong,
   Maryland!
Come! for thy dalliance does thee wrong,
   Maryland!
Come to thine own heroic throng
Walking with Liberty along,
And chant thy dauntless slogan-song,
   Maryland, my Maryland! 50

I see the blush upon thy cheek,
      Maryland!
For thou wast ever bravely meek,
      Maryland!
But lo! there surges forth a shriek,
From hill to hill, from creek to creek,
Potomac calls to Chesapeake,
      Maryland, my Maryland!

Thou wilt not yield the Vandal toll,
      Maryland!   60
Thou wilt not crook to his control,
      Maryland!
Better the fire upon thee roll,
Better the shot, the blade, the bowl,
Than crucifixion of the soul,
      Maryland, my Maryland!

I hear the distant thunder-hum,
      Maryland!
The Old Line bugle, fife, and drum,
      Maryland!   70
She is not dead, nor deaf, nor dumb;
Huzza! she spurns the Northern scum!
She breathes—she burns! she'll come! she'll come!
      Maryland, my Maryland!
              JAMES RYDER RANDALL

THE BONNIE BLUE FLAG[73]

inspiring-Patriotic note, Rythmical

We are a band of brothers, and native to the soil,
Fighting for our liberty, with treasure, blood and toil;
   And when our rights were threatened, the cry rose near and
     far:
Hurrah for the Bonnie Blue Flag that bears a Single Star!

Chorus:

Hurrah! Hurrah! for Southern rights, Hurrah!
Hurrah for the Bonnie Blue Flag that bears a Single Star!

As long as the Union was faithful to her trust,
Like friends and like brethren kind were we and just;
    But now when Northern treachery attempts our rights to
        mar,
    We hoist on high the Bonnie Blue Flag that bears a Single
        Star.   [Chorus]   10

First gallant South Carolina nobly made the stand;
Then came Alabama, who took her by the hand;
    Next, quickly Mississippi, Georgia, and Florida,
    All raised on high the Bonnie Blue Flag that bears a Single
        Star.   [Chorus]

Ye men of valor, gather round the banner of the right,
Texas and fair Louisiana, join us in the fight:
    Davis, our loved President, and Stephens, statesman rare,
    Now rally round the Bonnie Blue Flag that bears a Single
        Star.   [Chorus]

And here's to brave Virginia! The Old Dominion State
With the young Confederacy at length has linked her fate;   20
    Impelled by her example, now other States prepare
    To hoist on high the Bonnie Blue Flag that bears a Single
        Star.   [Chorus]

Then cheer, boys, cheer, raise the joyous shout,
For Arkansas and North Carolina now have both gone out;
    And let another rousing cheer for Tennessee be given—
    The Single Star of the Bonnie Blue Flag has grown to be
        eleven.   [Chorus]

Then, here's to our Confederacy; strong we are and brave,
Like patriots of old we'll fight our heritage to save;
    And rather than submit to shame, to die we would prefer—
    So cheer again for the Bonnie Blue Flag that bears a Single
        Star!   30

Chorus:

Hurrah! Hurrah! for Southern rights, Hurrah!
Hurrah! for the Bonnie Blue Flag has gained the Eleventh
    Star.

HARRY McCARTHY

I'M A GOOD OLD REBEL[74]

1   O I'm a good old rebel,
        Now that's just what I am;
    For the "fair land of freedom,"
        I do not care a damn;
    I'm glad I fit against it,
        I only wish we'd won,
    And I don't want no pardon,
        For anything I done.

2   I hate the Constitution,
        This great republic too;   10
    I hate the freedman's buro,
        In uniforms of blue.
    I hate the nasty eagle,
        With all his brags and fuss;
    The lyin' thievin' Yankees,
        I hate 'em wuss and wuss.

3   I hate the Yankee nation
        And everything they do;
    I hate the Declaration
        Of Independence, too.   20

I hate the glorious Union,
'Tis dripping with our blood;
I hate the striped banner,
I fit it all I could.

4 I followed old Marse Robert
For four years near about,
Got wounded in three places,
And starved on Point Lookout.
I cotch the roomatism
A-campin' in the snow, 30
But if I killed a chance of Yankees,
I'd like to kill some mo'.

5 Three hundred thousand Yankees
Is stiff in Southern dust;
We got three hundred thousand
Before they conquered us;
They died of Southern fever,
And Southern steel and shot,
I wish it was three million
Instead of what we got. 40

6 I can't take up my musket
And fight 'em now no more;
But I ain't a-goin' to love 'em,
Now that is certain sure.
And I don't want no pardon
For what I was and am;
I won't be reconstructed,
And I don't give a damn.

INNES RANDOLPH

THE VIRGINIANS OF THE VALLEY[75]

The knightliest of the knightly race,
  Who, since the days of old,
Have kept the lamp of chivalry
  Alight in hearts of gold;
The kindliest of the kindly band,
  Who, rarely hating ease,
Yet rode with Spotswood round the land,
  And Raleigh round the seas.

Who climbed the blue Virginian hills,
  Against embattled foes,   10
And planted there, in valleys fair,
  The lily and the rose;
Whose fragrance lives in many lands,
  Whose beauty stars the earth,
And lights the hearts of many homes
  With loveliness and worth.

We thought they slept! the sons who kept
  The names of noble sires,
And slumbered while the darkness crept
  Around the vigil fires.   20
But still the Golden Horse-shoe Knights
  Their Old Dominion keep,
Whose foes have found enchanted ground,
  But not a knight asleep.
                        FRANCIS ORRAY TICKNOR

LITTLE GIFFEN[76]

Out of the focal and foremost fire,
Out of the hospital walls as dire,
Smitten of grapeshot and gangrene,
Eighteenth battle and he sixteen—

Specter such as you seldom see,
Little Giffen of Tennessee.

"Take him and welcome," the surgeon said;
"Not the doctor can help the dead!"
So we took him and brought him where
The balm was sweet in our summer air;   10
And we laid him down on a wholesome bed;
Utter Lazarus, heel to head!

And we watched the war with abated breath,
Skeleton boy against skeleton death!
Months of torture, how many such!
Weary weeks of the stick and crutch,—
And still a glint in the steel-blue eye
Told of a spirit that wouldn't die,

And didn't! Nay! more! in death's despite
The crippled skeleton learned to write—   20
"Dear mother!" at first, of course, and then
"Dear Captain!" inquiring about the men.
Captain's answer: "Of eighty and five,
Giffen and I are left alive."

"Johnston pressed at the front," they say;—
Little Giffen was up and away!
A tear, his first, as he bade good-by,
Dimmed the glint of his steel-blue eye.
"I'll write, if spared!" There was news of fight,
But none of Giffen—he did not write!   30

I sometimes fancy that were I King
Of the courtly Knights of Arthur's ring,
With the voice of the minstrel in mine ear
And the tender legend that trembles here,
I'd give the best on his bended knee—
The whitest soul of my chivalry—
For Little Giffen of Tennessee.

FRANCIS ORRAY TICKNOR

ZOLLICOFFER[77]

First in the fight, and first in the arms,
    Of the white-winged angels of glory,
With the heart of the South at the feet of God,
    And his wounds to tell the story.

For the blood that flowed from his hero heart
    On the spot where he nobly perished,
Was drunk by the earth as a sacrament,
    In the holy cause he cherished.

In heaven a home, with the brave and blessed,
    And for his soul's sustaining,   10
The apocalyptic eyes of Christ,
    And nothing on earth remaining,

But a handful of dust in the land of his choice,
    A name in song and story,
And Fame to shout, with her brazen voice:
    "DIED ON THE FIELD OF GLORY."
                                    HENRY LYNDON FLASH

LEE TO THE REAR[78]

Dawn of a pleasant morning in May,
Broke through the wilderness cool and grey,
While perched in the tallest tree-tops, the birds
Were carolling Mendelssohn's "Songs without words."

Far from the haunts of men remote,
The brook brawled on with a liquid note,
And Nature, all tranquil and lovely, wore
The smile of the spring, as in Eden of yore.

Little by little as daylight increased,
And deepened the roseate flush in the East—   10

Little by little did morning reveal
Two long glittering lines of steel;

Where two hundred thousand bayonets gleam,
Tipped with the light of the earliest beam,
And the faces are sullen and grim to see,
In the hostile armies of Grant and Lee.

All of a sudden, ere rose the sun,
Pealed on the silence the opening gun—
A little white puff of smoke there came,
And anon the valley was wreathed in flame.   20

Down on the left of the rebel lines,
Where a breastwork stands in a copse of pines,
Before the rebels their ranks can form,
The Yankees have carried the place by storm.

Stars and Stripes on the salient wave,
Where many a hero has found a grave,
And the gallant Confederates strive in vain
The ground they have drenched with their blood to regain!

Yet louder the thunder of battle roared—
Yet a deadlier fire on the columns poured—   30
Slaughter infernal rode with despair,
Furies twain, through the murky air.

Not far off in the saddle there sat,
A grey-bearded man in a black slouched hat;
Not much moved by the fire was he,
Calm and resolute Robert Lee.

Quick and watchful he kept his eye
On the bold rebel brigades close by,—
Reserves, that were standing (and dying) at ease,
While the tempest of wrath toppled over the trees.   40

For still with their loud, deep, bull-dog bay,
The Yankee batteries blazed away,
And with every murderous second that sped
A dozen brave fellows, alas! fell dead.

The grand old grey-beard rode to the space
Where death and his victims stood face to face,
And silently waved his old slouched hat—
A world of meaning there was in that!

"Follow me! Steady! We'll save the day!"
This, was what he seemed to say;   50
And to the light of his glorious eye
The bold brigades thus made reply—

"We'll go forward, but you must go back"—
And they moved not an inch in the perilous track:
"Go to the rear, and we'll send them to h——!"
And the sound of the battle was lost in their yell.

Turning his bridle, Robert Lee
Rode to the rear. Like the waves of the sea,
Bursting the dikes in their overflow,
Madly his veterans dashed on the foe.   60

And backward in terror that foe was driven,
Their banners rent and their columns riven,
Wherever the tide of battle rolled
Over the Wilderness, wood and wold.

Sunset out of a crimson sky,
Streamed o'er a field of ruddier dye,
And the brook ran on with a purple stain,
From the blood of ten thousand foemen slain.

Seasons have passed since that day and year—
Again o'er its pebbles the brook runs clear,   70

And the field in a richer green is drest
Where the dead of a terrible conflict rest.

Hushed is the roll of the rebel drum,
The sabres are sheathed, and the cannon are dumb,
And Fate, with his pitiless hand has furled
The flag that once challenged the gaze of the world;

But the fame of the Wilderness fight abides;
And down into history grandly rides,
Calm and unmoved as in battle he sat,
The grey-bearded man in the black slouched hat.   80

JOHN REUBEN THOMPSON

STONEWALL JACKSON'S WAY[79]

Come, men, stack arms! Pile on the rails,
   Stir up the camp-fire bright;
No matter if the canteen fails,
   We'll make a roaring night.
Here Shenandoah brawls along,
Here burly Blue Ridge echoes strong,
To swell the brigade's rousing song,
   Of "Stonewall Jackson's way."

We see him now—the old slouched hat
   Cocked o'er his eye askew;   10
The shrewd, dry smile—the speech so pat,
   So calm, so blunt, so true.
The "Blue-Light Elder" knows 'em well.
Says he, "That's Banks, he's fond of shell;
Lord save his soul! We'll give him—" well,
   That's "Stonewall Jackson's way."

Silence! ground arms! kneel all! caps off!
   Old Blue Light's going to pray;

Strangle the fool that dares to scoff.
   Attention! it's his way!   20
Appealing from his native sod,
"Hear us, in power, Almighty God!
Lay bare thine arm, stretch forth thy rod,
   Amen." That's Stonewall's way.

He's in the saddle now! Fall in!
   Steady, the whole brigade!
Hill's at the ford, cut off; we'll win
   His way with ball and blade.
What matter if our shoes are worn?
What matter if our feet are torn?   30
Quick step! we're with him ere the dawn!
   That's Stonewall Jackson's way.

The sun's bright glances rout the mists
   Of morning—and, by George!
Here's Longstreet struggling in the lists,
   Hemmed in an ugly gorge,
Pope and his Yankees, whipped before,
"Bayonets and grape!" hear Stonewall roar.
"Charge, Stuart! pay off Ashby's score,
   In Stonewall Jackson's way."   40

Ah! maiden, wait, and watch, and yearn,
   For news of Stonewall's band!
Ah! widow, read with eyes that burn
   That ring upon thy hand!
Ah! wife, sew on, pray on, hope on!
Thy life shall not be all forlorn;
The foe had better ne'er been born
   That gets in Stonewall's way.

                       JOHN WILLIAMSON PALMER

THE SHADE OF THE TREES[80]

What are the thoughts that are stirring his breast?
  What is the mystical vision he sees?
"Let us pass over the river and rest
  Under the shade of the trees."

Has he grown sick of his toils and his tasks?
  Sighs the worn spirit for respite or ease?
Is it a moment's cool halt that he asks
  Under the shade of the trees?

Is it the gurgle of waters whose flow
  Ofttime has come to him borne on the breeze,   10
Memory listens to, lapsing so low,
  Under the shade of the trees?

Nay—though the rasp of the flesh was so sore,
  Faith, that had yearnings far keener than these,
Saw the soft sheen of the Thitherward Shore,
  Under the shade of the trees;—

Caught the high psalms of ecstatic delight,
  Heard the harps harping like soundings of seas,
Watched earth's assoiled ones walking in white
  Under the shade of the trees.   20

O, was it strange he should pine for release,
  Touched to the soul with such transports as these,
He who so needed the balsam of peace,
  Under the shade of the trees?

Yes, it was noblest for him—it was best
  (Questioning naught of our Father's decrees)
There to pass over the river and rest
  Under the shade of the trees!

                    MARGARET JUNKIN PRESTON

"THE BRIGADE MUST NOT KNOW, SIR!"

"Who've ye got there?" "Only a dying brother,
   Hurt in the front just now."
"Good boy! he'll do. Somebody tell his mother
   Where he was killed, and how."

"Whom have you there?" "A crippled courier, Major,
   Shot by mistake, we hear;
He was with Stonewall." "Cruel work they've made here;
   Quick with him to the rear!"

"Well, who comes next?" "Doctor, speak low, speak low, sir;
   Don't let the men find out!   10
It's STONEWALL!" "God!" "The brigade must not know, sir,
   While there is a foe about!"

Whom have we here—shrouded in martial manner,
   Crowned with a martyr's charm?
A grand dead hero, in a living banner,
   Born of his heart and arm:

The heart whereon his cause hung—see how clingeth
   That banner to his bier!
The arm wherewith his cause struck—hark! how ringeth
   His trumpet in their rear!   20

What have we left? His glorious inspiration,
   His prayers in council met;
Living, he laid the first stones of a nation;
   And dead, he builds it yet.

                                    ANONYMOUS

THE BAND IN THE PINES[81]

Oh, band in the pine-wood, cease!
    Cease with your splendid call;
The living are brave and noble,
    But the dead were bravest of all!

They throng to the martial summons,
    To the loud triumphant strain;
And the dear bright eyes of long-dead friends
    Come to the heart again.

They come with the ringing bugle,
    And the deep drum's mellow roar;   10
Till the soul is faint with longing
    For the hands we clasp no more!

Oh, band in the pine-wood, cease!
    Or the heart will melt in tears,
For the gallant eyes and the smiling lips
    And the voices of old years!

JOHN ESTEN COOKE

THE FOE AT THE GATES[82]

Ring round her! children of her glorious skies,
    Whom she hath nursed to stature proud and great;
Catch one last glance from her imploring eyes,
    Then close your ranks and face the threatening fate.

Ring round her! with a wall of horrent steel
    Confront the foe, nor mercy ask nor give;
And in her hour of anguish let her feel
    That ye can die whom she has taught to live.

Ring round her! swear, by every lifted blade,
    To shield from wrong the mother who gave you birth;

That never violent hand on her be laid,   11
    Nor base foot desecrate her hallowed hearth.

Curst be the dastard who shall halt or doubt!
    And doubly damned who casts one look behind!
Ye who are men! with unsheathed sword, and shout,
    Up with her banner! give it to the wind!

Peal your wild slogan, echoing far and wide,
    Till every ringing avenue repeat
The gathering cry, and Ashley's angry tide
    Calls to the sea-waves beating round her feet.   20

Sons, to the rescue! spurred and belted, come!
    Kneeling, with clasp'd hands, she invokes you now
By the sweet memories of your childhood's home,
    By every manly hope and filial vow,

To save her proud soul from that loathèd thrall
    Which yet her spirit cannot brook to name;
Or, if her fate be near, and she must fall,
    Spare her—she sues—the agony and shame.

From all her fanes let solemn bells be tolled;
    Heap with kind hands her costly funeral pyre,   30
And thus, with pæan sung and anthem rolled,
    Give her unspotted to the God of Fire.

Gather around her sacred ashes then,
    Sprinkle the cherished dust with crimson rain,
Die! as becomes a race of free-born men,
    Who will not crouch to wear the bondman's chain.

So, dying, ye shall win a high renown,
    If not in life, at least by death, set free;
And send her fame through endless ages down—
    The last grand holocaust of Liberty.   40
                          JOHN DICKSON BRUNS

STACK ARMS[83]

I

"Stack Arms!" I've gladly heard the cry
  When, weary with the dusty tread
Of marching troops, as night drew nigh
  I sank upon my soldier's bed
And calmly slept: the starry dome
  Of heaven's blue arch my canopy,
And mingled with my dreams of home
  The thoughts of peace and liberty.

II

"Stack Arms!" I've heard it, when the shout
  Exulting, rang along our line,   10
Of foes hurled back in bloody rout,
  Captured, dispersed; its tones divine
Then came to mine enraptured ear,
  Guerdon of duty nobly done,
And glistened on my cheek, the tear
  Of grateful joy for victory won.

III

"Stack Arms!" In faltering accents, slow
  And sad, it creeps from tongue to tongue,
A broken, murmuring wail of woe,
  From manly hearts by anguish wrung: 20
Like victims of a midnight dream,
  We move, we know not how nor why,
For life and hope but phantoms seem,
  And it were a relief—to die.

                              JOSEPH BLYTH ALLSTON

DREAMING IN THE TRENCHES[84]

I picture her there in the quaint old room,
    Where the fading fire-light starts and falls,
Alone in the twilight's tender gloom
    With the shadows that dance on the dim-lit walls.

Alone, while those faces look silently down
    From their antique frames in a grim repose—
Slight scholarly Ralph in his Oxford gown,
    And stanch Sir Alan, who died for Montrose.

There are gallants gay in crimson and gold,
    There are smiling beauties with powdered hair,   10
But she sits. there, fairer a thousand-fold,
    Leaning dreamily back in her low arm-chair.

And the roseate shadows of fading light
    Softly clear steal over the sweet young face,
Where a woman's tenderness blends tonight
    With the guileless pride of a knightly race.

Her small hands lie clasped in a listless way
    On the old *Romance*—which she holds on her knee—
Of *Tristram*, the bravest of knights in the fray,
    And *Iseult*, who waits by the sounding sea.   20

And her proud, dark eyes wear a softened look
    As she watches the dying embers fall:
Perhaps she dreams of the knight in the book,
    Perhaps of the pictures that smile on the wall.

What fancies, I wonder, are thronging her brain,
    For her cheeks, flush warm with a crimson glow!
Perhaps—ah! me, how foolish and vain!
    But I'd give my life to believe it so!

Well, whether I ever march home again
  To offer my love and a stainless name,   30
Or whether I die at the head of my men—
  I'll be true to the end all the same.

WILLIAM GORDON MCCABE

THE LAND WHERE WE WERE DREAMING[85]

Fair were our nation's visions, and as grand
As ever floated out of fancy-land;
  Children were we in simple faith,
  But god-like children, whom nor death,
  Nor threat of danger drove from honor's path—
    In the land where we were dreaming!

Proud were our men as pride of birth could render,
As violets our women pure and tender;
  And when they spoke, their voices' thrill
  At evening hushed the whip-poor-will;   10
  At morn the mocking bird was mute and still,
    In the land where we were dreaming!

And we had graves that covered more of glory,
Than ever taxed the lips of ancient story;
  And in our dream we wove the thread
  Of principles for which had bled,
  And suffered long our own immortal dead,
    In the land where we were dreaming!

Tho' in our land we had both bond and free,
Both were content, and so God let them be;   20
  Till Northern glances, slanting down,
  With envy viewed our harvest sun—
  But little recked we, for we still slept on,
    In the land where we were dreaming!

Our sleep grew troubled, and our dreams grew wild;
Red meteors flashed across our heaven's field;

Crimson the Moon; between the Twins
Barbed arrows flew in circling lanes
Of light; red Comets tossed their fiery manes
    O'er the land where we were dreaming!   30

Down from her eagle height smiled Liberty,
And waved her hand in sign of victory;
    The world approved, and everywhere,
    Except where growled the Russian bear,
    The brave, the good and just gave us their prayer,
        For the land where we were dreaming!

High o'er our heads a starry flag was seen,
Whose field was blanched, and spotless in its sheen;
    Chivalry's cross its union bears,
    And by his scars each vet'ran swears   40
    To bear it on in triumph through the wars,
        In the land where we were dreaming!

We fondly thought a Government was ours—
We challenged place among the world's great powers;
    We talk'd in sleep of rank, commission,
    Until so life-like grew the vision,
    That he who dared to doubt but met derision,
        In the land where we were dreaming!

A figure came among us as we slept—
At first he knelt, then slowly rose and wept;   50
    Then gathering up a thousand spears,
    He swept across the field of Mars,
    Then bowed farewell, and walked behind the stars,
        From the land where we were dreaming!

We looked again, another figure still
Gave hope, and nerved each individual will;
    Erect he stood, as clothed with power;
    Self-poised, he seemed to rule the hour,

With firm, majestic sway—of strength a tower,
    In the land where we were dreaming!   60

As while great Jove, in bronze, a warder god,
Gazed eastward from the Forum where he stood,
    Rome felt herself secure and free—
    So Richmond, we, on guard for thee,
    Beheld a bronzèd hero, god-like Lee,
        In the land where we were dreaming!

As wakes the soldier when the alarum calls—
As wakes the mother when her infant falls—
    As starts the traveler when around
    His sleepy couch the fire-bells sound—   70
    So woke our nation with a single bound—
        In the land where we were dreaming!

Woe! woe! is us, the startled mothers cried,
While we have slept, our noble sons have died!
    Woe! woe! is us, how strange and sad,
    That all our glorious visions fled,
    Have left us nothing real but our dead,
        In the land where we were dreaming!

And are they really dead, our martyred slain?
No, Dreamers! Morn shall bid them rise again;   80
    From every plain—from every height—
    On which they seemed to die for right,
    Their gallant spirits shall renew the fight,
        In the land where we were dreaming!

Unconquered still in soul, tho' now o'er-run,
In peace, in war, the battle's just begun!
    Once this Thyestean banquet o'er,
    Grown strong the few who bide the hour,
    Shall rise and hurl its drunken guests from power,
        In the land where we were dreaming!   90

DANIEL BEDINGER LUCAS

noted for 2 poems

very minor

Catholic priest

ABRAM JOSEPH RYAN

Abram Joseph Ryan was born in Norfolk, Virginia, August 15, 1836. His parents, John Thady and Mary Hartigan Ryan, had emigrated from Ireland a few years before. The family soon moved to St. Louis, where Abram was educated in Catholic schools, and then to Maryland, where he was educated for the priesthood. He was ordained shortly before the Civil War, and he served intermittently as chaplain throughout the conflict: at Nashville and Clarksville, Tennessee; at New Orleans, where in the winter of 1862–63 he ministered to sufferers of the smallpox epidemic. After the war he edited *The Star*, a weekly Catholic paper in New Orleans, but he soon relinquished this to wander over the South: to Knoxville for a few months, then to Augusta, where he founded the weekly *Banner of the South*. For this magazine he wrote most of his Civil War poems. He went from Augusta to Mobile, where he was pastor of St. Mary's Church, but in 1880 he resigned to travel in Europe and to lecture in the North with the purpose of aiding certain Southern charities. In Baltimore was published his *Poems: Patriotic, Religious, and Miscellaneous;* in fifteen years it went through twenty-five editions. Although a few additional poems were added in later editions, this was his only volume of poetry. Later he entered a Franciscan monastery in Louisville, where he was writing a life of Christ at the time of his death, April 22, 1886.

THE CONQUERED BANNER[86]

Always Remembered

Furl to flag

Furl that Banner, for 'tis weary;
Round its staff 'tis drooping dreary;
    Furl it, fold it, it is best:
For there's not a man to wave it,
And there's not a sword to save it,
And there's not one left to lave it
In the blood which heroes gave it;
And its foes now scorn and brave it;
    Furl it, hide it—let it rest.

Take that Banner down, 'tis tattered;   10
Broken is its staff and shattered;
And the valiant hosts are scattered,
  Over whom it floated high.
Oh! 'tis hard for us to fold it;
Hard to think there's none to hold it;
Hard that those, who once unrolled it,
  Now must furl it with a sigh.

Furl that Banner—furl it sadly;
Once ten thousands hailed it gladly,
And ten thousands wildly, madly,   20
  Swore it should forever wave;
Swore that foeman's sword should never
Hearts like theirs entwined dissever,
Till that flag should float forever
  O'er their freedom, or their grave!

Furl it! for the hands that grasped it,
And the hearts that fondly clasped it,
  Cold and dead are lying low;
And that Banner—it is trailing!
While around it sounds the wailing   30
  Of its people in their woe.

For, though conquered, they adore it!
Love the cold, dead hands that bore it!
Weep for those who fell before it!
Pardon those who trailed and tore it!
But, oh! wildly they deplore it,
  Now who furl and fold it so.

Furl that Banner! True, 'tis gory,
Yet 'tis wreathed around with glory,
And 'twill live in song and story,   40
  Though its folds are in the dust:
For its fame on brightest pages,

Penned by poets and by sages,
Shall go sounding down the ages—
    Furl its folds though now we must.

Furl that Banner, softly, slowly,
Treat it gently—it is holy—
    For it droops above the dead.
Touch it not—unfold it never,
Let it droop there, furled forever,   50
    For its people's hopes are dead!

THE SWORD OF ROBERT LEE

Forth from its scabbard pure and bright,
    Flashed the sword of Lee!
Far in the front of the deadly fight
High o'er the brave in the cause of Right
Its stainless sheen like a beacon light
    Led us to Victory.

    Out of its scabbard where full long
        It slumbered peacefully,—
    Roused from its rest by the battle's song,
    Shielding the feeble, smiting the strong,   10
    Guarding the right, avenging the wrong,
        Gleamed the sword of Lee.

Forth from its scabbard high in air
    Beneath Virginia's sky—
And they who saw it gleaming there
And knew who bore it knelt to swear,
That where that sword led, they would dare
    To follow and to die.

    Out of its scabbard!—never hand
        Waved sword from stain as free,   20
    Nor purer sword led braver band,

Nor braver bled for a brighter land,
Nor brighter land had a Cause so grand,
Nor cause a chief like Lee.

Forth from its scabbard! how we prayed,
That sword might victor be;—
And when our triumph was delayed,
And many a heart grew sore afraid,
We still hoped on while gleamed the blade
Of noble Robert Lee.   30

Forth from its scabbard! all in vain
Bright flashed the sword of Lee;—
'Tis shrouded now in its sheath again,
It sleeps the sleep of our noble slain;
Defeated yet without a stain,
Proudly and peacefully.

A LAND WITHOUT RUINS

"A land without ruins is a land without memories—a land without
memories is a land without history. A land that wears a laurel crown may
be fair to see; but twine a few sad cypress leaves around the brow of any
land, and be that land barren, beautiless and bleak, it becomes lovely in
its consecrated coronet of sorrow, and it wins the sympathy of the heart
and of history. Crowns of roses fade—crowns of thorns endure. Cal-
varies and crucifixions take deepest hold of humanity—the triumphs of
might are transient—they pass and are forgotten—the sufferings of right
are graven deepest on the chronicle of nations."

Yes, give me the land where the ruins are spread,
And the living tread light on the hearts of the dead;
Yes, give me a land that is blest by the dust
And bright with the deeds of the down-trodden just.
Yes, give me the land where the battle's red blast
Has flashed to the future the fame of the past;
Yes, give me the land that hath legends and lays
That tell of the memories of long vanished days;
Yes, give me a land that hath story and song,
Enshrine the strife of the right with the wrong;   10

Yes, give me a land with a grave in each spot
And names in the graves that shall not be forgot;
Yes, give me the land of the wreck and the tomb—
There is grandeur in graves—there is glory in gloom;
For out of the gloom future brightness is born
As after the night comes the sunrise of morn;
And the graves of the dead with the grass overgrown
May yet form the footstool of liberty's throne,
And each single wreck in the war-path of might,
Shall yet be a rock in the temple of right.   20

SONG OF THE MYSTIC

I walk down the Valley of Silence,—
   Down the dim, voiceless valley alone!
And I hear not the fall of a footstep
   Around me save God's and my own;
And the hush of my heart is as holy
   As hovers where angels have flown!

Long ago—was I weary of voices
   Whose music my heart could not win;
Long ago I was weary of noises
   That fretted my soul with their din;   10
Long ago was I weary of places
   Where I met but the human—and sin.

I walked in the world with the worldly;
   I craved what the world never gave;
And I said: "In the world each Ideal,
   That shines like a star on life's wave;
Is wrecked on the shores of the Real,
   And sleeps like a dream in a grave."

And still did I pine for the Perfect,
   And still found the False with the True;   20
I sought 'mid the Human for Heaven,
   But caught a mere glimpse of its Blue:

And I wept when the clouds of the mortal
   Veiled even that glimpse from my view.

And I toiled on heart-tired of the Human;
   And I moaned 'mid the mazes of men;
Till I knelt long ago at an altar
   And heard a voice call me;—since then
I walk down the Valley of Silence
   That lies far beyond mortal ken.   30

Do you ask what I found in the Valley?
   'Tis my Trysting Place with the Divine.
And I fell at the feet of the Holy,
   And above me a voice said: "Be mine."
And there arose from the depths of my spirit
   An echo—"My faith shall be thine."

Do you ask how I live in the Valley?
   I weep—and I dream—and I pray.
But my tears are as sweet as the dewdrops
   That fall on the roses in May;   40
And my prayer, like a perfume from Censers,
   Ascendeth to God night and day.

In the hush of the Valley of Silence
   I dream all the songs that I sing;
And the music floats down the dim Valley,
   Till each finds a word for a wing,
That to hearts, like the Dove of the Deluge,
   A message of Peace they may bring.

But far on the deep there are billows
   That never shall break on the beach;   50
And I have heard songs in the Silence
   That never shall float into speech;
And I have had dreams in the Valley
   Too lofty for language to reach.

And I have seen Thoughts in the Valley,—
　　Ah me! how my spirit was stirred!
And they wear holy veils on their faces,—
　　Their footsteps can scarcely be heard:
They pass through the Valley, like Virginis
　　Too pure for the touch of a word!　　　　　　　　　60

Do you ask me the place of the Valley?
　　Ye hearts that are harrowed by Care!
It lieth afar between mountains
　　And God and his angels are there:
And one is the dark mount of Sorrow,
　　And one,—the bright mountain of Prayer!

SIDNEY LANIER

Sidney Clopton Lanier, the oldest of three children of Robert
Sampson and Mary Jane Anderson Lanier, was born in Macon,
Georgia, February 3, 1842. His father was a lawyer, his grandfather a moderately wealthy hotelkeeper; among his earlier
ancestors probably were the famous musicians who enjoyed
the patronage of Queen Elizabeth and the Stuarts; one of them,
Nicholas Lanier, wrote music for the masques of Ben Jonson,
and another was most lavishly praised by Samuel Pepys as
"the best company for musique I ever was in in my life."
Sidney's parents were more prosaic people, but his father was
a well-read man chiefly noted for his "courtesy and refinement,"
and his mother was an accomplished musician. Love for music
was the dominant influence in Sidney's early life: "he could not remember the time when he could not play upon almost any musical instrument." He received his early education in a private
academy and in 1857 he entered the sophomore class of Oglethorpe University. Although it seemed to him later "a farcical
college," Oglethorpe and at least one professor, Dr. James
Woodrow, awakened in Lanier a desire for more intensive
study. After graduation he taught there one year, wavering
between the strong desires to be a professional musician, to
study in Germany, or to please his family by following the
conventional study of law.

This indecision was settled for him by war, and in April, 1861, he joined the Macon Volunteers. He fought in the seven days' battle that culminated with Malvern Hill, and served, with his brother Clifford, as mounted scout along the James River. In August, 1864, he was transferred to a blockade-runner. On November 2 he was captured and imprisoned at Point Lookout, Maryland, for four months. While in prison he entertained his comrades by playing on his flute. There he formed a lasting friendship with John Banister Tabb, and translated a few poems from the German of Heine and Herder. There also the tuberculosis from which he never recovered made its appearance, and he almost died during the voyage south to Virginia. After he recovered he was forced to make the long journey through the Carolinas to Macon chiefly on foot.

Life was hard for him. Yet he decided that, come what might, he would not settle himself "down to be a third-rate struggling lawyer for the balance of my little life." In 1867 his novel *Tiger Lilies* was published; in December of that year he married Mary Day. He continued to write poetry and music, but writing paid him so little that he was forced to tutor in private families and to work as a hotel clerk in Montgomery. The days of reconstruction he called "dark raven days," and he wrote to Bayard Taylor that "pretty much the whole of life has been merely not dying." He had decided to practice law, and was studying in his father's office, when he suffered his first hemorrhage of the lungs, and he began, with a trip to Texas, his frequent journeys in search of a place where he might regain his health and make a living.

In 1873 he became the flutist in the Peabody Orchestra in Baltimore, and for three years made a sparse living through music. His poems "Corn" and "The Symphony" led his friend Bayard Taylor to ask Lanier to write the Centennial Cantata for the Philadelphia Exposition of 1876, a commission that brought him much favorable attention, which was increased with the publication of his first book of poems in the same year. In 1879 he became lecturer in English literature at Johns Hopkins University, and began the critical studies on prosody and literature that were published as *The Science of English Verse* (1880) and *The English Novel* (1883). Also, to eke out his small salary, he wrote a group of "potboilers" for children.

But he was overtaxing a frail physique, and he died of tuberculosis on September 7, 1881.

SONG FOR "THE JACQUERIE"[87]

The hound was cuffed, the hound was kicked,
O' the ears was cropped, o' the tail was nicked,
(*All.*)   Oo-hoo-o, howled the hound.
The hound into his kennel crept;
He rarely wept, he never slept.
His mouth he always open kept
        Licking his bitter wound,
            The hound,
(*All.*)   U-lu-lo, *howled the hound.*

A star upon his kennel shone   10
That showed the hound a meat-bare bone.
(*All.*)   O hungry was the hound!
The hound had but a churlish wit.
He seized the bone, he crunched, he bit.
"An thou wert Master, I had slit
        Thy throat with a huge wound,"
            Quo' hound.
(*All.*)   O, angry was the hound.

The star in castle-window shone,
The Master lay abed, alone.   20
(*All.*)   Oh ho, why not? quo' hound.
He leapt, he seized the throat, he tore
The Master, head from neck, to floor,
And rolled the head i' the kennel door,
        And fled and salved his wound,
            Good hound!
(*All.*)   U-lu-lo, *howled the hound.*

Love = sole music master [handwritten]

THE SYMPHONY[88]

takes up theme of trade + business [handwritten]

"O Trade! O Trade! would thou wert dead!
The Time needs heart—'tis tired of head:
We're all for love," the violins said.

love of money [handwritten]

"Of what avail the rigorous tale
Of bill for coin and box for bale?
Grant thee, O Trade! thine uttermost hope:
Level red gold with blue sky-slope,
And base it deep as devils grope:

oppression of poor [handwritten]

When all's done, what hast thou won
Of the only sweet that's under the sun?   10
Ay, canst thou buy a single sigh
Of true love's least, least ecstasy?"
Then, with a bridegroom's heart-beats trembling,
All the mightier strings assembling
Ranged them on the violins' side
As when the bridegroom leads the bride,
And, heart in voice, together cried:
"Yea, what avail the endless tale
Of gain by cunning and plus by sale?
Look up the land, look down the land   20
The poor, the poor, the poor, they stand
Wedged by the pressing of Trade's hand
Against an inward-opening door
That pressure tightens evermore:
They sigh a monstrous foul-air sigh
For the outside leagues of liberty,
Where Art, sweet lark, translates the sky
Into a heavenly melody.
'Each day, all day' (these poor folks say),
'In the same old year-long, drear-long way,   30
We weave in the mills and heave in the kilns,
We sieve mine-meshes under the hills,
And thieve much gold from the Devil's bank tills,
To relieve, O God, what manner of ills?—

The beasts, they hunger, and eat, and die;
And so do we, and the world's a sty;
Hush, fellow-swine: why nuzzle and cry?
Swinehood hath no remedy
Say many men, and hasten by,
Clamping the nose and blinking the eye.   40
But who said once, in the lordly tone,
Man shall not live by bread alone
But all that cometh from the Throne?
    Hath God said so?
    But Trade saith *No:*
And the kilns and the curt-tongued mills say *Go!*
There's plenty that can, if you can't: we know.
Move out, if you think you're underpaid.
The poor are prolific; we're not afraid;
    Trade is trade.'"   50
Thereat this passionate protesting
Meekly changed, and softened till
It sank to sad requesting
And suggesting sadder still:
"And oh, if men might some time see
How piteous-false the poor decree
That trade no more than trade must be!
Does business mean, *Die, you—live, I?*
Then 'Trade is trade' but sings a lie:
'Tis only war grown miserly.   60
If business is battle, name it so;
War-crimes less will shame it so,
And widows less will blame it so.
Alas, for the poor to have some part
In yon sweet living lands of Art,
Makes problem not for head, but heart.
Vainly might Plato's brain revolve it:
Plainly the heart of a child could solve it."

And then, as when from words that seem but rude
We pass to silent pain that sits abroad   70

Back in our heart's great dark and solitude,
So sank the strings to gentle throbbing
Of long chords change-marked with sobbing—
Motherly sobbing, not distinctlier heard
Than half wing-openings of the sleeping bird,
Some dream of danger to her young hath stirred.
Then stirring and demurring ceased, and lo!
Every least ripple of the strings' song-flow
Died to a level with each level bow
And made a great chord tranquil-surfaced so,   80
As a brook beneath his curving bank doth go
To linger in the sacred dark and green
Where many boughs the still pool overlean
And many leaves make shadow with their sheen.
 But presently
A velvet flute-note fell down pleasantly
Upon the bosom of that harmony,
And sailed and sailed incessantly,
As if a petal from a wild-rose blown
Had fluttered down upon that pool of tone   90
And boatwise dropped o' the convex side
And floated down the glassy tide
And clarified and glorified
The solemn spaces where the shadows bide.
From the warm concave of that fluted note
Somewhat, half song, half odor, forth did float,
As if a rose might somehow be a throat:
"When Nature from her far-off glen
Flutes her soft messages to men,
  The flute can say them o'er again;   100
  Yea, Nature, singing sweet and lone,
Breathes through life's strident polyphone
The flute-voice in the world of tone.
  Sweet friends,
  Man's love ascends
To finer and diviner ends
Than man's mere thought e'er comprehends

For I, e'en I,
As here I lie,
A petal on a harmony,   110
Demand of Science whence and why
Man's tender pain, man's inward cry,
When he doth gaze on earth and sky?
I am not overbold:
      I hold
Full powers from Nature manifold.
I speak for each no-tonguéd tree
That, spring by spring, doth nobler be,
And dumbly and most wistfully
His mighty prayerful arms outspreads   120
Above men's oft-unheeding heads,
And his big blessing downward sheds.
I speak for all-shaped blooms and leaves,
Lichens on stones and moss on eaves,
Grasses and grains in ranks and sheaves;
Broad-fronded ferns and keen-leaved canes,
And briery mazes bounding lanes,
And marsh-plants, thirsty-cupped for rains,
And milky stems and sugary veins;
For every long-armed woman-vine   130
That round a piteous tree doth twine;
For passionate odors, and divine
Pistils, and petals crystalline;
All purities of shady springs,
All shynesses of film-winged things
That fly from tree-trunks and bark-rings;
All modesties of mountain-fawns
That leap to covert from wild lawns,
And tremble if the day but dawns;
All sparklings of small beady eyes   140
Of birds, and sidelong glances wise
Wherewith the jay hints tragedies;
All piquancies of prickly burs,
And smoothnesses of downs and furs

Of eiders and of minevers;
All limpid honeys that do lie
At stamen-bases, nor deny
The humming-birds' fine roguery,
Bee-thighs, nor any butterfly;
All gracious curves of slender wings,   150
Bark-mottlings, fibre-spiralings,
Fern-wavings and leaf-flickerings;
Each dial-marked leaf and flower-bell
Wherewith in every lonesome dell
Time to himself his hours doth tell;
All tree-sounds, rustlings of pine-cones,
Wind-sighings, doves' melodious moans,
And night's unearthly under-tones;
All placid lakes and waveless deeps,
All cool reposing mountain-steeps,   160
Vale-calms and tranquil lotos-sleeps;—
Yea, all fair forms, and sounds, and lights,
And warmths, and mysteries, and mights,
Of Nature's utmost depths and heights,
—These doth my timid tongue present,
Their mouthpiece and leal instrument
And servant, all love-eloquent.
I heard, when '*All for love*' the violins cried:
So, Nature calls through all her system wide,
Give me thy love, O man, so long denied.   170
Much time is run, and man hath changed his ways,
Since Nature, in the antique fable-days,
Was hid from man's true love by proxy fays,
False fauns and rascal gods that stole her praise.
The nymphs, cold creatures of man's colder brain,
Chilled Nature's streams till man's warm heart was fain
Never to lave its love in them again.
Later, a sweet Voice *Love thy neighbor* said;
Then first the bounds of neighborhood outspread
Beyond all confines of old ethnic dread.   180
Vainly the Jew might wag his covenant head:

'*All men are neighbors*,' so the sweet Voice said.
So, when man's arms had circled all man's race,
The liberal compass of his warm embrace
Stretched bigger yet in the dark bounds of space;
With hands a-grope he felt smooth Nature's grace,
Drew her to breast and kissed her sweetheart face:
Yea man found neighbors in great hills and trees
And streams and clouds and suns and birds and bees
And throbbed with neighbor-loves in loving these.   190
But oh, the poor! the poor! the poor!
That stand by the inward-opening door
Trade's hand doth tighten ever more,
And sigh their monstrous foul-air sigh
For the outside hills of liberty,
Where Nature spreads her wild blue sky
For Art to make into melody!
Thou Trade! thou king of the modern days!
        Change thy ways,
        Change thy ways;   200
Let the sweaty laborers file
        A little while,
        A little while,
Where Art and Nature sing and smile.
Trade! is thy heart all dead, all dead?
And hast thou nothing but a head?
I'm all for heart," the flute-voice said,
And into sudden silence fled,
Like as a blush that while 'tis red
Dies to a still, still white instead.   210

    Thereto a thrilling calm succeeds,
Till presently the silence breeds
A little breeze among the reeds
That seems to blow by sea-marsh weeds:
Then from the gentle stir and fret
Sings out the melting clarionet,

Like as a lady sings while yet
Her eyes with salty tears are wet.
"O Trade! O Trade!" the Lady said,
"I too will wish thee utterly dead   220
If all thy heart is in thy head.
For O my God! and O my God!
What shameful ways have women trod
At beckoning of Trade's golden rod!
Alas when sighs are traders' lies,
And heart's-ease eyes and violet eyes
          Are merchandise!
O purchased lips that kiss with pain!
O cheeks coin-spotted with smirch and stain!
O trafficked hearts that break in twain!   230
—And yet what wonder at my sisters' crime?
So hath Trade withered up Love's sinewy prime,
Men love not women as in olden time.
Ah, not in these cold merchantable days
Deem men their life an opal gray, where plays
The one red Sweet of gracious ladies'-praise.
Now, comes a suitor with sharp prying eye—
Says, *Here, you Lady, if you'll sell, I'll buy:*
Come, heart for heart—a trade? What! weeping? why?
Shame on such wooers' dapper mercery!   240
I would my lover kneeling at my feet
In humble manliness should cry, *O sweet!*
I know not if thy heart my heart will greet:
I ask not if thy love my love can meet:
Whate'er thy worshipful soft tongue shall say,
I'll kiss thine answer, be it yea or nay:
I do but know I love thee, and I pray
To be thy knight until my dying day.
Woe him that cunning trades in hearts contrives!
Base love good women to base loving drives.   250
If men loved larger, larger were our lives;
And wooed they nobler, won they nobler wives."

There thrust the bold straightforward horn
To battle for that lady lorn.
With heartsome voice of mellow scorn,
Like any knight in knighthood's morn.
   "Now comfort thee," said he,
      "Fair Lady.
For God shall right thy grievous wrong,
And man shall sing thee a true-love song,   260
Voiced in act his whole life long,
   Yea, all thy sweet life long,
      Fair Lady.
Where's he that craftily hath said,
The day of chivalry is dead?
I'll prove that lie upon his head,
   Or I will die instead,
      Fair Lady.
Is Honor gone into his grave?
Hath Faith become a caitiff knave,   270
And Selfhood turned into a slave
   To work in Mammon's cave,
      Fair Lady?
Will Truth's long blade ne'er gleam again?
Hath Giant Trade in dungeons slain
All great contempts of mean-got gain
   And hates of inward stain,
      Fair Lady?
For aye shall name and fame be sold,
And place be hugged for the sake of gold,   280
And smirch-robed Justice feebly scold
   At Crime all money-bold,
     Fair Lady?
Shall self-wrapt husbands aye forget
Kiss-pardons for the daily fret
Wherewith sweet wifely eyes are wet—
   Blind to lips kiss-wise set—
      Fair Lady?
Shall lovers higgle, heart for heart,

Till wooing grows a trading mart 290
Where much for little, and all for part,
   Make love a cheapening art,
       Fair Lady?
Shall woman scorch for a single sin
That her betrayer may revel in,
And she be burnt, and he but grin
   When that the flames begin,
       Fair Lady?
Shall ne'er prevail the woman's plea,
We maids would far, far whiter be 300
If that our eyes might sometimes see
   Men maids in purity,
       Fair Lady?
Shall Trade aye salve his conscience-aches
With jibes at Chivalry's old mistakes—
The wars that o'erhot knighthood makes
   For Christ's and ladies' sakes,
       Fair Lady?
Now by each knight that e'er hath prayed
To fight like a man and love like a maid, 310
Since Pembroke's life, as Pembroke's blade,
   I' the scabbard, death was laid,
       Fair Lady,
I dare avouch my faith is bright
That God doth right and God hath might.
Nor time hath changed His hair to white,
   Nor His dear love to spite,
       Fair Lady.
I doubt no doubts: I strive, and shrive my clay,
And fight my fight in the patient modern way 320
For true love and for thee—ah me! and pray
   To be thy knight until my dying day,
       Fair Lady."
Made end that knightly horn, and spurred away
Into the thick of the melodious fray.

And then the hautboy played and smiled,
And sang like any large-eyed child,
Cool-hearted and all undefiled.
     "Huge Trade! he said,
"Would thou wouldst lift me on thy head   330
And run where'er my finger led!
Once said a Man—and wise was He—
Never shalt thou the heavens see,
Save as a little child thou be."
Then o'er sea-lashings of commingling tunes
The ancient wise bassoons,
     Like weird
     Gray-beard
Old harpers sitting on the high sea-dunes,
     Chanted runes: 340
"Bright-waved gain, gray-waved loss,
The sea of all doth lash and toss,
One wave forward and one across:
But now 'twas trough, now 'tis crest,
And worst doth foam and flash to best,
     And curst to blest.

Life! Life! thou sea-fugue, writ from east to west,
     Love, Love alone can pore
     On thy dissolving score
     Of harsh half-phrasings,   350
       Blotted ere writ,
     And double erasings
     Of chords most fit.

Yea, Love, sole music-master blest,
May read thy weltering palimpsest.
To follow Time's dying melodies through,
And never to lose the old in the new,
And ever to solve the discords true—
     Love alone can do.
And ever Love hears the poor-folks' crying,   360

And ever Love hears the women's sighing,
And ever sweet knighthood's death-defying,
And ever wise childhood's deep implying,
But never a trader's glozing and lying.

And yet shall Love himself be heard,
Though long deferred, though long deferred:
O'er the modern waste a dove hath whirred:
Music is Love in search of a word."

SONG OF THE CHATTAHOOCHEE[89]

Out of the hills of Habersham,
    Down the valleys of Hall,
I hurry amain to reach the plain,
Run the rapid and leap the fall,
Split at the rock and together again,
Accept my bed, or narrow or wide,
And flee from folly on every side
With a lover's pain to attain the plain
        Far from the hills of Habersham,
        Far from the valleys of Hall.   10

All down the hills of Habersham,
    All through the valleys of Hall,
The rushes cried *Abide, abide*,
The willful waterweeds held me thrall,
The laving laurel turned my tide,
The ferns and the fondling grass said *Stay*,
The dewberry dipped for to work delay,
And the little reeds sighed *Abide, abide*,
        Here in the hills of Habersham,
        Here in the valleys of Hall.   20

High o'er the hills of Habersham,
    Veiling the valleys of Hall,
The hickory told me manifold

Fair tales of shade, the poplar tall
Wrought me her shadowy self to hold,
The chestnut, the oak, the walnut, the pine,
Overleaning, with flickering meaning and sign,
Said, *Pass not, so cold, these manifold*
        Deep shades of the hills of Habersham,
        These glades in the valleys of Hall.   30

        And oft in the hills of Habersham,
        And oft in the valleys of Hall,
The white quartz shone, and the smooth brook-stone
Did bar me of passage with friendly brawl,
And many a luminous jewel lone
—Crystals clear or a-cloud with mist,
Ruby, garnet and amethyst—
Made lures with the lights of streaming stone
        In the clefts of the hills of Habersham,
        In the beds of the valleys of Hall.   40

        But oh, not the hills of Habersham,
        And oh, not the valleys of Hall
Avail: I am fain for to water the plain.
Downward the voices of Duty call—
Downward, to toil and be mixed with the main,
The dry fields burn, and the mills are to turn,
And a myriad flowers mortally yearn,
And the lordly main from beyond the plain
        Calls o'er the hills of Habersham,
        Calls through the valleys of Hall.   50

THE STIRRUP-CUP[90]

Death, thou'rt a cordial old and rare:
Look how compounded, with what care!
Time got his wrinkles reaping thee
Sweet herbs from all antiquity.

David to this distillage went,
Keats, and Gotama excellent,
Omar Khayyam, and Chaucer bright,
And Shakspere for a king-delight.

Then, Time, let not a drop be spilt:
Hand me the cup whene'er thou wilt: 10
'Tis thy rich stirrup-cup to me;
I'll drink it down right smilingly.

THE REVENGE OF HAMISH[91]

It was three slim does and a ten-tined buck in the bracken lay;
    And all of a sudden the sinister smell of a man,
    Awaft on a wind-shift, wavered and ran
Down the hill-side and sifted along through the bracken and
        passed that way.

Then Nan got a-tremble at nostril; she was the daintiest doe;
    In the print of her velvet flank on the velvet fern
    She reared, and rounded her ears in turn.
Then the buck leapt up, and his head as a king's to a crown
        did go

Full high in the breeze, and he stood as if Death had the form
        of a deer;
    And the two slim does long lazily stretching arose,   10
    For their day-dream slowlier came to a close,
Till they woke and were still, breath-bound with waiting and
        wonder and fear.

Then Alan the huntsman sprang over the hillock, the hounds
        shot by,
    The does and the ten-tined buck made a marvellous bound,
    The hounds swept after with never a sound,
But Alan loud winded his horn in sign that the quarry was nigh.

For at dawn of that day proud Maclean of Lochbuy to the hunt
    had waxed wild,
    And he cursed at old Alan till Alan fared off with the hounds
    For to drive him the deer to the lower glen-grounds:
"I will kill a red deer," quoth Maclean, "in the sight of the wife
    and the child."   20

So gayly he paced with the wife and the child to his chosen
    stand;
    But he hurried tall Hamish the henchman ahead: "Go turn,"—
    Cried Maclean—"if the deer seek to cross to the burn,
Do thou turn them to me: nor fail, lest thy back be red as thy
    hand."

Now hard-fortuned Hamish, half blown of his breath with the
    height of the hill,
    Was white in the face when the ten-tined buck and the does
    Drew leaping to burn-ward; huskily rose
His shouts, and his nether lip twitched, and his legs were
    o'er-weak for his will.

So the deer darted lightly by Hamish and bounded away to the
    burn.
    But Maclean never bating his watch tarried waiting below   30
    Still Hamish hung heavy with fear for to go
All the space of an hour; then he went, and his face was greenish
    and stern,

And his eye sat back in the socket, and shrunken the eye-balls
    shone,
    As withdrawn from a vision of deeds it were shame to see.
    "Now, now, grim henchman, what is 't with thee?"
Brake Maclean, and his wrath rose red as a beacon the wind
    hath upblown.

"Three does and a ten-tined buck made out," spoke Hamish,
    full mild,

"And I ran for to turn, but my breath it was blown, and they
    passed;
  I was weak, for ye called ere I broke me my fast."
Cried Maclean: "Now a ten-tined buck in the sight of the wife
    and the child   40

I had killed if the gluttonous kern had not wrought me a snail's
    own wrong!"
  Then he sounded, and down came kinsmen and clansmen all:
  "Ten blows, for ten tine, on his back let fall,
And reckon no stroke if the blood follow not at the bite of
    thong!"

So Hamish made bare, and took him his strokes; at the last he
    smiled.
  "Now I'll to the burn," quoth Maclean, "for it still may be,
  If a slimmer-paunched henchman will hurry with me,
I shall kill the ten-tined buck for a gift to the wife and the child!"

Then the clansmen departed, by this path and that; and over
    the hill
  Sped Maclean with an outward wrath for an inward shame;
  And that place of the lashing full quiet became;   51
And the wife and the child stood sad; and bloody-backed
    Hamish sat still.

But look! red Hamish has risen: quick about and about turns
    he.
  "There is none betwixt me and the crag-top!" he screams
    under breath.
  Then, livid as Lazarus lately from death,
He snatches the child from the mother, and clambers the crag
    toward the sea.

Now the mother drops breath; she is dumb, and her heart goes
    dead for a space,

Till the motherhood, mistress of death, shrieks, shrieks
     through the glen,
   And that place of the lashing is live with men,
And Maclean, and the gillie that told him, dash up in a desperate
     race.   60

Not a breath's time for asking; an eye-glance reveals all the tale
     untold.
   They follow mad Hamish afar up the crag toward the sea,
   And the lady cries: "Clansmen, run for a fee!—
Yon. castle and lands to the two first hands that shall hook him
     and hold

Fast Hamish back from the brink!"—and ever she flies up the
     steep,
   And the clansmen pant, and they sweat, and they hostle and
     strain.
   But, mother, 'tis vain; but, father, 'tis vain;
Stern Hamish stands bold on the brink, and dangles the child
     o'er the deep.

Now a faintness falls on the men that run, and they all stand
     still.
   And the wife prays Hamish as if he were God, on her
     knees,   70
   Crying: "Hamish! O Hamish! but please, but please
For to spare him!" and Hamish still dangles the child, with a
     wavering will.

On a sudden he turns; with a sea-hawk scream, and a gibe, and
     a song,
   Cries: "So; I will spare ye the child if, in sight of ye all,
   Ten blows on Maclean's bare back shall fall,
And ye reckon no stroke if the blood follow not at the bite of
     the thong!"

Then Maclean he set hardly his tooth to his lip that his tooth
     was red,

Breathed short for a space, said: "Nay, but it never shall be!
Let me hurl off the damnable hound in the sea!"
But the wife: "Can Hamish go fish us the child from the sea,
if dead? 80

Say yea!—Let them lash *me*, Hamish?"—"Nay!"—"Husband,
the lashing will heal;
But, oh, who will heal me the bonny sweet bairn in his grave?
Could ye cure me my heart with the death of a knave?
Quick! Love! I will bare thee—so—kneel!" Then Maclean
'gan slowly to kneel

With never a word, till presently downward he jerked to the
earth.
Then the henchman—he that smote Hamish—would tremble
and lag;
"Strike, hard!" quoth Hamish, full stern, from the crag;
Then he struck him, and "One!" sang Hamish, and danced
with the child in his mirth.

And no man spake beside Hamish; he counted each stroke with
a song.
When the last stroke fell, then he moved him a pace down the
height, 90
And he held forth the child in the heartaching sight
Of the mother, and looked all pitiful grave, as repenting a
wrong.

And there as the motherly arms stretched out with the thanks-
giving prayer—
And there as the mother crept up with a fearful swift pace,
Till her finger nigh felt of the bairnie's face—
In a flash fierce Hamish turned round and lifted the child in
the air,

And sprang with the child in his arms from the horrible height
in the sea,

Shrill screeching, "Revenge!" in the wind-rush; and pallid
    Maclean,
  Age-feeble with anger and impotent pain,
Crawled up on the crag, and lay flat, and locked hold of dead
    roots of a tree—   100

And gazed hungrily o'er, and the blood from his back drip-
    dripped in the brine,
  And a sea-hawk flung down a skeleton fish as he flew,
  And the mother stared white on the waste of blue,
And the wind drove a cloud to seaward, and the sun began to
    shine.

HYMNS OF THE MARSHES [92]

I. SUNRISE [93]

unfinished

In my sleep I was fain of their fellowship, fain
  Of the live-oak, the marsh, and the main.
The little green leaves would not let me alone in my sleep;
Up-breathed from the marshes, a message of range and of sweep,
Interwoven with waftures of wild sea-liberties, drifting,
    Came through the lapped leaves sifting, sifting,
        Came to the gates of sleep.
Then my thoughts, in the dark of the dungeon-keep
Of the Castle of Captives hid in the City of Sleep,
Upstarted, by twos and by threes assembling:
    The gates of sleep fell a-trembling   10
Like as the lips of a lady that forth falter *yes*,
        Shaken with happiness:
    The gates of sleep stood wide.

*norfork
florida
ga
marshes*

I have waked, I have come, my beloved! I might not abide:
I have come ere the dawn, O beloved, my live-oaks, to hide
    In your gospelling glooms,—to be
As a lover in heaven, the marsh my marsh and the sea my sea.

Tell me, sweet burly-bark'd, man-bodied Tree
That mine arms in the dark are embracing, dost know   20
From what fount are these tears at thy feet which flow?
They rise not from reason, but deeper inconsequent deeps.
      Reason's not one that weeps.
    What logic of greeting lies
Betwixt dear over-beautiful trees and the rain of the eyes?

O cunning green leaves, little masters! like as ye gloss
All the dull-tissued dark with your luminous darks that emboss
The vague blackness of night into pattern and plan,
      So,
  (But would I could know, but would I could know,)   30
With your question embroid'ring the dark of the question of
    man,—
So, with your silences purfling this silence of man
While his cry to the dead for some knowledge is under the ban,
      Under the ban,—
      So, ye have wrought me
Designs on the night of our knowledge,—yea, ye have taught
    me,
      So,
    That haply we know somewhat more than we know.

      Ye lispers, whisperers, singers in storms,
      Ye consciences murmuring faiths under forms,   40
      Ye ministers meet for each passion that grieves,
      Friendly, sisterly, sweetheart leaves,
Oh, rain me down from your darks that contain me
Wisdoms ye winnow from winds that pain me,—
Sift down tremors of sweet-within-sweet
That advise me of more than they bring,—repeat
Me the woods-smell that swiftly but now brought breath
From the heaven-side bank of the river of death,—
    Teach me the terms of silence,—preach me
    The passion of patience,—sift me,—impeach me,—   50
      And there, oh there

As ye hang with your myriad palms upturned in the air,
          Pray me a myriad prayer.

     My gossip, the owl,—is it thou
That out of the leaves of the low-hanging bough,
     As I pass to the beach, art stirred?
       Dumb woods, have ye uttered a bird?
       . . . .

Reverend Marsh, low-couched along the sea,
  Old chemist, rapt in alchemy,
     Distilling silence,—lo,   60
That which our father-age had died to know—
  The menstruum that dissolves all matter—thou
Hast found it: for this silence, filling now
The globéd clarity of receiving space,
This solves us all: man, matter, doubt, disgrace,
Death, love, sin, sanity,
Must in yon silence' clear solution lie.
Too clear! That crystal nothing who'll peruse?
The blackest night could bring us brighter news.
Yet precious qualities of silence haunt   70
Round these vast margins, ministrant.
Oh, if thy soul's at latter gasp for space,
With trying to breathe no bigger than thy race
Just to be fellow'd, when that thou hast found
No man with room, or grace enough of bound
To entertain that New thou tell'st, thou art,—
'Tis here, 'tis here thou canst unhand thy heart
And breathe it free, and breathe it free,
By rangy marsh, in lone sea-liberty.

The tide's at full: the marsh with flooded streams   80
Glimmers, a limpid labyrinth of dreams.
Each winding creek in grave entrancement lies
A rhapsody of morning-stars. The skies
Shine scant with one forked galaxy,—
The marsh brags ten: looped on his breast they lie.

Oh, what if a sound should be made!
Oh, what if a bound should be laid
To this bow-and-string tension of beauty and silence a-spring,—
To the bend of beauty the bow, or the hold of silence the string!
I fear me, I fear me yon dome of diaphanous gleam   90
Will break as a bubble o'er-blown in a dream,—
Yon dome of too-tenuous tissues of space and of night,
Over-weighted with stars, over-freighted with light,
Over-sated with beauty and silence, will seem
　　But a bubble that broke in a dream,
If a bound of degree to this grace be laid,
　　　　Or a sound or a motion made.

But no: it is made: list! somewhere,—mystery, where?
　　　　In the leaves? in the air?
In my heart? is a motion made: 100
'Tis a motion of dawn, like a flicker of shade on shade.
In the leaves 'tis palpable: low multitudinous stirring
Upwinds through the woods; the little ones, softly conferring,
Have settled my lord's to be looked for; so; they are still;
But the air and my heart and the earth are a-thrill,—
And look where the wild duck sails round the bend of the river,—
　　And look where a passionate shiver
　　Expectant is bending the blades
Of the marsh-grass in serial shimmers and shades,—
And invisible wings, fast fleeting, fast fleeting,   110
　　　　Are beating
The dark overhead as my heart beats,—and steady and free
Is the ebb-tide flowing from marsh to sea—
　　(Run home, little streams,
　With your lapfulls of stars and dreams),—
And a sailor unseen is hoisting a-peak,
For list, down the inshore curve of the creek
　　How merrily flutters the sail,—
And lo, in the East! Will the East unveil?
The East is unveiled, the East hath confessed   120
A flush: 'tis dead; 'tis alive: 'tis dead, ere the West

Was aware of it: nay, 'tis abiding, 'tis unwithdrawn:
   Have a care, sweet Heaven! 'Tis Dawn.

Now a dream of a flame through that dream of a flush is up rolled:
   To the zenith ascending, a dome of undazzling gold
Is builded, in shape as a bee-hive, from out of the sea:
The hive is of gold undazzling, but oh, the Bee,
   The star-fed Bee, the build-fire Bee,
   Of dazzling gold is the great Sun-Bee
That shall flash from the hive-hole over the sea.   130

    Yet now the dew-drop, now the morning gray,
    Shall live their little lucid sober day
    Ere with the sun their souls exhale away.
Now in each pettiest personal sphere of dew
The summ'd morn shines complete as in the blue
Big dew-drop of all heaven: with these lit shrines
O'er-silvered to the farthest sea-confines,
The sacramental marsh one pious plain
Of worship lies. Peace to the ante-reign
Of Mary Morning, blissful mother mild,   140
Minded of nought but peace, and of a child.
Not slower than Majesty moves, for a mean and a measure
Of motion,—not faster than dateless Olympian leisure
Might pace with unblown ample garments from pleasure to
              pleasure,—
The wave-serrate sea-rim sinks unjarring, unreeling,
    Forever revealing, revealing, revealing,
Edgewise, bladewise, halfwise, wholewise,—'tis done!
      Good-morrow, lord Sun!
With several voice, with ascription one,
The woods and the marsh and the sea and my soul   150
Unto thee, whence the glittering stream of all morrows doth roll,
Cry good and past-good and most heavenly morrow, lord Sun.

O Artisan born in the purple,—Workman Heat,—
Parter of passionate atoms that travail to meet

And be mixed in the death-cold oneness,—innermost Guest
At the marriage of elements,—fellow of publicans,—blest
King in the blouse of flame, that loiterest o'er
The idle skies yet laborest fast evermore,—
Thou, in the fine forge-thunder, thou, in the beat
Of the heart of a man, thou Motive,—Laborer Heat: 160
Yea, Artist, thou, of whose art yon sea's all news,
With his inshore greens and manifold mid-sea blues,
Pearl-glint, shell-tint, ancientest perfectest hues
Ever shaming the maidens,—lily and rose
Confess thee, and each mild flame that glows
In the clarified virginal bosoms of stones that shine,
       It is thine, it is thine:

Thou chemist of storms, whether driving the winds a-swirl
Or a-flicker the subtiler essences polar that whirl
In the magnet earth,—yea, thou with a storm for a heart,   170
Rent with debate, many-spotted with question, part
From part oft sundered, yet ever a globéd light,
Yet ever the artist, ever more large and bright
Than the eye of a man may avail of:—manifold One,
I must pass from thy face, I must pass from the face of the Sun:
Old Want is awake and agog, every wrinkle a-frown;
The worker must pass to his work in the terrible town:
But I fear not, nay, and I fear not the thing to be done;
   I am strong with the strength of my lord the Sun:
How dark, how dark soever the race that must needs be run, 180
       I am lit with the Sun.

Oh, never the mast-high run of the seas
      Of traffic shall hide thee,
Never the hell-colored smoke of the factories
      Hide thee,
Never the reek of the time's fen-politics
      Hide thee,
And ever my heart through the night shall with knowledge
      abide thee,
And ever by day shall my spirit, as one that hath tried thee,

Labor, at leisure, in art,—till yonder beside thee   190
   My soul shall float, friend Sun,
      The day being done.

II. INDIVIDUALITY [94]

Sail on, sail on, fair cousin Cloud:
Oh loiter hither from the sea.
      Still-eyed and shadow-brow'd,
Steal off from yon far-drifting crowd,
And come and brood upon the marsh with me.

Yon laboring low horizon-smoke,
Yon stringent sail, toil not for thee
      Nor me; did heaven's stroke
The whole deep with drown'd commerce choke,
No pitiless tease of risk or bottomry   10

Would to thy rainy office close
Thy will, or lock mine eyes from tears,
      Part wept for traders'-woes,
Part for that ventures mean as those
In issue bind such sovereign hopes and fears.

—Lo, Cloud, thy downward countenance stares
Blank on the blank-faced marsh, and thou
      Mindest of dark affairs;
Thy substance seems a warp of cares;
Like late wounds run the wrinkles on thy brow.   20

Well may'st thou pause, and gloom, and stare,
A visible conscience: I arraign
      Thee, criminal Cloud, of rare
Contempts on Mercy, Right, and Prayer,—
Of murders, arsons, thefts,—and of nameless stain.

(Yet though life's logic grow as gray
As thou, my soul's not in eclipse.)

Cold Cloud, but yesterday
Thy lightning slew a child at play,
And then a priest with prayers upon his lips   30

For his enemies, and then a bright
Lady that did but ope the door
   Upon the storming night
To let a beggar in,—strange spite,—
And then thy sulky rain refused to pour

Till thy quick torch a barn had burned
Where twelve months' store of victual lay,
   A widow's sons had earned;
Which done, thy floods with winds returned,—
The river raped their little herd away.   40

What myriad righteous errands high
Thy flames *might* run on! In that hour
   Thou slewest the child, oh why
Not rather slay Calamity,
Breeder of Pain and Doubt, infernal Power?

Or why not plunge thy blades about
Some maggot politician throng
   Swarming to parcel out
The body of a land, and rout
The maw-conventicle, and ungorge Wrong?   50

> *What the cloud doeth*
> *The Lord knoweth,*
> *The cloud knoweth not.*
> *What the artist doeth,*
> *The Lord knoweth;*
> *Knoweth the artist not?*

Well-answered!—O dear artists, ye
—Whether in forms of curve or hue
   Or tone your gospels be—

Say wrong *This work is not of me,*   60
But God: it is not true, it is not true.

Awful is Art because 'tis free.
The artist trembles o'er his plan
        Where men his Self must see.
Who made a song or picture, he
Did it, and not another, God nor man.

My Lord is large, my Lord is strong:
Giving, He gave: my me is mine.
        How poor, how strange, how wrong,
To dream He wrote the little song   70
I made to Him with love's unforced design!

Oh, not as clouds dim laws have plann'd
To strike down Good and fight for Ill,—
        Oh, not as harps that stand
In the wind and sound the wind's command:
Each artist—gift of terror!—owns his will.

For thee, Cloud,—if thou spend thine all
Upon the South's o'er-brimming sea
        That needs thee not; or crawl
To the dry provinces, and fall   80
Till every convert clod shall give to thee

Green worship; if thou grow or fade,
Bring on delight or misery,
        Fly east or west, be made
Snow, hail, rain, wind, grass, rose, light, shade;
What matters it to thee? There is no thee.

Pass, kinsman Cloud, now fair and mild:
Discharge the will that's not thine own.
        I work in freedom wild,
But work, as plays a little child,   90
Sure of the Father, Self, and Love, alone.

III. MARSH SONG—AT SUNSET [95]

Over the monstrous shambling sea,
        Over the Caliban sea,
Bright Ariel-cloud, thou lingerest:
Oh wait, oh wait, in the warm red West,—
        Thy Prospero I'll be.

Over the humped and fishy sea,
        Over the Caliban sea
O cloud in the West, like a thought in the heart
Of pardon, loose thy wing, and start,
        And do a grace for me.   10

Over the huge and huddling sea,
        Over the Caliban sea,
Bring hither my brother Antonio,—Man,—
My injurer: night breaks the ban:
        Brother, I pardon thee.

characteristics

2 best known

IV. THE MARSHES OF GLYNN [96]

1 - desc.
2 rythm
3 thought

Glooms of the live-oaks, beautiful-braided and woven
With intricate shades of the vines that myriad-cloven
    Clamber the forks of the multiform boughs,—
            Emerald twilights,—
            Virginal shy lights,
Wrought of the leaves to allure to the whisper of vows,
When lovers pace timidly down through the green colonnades
Of the dim sweet woods, of the dear dark woods,
    Of the heavenly woods and glades,
That run to the radiant marginal sand-beach within   10
        The wide sea-marshes of Glynn;—

Beautiful glooms, soft dusks in the noon-day fire,—
Wildwood privacies, closets of lone desire,

Chamber from chamber parted with wavering arras of leaves,—
Cells for the passionate pleasure of prayer to the soul that
    grieves,
Pure with a sense of the passing of saints through the wood,
Cool for the dutiful weighing of ill with good;—

O braided dusks of the oak and woven shades of the vine,
While the riotous noon-day sun of the June-day long did shine
Ye held me fast in your heart and I held you fast in mine;   20
But now when the noon is no more, and riot is rest,
And the sun is a-wait at the ponderous gate of the West,
And the slant yellow beam down the wood-aisle doth seem
Like a lane into heaven that leads from a dream,—
Ay, now, when my soul all day hath drunken the soul of the oak,
And my heart is at ease from men, and the wearisome sound
    of the stroke
  Of the scythe of time and the trowel of trade is low,
    And belief overmasters doubt, and I know that I know,
    And my spirit is grown to a lordly great compass within,
That the length and the breadth and the sweep of the marshes
    of Glynn   30
Will work me no fear like the fear they have wrought me of
    yore
When length was fatigue, and when breadth was but bitterness
    sore,
And when terror and shrinking and dreary unnamable pain
Drew over me out of the merciless miles of the plain,—

Oh, now, unafraid, I am fain to face
  The vast sweet visage of space.
To the edge of the wood I am drawn, I am drawn,
Where the gray beach glimmering runs, as a belt of the dawn,
  For a mete and a mark
    To the forest-dark:—   40
         So:
Affable live-oak, leaning low,—
Thus—with your favor—soft, with a reverent hand,

(Not lightly touching your person, Lord of the land!)
Bending your beauty aside, with a step I stand
On the firm-packed sand,
        Free
By a world of marsh that borders a world of sea.
  Sinuous southward and sinuous northward the shimmering
    band
    Of the sand-beach fastens the fringe of the marsh to the
      folds of the land.   50
Inward and outward to northward and southward the beach-
    lines linger and curl
As a silver-wrought garment that clings to and follows the
    firm sweet limbs of a girl.
Vanishing, swerving, evermore curving again into sight,
Softly the sand-beach wavers away to a dim gray looping of
    light.
And what if behind me to westward the wall of the woods
    stands high?
The world lies east: how ample, the marsh and the sea and the
    sky!
A league and a league of marsh-grass, waist-high, broad in the
    blade,
Green, and all of a height, and unflecked with a light or a shade,
Stretch leisurely off, in a pleasant plain,
To the terminal blue of the main.   60

Oh, what is abroad in the marsh and the terminal sea?
  Somehow my soul seems suddenly free
From the weighing of fate and the sad discussion of sin,
By the length and the breadth and the sweep of the marshes of
    Glynn.

Ye marshes, how candid and simple and nothing-withholding
    and free
Ye publish yourselves to the sky and offer yourselves to the sea!
Tolerant plains, that suffer the sea and the rains and the sun,
Ye spread and span like the catholic man who hath mightily won

God out of knowledge and good out of infinite pain
And sight out of blindness and purity out of a stain.   70

As the marsh-hen secretly builds on the watery sod,
Behold I will build me a nest on the greatness of God:
I will fly in the greatness of God as the marsh-hen flies
In the freedom that fills all the space 'twixt the marsh and the
          skies:
By so many roots as the marsh-grass sends in the sod
I will heartily lay me a-hold on the greatness of God:
Oh, like to the greatness of God is the greatness within
The range of the marshes, the liberal marshes of Glynn.

And the sea lends large, as the marsh: lo, out of his plenty
          the sea
Pours fast: full soon the time of the flood-tide must be: 80
Look how the grace of the sea doth go
About and about through the intricate channels that flow
               Here and there,
                    Everywhere,
Till his waters have flooded the uttermost creeks and the low-
          lying lanes,
And the marsh is meshed with a million veins,
That like as with rosy and silvery essences flow
     In the rose-and-silver evening glow.
                    Farewell, my lord Sun!
The creeks overflow: a thousand rivulets run   90
'Twixt the roots of the sod; the blades of the marsh-grass stir;
Passeth a hurrying sound of wings that westward whirr;
Passeth, and all is still; and the currents cease to run;
And the sea and the marsh are one.

How still the plains of the waters be!
The tide is in his ecstasy.
The tide is at his highest height:
                    And it is night.

And now from the Vast of the Lord will the waters of sleep
Roll in on the souls of men, 100
But who will reveal to our waking ken
The forms that swim and the shapes that creep
    Under the waters of sleep?
And I would I could know what swimmeth below when the tide
   comes in
On the length and the breadth of the marvellous marshes of
   Glynn.

A BALLAD OF TREES AND THE MASTER[97]

Into the woods my Master went,
Clean forspent, forspent.
Into the woods my Master came,
Forspent with love and shame.
But the olives they were not blind to Him,
The little gray leaves were kind to Him:
The thorn-tree had a mind to Him
When into the woods He came.

Out of the woods my Master went,
And he was well content. 10
Out of the woods my Master came,
Content with death and shame.
When Death and Shame would woo Him last,
From under the trees they drew Him last:
'Twas on a tree they slew Him—last
When out of the woods He came.

JOHN BANISTER TABB

  John Banister Tabb, the third child of Thomas Yelverton
and Marianna Bertrand Archer Tabb, was born at "The Forest,"
the family estate at Mattoax, near Richmond, Virginia, March
22, 1845. In his childhood he suffered from a weak body and
weak eyes, and he had always with him a black slave-boy. He

was educated at home by a tutor. When the war began, his older brother and his tutor both enlisted, but John was too young and too frail for active service. Despite these handicaps, he joined a blockade-runner in the second year of war. On some of these trips he visited London and Paris, and ran the blockade at least twenty-one times. Only a severe fever which incapacitated him prevented Tabb from being on the *Robert E. Lee* when it was captured in 1863; in June of 1864, while serving on the *Siren*, he was captured and sent to Point Lookout, Maryland. For two months he suffered from diarrhœa, in a prison where men died at the rate of fifteen or twenty a day. Here he met Sidney Lanier, and Lanier's friendship was the one bright spot in prison life; to him Tabb dedicated his second book of poems. Early in 1865 he was exchanged, and joined his brother's regiment in the defense of Richmond.

After the war Tabb studied for a year in Baltimore. He was at that time an Episcopalian, and either while there or while teaching at St. Paul's School he determined to prepare for the Episcopalian ministry. For a few months he taught at Racine College, in Wisconsin, leaving because of his sister's illness. With several close friends Tabb turned to Catholicism, in 1872, and immediately decided to study for the priesthood—a decision which temporarily alienated him from his family. He graduated from St. Charles College in 1875, but instead of being ordained he went as teacher to St. Peter's Boys School in Richmond. Three years later he returned to St. Charles College as a teacher, but he was not ordained until 1884. By that time he had published a volume of poems (in Baltimore, 1882) and had also acquired a reputation as a wit. He delighted in sending satirical or punning verses, with illustrations of his own invention, to his friends. In general his life was uneventful: he taught English at St. Charles until his death. His first volume of poems to attract attention was published in 1894, and ten volumes, including an English edition selected by Alice Meynell, were published during his lifetime. Two posthumous volumes—one a complete collection of his poems—have been issued. In 1908 the weak eyes that had long troubled Father Tabb began to fail completely, and for a year before his death on November 19, 1909, he was totally blind.

KILDEE

Kildee! Kildee! far o'er the lea
    At twilight comes the cry.
Kildee! a marsh-mate answereth
    Across the shallow sky.

Kildee! Kildee! thrills over me
    A rhapsody of light,
As star to star gives utterance
    Between the day and night.

Kildee! Kildee! O Memory,
    The twin birds, Joy and Pain,   10
Like shadows parted by the sun,
    At twilight meet again!

COMPENSATION

How many an acorn falls to die
    For one that makes a tree!
How many a heart must pass me by
    For one that cleaves to me!

How many a suppliant wave of sound
    Must still unheeded roll
For one low utterance that found
    An echo in my soul!

THE DEPARTED

They cannot wholly pass away,
    How far soe'er above;
Nor we, the lingerers, wholly stay
    Apart from those we love;

For spirits in eternity,
　　As shadows in the sun,
Reach backward into time, as we,
　　Like lifted clouds, reach on.

EVOLUTION

Out of the dusk a shadow,
　　Then a spark;
Out of the cloud a silence,
　　Then a lark;

Out of the heart a rapture,
　　Then a pain;
Out of the dead, cold ashes,
　　Life again.

THE SNOW-BIRD

When snow, like silence visible,
　　Hath hushed the summer bird,
Thy voice, a never-frozen rill
　　Of melody, is heard.

But when from winter's lethargy
　　The buds begin to blow,
Thy voice is mute, and suddenly
　　Thou vanishest like snow.

MY SECRET

'Tis not what I am fain to hide
　　That doth in deepest darkness dwell,
But what my tongue hath often tried,
　　Alas, in vain to tell.

MATINS

Still sing the morning stars remote
    With echoes now unheard
Save in the scintillating note
    Of some dawn-wakened bird

Whose heart, a fountain of the light,
    Prolongs the limpid strain
Till on the borderland of night
    The stars begin again.

GOING BLIND

Back to the primal gloom
    Where life began,
As to my mother's womb
    Must I a man
    Return:
Not to be born again,
    But to remain;
And in the School of Darkness learn
    What mean
"The things unseen."

10

IRWIN RUSSELL

Irwin Russell was born June 3, 1853, in Port Gibson, Mississippi. His parents, Dr. William McNab and Elizabeth Allen Russell, soon moved to St. Louis. Irwin was a frail, precocious child, capable at six of understanding Milton's poetry, but his formal education was interrupted by the Civil War. At the outbreak of hostilities Dr. Russell returned to Port Gibson; after the war he moved back to St. Louis and remained there until Irwin graduated from St. Louis University in 1869. Back once more at Port Gibson, Irwin studied law under Judge

L. N. Baldwin, and dabbled with poetry—his first poem, "A Chinese Tale," dealing with the origin of foot-binding. In the next eight years he practiced law intermittently, worked on newspapers, and occasionally ran off to New Orleans where he lived with sailors and acquired a fondness for strong drink. In 1877 he became Judge Baldwin's assistant, but the following year, during an epidemic of yellow fever, he assisted his father as nurse and medical assistant. His fiancée, Dora Donald, died in the epidemic, and his father, worn out by exertion during the plague, died soon after. Irwin apparently went to pieces under this double catastrophe. He went to New York, where he was welcomed by H. C. Bunner and Richard Watson Gilder. Although his negro poetry had made him something of a celebrity, he was sick and penniless and could find no work. In August, 1879, he worked his way by boat to New Orleans, where he worked on the New Orleans *Times* until his death, December 23, 1879. A melancholy poem, "The Cemetery," published ten days before his death, presaged his end.

Russell's poems were collected and published in book form, with a preface by Joel Chandler Harris, in 1888.

CHRISTMAS-NIGHT IN THE QUARTERS

When merry Christmas-day is done,
And Christmas-night is just begun;
While clouds in slow procession drift
To wish the moon-man "Christmas gift,"
Yet linger overhead, to know
What causes all the stir below.
At Uncle Johnny Booker's ball
The darkies hold high carnival.
From all the country-side they throng,
With laughter, shouts, and scraps of song—   10
Their whole deportment plainly showing
That to "the frolic" they are going.
Some take the path with shoes in hand,
To traverse muddy bottom-land;
Aristocrats their steeds bestride—
Four on a mule, behold them ride!

And ten great oxen draw apace
The wagon from "de oder place,"
With forty guests, whose conversation
Betokens glad anticipation.   20
Not so with him who drives: old Jim
Is sagely solemn, hard and grim,
And frolics have no joys for him.
He seldom speaks, but to condemn—
Or utter some wise apothegm—
Or else, some crabbed thought pursuing,
Talk to his team, as now he's doing:

———

Come up heah, Star! Yee-bawee!
    You alluz is a-laggin'—
Mus' be you think I's dead,   30
    And this de huss you's draggin'—
You's mos' too lazy to draw yo' bref,
    Let 'lone drawin' de waggin.

Dis team—quit bel'rin, sah!
    De ladies don't submit 'at—
Dis team—you ol' fool ox,
    You heah me tell you quit 'at?
Dis team's des like de 'Nited States;
    Dat's what I's tryin' to git at!

De people rides behind   40
    De pollytishners haulin'—
Sh'u'd be a well-bruk ox,
    To foller dat ar callin'—
An' sometimes nuffin won't do dem steers
    But what dey mus' be stallin'!

Woo bahgh! Buck-kannon! Yes, sah,
    Sometimes dey will be stickin';
An' den, fus thing dey knows,
    Dey takes a rale good lickin'—

De folks gits down: an' den watch out   50
  For hommerin' an' kickin'.

Dey blows upon dey hands,
  Den flings 'em wid de nails up,
Jumps up an' cracks dey heels,
  An' pruzntly dey sails up,
An' makes dem oxen hump deyself,
  By twistin' all dey tails up!

In this our age of printer's ink,
'Tis books that show us how to think—
The rule reversed, and set at naught,   60
That held that books were born of thought;
We form our minds by pedant's rules;
And all we know, is from the schools;
And when we work, or when we play,
We do it in an ordered way—
And Nature's self pronounce a ban on,
Whene'er she dares transgress a canon.
Untrammeled thus, the simple race is,
That "works the craps" on cotton-places!
Original in act and thought,   70
Because unlearned and untaught,
Observe them at their Christmas party.
How unrestrained their mirth—how hearty!
How many things they say and do,
That never would occur to you!
See Brudder Brown—whose saving grace
Would sanctify a quarter-race—
Out on the crowded floor advance,
To "beg a blessin' on dis dance."

A BLESSING ON THE DANCE

O Mahsr! let dis gath'rin' fin' a blessin' in yo' sight!   80
Don't jedge us hard for what we does—you knows it's Chris-
    mus night;

An' all de balunce ob de yeah, we does as right's we kin—
Ef dancin's wrong—oh, Mahsr, let de time excuse de sin!

We labors in de vineya'd—workin' hard, and workin' true—
Now, shorely you won't notus ef we eats a grape or two,
An' takes a leetle holiday—a leetle restin'-spell—
Bekase, nex' week, we'll start in fresh, an' labor twicet as well.

Remember, Mahsr,—min' dis, now—de sinfulness ob sin
Is pendin' 'pon de sperret what we goes an' does it in;
An' in a righchis frame ob min' we's gwine to dance an' sing; 90
A-feelin' like King David, when he cut de pigeon-wing.

It seems to me—indeed it do—I mebbe mout be wrong—
That people raly *ought* to dance, when Chrismus comes along;
Des dance bekase dey's happy—like de birds hops in de trees;
De pine-top fiddle soundin' to de blowin' ob de breeze.

We has no ark to dance afore, like Isrul's prophet king;
We has no harp to soun' de cords, to holp us out to sing;
But cordin' to de gif's we has we does de bes' we knows—
An' folks don't 'spise de vi'let-flow'r bekase it aint de rose.

You bless us, please sah, eben ef we's doin' wrong to-night; 100
Kase den we'll need de blessin' more'n ef we's doin' right;
An' let de blessin' stay wid us, untell we comes to die,
An' goes to keep our Chrismus wid dem sheriffs in de sky!

Yes, tell dem preshis anjuls we's a-gwine to jine 'em soon:
Our voices we's a-trainin' for to sing de glory tune;
We's ready when you wants us, an' it aint no matter when—
O Mahsr! call yo' chillen soon, an' take 'em home! Amen.

———

The rev'rend man is scarcely through,
When all the noise begins anew,
And with such force assaults the ears,   110
That through the din one hardly hears

Old Fiddling Josey "sound his A"—
Correct the pitch—begin to play—
Stop, satisfied,—then, with the bow,
Rap out the signal dancers know:

Git yo' pardners, fust kwattillion!
 Stomp yo' feet, an' raise 'em high;
Tune is: "Oh! dat water-million!
 Gwine to git to home bime-bye."

S'lute yo' pardners! scrape perlitely—   120
 Don't be bumpin' gin de res'—
Balance all! now, step out rightly;
 Alluz dance yo' lebbel bes'.

Fo'w'ad foah! whoop up, niggers!
 Back ag'in! don't be so slow—
Swing cornahs! min' de figgers:
 When I hollers, den yo' go.

Top ladies cross ober!
 Hol' on, till I takes a dram—
Gemmen solo! yes, *I*'s sober—   130
 Kaint say how de fiddle am—

Hands around! hol' up yo' faces,
 Don't be lookin' at yo' feet!
Swing yo' pardners to yo' places!
 Dat's de way—dat's hard to beat.

Sides fo'w'd!—when you's ready—
 Make a bow as low's you kin!
Swing acrost wid opp'site lady!
 Now we'll let you swap ag'in:

Ladies change!—shet up dat talkin'—   140
 Do yo' talkin' arter while—

Right an' lef'!—don't want no walkin'—
      Make yo' steps, an' show yo' style!

And so the "set" proceeds—its length
Determined by the dancers' strength;
And all agreed to yield the palm
For grace and skill, to "Georgy Sam,"
Who stamps so hard, and leaps so high,
"Des watch him!" is the wond'ring cry—
"De nigger mus' be, for a fac',   150
Own cousin to a jumpin'-jack!"
On, on, the restless fiddle sounds—
Still chorused by the curs and hounds—
Dance after dance succeeding fast,
Till "supper" is announced at last.
That scene—but why attempt to show it?
The most inventive modern poet,
In fine new words whose hope and trust is,
Could form no phrase to do it justice!
When supper ends—that is not soon—   160
The fiddle strikes the same old tune;
The dancers pound the floor again,
With all they have of might and main;
Old gossips, *almost* turning pale,
Attend Aunt Cassy's gruesome tale
Of conjurors, and ghosts, and devils,
That in the smoke-house hold their revels;
Each drowsy baby droops its head,
Yet scorns the very thought of bed:—
So wears the night; and wears so fast,   170
All wonder when they find it passed,
And hear the signal sound, to go,
From what few cocks are left to crow.
Then, one and all, you hear them shout:
"Hi! Booker! fotch de banjo out,
An' gib us *one* song 'fore we goes—
One ob de berry bes' you knows!"

Responding to the welcome call,
He takes the banjo from the wall,
And tunes the strings with skill and care—   180
Then strikes them with a master's air;
And tells, in melody and rhyme,
This legend of the olden time:

THE FIRST BANJO

Go 'way, fiddle!—folks is tired o' hearin' you a-squawkin',
Keep silence fur yo' betters—don't you heah de banjo talkin'?
About de 'possum's tail she's gwine to lecter—ladies, listen!
About de ha'r what isn't dar, and why de ha'r is missin':

"Dar's gwine to be a oberflow," said Noah, lookin' solemn—
For Noah tuk the "Herald," an' he read de ribber column—
An' so he sot his hands to work a-cl'arin' timber-patches,   190
An' 'lowed he's gwine to build a boat to beat de steameh "Natchez."

Ol' Noah kep' a-nailin', an' a-chippin', an' a-sawin';
An' all de wicked neighbors kep' a-laughin' an' a-pashawin';
But Noah didn't min' 'em—knowin' whut wus gwine to happen;
An' forty days an' forty nights de rain it kep' a-drappin'.

Now, Noah had done cotched a lot ob ebry sort o' beas'es—
Ob all de shows a-trabbelin', it beat 'em all to pieces!
He had a Morgan colt, an' sebral head o' Jarsey cattle—
An' druv' 'em 'board de Ark as soon's he heered de thunder rattle.

Den sech anoder fall ob rain!—it come so awful hebby,   200
De ribber riz immejitly, an' busted troo de lebbee;
De people all wus drownded out—'cep' Noah an' de critters,
An' men he'd hired to work de boat—an' one to mix de bitters.

De Ark she kep' a-sailin', an' a-sailin', *an'* a-sailin';
De lion got his dander up, an' like to bruk de palin'—

De sarpints hissed—de painters yelled—tell, what wid all de
  fussin',
You c'u'dn't hardly heah de mate a-bossin' 'roun' an' cussin'.

Now, Ham, de only nigger whut wuz runnin' on de packet,
Got lonesome in de barber-shop, an' c'u'dn't stan' de racket;
An' so, for to amuse he-se'f, he steamed some wood an' bent it,
An' soon he had a banjo made—de fust dat wus invented.   211

He wet de ledder, stretched it on; made bridge, an' screws an'
  apron;
An' fitted in a proper neck—'twuz berry long an' tap'rin';
He tuk some tin, an' twisted him a thimble for to ring it;
An' den de mighty question riz: how wuz he gwine to string it?

De' possum had as fine a tail as dis dat I's a-singin';
De ha'rs so long, an' thick, an' strong,—des fit for banjo-
  stringin';
Dat nigger shaved 'em off as short as wash-day-dinner graces;
An' sorted ob 'em by de size, frum little E's to basses.

He strung her, tuned her, struck a jig,—'twus "Nebber min' de
  wedder"—   220
She soun' like forty-lebben bands a-playin' all togedder;
Some went to pattin'; some to dancin';—Noah called de figgers—
An' Ham he sot an' knocked de tune, de happiest ob niggers!

Now, sence dat time—it's mighty strange—dere's not de
  slightes' showin'
Ob any ha'r at all upon the 'possum's tail a-growin';
An' curi's, too,—dat nigger's ways: his people nebber los' 'em—
For whar you finds de nigger—dar's de banjo an' de 'possum!

The night is spent; and as the day
Throws up the first faint flash of gray,
The guests pursue their homeward way;   230
And through the field beyond the gin,

Just as the stars are going in,
See Santa Claus departing—grieving—
His own dear Land of Cotton leaving.
His work is done—he fain would rest,
Where people know and love him best—
He pauses—listens—looks about—
But go he must: his pass is out;
So, coughing down the rising tears,
He climbs the fence and disappears.   240
And thus observes a colored youth—
(The common sentiment, in sooth):
"Oh! what a blessin' 'wo'u'd ha' been,
Ef Santa had been born a twin!
We'd hab two Chrismuses a yeah—
Or p'r'aps *one* brudder'd *settle* heah'!"

LIZETTE WOODWORTH REESE

Lizette Woodworth Reese, the daughter of David and Louisa
Reese, was born in Waverly, Maryland, January 9, 1856, of
mixed English and German parentage. She was educated chiefly
in private schools, and at seventeen she became a teacher.
After teaching for a number of years in schools in Waverly and
Baltimore, in 1901 she began teaching English in Western
High School, Baltimore, where she remained until her retirement in 1921. A bronze tablet, inscribed with her most famous
poem, "Tears," was presented to the school by alumni in
1923.

Her poetry seems, at first glance, as uneventful as her life,
but it has a surprising range beneath its even surfaces. Her
first book, *A Branch of May* (1887), dealt mainly with the roads
and trees and country life of her own county, which she knew
so well; and her later volumes, although deepened in poetic
power and emotional intensity, have never departed far from her
original subject matter. In 1929 she published her autobiography, *A Victorian Village*—the quiet record of a woman who
could see in nature and in small things all the material needed for
poetry or for life.

APRIL WEATHER

Oh, hush, my heart, and take thine ease,
　For here is April weather!
The daffodils beneath the trees
　Are all a-row together.

The thrush is back with his old note;
　The scarlet tulip blowing;
And white—ay, white as my love's throat—
　The dogwood boughs are growing.

The lilac bush is sweet again;
　Down every wind that passes,　　　　　　　　10
Fly flakes from hedgerow and from lane;
　The bees are in the grasses.

And Grief goes out, and Joy comes in,
　And Care is but a feather;
And every lad his love can win,
　For here is April weather.

TEARS

Her Most famous Poem

When I consider Life and its few years—
A wisp of fog betwixt us and the sun;
A call to battle, and the battle done
Ere the last echo dies within our ears;
A rose choked in the grass; an hour of fears;
The gusts that past a darkening shore do beat;
The burst of music down an unlistening street—
I wonder at the idleness of tears.
Ye old, old dead, and ye of yesternight,
Chieftains, and bards, and keepers of the sheep,　　10
By every cup of sorrow that you had,
Loose me from tears, and make me see aright

How each hath back what once he stayed to weep;
Homer his sight, David his little lad!

WAITING

They swear the dead come back at night,
Who once were women and men,
And sob and cry in the strange weather,
To be let in again.

Out by the straggling thorn I wait,
But you are not come yet;
So it must be that I remember,
And that you forget.

SPICEWOOD

The spicewood burns along the gray, spent sky,
In moist, unchimneyed places, in a wind,
That whips it all before, and all behind,
Into one thick, rude flame, now low, now high.
It is the first, the homeliest thing of all—
At sight of it, the lad that by it fares,
Whistles afresh his foolish town-caught airs—
A thing so honey-colored and so tall!
It is as though the young Year, ere he pass,
To the white riot of the cherry tree,   10
Would fain accustom us, or here, or there,
To his new sudden ways with bough and grass,
So starts with what is humble, plain to see
And all familiar as a cup, a chair.

OLD SAUL

I cannot think of any word
    To make it plain to you,
How white a thing the hawthorn bush
    That delicately blew

Within a crook of Tinges Lane;
  Each May Day there it stood;
And lit a flame of loveliness
  For the small neighborhood.

So fragile-white a thing it was,
  I cannot make it plain;   10
Or the sweet fumbling of the bees,
  Like the break in a rain.

Old Saul lived near. And this his life:—
  To cobble for his bread;
To mourn a tall son lost at sea;
  A daughter worse than dead.

And so, in place of all his lack,
  He set the hawthorn tree;
Made it his wealth, his mirth, his god,
  His Zion to touch and see.   20

Born English he. Down Tinges Lane
  His lad's years came and went;
He saw out there behind his thorn,
  A hundred thorns of Kent.

At lovers slipping through the dusk
  He shook a lover's head;
Grudged them each flower. It was too white
  For any but the dead.

Once on a blurred, wet, silver day
  He said to two or three: 30
"Folks, when I go, pluck yonder bloom
  That I may take with me."

But it was winter when he went,
  The road wind-drenched and torn;
They laid upon his coffin lid
  A wreath made all of thorn.

TODAY

Is there but emptiness from sky to sky;
A hollow where we pass,
Along the simple grass?
Stirs not some intimate foot as we draw nigh?
Or is Today grown but a lantern light,
That throws at the dark's edge,
Upon some village hedge,
A petty red, then dwindles into night?

The House decays, but in the April rain,
Long after, where it stood,   10
Betwixt the sea and wood,
Purple as yore, its violets remain.
Long after, hoarded in the ancestral town,
The new folk find it there,
In carvèd shelf or chair,
Or candlesticks whose gilt is turning brown.

Thus is it with our Pasts; they go; they stay;
They go, yet leave behind,
Some wealth, dear, starry, kind,
For common folk to gather day by day: 20
There is no moment which dies unforgot;
For when the last is flown,
The very churls do own,
More wars than Troy, more towers than Camelot.

Yet not alone the vanished years are fair;
There are two spirits keep,
Where men do work or sleep,
Down rutty lane, or in the roof-girt square;
Their looks are gentle, for they come to bless;
With brooding eyes they see,   30

The Best for you and me;
And one is Awe and one is Loveliness.

From wonder unto wonder do we go;
Faith, fervors, quests, desires,
Youth's brief entrancing fires,
The deeper moods of deeper years we know;
We need but lift our bare, expectant hands;
The mists break and are gone;
Sounds, scents, visions of dawn
Surge toward us from the old, unalien lands.   40

The wonder of this life that hurries by!—
Loves, wrecks, deceits, and woes,
Pomps, marketings and shows,
So close to earth, yet closer to the sky.
This you and I—forgetting and forgot;
Yet shall we plan, dream, slay,
Or, sudden on a day,
Grasp at the wheeling suns and perish not.

This mystery forever at the door!—
Familiar as the air,   50
And sacred as a prayer,
Forever new and yet forever hoar—
This you and I—blown past the village pane,
And down to darkness thrust,
A little simple dust,
That still shall rise and serve its God again.

What go into the making of a song?
A thousand years agone,
And more that are to dawn,
And this one moment pulsing strange and strong;   60
And every moment, be it near or far,
Joy-lit, or drab with woe,

And every great and low,
The rose, the worm, the tempest, and the star.

The cry of Sorrow gathering her sheaves;
The laughter full and low,
Of the rude folk that sow,
A windy hour under thin country eaves;
The shout of Singers marching in their might,
To viol and to horn,   70
Far up the steeps of morn,
To the white levels of perpetual light.

First love, that in the young days has us thrall;
The festival; the flower;
The wet, autumnal hour;
The last fight waging by the broken wall—
These, these and more. For hark! all wrong, all right;
The fear that drove men back,
The dream along the track,
The foot that slipped, the heart that took the height! 80

Oh, wonder of a song! Along it pour
A thousand years to be,
The fair, the rude, the free,
Like wind adown the hollow of a shore:
Out of their hearts shall come a kindlier Plan;
Out of our fathers' creeds,
A better for our needs,
Out of the ancestral throng a nobler Man.

Oh, life! oh, song! Oh, the long awe of spring!
A little shines the light;   90
Then lo, to left, to right,
Across the garden flags some baffling thing!—
See the round scarlet leap from April clod:
Empty we turn away,

Dared by that bit of clay;
For tulips still are tulips, God still God.

Some ancient sense of Beauty haunts us still;
The pangs of Life and Art,
Lie sharp about the heart;
Sudden we feel the unescapable thrill:　　100
One instant naught—the next, a pageant nigh!
Out in the naked street,
The sound of lonely feet;
In ordered splendor all our dreams march by.

A book can hold us, or a snatch of sea,
Or lilies by a wall;
A comrade at dewfall,
Can from his violin such chords set free,
To such quick, searching notes give instant tongue,
To woods, darks, sailing ships;　　110
The sobs start to our lips—
How long, how long it is since we were young!

He plays. Under the clear and ruddy sky,
And there in the dewfall,
The oldest things of all,
Go gleaming past, and as they go, they cry—
Love, Longing, Tears, and gray Remembering;
A foot, a voice, a face!—
And there, in some dim place,
The little honey-colored flowers of spring.　　120

To every age some mystery all its own,
That makes its dullest air,
A something hushed and fair;
Down every age some breath of Beauty blown
Each day is but a pool within the grass,
A haunted, gusty thing,
Of ancient fashioning,
Where earth and heaven do meet as in a glass.

Kent. Poet 1865 stimulated would go out
1st job cashier in poolroom,

MADISON CAWEIN

Madison Julius Cawein was born in Louisville, Kentucky, March 23, 1865. His father William was of French Huguenot descent, his mother, Christiana Stelsly Cawein, of German parentage. From his father, who gathered herbs and compounded medicines, Madison got a love for the outdoors, with an accurate knowledge of Kentucky's flora and fauna; from his mother, a decided interest in spiritualism and the supernatural. He graduated as class poet in 1886 from the Louisville Male High School. Knowing nothing of business yet confronted with the necessity of making a living, Cawein worked for several years as cashier in a poolroom. While working there he wrote and published his first volume of poetry, *Blooms of the Berry* (1887), a volume which William Dean Howells praised generously. This encouragement led Cawein the following year to dedicate his second volume of poems to Howells. To escape from the poolroom he became a stock-broker and real-estate man—an occupation which he made very profitable although he devoted only each morning to it; the afternoon he reserved for writing, and he usually went into the woods to compose his poems. In 1902 Sir Edmund Gosse wrote an introduction for a carefully selected English edition of his work, *Kentucky Poems*. Cawein married Gertrude Foster McKelvey, June 4, 1903, and amassed through writing and stock speculation a small fortune, most of which he lost after 1906. Too prolific, little given to revision, Cawein published thirty-six volumes, some of them partially in prose, and some representing selections from earlier volumes. In 1911 he began to suffer from poverty and from ill health; on December 8, 1914, he died suddenly from a fall in his bathroom. Whether his death resulted from striking his head on the tub, or from a stroke of apoplexy, remains unknown.

School of imagist good Example

SNOW

use of large Pictures   *tone Poem*

The moon, like a round device
On a shadowy shield of war,
Hangs white in a heaven of ice
With a solitary star.

The wind has sunk to a sigh,
And the waters are stern with frost;
And gray, in the eastern sky,
The last snow-cloud is lost.

White fields, that are winter-starved,
Black woods, that are winter-fraught,   10
Cold, harsh as a face death-carved,
With the iron of some black thought.

AUBADE[98]

Awake! the dawn is on the hills!
    Behold, at her cool throat a rose,
    Blue-eyed and beautiful she goes,
Leaving her steps in daffodils.—
Awake! arise! and let me see
    Thine eyes, whose deeps epitomize
All dawns that were or are to be,
    O love, all Heaven in thine eyes!—
Awake! arise! come down to me!

Behold! the dawn is up: behold!   10
    How all the birds around her float,
    Wild rills of music, note on note,
Spilling the air with mellow gold.—
Arise! Awake! and, drawing near,
    Let me but hear thee and rejoice!
Thou, who keep'st captive, sweet and clear,
    All song, O love, within thy voice!
Arise! awake! and let me hear!

See, where she comes, with limbs of day,
    The dawn! with wild-rose hands and feet,   20
    Within whose veins the sunbeams beat,
And laughters meet of wind and ray.
Arise! come down! and, heart to heart,

Love, let me clasp in thee all these—
The sunbeam, of which thou art part,
    And all the rapture of the breeze!—
Arise! come down! loved that thou art!

PROTOTYPES

Whether it be that we in letters trace
The pure exactness of a wood bird's strain,
And name it song; or with the brush attain
The high perfection of a wildflower's face;
Or mold in difficult marble all the grace
We know as man; or from the wind and rain
Catch elemental rapture of refrain
And mark in music to due time and place:
The aim of Art is Nature; to unfold
Her truth and beauty to the souls of men   10
In close suggestions; in whose forms is cast
Nothing so new but 'tis long eons old;
Nothing so old but 'tis as young as when
The mind conceived it in the ages past.

THE WINDS

Those hewers of the clouds, the Winds,—that lair
At the four compass points,—are out tonight;
I hear their sandals trample on the height,
I hear their voices trumpet through the air:
Builders of storm, God's workmen, now they bear,
Up the steep stair of sky, on backs of might,
Huge tempest bulks, while,—sweat that blinds their sight,—
The rain is shaken from tumultuous hair:
Now, sweepers of the firmament, they broom,
Like gathered dust, the rolling mists along   10
Heaven's floors of sapphire; all the beautiful blue
Of skyey corridor and celestial room
Preparing, with large laughter and loud song,
For the white moon and stars to wander through.

KU KLUX

We have sent him seeds of the melon's core,
And nailed a warning upon his door:
By the Ku Klux laws we can do no more.

Down in the hollow, 'mid crib and stack,
The roof of his low-porched house looms black;
Not a line of light at the door-sill's crack.

Yet arm and mount! and mask and ride!
The hounds can sense though the fox may hide!
And for a word too much men oft have died.

The clouds blow heavy toward the moon.   10
The edge of the storm will reach it soon.
The kildee cries and the lonesome loon.

The clouds shall flush with a wilder glare
Than the lightning makes with its angled flare,
When the Ku Klux verdict is given there.

In the pause of the thunder rolling low,
A rifle's answer—who shall know
From the wind's fierce hurl and the rain's black blow?

Only the signature, written grim
At the end of the message brought to him—   20
A hempen rope and a twisted limb.

So arm and mount! and mask and ride!
The hounds can sense though the fox may hide!—
For a word too much men oft have died.

Sympathetic Picture

THE MAN HUNT

The woods stretch deep to the mountain side,
And the brush is wild where a man may hide.

They have brought the bloodhounds up again
To the roadside rock where they found the slain.

They have brought the bloodhounds up, and they
Have taken the trail to the mountain way.

Three times they circled the trail and crossed;
And thrice they found it and thrice they lost.

Now straight through the trees and the underbrush
They follow the scent through the forest's hush.   10

And their deep-mouthed bay is a pulse of fear
In the heart of the wood that the man must hear.

The man who crouches among the trees
From the stern-faced men who follow these.

A huddle of rocks that the ooze has mossed,
And the trail of the hunted again is lost.

An upturned pebble; a bit of ground
A heel has trampled—the trail is found.

And the woods reëcho the bloodhounds' bay
As again they take to the mountain way.   20

A rock; a ribbon of road; a ledge,
With a pine tree clutching its crumbling edge.

A pine, that the lightning long since clave,
Whose huge roots hollow a ragged cave.

A shout; a curse; and a face aghast;
The human quarry is laired at last.

The human quarry with clay-clogged hair
And eyes of terror who waits them there.

That glares and crouches and rising then
Hurls clods and curses at dogs and men.　　30

Until the blow of a gun-butt lays
Him stunned and bleeding upon his face.

A rope; a prayer; and an oak-tree near,
And a score of hands to swing him clear.

A grim, black thing for the setting sun
And the moon and the stars to gaze upon.

DESERTED

The old house leans upon a tree
　　Like some old man upon a staff:
The night wind in its ancient porch
　　Sounds like a hollow laugh.

The heaven is wrapped in flying clouds
　　As grandeur cloaks itself in gray:
The starlight flitting in and out,
　　Glints like a lanthorn ray.

The dark is full of whispers.　Now
　　A fox-hound howls: and through the night,　10
Like some old ghost from out its grave,
　　The moon comes misty white.

THE MOUNTAIN STILL

I. THE MOONSHINER

He leans far out and watches: down below
The road seems but a ribbon through the trees:
The bluff, from which he gazes, whence he sees
Some ox-team or some horseman come and go,
Is briered with brush. A man comes riding slow
Around a bend of road. Against his knees
The branches whip. He sits at careless ease.
It is the sheriff, armed for any foe.
A detonation tears the echoes from
Each pine-hung crag; upon the rider's brow   10
A smear of red springs out; he shades it now,
His grey eyes on the bluff. The crags are dumb.
Smoke wreathes one spot. The sheriff, with a cough,
Marks well that place, and then rides slowly off.

II. THE SHERIFF

Night and the mountain road: a crag where burns
What seems a star, low down: three men that glide
From tree and rock towards it: one a guide
For him who never from his purpose turns,
Who stands for law among these mountain kerns.
At last the torchlit cave, along whose side   20
The still is seen, and men who have defied
The law so long—law, who the threshold spurns
With leveled weapons now. . . . Wolves in a den
Fight not more fiercely than these fought; wild fear
In every face, and rage and pale surprise.
The smoke thins off, and in the cave four men
Lie dead or dying; one that mountaineer,
And one the sheriff with the fearless eyes.

Patterns his poetry on middle ages or
Classical themes. - clearly imitative
William Alexander Percy ~~not~~ *soon after* ~~1930~~ 229
mississippi Poet -

WILLIAM ALEXANDER PERCY

William Alexander Percy, the son of United States Senator
Leroy and Camille Bourges Percy, was born in Greeneville,
Mississippi, May 14, 1885. He received his A.B. degree from the
University of the South in 1904, his LL.B. degree from Harvard
in 1908. With the exception of three years during the war—
in 1916 with the Relief Commission in Belgium, 1917–19 as
lieutenant and captain in the American Expeditionary Force—
he has practiced law in Greeneville, and farmed. In 1915 he
published his first books of poetry, *Sappho in Levkas*, and he
has since published two other volumes. He also has acted as
editor for the Yale Series of Younger Poets. In 1930 his
Selected Poems, containing the best of the poems from his
three books, with a few new ones, appeared. His work is
quiet, traditional in form, and much of it goes back to the
Middle Ages or to classical times for subject matter, but underneath his quiet traditional forms will be found some of the best
poetical writing in modern times.

Quiet, Calm, tone

OVERTONES

I heard a bird at break of day
    Sing from the autumn trees
A song so mystical and calm,
    So full of certainties,
No man, I think, could listen long
    Except upon his knees.
Yet this was but a simple bird
    Alone, among dead trees.

THE WANDERER

I have grown weary of the open sea,
The chartless ways, the storms, the loneliness,
The coast that topples, tall and shelterless—
Weary of faring where all things are free!

Yet once the open sea was all romance,
Purple and olive-stained and golden-scaled;
And every breeze from some adventure hailed,
And shoals were silver for the moon to dance.

The cliffs were only tall to keep untrod
The kingdom of the fay hung high in air,   10
And every storm was but Poseidon's dare,
And brave it was to battle with a god.

Ah, blithe it was when the mad night was done
And day with flying hair woke wild and white,
To see the salty sail loom in the light
And know one battle more was bravely won.

Then these were magic seas that ever rang
With melodies, now wild, now sweet, now glad;
At dusk the drifting choirs unseen were sad
And in the lulls of night the sirens sang.   20

They sing no more; the colors now are grey;
The cliffs defend not fairyland, but home;
And when th' impenitent, hoar sea has clomb
The clouds, I have no heart to sing or pray.

Oh, I am weary of the open sea,
Vigils and storms and watches without name,
The ache of long resistance without aim,
The fetters of the fetterless and free.

There is some haven that no tempest mars,
Some brown-hilled harbor, hushed and clear and deep,   30
Where tired evening may sit down and weep,
And, waking, find not water there but stars.

There would I creep at last ere day is done,
With ashen sail dropped down and cordage white;
There rest secure, there find before the night
A little hour of peace, a little sun!

CHORUS

(After the Greek)

Surely in no benignant mood
The gods have fashioned us, but craftily
    To send us homing to the sod
Wise only in our own futility.

    With hyacinthine brows of youth,
We enter life as to a festival;
    But, ere the feast is spread, the gods
Snatch back the wine, the song, the coronal.

    And, lustreless, we turn, afraid,
Turn to the sole vouchsafèd heritage,   10
    And in the shaken darkness clutch
The disenchanted ledges of old age.

IN NEW YORK

I. ON SUNDAY MORNING

Far, far from here the church bells ring,
    As when I was a child,
And there is one I dearly love
    Walks in the sunlight mild.
To church she goes, and with her once
    I went, a little child.

The church bells ring far, far away,
    The village streets are bright,
The sunlight falls in slanting bars
    And fills the church with light.   10
And I remember when I knelt
    Beside her, in delight.

There's something lost, there's something lost,
    Some wisdom has beguiled!

My heart has flown a thousand miles
    And in the sunlight mild
I kneel and weep beside her there
    As she prays for her child.

2. THE SONG YOU LOVE

When I have sung the sweet songs and the sad,
The songs of magic drifting from above,
The trumpet songs that shout across men's souls,
The sleep-song, breasted softer than the dove,
Still there will be one song I have not sung—
    The song you love, the song you love.

What are the torches of the world to you,
The words that comfort men and calm their fears?
What are the stars with their strange harmonies,
Or fate that shadows all, or death that jeers?   10
There must be laughter in the song you love
    And at the end there must be tears.

When I have come to that green place we know
Where cedars stand that have no faith in spring,
Where through the utter peace of afternoon
The mocking-birds their heartless raptures fling,
Long after it is dust, one heart there'll be
    Restless with words it could not sing.

3. WEARINESS

I sometimes think Thou art my secret love;
But not to-night. . . . To-night I have the need
Of human tenderness; not hovering wings,
But one warm breast where I may lay my head
And close my eyes. For I am tired to-night. . . .
The park was full of lovers,
And such a slender moon looked down on them. . . .
For one kiss of one mouth, free-given, I
Would give—what's left of me to-night

To the last dream!   10
Art Thou a jealous god?
Dost think to force by loneliness
Unwilling love to Thee?
Beware, beware! The winds of madness blow
Strong, strong on nights like these! . . .
Thou dost deny me what's of life most sweet,
The bending head and lovely eyes of love—
Then give, beseech Thee, give me sleep.

4. IN THE NIGHT

Drifting, groping
For delight;
Longing, hoping
All the night.
Perfume of
Blossomed hair—
Where is love?
Ah, no, not there! . . .
Not there.

Turning, turning,   10
Sleepless-eyed,
Something burning
At my side—
Winds that sweep
Poppied hair,
Where is sleep?
Ah, no, not there! . . .
Not there?

5. HOME

I have a need of silence and of stars:
Too much is said too loudly; I am dazed.
The silken sound of whirled infinity
Is lost in voices shouting to be heard.
I once knew men as earnest and less shrill.

An undermeaning that I caught I miss
Among these ears that hear all sounds save silence,
These eyes that see so much but not the sky,
These minds that gain all knowledge but no calm.
If suddenly the desperate music ceased,   10
Could they return to life? or would they stand
In dancers' attitudes, puzzled, polite,
And striking vaguely hand on tired hand
For an encore, to fill the ghastly pause?
I do not know. Some rhythm there may be
I cannot hear. But I—oh, I must go
Back where the breakers of deep sunlight roll
Across flat fields that love and touch the sky;
Back to the more of earth, the less of man,
Where there is still a plain simplicity,   20
And friendship, poor in everything but love,
And faith, unwise, unquestioned, but a star.
Soon now the peace of summer will be there
With cloudy fire of myrtles in full bloom;
And when the marvelous wide evenings come,
Across the molten river one can see
The misty willow-green of Arcady.
And then—the summer stars. . . . I will go home.

DuBOSE HEYWARD

DuBose Heyward, the son of Edwin W. and Jane DuBose
Heyward, was born in Charleston, South Carolina, August 31,
1885. He was educated in the public schools of the city, and
for years struggled with mediocre success to make a living.
He helped to organize the Poetry Society of South Carolina,
and his earlier writing was mainly poetry. In collaboration
with Hervey Allen he wrote *Carolina Chansons* (1922), an attempt to catch in verse the local color of Charleston and of the
Carolina mountains. In 1923 he married the playwright, Dor-
othy Hartzell Kuhns. The following year he published another
volume of poems, but it was with his novel of a crippled Negro,
Porgy (1925), that he gained wide recognition. Since that time

Heyward has written little poetry, but has busied himself with dramatizing *Porgy* (assisted by his wife), and with writing novels of the mountain whites, the Charleston Negroes, and the Charleston society of pre-Civil War days.

DUSK

They tell me she is beautiful, my city,
That she is colorful and quaint; alone
Among the cities. But I—I who have known
Her tenderness, her courage, and her pity;
Have felt her forces mold me, mind and bone,
Life after life, up from her first beginning—
How can I think of her in wood and stone!
To others she has given of her beauty:
Her gardens, and her dim old faded ways;
Her laughter, and her happy drifting hours;   10
Glad spendthrift April, squandering her flowers;
The sharp still wonder of her autumn days;
Her chimes, that shimmer from St. Michael's steeple
Across the deep maturity of June
Like sunlight slanting over open water
Under a high blue listless afternoon.
But when the dusk is deep upon the harbor,
She finds me where her rivers meet and speak,
And while the constellations gem the silence
High overhead, her cheek is on my cheek.   20
I know her in the thrill behind the dark
When sleep brims all her silent thoroughfares.
She is the glamour in the quiet park
That kindles simple things like grass and trees;
Wistful and wanton as her sea-born airs,
Bringer of dim rich age-old memories.
Out on the gloom-deep water, when the nights
Are choked with fog, and perilous, and blind,
She is the faith that tends the calling lights.
Hers is the stifled voice of harbor bells,   30

Muffled and broken by the mist and wind.
Hers are the eyes through which I look on life
And find it brave and splendid. And the stir
Of hidden music shaping all my songs,
And these my songs, my all, belong to her.

PRODIGAL

Some day, when the stern seeker in my brain
Has ceased to drive me stumbling through the dark,
Dropping dead cinders for each faint new spark,
Only to see the new one wax and wane;
When all my dreams are numbered with the slain;
And wisdom, that egregious patriarch,
Has told his last half truth, and left me stark:
I shall go home, I shall go home again.

Laughter will greet me, waiting in the hall;
And friendships will come trooping down the stairs,   10
Sweet as old rose leaves wrinkled in a jar.
Battles and loves will move me not at all.
There will be juleps, billiards, family prayers,
And a clean passport for another star.

SINGLE POEMS

OUR ANGLO-SAXON TONGUE[99]

Good is the Saxon speech! clear, short, and strong,
Its clean-cut words, fit both for prayer and song;
Good is this tongue for all the needs of life;
Good for sweet words with friend, or child, or wife.
Seax—short word—and like a sword its sway
    Hews out a path 'mid all the forms of speech,
    For in itself it hath the power to teach
Itself, while many tongues slow fade away.

'Tis good for laws; for vows of youth and maid;
Good for the preacher; or shrewd folk in trade;   10
Good for sea-calls when loud the rush of spray;
Good for war-cries where men meet hilt to hilt,
And man's best blood like new-trod wine is spilt,—
Good for all times, and good for what thou wilt!

JAMES BARRON HOPE

TO MY FATHER[100]

WRITTEN ON HIS FIFTY-SIXTH BIRTHDAY

It matters not that Time has shed
His thawless snow upon your head,
For he maintains, with wondrous art,
Perpetual summer in your heart.

WILLIAM HAMILTON HAYNE

SAM DAVIS[101]

"Tell me his name and you are free,"
The General said, while from the tree
The grim rope dangled threat'ningly.

The birds ceased singing—happy birds,
That sang of home and mother-words,
The sunshine kissed his cheek—dear sun;
It loves a life that's just begun!
The very breezes held their breath
To watch the fight twixt life and death.
And O, how calm and sweet and free,   10
Smiled back the hills of Tennessee!
Smiled back the hills, as if to say,
"O, save your life for us to-day."

"Tell me his name and you are free,"
The General said, "and I shall see

You safe within the rebel line—
I'd love to save such life as thine."

A tear gleamed down the ranks of blue—
(The bayonets were tipped with dew),
Across the rugged cheek of war   20
God's angels rolled a teary star.
The boy looked up—'twas this they heard:
"And would you have me break my word?"

A tear stood in the General's eye!
"My boy, I hate to see thee die—
Give me the traitor's name and fly!"

Young Davis smiles, as calm and free
As He who walked on Galilee:
"Had I a thousand lives to live,
Had I a thousand lives to give,   30
I'd lose them, nay, I'd gladly die
Before I'd live one life, a lie!"
He turned—for not a soldier stirred—
"Your duty, men—I gave my word."

The hills smiled back a farewell smile,
The breeze sobbed o'er his hair awhile,
The birds broke out in sad refrain,
The sunbeams kissed his cheek again—
Then, gathering up their blazing bars,
They shook his name among the stars.   40

O Stars, that now his brothers are,
O Sun, his sire in truth and light,
Go tell the list'ning worlds afar
Of him who died for truth and right!
For martyr of all martyrs he
Who dies to save an enemy!
                                    JOHN TROTWOOD MOORE

OPPORTUNITY[102]

They do me wrong who say I come no more
  When once I knock and fail to find you in;
For every day I stand outside your door,
  And bid you wake, and rise to fight and win.

Wail not for precious chances passed away,
  Weep not for golden ages on the wane!
Each night I burn the records of the day—
  At sunrise every soul is born again!

Laugh like a boy at splendors that have sped,
  To vanished joys be blind and deaf and dumb;   10
My judgments seal the dead past with its dead,
  But never bind a moment yet to come.

Though deep in mire, wring not your hands and weep;
  I lend my arm to all who say "I can!"
No shame-faced outcast ever sank so deep,
  But yet might rise and be again a man!

Dost thou behold thy lost youth all aghast?
  Dost reel from righteous Retribution's blow?
Then turn from blotted archives of the past,
  And find the future's pages white as snow.   20

Art thou a mourner? Rouse thee from thy spell;
  Art thou a sinner? Sins may be forgiven;
Each morning gives thee wings to flee from hell,
  Each night a star to guide thy feet to heaven.
                                        WALTER MALONE

LUTE AND FURROW[103]

I

The winter has grown so still
I can stand at the foot of the hill
Where the stream beneath the bridge
Is dry as a heart after grief,
And hear at the top of the ridge
The wind as it lifts a leaf.

At last there is time, I say;
I will shut out the strife to-day;
I will take up my pen and once more
Meet that stranger, my soul, nor be dumb   10
As when earth was the whirlwind's floor,
And Life at her loom sat numb.

Springs, many as ever have been,
On sandals of moss shall slip in;
There is time for the laugh we would fling,
For the wiping of dust from our stars,
For a bee on his marketing wing,
For the forester wind's wild wares.

Comes the joy and the rushing pulse
That in beauty's beginning exults;   20
Then the weight tied fast to the heart;
The doubt that deadens the dawn;
And the raining sting and the smart
Of invisible whips laid on.

II

What is this sudden gaiety that shakes the greyest boughs?
A voice is calling fieldward, 'tis time to start the ploughs!
To set the furrows rolling while all the old crows nod,
And deep as life, the kernel, to cut the golden sod!
The pen, let nations have it,—we'll plough awhile for God.

When half the things that must be done are greater than our
    art, 30
And half the things that must be done are smaller than our heart,
And poorest gifts are dear to burn on altars unrevealed,
Like music comes the summons, the challenge from the weald,—
"They tread immortal measure who make a mellow field!"

The planet may be pleasant, alluring in its way;
But let the ploughs be idle, and none of us can stay.
Here's where there is no doubting, no ghosts uncertain stalk,
A-travelling with the plough beam, beneath the sailing hawk,
Cutting the furrow deep and true where Destiny will walk.

III

The winter has grown so still 40
I can pause and pluck what I will
From the arms of Time as he goes.
All the poems with beauty half-hid,
Yet touching my haste like a rose,
May fall to me now if I bid.

There's the book whose pages shall read
Like the hearts of old friends, who will need
For its quaint flowered paths no guide,
And into the late, sweet night
Will smile as they lay it aside— 50
The book that they once meant to write;

And one that may haunt a strange road,
Like a voice blown low from a wood,
And be song to the wanderer there,
Till the inn is a dark thing and cold,
And the night is a roof-tree dear,
And the moon his hearth of warm gold;

And that other whose music may be
As a flight of birds to the sea;

To the far island beaches made brave   60
With the feet of to-morrows; where strain
The lifters of stone from the grave
Of the world we have dreamed us and slain.

IV

Reproach is upon me; I almost grasp the pen;
When comes a laugh like daybreak, and "Winter's broke," says
    Len.
His eye is like a highpriest's as glowingly he 'lows
He saw a bat by daylight fly roun' the pigeon-house.
"Ain't no time now for foolin', we got to start the ploughs."

We'll set the furrows rolling, and drop the yellow corn;
We'll plough along the universe that babies may be born.   70
Ay, no more time for fooling, here's task without a bound;
It's not the tame old earth now that's spinning us around;
It's Jupiter and Neptune when the plough is in the ground.

How light, how light the heart grows with something surely
    done!
When all the ploughs are going, and all the tasks are one!
Then Fame's a lass that smirks too late; the sun's a brother
    lout;
The moon's a lantern in our hand; the stars are fieldmen stout.
Oh, luck to die in ploughing time,—'twill be just one step out!
                                    OLIVE TILFORD DARGAN

ONE END OF LOVE[104]

"It is long since we met," she said.
I answered, "Yes."

                    She is not fair,
But very old now, and no gold
Gleams in that scant gray withered hair
Where once much gold was: and, I think,
Not easily might one bring tears

Into her eyes, which have become
Like dusty glass.

        " 'Tis thirty years,"
I said. "And then the war came on
Apace, and our young King had need   10
Of men to serve him oversea
Against the heathen. For their greed,
Puffed up at Tunis, troubles him—"
She said: "This week my son is gone
To him at Paris with his men."
And then: "You never married, John?"
I answered, "No." And so we sate
Musing a while.

        Then with his guests
Came Robert; and his thin voice broke
Upon my dream, with the old jests,   20
No food for laughter now: and swore
We must be friends now that our feud
Was overpast.

        "We are grown old—
Eh, John?" he said. "And, by the Rood!
'Tis time we were at peace with God
Who are not long for this world."

           "Yea,"
I answered; "we are old." And then,
Remembering that April day
At Calais, and that hawthorn field
Wherein we fought long since, I said: 30
"We are friends now."

        And she sate by,
Scarce heeding. Thus the evening sped.

And we ride homeward now, and I
Ride moodily; my palfrey jogs
Along a rock-strewn way the moon
Lights up for us; yonder the bogs

Are curdled with thin ice; the trees
Are naked; from the barren wold
The wind comes like a blade aslant
Across a world grown very old.   40

JAMES BRANCH CABELL

ICARUS IN NOVEMBER[105]

There is a moment blind with light, split by the hum
    Of something struck and shaken otherwhere,
And if breath's pausing stills the heartbeat and the dumb
    Wet trees clutch every leaf, then on the air
Will blow slow, small, and keen, and faster, greater, higher,
    The hissing whoop of wind through timeless wings
A thuttering drum-beat round a cold immortal fire
    Half-muffling such a mortal cry as brings
    Fear to the lonely soul's imaginings,
A crescent wailing, and the little heart inclined   10
Hears Icarus, and how the chill gale moans behind.

Who said, O Sun, to Icarus that he must fly
    Or fall who dropped on this green wave at last?
Who fed him bitter aether from the tenuous sky
    Whirled in his winged mind all that is past
And pointed four directions to his stumbling soul?
    Quibbled the whence how where when who and what
Till golden antlers blossomed and the Tree was whole
    And Dian poised, and Icarus forgot
    What Icarus had been, and what had not,   20
And searching lost the hope that Icarus designed
And seeing, never saw that Icarus was blind?

O Icarus is fallen, alabaster foam
    Hangs stilly, still, *Icare est chut ici*,
White tangent to the green wave's arc he's shotten home
    Man-bird, sky-arrow to the unriddling sea,

Who was so questing, still unsated, lost to act,
    Quartered the zig-zag sky for beauty's use,
Swooped, soared, sailed, wheeled and turned and sudden
    stooped on fact
    Or use's beauty or the keen mind's loose   30
    Hot ions streaming in a fluent sluice,
Heedless that Icarus must fall against the wind
Echoing, ever falling in the hollow mind.

Sun of my night, lamp of my not uncertain void,
    Here Icarus is fallen, here he lies.
O fallen Icarus, whose fleshly eyes alloyed
    The fire and solar gold and still are eyes
Give me some manner back the brain, the hardiness—
    If Icarus is fallen once he flew.
Hard-taloned on the sunward wrist he scorned the jess   40
    Pressed on his quarry in aethereal blue.
    Icare est chut ici, and still he knew
Less where the heron went than what he hoped to find
And more the cloven hoof-print than the frightened hind.
                    ALEC B. STEVENSON

CALE YOUNG RICE

Cale Young Rice, the son of Laban M. and Martha Lacy Rice, was born in Dixon, Kentucky, December 7, 1872. When he was six, his family moved to Evansville, Indiana, where he attended the public school for ten years. He received his A.B. degree from Cumberland University in 1893; his A.M. from Harvard in 1896. His home since that time has been in Louisville, but he has wandered all over the world, and his poems deal with many lands. In 1902 he married the popular novelist, Alice Caldwell Hegan, author of *Mrs. Wiggs of the Cabbage Patch*. His life has been relatively uneventful. He has written seven poetic dramas, twenty-one volumes of poetry, and five volumes of prose.

FROM A FELUCCA

A white tomb in the desert,
An Arab at his prayers
Beside the Nile's dark water,
Where the lone camel fares.
An ibis on the sunset,
A slow shadouf at rest,
And in the caravansary
Low music for the guest.

Above the tawny city
A gleam of minarets,   10
Resounding the muezzin's
Clear call as the sun sets.
A mystery, a silence,
A breathing of strange balm,
A peace with Allah on the wind
And on the sky his calm.

DANIEL BOONE'S LAST LOOK WESTWARD

I'm only four score year, my sons, and a few
To fill the measure up. And so I shouldn't
Be shut here like an old hound by the fire
To dream of deeds I still have wind to do.
Maybe I have performed enough for one man;
For there's Kentucky cut from the wilderness
And sewed fast to the States by law and order—
Which I'm not sayin' isn't good for them
Who like pullin' in harness with their neighbors.
But I keep seein' trails,—runnin' to westward   10
And northwest,—Indian-footed trails
That no white man has ever pierced an eye through;
And beyond them are prairie lands and forests
Which settlers comin' after me could scalp

And sell, if silver is the game they're seekin':
And the Almighty means my eyes to see them,
Else He'd have made my sight dim and rheumy
By now—and where's the deer or bear that gambols
Before my gun and goes away to say so?

It's kind of shiftless maybe, I'll allow,   20
To want to keep always *beyond* the settlements
Not *in* them: ten near families is too many.
But the Lord never meant the plow to be
My instrument: I get to the end of a furrow
And there's the wilderness waitin', all creation,
And I just have to find a path across it—
As your ma, there, knows; though I never could tell her
The reason, till they took Kentucky in.
And then I saw the cunnin' to be wise
With animals and savages was more   30
Than love of powder and shot; and that God used
My axe to hew a realm out. And there's more realms
Yet to be hewed—and God's grindin' the axes,
I'll tell you that. For, young Lewis and Clark,
Sons of my two old friends, are comin' tomorrow
With unblazed trails of the Northwest in their eyes;
And who knows but that land's as big as Kentucky
And Illinois too; and that they're comin'
For more than to look at an old hound by the fire?
There's one run in me yet; and if I died   40
Somewhere upon a far new trail with them,
There's a coffin-board saved—and I'd sleep better . . .
Unless your ma, this time, wouldn't be willin'
To pack my kit and draw the latch of the door.

She won't, eh? Then it's dodderin' here, I reckon,
And dreamin'. Put a fresh log on, and let be.
Young Lewis and Clark will need a-many like me, though,
Before they hew that Northwest into the world.

THE CONTESSA TO HER JUDGES

(PALERMO)

Do not suppose that I confess
    I sinned—I who have killed him!
For did he not go nightly there
    To her balcony and sing—
Until she bade him up to her
    And in her arms stilled him,
Then sent him back with lies of love
    To me—a shameless thing?

Do not suppose that I confess:
    Not unto God, the Father,   10
Sitting, with mercy in His eyes,
    And ready to shrive all,
And shrinking not away from me,
    But listening to me rather,
Would I say, 'I am on sin's flood,
    Save me, or I am drowned!'

Ah no. . . . For had he that I loved
    But said, 'I love *her* better;
You are my wife—but Beauty reigns
    As mistress of men's soul!'   20
I would have scorned to spill her cup
    Of joy—but would have let her
Clasp it to her and drink of it
    Whatever he should dole.

Yes, had he only dealt me fair,
    But once, and not pretended,
While I with ready doting still
    Gave all of soul or flesh—
With a belief I blush for now,
    We might at last have ended   30

> Merely as many have before,
>   Not in this bloody mesh!
>
> For love has too its Holy Ghost
>   To sin against, past pardon;
> Love too, and I in killing him
>   Have done no more a wrong
> Than Christ will, when He comes again
>   From Paradise, to harden
> His heart against all blasphemy
>   That surges from Hell's throng.
>
> 40

JOHN GOULD FLETCHER

John Gould Fletcher, the only son and oldest child of John Gould and Adolphine Krause Fletcher, was born in Little Rock, Arkansas, January 3, 1886. His father had served with distinction in the Civil War, advancing from private to captain and being cited for gallantry at the battle of Stone River; his mother was of German-Danish descent. The early life of John Gould Fletcher was redolent of the traditions of the ante-bellum South: when he was four years old his father purchased the Pike House, old home of the distinguished poet and soldier, Albert Pike. This house, he wrote, "exerted a powerful influence on my childhood, and I may truly say that I have never fully gotten away from it." He was brought up carefully, and educated at home until he was ten years old. A public school education was followed by one year at Andover and four years at Harvard, which he left in 1907 without taking a degree.

He accompanied an archaeological expedition to the Southwest, with the idea of becoming an archaeologist, but soon abandoned this idea. Deciding that "the United States held nothing of interest for me," he went to Europe in 1908, and, with occasional trips to this country, remained there until 1930. In England he continued to write poetry and in 1913 five books of his poems were published. These works were neglected by readers and critics; not until the publication of *Irradiations* (1915) and *Goblins and Pagodas* (1916) did Fletcher become widely known. He was by that time a leading member of the "Imagist" group, a friend of Ezra Pound and Amy Lowell, and one of the foremost writers of experimental verse. In 1916 he married Florence Emily Arbuthnot of London; two children were born to them.

Granite and Breakers, more native to his own country than his earlier poems, appeared in 1921, and with it appeared a definitely philosophical note, to be followed in later poems by a note at once mystical and prophetic. Fletcher also began to translate from the French, and to write prose on such varied subjects as *The Two Frontiers* (1930), contrasting America and Russia, a biography of Captain John Smith, and a provocative article on education for *I'll Take My Stand*. In 1930 he returned to America and to the South to live, and his later poems and prose have affirmatively treated the legends and subjects of the South, with an underlying philosophy that men must get back to an agrarian way of life.

WHITE SYMPHONY[106]

I

Forlorn and white,
Whorls of purity about a golden chalice,
Immense the peonies
Flare and shatter their petals over my face.

They slowly turn paler,
They seem to be melting like blue-gray flakes of ice,
Thin greyish shivers
Fluctuating mid the dark green lance-thrust of the leaves.

Like snowballs tossed,
Like soft white butterflies,
The peonies poise in the twilight.   10
And their narcotic insinuating perfume
Draws me into them
Shivering with the coolness,
Aching with the void.
They kiss the blue chalice of my dreams
Like a gesture seen for an instant and then lost forever.

* * *

Outwards the petals
Thrust to embrace me,
Pale daggers of coldness   20
Run through my aching breast.

Outwards, still outwards,
Till on the brink of twilight
They swirl downwards silently,
Flurry of snow in the void.

                    *   *   *

Outwards, still outwards,
Till the blue walls are hidden,
And in the blinding white radiance
Of a whirlpool of clouds, I awake.

Like spraying rockets   30
My peonies shower
Their glories on the night.

Wavering perfumes,
Drift about the garden;
Shadows of the moonlight,
Drift and ripple over the dew-gemmed leaves.

Soar, crash, and sparkle,
Shoal of stars drifting
Like silver fishes,
Through the black sluggish boughs.   40

Towards the impossible,
Towards the inaccessible,
Towards the ultimate,
Towards the silence,
Towards the eternal,
These blossoms go.

The peonies spring like rockets in the twilight,
And out of them all I rise.

II

Downwards through the blue abyss it slides,
The white snow-water of my dreams   50
Downwards crashing from slippery rock
Into the boiling chasm:
In which no eye dare look, for it is the chasm of death.

Upwards from the blue abyss it rises,
The chill water-mist of my dreams;
Upwards to greyish weeping pines,
And to skies of autumn ever about my heart,

It is blue at the beginning,
And blue-white against the grey-greenness;
It wavers in the upper air,   60
Catching unconscious sparkles, a rainbow-glint of sunlight,
And fading in the sad depths of the sky.

Outwards rush the strong pale clouds,
Outwards and ever outwards;
The blue-grey clouds indistinguishable one from another:
Nervous, sinewy, tossing their arms and brandishing,
Till on the blue serrations of the horizon
They drench with their black rain a great peak of changeless
    snow.

* * *

As evening came on, I climbed the tower,
To gaze upon the city far beneath: 70
I was not weary of day; but in the evening
A white mist assembled and gathered over the earth
And blotted it from sight.

But to escape:
To chase with the golden clouds galloping over the horizon:
Arrows of the northwest wind

Stinging amid them,
Ruffling up my hair!

As evening came on the distance altered,
Pale wavering reflections arose from out the city,   80
Like sighs or the beckoning of half-invisible hands.
Monotonously and sluggishly they crept upwards
A river that had spent itself in some chasm,
And dwindled and foamed at last at my weary feet.

Autumn! Golden fountains,
And the winds neighing
Amid the monotonous hills:
Desolation of the old gods,
Rain that lifts and rain that moves away;
In the green-black torrent   90
Scarlet leaves.

It was now perfectly evening:
And the tower loomed like a gaunt peak in mid-air
Above the city: its base was utterly lost.
It was slowly coming on to rain,
And the immense columns of white mist
Wavered and broke before the faint-hurled spears.

I will descend the mountains like a shepherd,
And in the folds of tumultuous misty cities,
I will put all my thoughts, all my old thoughts, safely to sleep.
For it is already autumn,   101
O whiteness of the pale southwestern sky!
O wavering dream that was not mine to keep!

* * *

In midnight, in mournful moonlight,
By paths I could not trace,
I walked in the white garden,
Each flower had a white face.

Their perfume intoxicated me: thus I began my dream.

I was alone; I had no one to guide me,
But the moon was like the sun: 110
It stooped and kissed each waxen petal,
One after one.

Green and white was that garden: diamond rain hung in the
        branches,
You will not believe it!

In the morning, at the dayspring,
I wakened, shivering; lo,
The white garden that blossomed at my feet
Was a garden hidden in snow.

It was my sorrow to see that all this was a dream.

                                III

Blue, clogged with purple,   120
Mists uncoil themselves:
Sparkling to the horizon,
I see the snow alone.

In the deep blue chasm,
Boats sleep under gold thatch;
Icicle-like trees fret
Faintly rose-touched sky.

Under their heaped snow-eaves,
Leaden houses shiver.
Through thin blue crevasses,   130
Trickles an icy stream.

The pines groan white-laden,
The waves shiver, struck by the wind;

Beyond from treeless horizons,
Broken snow-peaks crawl to the sea.

* * *

Wearily the snow glares,
Through the grey silence, day after day,
Mocking the colourless cloudless sky
With the reflection of death.

There is no smoke through the pine tops,   140
No strong red boatmen in pale green reeds,
No herons to flicker an instant,
No lanterns to glow with gay ray.

No sails beat up to the harbour,
With creaking cordage and sailors' song.
Somnolent, bare-poled, indifferent,
They sleep, and the city sleeps.

Mid-winter about them casts,
Its dreary fortifications:
Each day is a gaunt grey rock,   150
And death is the last of them all.

* * *

Over the sluggish snow,
Drifts now a pallid weak shower of bloom;
Boredom of fresh creation,
Death-weariness of old returns.

White, white blossom,
Fall of the shattered cups day on day:
Is there anything here that is not ancient,
That has not bloomed a thousand years ago?

Under the glare of the white-hot day,   160
Under the restless wind-rakes of the winter,
White blossom or white snow scattered,
And beneath them, dark, the graves.

Dark graves never changing,
White dream drifting, never changing above them:
O that the white scroll of heaven might be rolled up,
And the naked red lightning thrust at the smouldering earth!

DOWN THE MISSISSIPPI

I. EMBARKATION

Dull masses of dense green,
The forests range their sombre platforms;
Between them silently, like a spirit,
The river finds its own mysterious path.

Loosely the river sways out, backward, forward,
Always fretting the outer side;
Shunning the invisible focus of each crescent,
Seeking to spread into shining loops over fields.

Like an enormous serpent, dilating, uncoiling,
Displaying a broad scaly back of earth-smeared gold;   10
Swaying out sinuously between the dull motionless forests,
As molten metal might glide down the lip of a vase of dark
     bronze;

It goes, while the steamboat drifting out upon it,
Seems now to be floating not only outwards but upwards;
In the flight of a petal detached and gradually moving skyward
Above the pink explosion of the calyx of the dawn.

II. HEAT

As if the sun had trodden down the sky,
Until no more it holds living air, but only humid vapour,
Heat pressing upon earth with irrestible languor,
Turns all the solid forest into half-liquid smudge.   20

The heavy clouds like cargo-boats strain slowly against its
     current;

And the flickering of the haze is like the thunder of ten thousand
    paddles
Against the heavy wall of the horizon, pale-blue and utterly
    windless,
Whereon the sun hangs motionless, a brassy disc of flame.

III. FULL MOON

Flinging its arc of silver bubbles, quickly shifts the moon
From side to side of us as we go down its path;
I sit on the deck at midnight and watch it slipping and sliding,
Under my tilted chair, like a film of spilt water.
It is weaving a river of light to take the place of this river;
A river where we shall drift all night, then come to rest in its
    shallows;   30
And then I shall wake from my drowsiness and look down from
    some dim treetop
Over white lakes of cotton, like moonfields on every side.

IV. THE MOON'S ORCHESTRA

When the moon lights up
Its dull red campfire through the trees;
And floats out, like a white balloon,
Into the blue cup of the night, borne by a casual breeze;
The moon-orchestra then begins to stir.
Jiggle of fiddles commence their crazy dance in the darkness.
Crickets churr
Against the stark reiteration of the rusty flutes which frogs 40
Puff at from rotted logs
In the swamp.
And then the moon begins her dance of frozen pomp
Over the lightly quivering floor of the flat and mournful river.
Her white feet slightly twist and swirl.
She is a mad girl
In an old unlit ballroom
Whose walls, half-guessed at through the gloom,
Are hung with the rusty crape of stark black cypress

Which show, through gaps and tatters, red stains half hidden
  away.   50

negro

V. THE STEVEDORES

Frieze of warm bronze that glides with catlike movements
Over the gangplank poised and yet awaiting,
The sinewy thudding rhythm of forty shuffling feet *loading cotton*
Falling like muffled drumbeats on the stillness. *humming a song as they wor*
O roll the cotton down,
Roll, roll the cotton down,
From the further side of Jordan,
O roll the cotton down!

And the river waits,
The river listens,   60
Chuckling little banjo-notes that break with a flop on the
  stillness;
And by the low dark shed that holds the heavy freights,
Two lonely cypress trees stand up and point with stiffened
  fingers *dead limbs*
Far southward where a single chimney stands out aloof in the
  sky.

VI. NIGHT LANDING

After the whistle's roar has bellowed and shuddered,
Shaking the sleeping town and the somnolent river,
The deep toned floating of the pilot's bell
Suddenly warns the engines.

They stop like heart-beats that abruptly stop,
The shore glides to us, in a wide low curve.   70

And then—supreme revelation of the river—
The tackle is loosed—the long gangplank swings outwards—
And poised at the end of it, half-naked beneath the searchlight,
A blue-black negro with gleaming teeth waits for his chance to
  leap.

VII. THE SILENCE

There is a silence I carry about with me always;
A silence perpetual, for it is self-created;
A silence of heat, of water, of unchecked fruitfulness
Through which each year the heavy harvests bloom, and burst
    and fall.

Deep, matted green silence of my South,
Often within the push and scorn of great cities,   80
I have seen that mile-wide waste of water swaying out to you,
And on its current glimmering, I am going to the sea.

There is a silence I have achieved: I have walked beyond its
    threshold;
I know it is without horizons, boundless, fathomless, perfect,
And some day maybe, far away,
I will curl up in it at last and sleep an endless sleep.

EARTH

I

Earth, let me speak to you,
Earth, let me listen to you;
Patient, brooding, melancholy;
Earth of many harvests.

Earth, let me rest upon you,
Earth, let me sleep upon you,
Deep, dark-bosomed mother,
Shaper of my life.

Mother of the grass
That grows and is mown in a season,   10
Mother of the tree
That abides for a hundred years in strength;

Mother of the man
Whose years fall swiftly as the grass,
Whose spirit stands yet as a tree
Unshattered by the gales;

Womb out of which I emerged,
Grave into which I must enter,
Hear me, mother of my song;
Give reply.   20

In the splendor of the morning
Hear my question:
"Why are not men made as Gods
That they may know the beauty of the earth?"

In the weariness of evening
Answer low:
"I am the ultimate mistress,
I open wide my arms that all may come."

II

Earth of bright harvest fields,
Rich, firm-breasted, fertile, yielding   30
Golden grain and gleaming flowers,
Song-birds, butterflies;

Orchard-bearing earth,
Chastely beautiful in the spring;
After the dense, dull showers of summer,
Glowing in pride, mature;

Flaming with scarlet fruit,
Heavy, firm, and sweet to the taste;
Flowing with wild berries
Sharp and bitter;   40

You are the giver of all life,
Bountiful, fruitful, worn with years,

Offering your body up
Still to the casual sun;

You are the grave that awaits me,
The peace that is greater than life's peace,
The curtain of silence that falls
Upon the close of the play.

III

Earth of dark battlefields,
Red-soaked burnt earth, crumbling, barren,   50
Earth under which the armies burrowed
As into living tombs;

Earth that is slashed and rent;
Shell-gouged, trench-torn, bruised, and battered,
Earth that is desolate,
A stark and horrible shape.

Weedy, forsaken earth,
Stagnant with scummy, rotting pools,
Earth where nothing flourishes
But the rat, the hawk, the crow;   60

You are the grave of my hopes,
You are the sterile harlot
Kissing me with the fierce kisses of death
That eat my lips and eyes;

You are the mother of new life,
Torn with the pangs of a monstrous birth,
The unforgettable shame
Through which we men renew.

IV

Dust returns to the dust,
And spirit goes back into spirit;   70
Who speaks with the tongue of the earth,
Earth only can set him free.

Of me the winds shall speak
When they cry with half-human voices,
For me the rains shall complain
In their long falling;

Through me the stars shall burn bright
Over desolate ruined cities;
Through me new cities shall rise,
Fair as the ones in my dreams.   80

My tears have dropped on the earth,
And the earth has received them.
My voice has called out to the earth,
Earth's silence will answer my speech.

My years turn to seaward now,
A river of sorrows, burdened, dark;
Fed by the clouds and tempests
Of other years.

I have buried my hopes in the earth,
As a man robbed of all but one treasure   90
Hides that away
In the hills;

I have looked far away to the future,
As a man who at sunset peers
Into the cloudy, smouldering west
Finds the faint evening star.

THE SWAN

Under a wall of bronze,
Where beeches dip and trail
Thin branches in the water,
With red-tipped head and wings,
A beaked ship under sail,
. There glides a great black swan.

Under the autumn trees
He goes. The branches quiver,
Dance in the wraith-like water,
Which ripples beneath the sedge   10
With the slackening furrow that glides
In his wake when he is gone:
The beeches bow dark heads.

Into the windless dusk,
Where in mist great towers stand
Guarding a lonely strand
That is bodiless and dim,
He speeds with easy stride;
And I would go beside,
Till the low brown hills divide   20
At last, for me and him.

THE BLACK ROCK *loneliness*

(To THOMAS HARDY)

I

Off the long headland, threshed about by round-backed
    breakers,
There is a black rock, standing high at the full tide;
Off the headland there is loneliness,
And the moaning of the ocean,
And the black rock standing alone.

In the orange wake of sunset,
When the winds have fallen silent,
And the shadows slip and meet together from the edges of the
    sea,
Settled down in the dark water,
Fragment of this earth abandoned,   10
Ragged and huge the black rock stands.

It is as if it listened,
Stood and listened very intently,
To the everlasting swish and boom and hiss of spray;
While afar off, to the westward,
Dark clouds silently are packed together,
With a dull red glow between.

It is listening, it is lonely;
For the sunlight
Showed it houses near the headland,   20
Distant trees and flowers.
For the sunlight caused to grow upon it blades of scanty grass
In the crannies of the granite
Here and there;
For the sunlight brought it back remembrance of a world
Long rejected
And long lost;
Showed it white sails near the coast,
Children laughing in the bay,
Signs of life and kinship with mankind   30
Long forgot.
Now the sunset leaves it there,
Bare, rejected, a black scrap of rock,
Battered by the tides,
Wallowing in the sea.

Bleak, adrift,
Shattered like a monstrous ship of stone
By the waters, on its voyage;
With no foot to touch its deck,
With no hand to stir its sails,   40
There it stands.

II

Gulls wheel near it in the sunlight,
White backs flash,
Grey wings eddy, curl, are lifted, swept away,

On a wave:
Gulls pass rapidly in the sunlight
Round about it.

But the black rock does not welcome them,
Knows by heart already all their cries;
Hears repeated for the millionth millionth time   50
All the bitterness of ocean
Spoken in their voices.

*not much love
harsh*

It still dreams of other things,
Of the cities and the fields,
And the lands near to the coast
Where the lonely grassy valleys
Filled with dun herds deeply browsing
Sweep in wide curves towards the sea:

It still holds the memory
Of the wild bees booming, murmuring   60
In the fields of thyme and clover,
And the shadows of broad trees
Towards noon:

It still lifts its huge scarred sides
Vainly, to the burning glare of noon,
With the memory of doom
Thick upon them;
And the hope that by some fate
It may come once more to be
Part of all the earth it had: 70

Freed from clamour of the waves,
From the broken planks and wreckage,
Drifting aimless, here and there,
With the tides;
Freed to share its life with earth,
And to be a dwelling place

For the outcast tribes of men
Once again.

III

In the morning,
When the dark clouds swirl swift over   80
From the southwest, dragging with them
Heavy curtains of grey rain,

The black rock rejoices.
All its little gullies drip with cool refreshing showers.
All its crannies, all its steeps,
All its meagre sheltered places
Fill with drip and tinkle of the rain.

But when afternoon amid the clouds
Leaves adrift cool patches of the sky,
Moving like smooth stretches of the sea   90
Between floes of polar snow;

Then the rock is all aflame;
Diamonds, emeralds, topazes,
Burn and shatter, till it seems
Like a garden filled with flowers.

Like a garden where the rapid wheeling lights
And brown shadows drift and sway and fall;
Spring and summer and red autumn chase each other
Moment after moment, over its face.

So, till sunset   100
Lifts once more its lonely crimson torch
Menacing and mournful, far away;
Then an altar left abandoned, it stands facing all the horizon
Whence the light departs:

Massive black and crimson towers,
Cities carven by the winds from out the clouds of sunset look
    at it;

It has dreamed them, it has made this sacrifice,
Now it sees their rapid passing,
Soon it will be bleak and all alone.

IV

Abrupt and broken rock,   110
Black rock, awash in the midst of the waters,
Lonely, aloof, abandoned,
Impotent to change;

Storm clouds drift off,
The sun strikes the hills far inland,
But you are forever tragic and apart,
Forever battling with the sea;

Till the waves have ground you to dust,
Till the ages are accomplished,
Till you have relinquished the last reluctant fragment   120
To the gnawing teeth of the wave.

I know the force of your patience,
Have shared your grim silent struggle,
The mad dream you have and will not abandon,
To cover your strength with gay flowers.

Keel of the world, apart,
I have lived with you.

Some men are soil of the earth;
Their lives are like harvest fields
Green in the spring, and gold in their season,   130
Then barren and mown;

But those whom my soul has loved
Are as barren rock standing off headlands,
Cherishing perhaps a few bitter wild flowers
That bloom in the granite year after year.

THE HOUSE TO THE MAN

Here is no easy fate, nor may you find
What you came forth to see—
Not solemn columns only
Nor the broad splendour of the sun
Dappling the wide white wall
With dancing patterns of shadow:
No, not these things shall reveal me, not the sweep of the
    lawn,
Nor the peace of the hall,
With its great cupboards flung open, the breadth of the doors
Forever unclosed: 10
Nor the croon of the slow dark voices, the patient unhurrying
    gait
Of those that in me once reposed.
These may forever wait,
Might in proud grace undisclosed,
But not the strength, the vast strength of foundations fixed to
    the earth,
Stone rooted to stone,
And the trees that whisper beyond, the solemn trees drearily
    swinging
Their aged incredible beards;
Spying upon the graveyard away off there in the corner;
These shall be mine: 20
These shall do as you feared;
Sapping the lives that live by them, burning them down,
Taking each one in its turn;
No liquor was ever brewed that could subdue them;
They shall go on
Ghost against man, till the last hand
Has smoothed back the lawn,
Dusted the chairs, made the feast ready
For the guest who never came.
Few men will know of this, few will spy closely yet love me

Still more deep, for the stains   31
Because they are clear, few will seek out still the cricket
Chirping on in the autumn rains.
Therefore I say it is better to let me go,
Better to break me down,
Shear the wall off, topple the trees with their burden,
Trek for the north, and begone;
Than to sit here still listlessly brooding on quiet,
Still aimless and wan,
While over the Southern fields swings the immitigable   40
Gold hawk of the great Sun.

JOHN CROWE RANSOM

John Crowe Ransom, the son of John James and Ella Crowe
Ransom, was born in Pulaski, Tennessee, April 30, 1888. He
received his B.A. degree from Vanderbilt University in 1909,
and as a Rhodes Scholar from Tennessee, his B.A. from Oxford
(taking the classical course) in 1913. He served for two years
as an artillery officer in France, and since that time has taught
English at Vanderbilt, with the exception of one year, 1931–32,
when he was a Guggenheim Fellow in England. His first
volume, *Poems About God,* appeared in 1919; it made use of
local Tennessee scenery and idiom in a striking manner. He
was one of the founders of the "Fugitive" group of poets
(which included Donald Davidson, Allen Tate, Merrill Moore,
Robert Penn Warren, and other talented poets), and helped
to publish the poetry magazine, *The Fugitive.* His second
volume, *Chills and Fever,* appeared in 1924; the same year, the
English poet Robert Graves selected from the two books a
group of poems and published them in England under the title
Grace After Meat. Since 1927, when *Two Gentlemen in Bonds*
appeared, Ransom has written little poetry, but in a book of
prose, *God without Thunder,* he has stated in striking and brilliant fashion his dissatisfaction, philosophically, with modern
science and weakened religion; he has helped to transform the
Fugitives into an agrarian group, which produced *I'll Take
My Stand,* and in his later writing he has consistently presented
these two philosophical ideas in persuasive prose.

SPECTRAL LOVERS

By night they haunted a thicket of April mist,
As out of the rich ground strangely come to birth,
Else two immaculate angels fallen on earth.
Lovers they knew they were, but why unclasped, unkissed?
Why should two lovers go frozen asunder in fear?
And yet they were, they were.

Over the shredding of an April blossom
Her thrilling fingers touched him quick with care;
Of many delicate postures she cast a snare;
But for all the red heart beating in the pale bosom,   10
Her face as of cunningly tinctured ivory
Was hard with an agony.

Stormed by the little batteries of an April night,
Passionate being the essences of the field,
Should the penetrable walls of the crumbling prison yield
And open her treasure to the first clamorous knight?
"This is the mad moon, and must I surrender all?
If he but ask it, I shall."

And gesturing largely to the very moon of Easter,
Mincing his steps, and swishing the jubilant grass,   20
And beheading some field-flowers that had come to pass,
He had reduced his tributaries faster,
Had not considerations pinched his heart
Unfitly for his art.

"Am I reeling with the sap of April like a drunkard?
Blessed is he that taketh this richest of cities;
But it is so stainless, the sack were a thousand pities;
This is that marble fortress not to be conquered,
Lest its white peace in the black flame turn to tinder
And an unutterable cinder."   30

They passed me once in April, in the mist.
No other season is it, when one walks and discovers
Two clad in the shapes of angels, being spectral lovers,
Trailing a glory of moon-gold and amethyst,
Who touch their quick fingers fluttering like a bird
Whose songs shall never be heard.

HERE LIES A LADY

touch of bitterness / modernism / flipness

Here lies a lady of beauty and high degree.
Of chills and fever she died, of fever and chills,
The delight of her husband, her aunts, an infant of three,
And of medicos marvelling sweetly on her ills.

For either she burned, and her confident eyes would blaze,
And her fingers fly in a manner to puzzle their heads—
What was she making? Why, nothing; she sat in a maze
Of old scraps of laces, snipped into curious shreds—

Or this would pass, and the light of her fire decline
Till she lay discouraged and cold as a thin stalk white and blown,
And would not open her eyes, to kisses, to wine;   11
The sixth of these states was her last; the cold settled down.

Sweet ladies, long may ye bloom, and toughly I hope ye may
    thole,
But was she not lucky? In flowers and lace and mourning,
In love and great honour we bade God rest her soul
After six little spaces of chill, and six of burning.

JUDITH OF BETHULIA

Beautiful as the flying legend of some leopard,
She had not yet chosen her great captain or prince
Depositary to her flesh, and our defence;
And a wandering beauty is a blade out of its scabbard.
You know how dangerous, gentlemen of threescore?
May you know it yet ten more.

Nor by process of veiling she grew the less fabulous.
Gray or blue veils, we were desperate to study
The invincible emanations of her white body,
And the winds at her ordered raiment were ominous.   10
Might she walk in the market, sit in the council of soldiers?
Only of the extreme elders.

But a rare chance was the girl's then, when the Invader
Trumpeted from the south, and rumbled from the north,
Beleaguered the city from four quarters of the earth,
Our soldiery too craven and sick to aid her—
Where were the arms could countervail his horde?
Her beauty was the sword.

She sat with the elders, and proved on their blear visage
How bright was the weapon unrusted in her keeping,   20
While he lay surfeiting on their harvest heaping,
Wasting the husbandry of their rarest vintage—
And dreaming of the broad-breasted dames for concubine?
These floated on his wine.

He was lapped with bay-leaves, and grass and fumiter weed,
And from under the wine-film encountered his mortal vision.
For even within his tent she accomplished his derision;
She loosed one veil and another, standing unafraid;
And he perished. Nor brushed her with even so much as a
    daisy?
She found his destruction easy.   30

The heathen are all perished. The victory was furnished,
We smote them hiding in our vineyards, barns, annexes,
And now their white bones clutter the holes of foxes,
And the chieftain's head, with grinning sockets, and varnished—
Is it hung on the sky with a hideous epitaphy?
No, the woman keeps the trophy.

May God send unto the virtuous lady her prince.
It is stated she went reluctant to that orgy,

Yet a madness fevers our young men, and not the clergy
Nor the elders have turned them unto modesty since.   40
Inflamed by that thought of her naked beauty with desire?
Yes, and chilled with fear and despair.

BLUE GIRLS 20th century

Twirling your blue skirts, travelling the sward
Under the towers of your seminary,
Go listen to your teachers old and contrary
Without believing a word.

Tie the white fillets then about your lustrous hair
And think no more of what will come to pass
Than bluebirds that go walking on the grass
And chattering on the air.

Practise your beauty, blue girls, before it fail;
And I will cry with my loud lips and publish   10
Beauty which all our power shall never establish,
It is so frail.

For I could tell you a story which is true;
I know a lady with a terrible tongue,
Blear eyes fallen from blue,
All her perfections tarnished—and yet it is not long
Since she was lovelier than any of you.

OUR TWO WORTHIES

All the here and all the there
Ring with the praises of the pair:
Jesus the Paraclete
And Saint Paul the Exegete.

Jesus proclaimed the truth.
Paul's missionary tooth

Shredded it fine, and made a paste,
No particle going to waste,
Kneaded it and caked it
And buttered it and baked it   10
(And indeed all but digested
While Jesus went to death and rested)
Into a marketable compound
Ready to lay on any wound,
Meet to prescribe to our distress
And feed unto our emptiness.

And this is how the pure Idea
Became our perfect panacea,
Both external and internal
And supernal and infernal.   20

What would the Originator have done
Without his Assisting One?
Would his truth have penetrated
If Paul had not fabricated?

When the great captains die
There is some faithful standing by
To whom the chieftain hands his sword.
Proud Paul received—a Word.

This was the man who, given his cause,
Gave constitution and by-laws,   30
Distinguished pedagogue
Who invaded the synagogue
And in a little while
Was proselyting the Gentile.

But what would there have been for Paul
If the Source had finished all?
He blessed the mighty Paraclete
For needing him, to miss defeat,

He couldn't have done anything
But for his Captain spiriting.   40

He knew that he was competen⸱
For any sort of punishment,
With his irresistible urge
To bare his back unto the scourge,
Teasing his own neck
In prodigious shipwreck;
Hunger and rats and gaol
Were mere detail.

Paul was every inch of him
Valiant as the Seraphim   50
And all he went among
Confessed his marvellous tongue,
And Satan fearing the man's spell
Embittered smote the gates of Hell.
So he finished his fight
And he too went from sight.

Then let no cantankerous schism
Corrupt this our catechism
But one and all let us repeat:
Who then is Jesus?   60
He is our Paraclete.
And Paul, out of Tarsus?
He is our Exegete.

AUTUMN LOVE

(ENGLISH SONNET OF ITALIAN PARTS)

Easter thaws no overwintered mind
With its pale burning. Centered in the cake
Of cold the heart fluttering can but ache
And wish the spring away. On an Easter wind
Came she, his lump of locked earth to unbind.
But too white shone the unseasoned lilies plucked

Which still the snows attainted, and no bees sucked,
And he refused her bosom, white and kind.

Great was summer; its fat boughs unshaken,
Its red and thirsting face, its frowzy plumes   10
That nodded, and its fervent rosy fumes.
She leaned like a rich flower to be taken,
But his cold Northern heart would not awaken
To her strong fire, and fevered with half-love
He trembled and went stealthy through the grove,
Leaving her gift ungathered and forsaken.

Vengeance struck with autumn; flapped its blear
And ragged banners; spilled the blossoms; grayed
The plumes and dusted with its cannonade.
Then warned of winter, of these disgraced and dear   20
Already wasting, and bright crowns grown sere,
He ran to seek her, and by the rushes found
Her sunken cold with treachery on the ground.
There they clung, in the ashes of the year.

Her tears filled up her eyes, and unconfessed
His tears lumpily thickening in the throat
Muffled his valiant pledges, every note.
By the sad yellow passage of the sun
They kissed in tears, and heard the fowler's gun
Bark at a few faint birds far from the nest.   30

JOHN PEALE BISHOP

John Peale Bishop, the son of Jonathan Peale and Margaret
Cochran Bishop, was born in Charles Town, West Virginia,
May 21, 1892. He was prepared for college in private and public
schools in West Virginia and in Maryland and attended Mercers-
burg Academy before entering Princeton. He graduated with the
class of 1917; that fall he joined the U. S. Army as lieutenant
of infantry and was in service two years, part of the time in

France. Until he went abroad to live after his marriage to Margaret Grosvenor Hutchins in June, 1922, he was managing editor of *Vanity Fair*. Since 1933 he has lived in the United States, mainly in New Orleans. In addition to his volumes of poetry, *Green Fruit* (1917) and *Now With His Love* (1933), he has contributed verse, sketches, and stories to various magazines. A volume of his stories, *Many Thousands Gone* (the title story was awarded the *Scribner's Magazine* first prize, 1930) was published in 1931.

BEYOND CONNECTICUT, BEYOND THE SEA

When I look into my sons' eyes I see
The color of seawater, blue
Under cold shores. Their bodies will be tall.
Their hair has come to them from far off
Washing like seaweed through diverse waters.

Tall with fair hair, they lived in islands
Who long had lived
Ravaging the shores: swords that arrived
Upon the rising wave
Slowly. Always they came westward.   10
Their stranded keels were sure in the sand.

(But back of bronze is stone, beyond the seamists
Is the silence of old lands and grave shards
Savage and then no longer human secrets.)

They came to the sea-isles. Beyond the sea
The silence of peninsulas of snow. I take
My name and blood from a poor boy
Stolen in the islands, whipped at sea,
And sold to a Connecticut farmer.

Eleazar Bishop lived to be old; he died   20
When old, still stooping over stones
That had come with Bethia, his wife. Dead

They dug him shallow and covered him over
With a clatter of stones from the uncleared hillside.

He left behind him tall seven sons.
Another Eleazar straddled stones
And did not find them fertile.

Thomas Bishop
Was bulleted by the British
In his revolutionary buttocks, climbing   30
A railfence at Breed's Hill.

Isaac Bishop strode upon a continent
And old still stared, at seventy years
Insatiable, upon the setting sun.

And John Bishop wandered south
When long war had burned the corn
And saw his sons stoned, little boys.

And Jonathan Bishop first aspired
To make that landscape desolate
In pigments black and green and white.   40

These are my bones, my bones that lie
Six skeletons underground
And clayed in ruin
On their hillsides keep
As winds are held in autumn rusted leaves
Aging their rustic names.

This is my blood, my blood that beats
In blithe boys' bodies
And shall yet run (O Death!)
Upon a bright inhabited star.   50

But more there are that lie
'Neath snows more northern than Connecticut

Or round the sea-isles drift, dissolved
To salt and drowned, dead bones that rise upon the surf
And prompt the sea to whispers.

THE MOTHERS

Sealights reflected on the rocks
And sunlight baffled by the waves:

O shores! what greens that waver in the shallows
What depths of being, invading blues,
What shadows under waves!

They sit like vast shadows on the rocks
They stand and are women on the sands.
Their hands are sober on the rocks
And in their eyes are myths conceived.

These hands have dug, their loins have laboured   10
These eyes have seen
The man that leaned above them, hasty,
They have known the hands that pushed their thighs apart
The ecstasy they have known and the burning
The heart against the heart
And the heart under the heart
The ecstasy they have known and the burden
The child's hand that gropes across the heart.

But now they sit by the seas
And are unmoved by the lisping sands   20
Or by the losing splendour of the shelly moon.

Our course, I think, is nearer to the sun.

Over their eyelids in etherial bronze
Deploy, Icarus! For among their rocks
Are deeps where a man might drown.

What shall we do? We are their sons,
Insane of courage, lost to will,
Failing, not fathers to our sons?

Serene, in the ears of the flesh they hear
The rude white-flashing rock-noise.   30
Their seas have not the fret of fortune.
In our appeasement is their peace.

When they set out upon these sands
It will be, huge feet, toward eternity.
With the calm march of night they will go
And to the assuagement of goddesses.

In what region, by what shores,
White marts and towers,
By what margins of what noisier seas
Do I think thee to be, my country?   40

After revolt, what triumphs and what deaths?

DONALD DAVIDSON

Donald Davidson was born in Campbellsville, Tennessee,
August 18, 1893. He received his B.A. and M.A. degrees from
Vanderbilt University, taught in high schools, served as an officer in France during the World War, and since that time has
taught English at Vanderbilt. He was one of the founders of
the Fugitives and helped to edit the magazine published by that
group of poets. As literary editor of the Nashville *Tennessean*
he conducted one of the best book review pages in the country,
until this feature was discontinued for financial reasons late in
1930; his own reviews were distinguished for a sanity and con-
sistency of viewpoint which led him, with others, to transform
the Fugitive group into exponents of agrarianism. His first
volume, *An Outland Piper* (1924), was fairly conventional in
form; his second, *The Tall Men* (1927), was a remarkable extended poem in blank verse which dealt with "a people, a state,

a passage of time, and one man's mind." Since this volume was published, Davidson has contributed essays to various magazines, and two illuminating essays on Southern literature to *I'll Take My Stand* and *Culture in the South*. Some of his later poems, especially "Lee in the Mountains," show a greater power than any of his earlier work.

REDIVIVUS

Thin lips can make a music;
Hateful eyes can see;
Crooked limbs go dancing
To a strange melody.

The probing knife of madness
Can start a dullard brain.
Cold cheeks can feel kisses
And warm with tears again.

The surly heart of clowns
Can crack with ecstasy;
Rootbound oaks toss limbs
If winds come fervently.

cry for something to awaken 10

Then let my skeleton soul
Writhe upward from the loam,
Drink red morning again,
And look gently home.

From THE TALL MEN

It was a hunter's tale that rolled like wind
Across the mountains once, and the tall men came
Whose words were bullets. They, by the Tennessee waters,
Talked with their rifles bluntly and sang to the hills
With a whet of axes. Smoke arose where smoke
Never had been before. The Red Man's lodges

Darkened suddenly with a sound of mourning.
Bison, cropping the blue-grass, raised their heads
To a strange wind that troubled them. The deer
Leaped in the thicket, vainly loathing the death   10
That stung without arrows. The great bear, hungry for cattle,
Nudged the rough logs of an unyielding pen
And returned no more, having seen the fangs
Of the snarling dogs and the bright knife of the hunter.
Looks were all westward, I have heard, and feet,
Firm in moccasins after the Indian fashion,
Moved with keen presence like the quiet stir
Of a ravenous spring. The lips of hunters awoke
With rumor of far lands till Carolina
Firesides were restless, till the tall Virginians hated   20
The easy warmth of houses, the too-many-peopled
World. In twos and threes the tall men
Strode in the valleys. Their palisades were pitched
In the Cumberland hills. They brought their teeming wives
To rock the hickory cradles and to mould
Bullets for words that said: "Give way, Red Man.
You have lived long enough. The seed is sown and covered
Which like the dragon's-teeth in a new soil
Shall sprout full-armed in tall men who fight
With a lazy smile, speaking from long rifles."   30

Something (call it civilization) crept
Across the mountains once, and left me here
Flung up from sleep against the breakfast table
Like numb and helpless driftwood. Through the trees
Where summer morning grows with a threat of drouth
I look back on the centuries (not quite two),
Rustling the morning paper and watching the clock.
On upper Sixth . . . some negroes . . . yesterday
Dug up old bones . . . and trash . . . while excavating . . .
Fundaments for the latest Towers of Babel!   40
An Indian grave, the state geologist says,
With beads and bear-tooth necklace and a few

Chipped flints and pots. Another grave?
What's that to me who have my teeth to wash
And a cigarette to light before I catch
A car at eight-fifteen with a paper folded
Neatly in my coat pocket. I must remember
Always to look before crossing. A man was killed
On this historic corner the other day
For failing to look while civilization crept *Modern*   50
Upon him with rubber wheels and a stench of gas.
But here no Indians lurk. The motorman
Knows perfectly what I want. The prisoned air,
Steel, and electricity obey his wrist,
And my soft proud body is borne on the smooth
Parallel rails into a city hoarse
With nine o'clock which brings the swivel-chair
And to the hungry brain the pelt of typewriters.

Some sort of a battle, would you call it, where
Words pass for bullets, dabbed in a scribble of ink?   60
Now here the hero sprawls while a little man
Purrs in a patent tone of voice and a sleek
Copyrighted smile. He has a Northern way
Of clipping his words, and with an inevitable curve
Of an arm in a business suit reveals cigars
In the tribal code. Then we are wreathed in smoke
Like friends. He says: "You are so tall, you men,
You Tennesseans. I've never seen so many
Tall fellows riding in elevators.
What makes you then so tall? Is it the cornbread   70
And the buttermilk, or is it in the air,
Or is it having to climb so many hills
That makes you stretch your legs?"

                              Why, since you ask,
Tallness is not in what you eat or drink
But in the seed of man. And I am minded
(Remembering an Indian grave) to speak

As only I can speak of what I am,
What were the loins that begot me, what the breasts
That suckled me in danger, what the blood
Running rebelliously within me still   80
Of the tall men who walked here when there were
No easy roads for walking or for riding. . . .

The curve of Mill Creek with its throat of moonlight
Dazzled McCrory's eyes and made him dream
Of how a girl's neck looks against the gray
Homespun at candle-lighting time.
Such fleshly thoughts were not his business,
And yet he thought them, gazing below his perch
At the dark logs of the station and the roof
Beneath which Phœbe slept, with her warm neck   90
Curved on a pillow. Outside it was cold
And tedious bother watching for the Indians
Who had not come and would not come, perhaps.
For it was already past the full of the moon;
The spies had skinned the country—all for nothing,
If he was any judge. It was plumb queer,
The way Buchanan had his dander up
And kept fifteen strong men away from harvest,
Waiting for Creeks and Cherokees to come.
Why couldn't he take the word of Indian fighters   100
Who'd never yet guessed wrong? McCrory's feet
Ached with the cold. He scuffed them on the bark.
The sentinel in the opposite shadow leaned
Lazily in his tower. The leaves of autumn
Roared and drooped, and the moon was midnight high.

A spatter of hoofbeats in the bottom-grass
Broke upward to the fort. McCrory jerked
Awake like a cat and saw a straggling herd
Of darting cattle, wild and snorting, crash
Through the plum-thickets and blackberry bushes. What   110
Had startled them? Maybe a prowling bear

Or a nosy wild-cat? Maybe something else,
A nosy Cherokee or Creek? His rifle
Slid on the steady logs. McCrory peered.

And there they were, the painted devils, slinking
Across a patch of sedge. His rifle split
September midnight dead in two. He saw
A feathered topknot sag and crumple. God!
A good shot! Now to get reloaded quickly,
Ram and fire again while in the bare   120
Closure of palisades the tall forms raced
Madly with rifles tall as a man to station,
Speaking hotly into the moonlight greetings
One-syllabled that were not gentle. Then
The hunters remembered their boasts. And useless they thought
Was the life on earth of the Creek and the Cherokee.
Unacata drooped already with neck
Bubbling his blood. And Talotiskee tripped
Like steer beneath the axe when the bullet grunted
Home in his breast. Easy shooting, they said,   130
Laying a cheek against the stock and slowly
Drawing a bead. They felt the steel grow hot
Against their hard palms, looked and fired and looked
While Sally Buchanan ducked beneath the loopholes,
Bringing them powder and ball and pouring whiskey
Out of a gourd. The bullets ripped and smacked
Around lean heads that had forgot to flinch,
And eyes that spotted flashes in the bush.
But now a torch lunged forward on the arm
Of Kiachatallee. The chief whose life was charmed   140
Despised the white men's rifles as he ran.
Leaping as a deer leaps, climbing as a squirrel
Climbs, he topped the flat low roof
And poked the flame against the tindery bark
While the lead spattered and the red devils whooped.
The hunters cursed and fretted when their bullets
Fell weak against the Indian medicine.

They could not draw a bead. McCrory said,
By God, I'll get him yet! and climbed his perch
Again, hurling his cap across the logs   150
And spitting for luck. He laid the barrel steady,
Smoothly gripping the trigger. The Indian jumped
Like a stricken deer. His falling arc of flame
Dashed on the groundward logs. McCrory strained
In an awkward cramp to get a second bead
While the dark form was scuffling desperately
To blow the dying torch. Then suddenly
The hunters knew the dawn and heard a boom
From northward hills where Nashboro was, and said,
It's Robertson with men and guns. But now,   160
Softly as night, the Red Men all had gone. . . .

I have not seen the legendary tree
Where D. BOON CILLED A BAR and lightly slept
With one eye open, leathery cheek on rifle.
Another tree I know, a veteran
Of storms and traffic on a city street,
Bulging its muscular trunk in the dreary middle
Of glib macadam, sending its roots in the deep
Stones of the world where earth and Tennessee
Are all the same. The tree divides the stream   170
Of motors roaring homeward on the hill.
Here, from the Natchez trail, the files of hunters
Warily lounged. And here war-parties met,
Pausing to spy the country, hooting like owls
In the forest twilight. Here I pass with looks
Too reminiscent for a clear impression
Of four-room bungalows fronting a concrete path
That radiates heat. And here I am besieged
By ghosts and shadows much too tall to be
The spirits of the little men who died   180
Respectably last week in a private hospital.
And I must let them speak as they know how. . . .

JOHN SEVIER

Xavier my name in the Gascon country till
My great-sires came to England, and were called
Sevier in the rough English speech, but lost
No chivalry of their ancient name. I loved
The praise of men in hunting-shirts who cheered
For Nolichucky Jack at Watauga Old Fields
And followed me through night and the dripping forest
To King's Mountain. We were the backwoods hornets   190
Crowding the rocky slopes and buzzing death
To that gaudy lion, Ferguson. Elsewhere
It was the same. The sword of the Lord and of Gideon
In my hands smote the Indian villages
To dust and ashes till I lived in peace,
Governing my country, loving my Bonny Kate,
And seeking the praise of men. But where are they?
Where are Shelby and Campbell? Where is Cosby?
Where are the rifles and the lean hunters
Who strode the long trail with me? Have they left   200
No tall sons to hate what should be hated
And love what should be loved—the praise of men
Speaking with quiet eyes behind long rifles?

ANDREW JACKSON

What makes men live but honor? I have felt
The bullet biting next to my heart and yet
I kept my life for honor's sake and killed
My enemy. And what else was the fire
That fed my sickly body when I shamed
The Tennesseans into victory
At Horseshoe Bend? What was it then but honor   210
That blazed too hot for British regulars
At New Orleans? Then all the people knew
That I was of their breed and trusted me.
Cowards and lies and little men will pass,
But honor, by the Eternal, will endure.

DAVID CROCKETT

The corn-shuckings and square dances, the fiddles,
The barrels of gin and whiskey, the jerked venison,
Juicy bear meat, hot corn pone, molasses,
And the girls giggling in corners—those are the things
That make life merry. But there came a time   220
When I neglected them all, and we made merry
(My Betsey and I) at a different kind of party,
Playing with powder and ball at the Alamo.
I regret nothing, not even the lies and jokes
I told in Congress. But what is this I hear?
Tennesseans, have you forgotten the songs
Of Old Zip Coon and Turkey in the Straw?

These are the words of ghosts. I was not there,
At Talledega, Horseshoe Bend, King's Mountain,
Not at Suwannee, Mobile, or Pensacola   230
In days when men were tall. I have not eaten
Acorns to still my hunger or followed the war-path
After a fiery leader tough as the hickory.
I have not heard the cry of the owl at night
With dreadful understanding. I have not seen
A friend plunge, furred with arrows, across his plough
Or heard the scream of a woman snatched from the hearth
By painted warriors. And when it was misty dawn
I was not by the ragged breastworks, priming my rifle,
Hearing the British drums beat. I have not sung   240
Old songs or danced old tunes. I have read a book.
I have loitered by graves. I have trod old floors,
Tiptoed through musty rooms and glanced at letters
Spread under glass and signed *Yr Obt Servant*,
And wistfully conned old platitudes in stone.
But shall I say the praise of men, bright honor,
The songs of my own race and the ways of fighters
Are something read in a book only, or graven
Only in stone and not in the hearts of men?

Speaking with words for bullets politely now 250
I move on rubber heels dividing parallel grooves
On the swept sidewalk. I with an evening paper
Folded neatly in my coat pocket salute the tree
And walk, a veteran of storms and traffic, home,
Where windows bloom with mellow lights against
A square slab of buildings. This is dusk
Where tall men humped on cushioned seats glide home
Impatiently. Feet in immaculate leather,
Silken-cased, urge down the throttle gently,
Speeding with effort only of ankle and wrist. 260
Seven o'clock in the twentieth century is
The hour of supper, not the hour of prayer,
And something (call it civilization) turns
A switch; a fan hums pianissimo,
Blowing old ghosts to outer darkness where
The bones of tall men lie in the Tennessee earth.

FIRE ON BELMONT STREET

(EPILOGUE TO *The Tall Men*)

He was a worthy citizen of the town.
"Where is the fire?" he babbled as he ran.
"The fire! The fire!" Spat between pursy breaths
He dropped his question, stuck his gross right hand
Against his watch-chain, ran, and stared, and sobbed,
Out Belmont Street? My God, that's where I live!
Stumbling with slow fat feet and tragic breath
While roaring sirens passed upon the wind.
And then I heard (What laughter!) blobs of heels
Pecking the night with hurry. Poor staccato, 10
Dragging a million feeble stumps across
The easy pavements while the flames went up,
Gobbling the roofs and sky. Beneath was earth.
Steady against all shouting, ground was waiting
Forever subtle, old. But walls dissolved
And houses quaked with Fire until I could

Endure no more, but ran, as clamorous
As all the plump mad mob, shouting like them:
"The fire," I cried. What fire? No gables burn,
Nor is that redness some unusual dawn   20
Sprawled against moonrise, nor a dragon's breath
Spurted from some old sewer you forgot,
Nor ghosts of Red Men that your fathers knew,
Come back with devil-medicine to bombard
Your bungalows. Choctaw and Cherokee
Lie where the spitting Decherd rifles planted
Under the Tennessee grass, their tired bones.
The fire! What fire? Why God has come alive
To damn you all, or else the smoke and soot
Have turned back to live coals again for shame   30
On this gray city, blinded, soiled, and kicked
By fat blind fools. The city's burning up?
Why, good! Then let her burn!
                                    But I'll say more,
Remembering other odds, a narrow place,
A shock of arms, a cry of gables burning.
And there were gathered in that long grim room
Of warriors sixty who called Hnaef their lord,
Who saw the gray wolf creeping in the wood
And heard the grind of linden shields afar;
Surrounded were, yet held the door and died   40
While the strange light of swords and helmets made
The place like day.
                                    But who will stand tonight,
Holding this other door against the press
Of brazen muscles? Who can conquer wheels
Gigantically rolled with mass of iron
Against frail human fingers? Who can quench
The white-hot fury of the tameless atoms
Bursting the secret jungle of their cells?
Oh, who can stay or ever chain the dull
Gnaw of the fiery smoke, eternally settling   50
Into the beating heart? There is no fire?

Only, perhaps, the breath of a Southern wind
That I have known too well in many a summer,
Drying the pulse, stopping the weary pulse,
Blowing the faint blood back in the curdled veins
Till there is no way to think of what might be
Better or worse. Yet maybe it were better
Climbing the tallest hill to cry at night:
"Citizens, awake! Fire is upon you, fire
That will not rest, invisible fire that feeds   60
On your quick brains, your beds, your homes, your steeples,
Fire in your sons' veins and in your daughters',
Fire like a dream of Hell in all your world.
Rush out into the night, take nothing with you,
Only your naked selves, your naked hearts.
Fly from the wrath of fire to the hills
Where water is and the slow peace of time."

There is a place where beech-trees droop their boughs
Down-slanting, and where the dark cedars grow
With stubborn roots threading the lichened rocks.   70
There the smooth limestone benches, rubbed
By warm primeval streams, yet hold the crystal
Forms of dead life. There on a summer's evening
The screech-owl quavers and unseen July-flies
Trill their thin songs. And there my father said
Pointing a low mound out to me, "My son,
Stand on this Indian's grave and plainly ask,
Indian, what did you die for? And he'll say,
Nothing!"
        So was it! So it is!
What did you die for? Nothing indeed nothing!   80
The seed of the white man grows on Indian graves,
Waxing in steel and stone, nursing the fire
That eats and blackens till he has no life
But in the fire that eats him. White man, remember,
Brother, remember Hnaef and his sixty warriors
Greedy for battle-joy. Remember the rifles

Talking men's talk into the Tennessee darkness
And the long-haired hunters watching the Tennessee hills
In the land of big rivers for something.

SOUTHWARD RETURNING

To you, Virginia, Tennessee,
To Georgia's red roads, to the past
That binds the delta and the sea
Your Southern sons return at last.

No more the always going forth
From ruin and our old regret,
No more the sundering of faiths
By some who taught us to forget.

For us, the long remembering
Of all our hearts have better known.   10
The darkness falls away, a door
Swings, and the traveler is home.

And no lock turns against the night.
None here but has his best desire:
Kinsmen and friends the miles around,
An old man's laughter by the fire,

Then in our fathers' house the sleep
Of sons who bide the calm night through,
The living near the long-lost dead
Who yonder without are sleeping too.   20

LEE IN THE MOUNTAINS

1865–1870

Walking into the shadows, walking alone
Where the sun falls through the ruined boughs of locusts
Up to the President's office. . . .

                                Hearing the voices
Whisper, *Hush it is General Lee!* And strangely
Hearing my own voice say *Good morning boys.*
(*Don't get up. You are early. It is long*
Before the bell. You will have long to wait
On these cold steps. . . .)
                        The young have time to wait.
But the soldiers' faces under the tossing flags
Lift no more by any road or field,   10
And I am spent with old wars and new sorrow.
Walking the rocky path, where the steps decay
And the paint cracks and grass eats on the stone.
It is not General Lee, young men . . .
It is Robert Lee in a dark civilian suit who walks,
An outlaw fumbling for the latch, a voice
Commanding in a dream where no flag flies.

My father's house is taken and his hearth
Left to the candle-drippings where the ashes
Whirl at a chimney-breath on the cold stone.   20
I can hardly remember my father's look, I cannot
Answer his voice as he calls farewell in the misty
Mounting where riders gather at gates.
He was old then—I was a child—his hand
Held out for mine, some daybreak snatched away,
And he rode out, a broken man. Now let
His lone grave keep, surer than cypress roots,
The vow I made beside him. God too late
Unseals to certain eyes the drift
Of time and the hopes of men and a sacred cause.   30
The fortune of the Lees goes with the land
Whose sons will keep it still. My mother
Told me much. She sat among the candles,
Fingering the *Memoirs*, now so long unread.
And as my pen moves on across the page
Her voice comes back, a murmuring distillation

Of old Virginia days now done to death,
The hurt of all that was and cannot be.

Why did my father write? I know he saw
History clutched as a wraith out of blowing mist   40
Where tongues are loud, and a glut of little souls
Laps at the too much blood and the burning house.
He would have his say, but I shall not have mine.
What I do is only a son's devoir
To a lost father. Let him only speak.
The rest must pass to men who never knew
(But on a written page) the strike of armies,
And never heard the long Confederate cry
Charge through the muzzling smoke or saw the bright
Eyes of the beardless boys go up to death.   50
It is Robert Lee who writes with his father's hand—
The rest must go unsaid and the lips be locked.

If all were told, as it cannot be told—
If all the dread opinion of the heart
Now could speak, now in the shame and torment
Lashing the bound and trampled States—

If a word were said, as it cannot be said—

I see clear waters run in Virginia's Valley
And in the house the weeping of young women
Rises no more. The waves of grain begin.   60
The Shenandoah is golden with new grain.
The Blue Ridge, lapped in a haze of light,
Thunders no more. The horse is at plough. The rifle
Returns to the chimney crotch and the hunter's hand.
And nothing else than this? Was it for this
That on an April day we stacked our arms
Obedient to a soldier's trust—to sink, to lie
Ground by heels of little men,

Forever maimed, defeated, lost, impugned?
And was I then betrayed? Did I betray?   70

If it were said, as still it might be said—
If it were said, and a word should run like fire,
Like living fire into the roots of grass,
The sunken flag would kindle on wild hills,
The brooding hearts would waken, and the **dream**
Stir like a crippled phantom under the pines,
And this torn earth would quicken into shouting
Beneath the feet of ragged men—   .

                                             The quill
Turns to the waiting page, the sword of Lee
Bows to the rust that cankers and the silence.   80

Among these boys whose eyes lift up to mine
Within grey walls where droning wasps repeat
A hollow reveille, I still must face
Day after day, the courier with his summons
Once more to surrender, now to surrender all.
Without arms or men I stand, but with knowledge only
I face what long I saw, before others knew,
When Pickett's men streamed back, and I heard the tangled
Cry of the Wilderness wounded, bloody with doom.

The mountains, once I said, in the little room   90
At Richmond, by the huddled fire, but still
The President shook his head. The mountains wait,
I said in the long beat and rattle of siege
At cratered Petersburg. Too late
We sought the mountains and those people came.
And Lee is in mountains now, beyond Appomattox,
Listening long for voices that never will speak
Again; hearing the hoofbeats come and go and fade
Without a stop, without a brown hand lifting
The tent-flap, or a bugle call at dawn,   100

Or ever on the long white road the flag
Of Jackson's quick brigades. I am alone,
Trapped, consenting, taken at last in mountains.

It is not the bugle now, or the long roll beating.
The simple stroke of a chapel bell forbids
The hurtling dream, recalls the lonely mind.
Young men, the God of your father is a just
And merciful God who in this blood once shed
On your green altars measures out all days,
And measures out the grace   110
Whereby alone we live;
And in His might He waits,
Brooding within the certitude of time,
To bring this lost forsaken valour
And the fierce faith undying
And the love quenchless
To flower among the hills to which we cleave,
To fruit upon the mountains whither we flee,
Never forsaking, never denying
His children and His children's children forever   120
Unto all generations of the faithful heart. Amen.

JOSEPHINE PINCKNEY

Josephine Lyons Pinckney, the daughter of Thomas and
Camilla Scott Pinckney, was born in Charleston, South Caro-
lina, January 25, 1895. She studied at Ashley Hall in Charleston, at the College of the City of Charleston, Columbia
University, and Radcliffe College. She helped to found the
Poetry Society of South Carolina, and has published one volume
of poems, chiefly about the country which she knows so well:
Sea-Drinking Cities (1927). She lives in Charleston, and writes
frequently for various magazines. In 1933 she contributed to
Culture in the South an article on social life in the South, significantly titled "Bulwarks against Change."

STREET CRIES

The dreamer turns.
Clear tones zig-zag like lightning
Through soft black sleep.
Thick walls of sleep are cracking. . . .
From streets immeasurably below
The vendors' voices leap,
The cool tunes flow:
"Turtle-eggs—turtle-eggs!"
Delicious quiet:
The sleeper turns . . .   10
"Turtle-eggs . . ."
Dreaming of steaming beaches . . .
The warm sand is wet,
Diggers' bodies bow
Clammy with salt and sweat;
Nests are hidden deep,
. . . turtle-eggs . . .
Round, creamy curds.
How good to dig in the fresh morning
While rosy beaches whiten   20
Quick with the young sea-birds!
Through glassy heat the beach-lines run
Quiver in misty sea and sun,
Gently-rocking sea and sun.

"I got honey,
I got um in de comb!"
June is honey-gold,
Oozing through shutters;
"Honey in de comb—"
An impish whistling tickles   30
The dreamer's muffled ears:
"I'm a po' boy long ways fum home—"
A clack and a clack of feet,

Words fountain up and fall,
Plash in the stony street;
Slow-dripping music trickles,—
"Honey . . . in . . . comb . . ."

Soft black sleep
Is barred with amber light;
The sleeper sighs . . .   40
Oh, sweet delight of love
Where is there such delight
As to love blindly—
Shut-eyed as flowers are at night!

A chorus sings,
A negro chorus, stately-moving,
Fruit-piled basket on head,
And perfect balancings,
Paeans to ripe earth harvested.
"Melons . . . musk-melons . . ."   50
Strophe—curve—return.
Round tones rolling,
Like fruit from horns of plenty,
Spiral down—lie mute,
Trampled by idle strolling.
"Water-water-water-melons . . .
Musk . . ."
Oh, such is love—dream-fruit!
On it the sleeper feeds
And loses all content   60
With daylight things,
Like Proserpine who ate pomegranate seeds
And back to darkness went . . .
And back to darkness went.

SEA-DRINKING CITIES

Sea-drinking cities have a moon-struck air;
Houses are topped with look-outs; as a dog
Looks up with dumb eyes asking, dormers stare
At stranger-vessels and swart cunning faces.
They are touched with long sleeping in the sea-born moon;
They have heard fabled sails slatting in the dark,
Clearing with no papers, unwritten in any log,
Light as thin leaves before the rough typhoon;
Keels trace a phospher-mark,
To follow to old ocean-drowned green places.   10

They never lose longing for the never-known,
These ocean-townships moored and hawsered fast,
They welcome ships, salt-jewelled venturers
That up over the curve of the world are blown
With sun-rise in their sails and gold-topped mast;
And in the evening they let them go again
With a twisted lip of pain,
Into the cavernous fog that folds and stirs;
They have not even a faint tenderness
For their own loveliness.   20

Their loveliness, as of an old tale told . . .
A harbor-goblet with wide-brimming lip
Where morning tumbles in shaken red and gold,
Trinketed and sun-bedizened they sip;
Their tiny tiles all twinkle, fire-bright;
Their strong black people bargain on the docks
In gaudy clothes that catch the beating light . . .
But all bewitched, old cities sit at gaze
Toward the wharves of Mogador . . . Gibraltar,
Where the shawl-selling Arab piles a blaze   30
Of fiery birds and flowers on Trade's heaped altar.
Sea-drunken sure are these,—

Towns that doze—dream—and never wake at all,
While the soft supple wind slides through the trees,
And the sun sleeps against the yellow wall.

ALLEN TATE

Read Poet

John Orley Allen Tate was born on November 19, 1899, in Fairfax County, Virginia, and was reared in Kentucky and Tennessee. He was educated in public and private schools in Louisville, Washington, D. C., and Nashville; he graduated from Vanderbilt University in 1922. That year he helped to found the Fugitives, and he became, at the same time, a free-lance writer—an independent position which he held until the fall of 1934, when he went as professor of English to South-western at Memphis. A brilliant biographer, he has steadily written of Southern men: *Stonewall Jackson* (1928) and *Jefferson Davis* (1929); a critic, he has contributed to *A Critique of Humanism*, to *I'll Take My Stand*, to various magazines, and has in preparation a study of Southern literature. But it is as a poet that Allen Tate is best and most deservedly known, for his two volumes, *Mr. Pope and Other Poems* (1928), and *Poems, 1928–1931* (1932), and for later works, as yet uncollected. In 1930, after two years in Europe on a Guggenheim Fellowship, he returned to live in Clarksville, Tennessee. Tate is married to Caroline Gordon, author of *Penhally*, a novel of the section in which they live.

MR. POPE

When Alexander Pope strolled in the city
Strict was the glint of pearl and gold sedans.
Ladies leaned out, more out of fear than pity;
For Pope's tight back was rather a goat's than man's.

One often thinks the urn should have more bones
Than skeletons provide for speedy dust;
The urn gets hollow, cobwebs brittle as stones
Weave to the funeral shell a frivolous rust.

And he who dribbled couplets like the snake
Coiled to a lithe precision in the sun,   10
Is missing. The jar is empty; you may break
It only to find that Mr. Pope is gone.

What requisitions of a verity
Prompted the wit and rage between his teeth
One cannot say: around a crooked tree
A mortal climbs whose name should be a wreath.

ODE TO THE CONFEDERATE DEAD[107]

Row after row with strict impunity
The headstones yield their names to the element,
The wind whirrs without recollection;
In the riven troughs the splayed leaves
Pile up, of nature the casual sacrament
To the seasonal eternity of death,
Then driven by the fierce scrutiny
Of heaven to their business in the vast breath,
They sough the rumor of mortality.

Autumn is desolation in the plot   10
Of a thousand acres, where these memories grow
From the inexhaustible bodies that are not
Dead, but feed the grass row after rich row:
Remember now the autumns that have gone—
Ambitious November with the humors of the year,
With a particular zeal for every slab,
Staining the uncomfortable angels that rot
On the slabs, a wing chipped here, an arm there:
The brute curiosity of an angel's stare
Turns you like them to stone,   20
Transforms the heaving air,
Till plunged to a heavier world below
You shift your sea-space blindly,
Heaving, turning like the blind crab.

   Dazed by the wind, only the wind
   The leaves flying, plunge

You know who have waited by the wall
The twilit certainty of an animal;
Those midnight restitutions of the blood
You know—the immitigable pines, the smoky frieze 30
Of the sky, the sudden call; you know the rage—
The cold pool left by the mounting flood—
The rage of Zeno and Parmenides.
You who have waited for the angry resolution
Of those desires that should be yours tomorrow,
You know the unimportant shrift of death
And praise the vision
And praise the arrogant circumstance
Of those who fall
Rank upon rank, hurried beyond decision—   40
Here by the sagging gate, stopped by the wall.

   Seeing, seeing only the leaves
   Flying, plunge and expire

Turn your eyes to the immoderate past,
Turn to the inscrutable infantry rising
Demons out of the earth—they will not last.
Stonewall, Stonewall—and the sunken fields of hemp
Shiloh, Antietam, Malvern Hill, Bull Run.
Lost in that orient of the thick and fast
You will curse the setting sun.   50

   Cursing only the leaves crying
   Like an old man in a storm

You hear the shout—the crazy hemlocks point
With troubled fingers to the silence which
Smothers you, a mummy, in time. The hound bitch
Toothless and dying, in a musty cellar
Hears the wind only.

Now that the salt of their blood
Stiffens the saltier oblivion of the sea,
Seals the malignant purity of the flood,
What shall we, who count our days and bow   60
Our heads with a commemorial woe,
In the ribboned coats of grim felicity,
What shall we say of the bones, unclean—
Their verdurous anonymity will grow—
The ragged arms, the ragged heads and eyes
Lost in these acres of the insane green?
The grey lean spiders come; they come and go;
In a tangle of willows without light
The singular screech-owl's bright
Invisible lyric seeds the mind   70
With the furious murmur of their chivalry.

We shall say only, the leaves
Flying, plunge and expire

We shall say only, the leaves whispering
In the improbable mist of nightfall
That flies on multiple wing:
Night is the beginning and the end,
And in between the ends of distraction
Waits mute speculation, the patient curse
That stones the eyes, or like the jaguar leaps   80
For his own image in a jungle pool, his victim.

What shall we say who have knowledge
Carried to the heart? Shall we take the act
To the grave? Shall we, more hopeful, set up the grave
In the house? The ravenous grave?

Leave now
The turnstile and the old stone wall:
The gentle serpent, green in the mulberry bush,
Riots with his tongue through the hush—
Sentinel of the grave who counts us all!

THE CROSS

There is a place that some men know,
I cannot see the whole of it,
Nor how I came there. Long ago
Flame burst out of a secret pit
Crushing the world with such a light
The day sky fell to moonless black,
The kingly sun to hateful night
For those, once seeing, turning back:
For love so hates mortality,
Which is the providence of life,   10
She will not let it blessèd be
But curses it with mortal strife,
Until beside the blinding rood
Within that world-destroying pit
—Like young wolves that have tasted blood,
Of death, men taste no more of it;
So blind, in so severe a place
(All life before in the black grave)
The last alternatives they face
Of life, without life to save,   20
Being from all salvation weaned—
A stag charged both at heel and head;
Who would come back is turned a fiend
Instructed by the fiery dead.

JOHN BROWN

John Brown of Ossawatomie
Who died to set Abstraction free
Stole Washington's gold-handled sword
Less for the gold than for the Lord;
Perhaps it would not much amuse
The General, could he hear the news.

SHADOW AND SHADE

The shadow streamed into the wall—
The wall, break-shadow in the blast;
We lingered wordless while a tall
Shade enclouded the shadow's cast.

The torrent of the reaching shade
Broke shadow into all its parts,
What then had been of shadow made
Found exigence in fits and starts

Where nothing properly had name
Save that still element, the air,
Burnt sea of universal frame
In which impounded now we were:

I took her hand, I shut her eyes,
And all her shadow clove with shade;
Shadow was crushed beyond disguise
But, being fear, was unafraid.

I asked fair shadow at my side:
"What more shall fiery shade require?"
We lay there, in the immense tide
Of shade and shadowy desire

And saw the dusk assail the wall,
The black surge mounting crash the stone.
"Companion of this lust, we fall,"
I said, "lest we should die alone."

MERRILL MOORE ~~omit~~

Merrill Moore, the oldest child of John Trotwood and Mary Daniel Moore, was born in Columbia, Tennessee, September 11, 1903. He was educated in Nashville—where his parents lived and his father served as state historian—graduating both from the college (1924) and the medical school (1928) of Vanderbilt University. He was one of the early members of the Fugitive group, contributing many sonnets to *The Fugitive* and other magazines—sonnets loose in form, a definite unit but without regard to the usual restrictions of the form, and broken according to natural divisions in the poem rather than by arbitrary division. He writes spontaneously, in what may be called an "American sonnet form." After graduation and interneship, Dr. Moore went to Boston for additional study and practice. In 1929 appeared his first book of poems, *The Noise That Time Makes;* in 1935, a second volume, *Six Sides to a Man.*

THE NOISE THAT TIME MAKES

The noise that Time makes in passing by
Is very slight but even you can hear it,
Having not necessarily to be near it,
Needing only the slightest will to try:

Hold the receiver of a telephone
To your ear when no one is talking on the line
And what may at first sound to you like the whine
Of wind over distant wires is Time's own
Garments brushing against a windy cloud.

That same noise again but not so well   10
May be heard by taking a small cockle-shell
From the sand and holding it against your head;

Then you can hear Time's footsteps as they pass
Over the earth brushing the eternal grass.

SHOT WHO? JIM LANE!

When he was shot he toppled to the ground
As if the toughened posts that were his thighs
Had felt that all that held them up were lies,

Weak lies, that suddenly someone had found
Out all that was true about them.

                  It did not seem
Like the crashing of a stalwart forest oak
But like a frail staff that a sharp wind broke
Or something insubstantial in a dream.

I never thought Jim Lane would fall like that.

He'd sworn that bullets must be gold to find him;   10
That when they came toward him he made them mind him
By means he knew,

              just as a barnyard cat
Can keep a pack of leaping dogs at bay
By concentrating and looking a certain way.

ROBERT PENN WARREN *omit*

Robert Penn Warren was born near Guthrie, Kentucky, in
1905. He received his B.A. degree from Vanderbilt University,
his M.A. from the University of California, and his B.Litt.
degree from New College, Oxford. His biography, *John Brown:
The Making of a Martyr*, appeared in 1929, and two years later
an essay on the Negro, "The Briar Patch," was published in
I'll Take My Stand. He has been represented by stories and
poems in *The American Caravan;* his poetry (not as yet collected
in book form), his stories, and his criticisms have appeared in
many magazines. After returning from Oxford in 1930, he
married and taught English for one year at Southwestern in
Memphis and for three years at Vanderbilt. In 1934 he began
to teach creative writing at Louisiana State University.

KENTUCKY MOUNTAIN FARM[108]

I. REBUKE OF THE ROCKS

Now on you is the hungry equinox,
O little stubborn people of the hill,
The season of the obscene moon whose pull
Disturbs the sod, the rabbit, the lank fox,
Moving the waters, the boar's dull blood,
And the acrid sap of the ironwood.

But breed no tender thing among the rocks.
Rocks are too old, under the mad moon,
Renouncing passion by the strength that locks
The eternal agony of fire in stone.   10

Then quit yourselves as stone, and cease
To break the weary stubble-field for seed;
Let not the naked cattle bear increase,
Let barley wither and the bright milk-weed.
Instruct the heart, lean men, of a rocky place
That even the little flesh and fevered bone
May keep the sweet sterility of stone.

II. AT THE HOUR OF THE BREAKING OF THE ROCKS

Beyond the wrack and eucharist of snow
The tortured and reluctant rock again
Receives the sunlight and the tarnished rain.
Such is the hour of sundering, we know,
Who on the hills have seen to stand and pass
Stubbornly the taciturn
Lean men that of all things alone
Were, not as water or the febrile grass,
Figured in kinship to the savage stone.

The hills are weary, the lean men have passed;   10
The rocks are stricken, and the frost has torn

Away their ridged fundaments at last,
So that the fractured atoms now are borne
Down shifting waters to the tall, profound
Shadow of the absolute deeps,
Wherein the spirit moves and never sleeps
That held the foot among the rocks, that bound
The tired hand upon the stubborn plow,
Knotted the flesh unto the hungry bone,
The red-bud to the charred and broken bough,   20
And strung the bitter tendons of the stone.

III. HISTORY AMONG THE ROCKS

There are many ways to die
Here among the rocks in any weather:
Wind, down the eastern gap, will lie
Level along the snow, beating the cedar,
And lull the drowsy head that it blows over
To start a crystalline, cold dream forever.

The hound's black paw will print the grass in May,
And sycamores rise down a dark ravine,
Where a creek in flood, sucking the rock and clay,
Will tumble the sycamore, the laurel, away.   10
Think how a body, naked and lean
And white as the splintered sycamore, would go
Tumbling and turning, hushed in the end,
With hair afloat in waters that gently bend
To ocean where the blind tides flow.

Under the shadow of ripe wheat,
By flat limestone, will coil the copperhead,
Fanged as the sunlight, hearing the reaper's feet.
But there are other ways, the lean men said:
In these autumn orchards once young men lay dead—   20
Grey coats, blue coats. Young men on the mountainside
Clambered, fought. Heels muddied the rocky spring.
Their reason is hard to guess, remembering

Blood on their black mustaches in moonlight,
Cold musket-barrels glittering with frost.
Their reason is hard to guess and a long time past;
The apple falls, falling in the quiet night.

JESSE STUART

Jesse Stuart was born in W-Hollow, near Riverton, Kentucky, in 1905. His people—the Hiltons, Meades, Penningtons, and Stuarts—all came from Virginia; all are mountaineers. For his education Stuart had to walk four miles, morning and night, to school in Riverton; after graduating from high school there he farmed and worked in the steel mills. He graduated from Lincoln Memorial College with the degree of A.B., and from Vanderbilt University in 1932 with an M.A. Since that time he has taught school in Fullerton, Kentucky.

Stuart's first volume of poems, *Man With the Bull-Tongue Plow*, was published in 1934. His poetry is of the mountains; of it he has written: "None of the work I have ever done took writing away from me. It was my first love back as far as I can remember, and it is still. Robert Burns put fire in me. When I check upon the past, I put Jesus Christ first, Robert Burns second, Shakespeare (for his sonnets and not his plays) third, and Job fourth."

YOUNG KENTUCKY

I

I came the Womack Road from Sandy Bridge
When red shoe-makes were nodding with the dew.
The sun rose even with the Seaton Ridge;
Under the leaves a golden ray came through.
A man with horse and buggy passed me by,
A jar-fly sang upon the weedy hill;
A mallard duck flew over with a cry,
A crow flew by with something in its bill.
I went the Womack Road from Sandy Bridge
When red shoe-makes were drinking back the dew.   10

The moon rose even with the Seaton Ridge;
Under the leaves a silver ray came through.
I could pick blackberries along the way,
For moonlight on the fields was bright as day.

II

The August sassafras leaves are turning red;
The black-oak leaves are getting tough and thick;
The corn is dying and the beans are dead;
The pasture grass is short, and cattle pick
The leaves from sprouts and reach between the wires,
And crane their necks to gather tall grass there.   20
The yellow leaves are dropping from green briars
Like drops of water fall on the field stones.
The summer blood is dripping from the trees;
The trees are in a windy autumn mood
To give their blood in drops of flying leaves—
It must hurt them to lose their summer blood.
The trees are drunk till Spring gives them new birth;
Their blood is whiskey for the thirsty earth.

III

O storm, rise up!—and lightning, cut the sky
And pour your water—wash the earth to ruts!   30
Oh, give earth water for the earth is dry,
The earth is dry—her lips and teeth and guts.
O lightning, rip the seams of dirty clouds
And tear the hearts out of the strongest oaks!
Oh, cover the dark womb of earth with shrouds
Of falling water, wind and fog and smoke!
O storm, rise up and hide the huts of men
And show your teeth of fire on muddy dark—
Show us just what the old earth might have been!
Oh rise up, storm, and let your thunder bark   40
And wake cold-blooded snakes and dusts of men!
Wake them—eternity is long and dark!

IV

The winter birds are roosting in the fodder,
I hear them twitter when I pass at night;
I hear September winds in low-lipped laughter
Combing the gray corn-stalks in white moonlight.
I see old stubble fields and fresh green weeds
Beneath old ferns and leaves and blades of fodder.
I see the timid rabbit coming out to feed
And then I see his playful mate come after.   50
I hear the long notes of the hunter's horn
Sound over silent hills in white moonlight—
It is not music like the wind in corn,
The notes are coarser than the warring fife.
And I have picked a solitary star
Above the pine-cone fire where hunters are.

V

I hate to leave springtime among the hills
Of dark Kentucky and her solitudes;
I love her blood-root and her daffodils,
I love fern-shaded water in beech woods,   60
And midnight singing of the whippoorwill,
And thin-piped music from the lean swamp frogs.
I love dark silence on a wooded hill
And mushrooms growing on old rotted logs.
I love the fox-fire glowing on wet leaves.
Then think, to all of these I say good-by—
To my Kentucky and my strong oak-trees,
To April night and the white starry sky.
I say farewell to these—farewell is long,
There may not be a new life and new song.   70

VI

The winds are kind to white bones on a hill—
The black snake loves to coil among white bones.
White bones are foot-rest for the whippoorwill;
White bones are a clean kind of pretty stones

And dust of one is quick growth for the weeds,
For round a pile of bones the weeds grow tall;
They get the kind of nourishment they need—
These barricades wherein the snakes may crawl.
Then let my bones lie open to the wind;
My dust give quick growth to the roots of weeds; 80
Let my eyes' socket-rims turn to the skies;
Let wind and weeds play the sweet violin.
This is the mountain requiem my dust needs
When on the surface of some hill it lies.

NEGRO SONGS AND SPIRITUALS

The negro songs included in this section are representative of one type of Southern poetry which has attained wide popularity in recent years. When capably sung (as by Roland Hayes or by the Fisk Jubilee Singers) these folk songs and spirituals have an artistic validity which mainly disappears when they are reduced to cold type: the music and the manner of singing are essential parts and provide a necessary background for the lyrics.

Few literary productions have been more overpraised. James Weldon Johnson wrote that "the Spirituals are purely and solely the creation of the American Negro . . . the Spirituals possess the fundamental characteristics of African music." This, of course, is nonsense. As George Pullen Jackson has clearly proved, in his highly intelligent contribution to this subject, the spirituals stem directly out of the camp-meeting songs, or "white spirituals" of the evangelistic sects. To give one example, an exact parallel can be found in the song "I'll Hear the Trumpet Sound," which James Weldon Johnson (Preface, *The Book of American Negro Spirituals*, 41–2) describes as "the Negro's innate expression of his own emotions and experiences"; it is only a reworked version of a white "fasola" song.* On the

---

*J. W. Johnson's version of the refrain:

> You may bury me in de east,
> You may bury me in de west
> But I'll hear de trumpet sound
> In-a dat mornin'.

basis of Jackson's study, and of Guy B. Johnson's *Folk Culture on St. Helena Island*, there is every reason to believe that Guy B. Johnson's conclusions were correct: "They are selections from white music, selections influenced by the Negro's African musical heritage." There was a gradual loosening of music and words: in some cases eighteenth-century poems or songs were reworked by the fasola singers, and these songs were in turn reworked by the Negroes, until the spirituals resulted.† And this was undoubtedly the origin of these songs—not, as James Weldon Johnson claims, "by sheer spiritual forces that African chants were metamorphosed into Spirituals; that upon the fundamental throb of African rhythms were reared these reaches of melody that rise above earth and soar into the pure, ethereal blue" (*op. cit.*, 21).

This does not weaken the value of the songs as music; as literature, they are chiefly of social value. The folk singers simply

---

differs from the white song only in that *the* is changed to *de*, and *in that morning* becomes *In-a dat morning*. Musically, the only change of importance is that the negroes have raised the seventh and injected a sharp sixth. (Jackson, *White Spirituals in the Southern Uplands*, pp. 254-5; the entire subject is discussed, pp. 243-302, with comparison of texts.)

† This example is taken from Jackson (*op. cit.*, p. 302):

Eighteenth-Century Hymn: poem by John Leland—

> Through grace I feel determined
> To conquer, though I die;
> *And then away to Jesus*
> *On wings of love I'll fly*, etc.

Its camp-meeting version—

> Through grace I feel determined
> To conquer, though I die;
> *And then away to Jesus*
> *On wings of love I'll fly.*

> *Chorus*

> Shout, O glory,
> *For I shall mount above the skies,*
> *When I hear the trumpet sound*
> *In that morning.*

Its Negro spiritual remnant—

> (J. W. Johnson, I, 182)
> Good ol' Christians in dat day,
> *Dey'll take wings and fly away,*
> *For to hear de trumpet soun'*
> *In dat mornin'.*

borrowed the handiest and most attractive music and words available; they transformed them to such an extent that the songs have become, in simple fact, their own. In some cases an individual Negro probably composed a spiritual, but in general this composition or reworking must have been the gradual variation and development of groups widely scattered, but probably compositions and variations were the result of gifted individuals within those groups. The persons have remained anonymous; the songs are folk creations, not individual works, and in work songs as well as religious songs they have tended to express the ideas of the race. If the examples given here cannot be called good poetry, they do at least represent great music, and they give some indication of the finest literary productions of the Southern Negro.

JOHN HENRY

When John Henry was a baby,
Sittin' on his daddy's knee,
He said, "O the Big Ben Tunnel
Will be the death of me."

John Henry told his captain,
"Lawd, a man ain't nothin' but a man,
But before I'll be driven by your old steam drill,
Lawd, I'd die with the hammer in my hand."

John Henry walked in the tunnel,
Had his captain by his side;   10
But the rock so tall, John Henry so small,
Lawd, he laid down his hammer and he cried.

John Henry's captain sat on a rock,
Says, "I believe my mountain's fallin' in."
John Henry turned around and said,
"It's my hammer fallin' in the wind."

John Henry said as he took his stand,
"This will be the end of me;"

But every foot the steam-drill drove,
John Henry's hammer drove three.   20

John Henry had a little woman,
Her name was Polly Ann.
When John Henry lay on his dyin' bed,
Polly drove steel like a man.

John Henry had just one only son,
He could stand in the palm of his hand.
The last words that John Henry said,
"Son, don't be a steel-drivin' man."

THE BOLL WEEVIL SONG

Oh, de boll weevil am a little black bug,
   Come from Mexico, dey say,
Come all de way to Texas, jus' a-lookin' foh a place to stay,
   Jus' a-lookin' foh a home, jus' a-lookin' foh a home.

De first time I seen de boll weevil,
   He was a-settin' on de square.
De next time I seen de boll weevil, he had all of his family dere.
   Jus' a-lookin' foh a home, jus' a-lookin' foh a home.

De farmer say to de weevil:
   "What make yo' head so red?"   10
De weevil say to de farmer, "It's a wondah I ain't dead,
   A-lookin' foh a home, jus' a-lookin' foh a home."

De farmer take de boll weevil,
   An' he put him in de hot san'.
De weevil say: "Dis is mighty hot, but I'll stan' it like a man,
   Dis'll be my home, it'll be my home."

De farmer take de boll weevil,
   An' he put him in a lump of ice;

De boll weevil say to de farmer: "Dis is mighty cool and nice,
  It'll be my home, dis'll be my home."   20

De farmer take de boll weevil,
  An' he put him in de fire.
De boll weevil say to de farmer: "Here I are, here I are,
  Dis'll be my home, dis'll be my home."

De boll weevil say to de farmer:
  "You better leave me alone;
I done eat all yo' cotton, now I'm goin' to start on yo' corn,
  I'll have a home, I'll have a home."

De merchant got half de cotton,
  De boll weevil got de res'.   30
Didn't leave de farmer's wife but one ole cotton dress,
  An' it's full of holes, it's full of holes.

De farmer say to de merchant:
  "We's in an awful fix;
De boll weevil et all de cotton up and lef' us only sticks,
  We's got no home, we's got no home."

De farmer say to de merchant:
  "We ain't made but only one bale,
And befoh we'll give yo' dat one we'll fight and go to jail,
  We'll have a home, we'll have a home."   40

An' if anybody should ax you
  Who it was dat make dis song,
Jus' tell 'em 'twas a big buck niggah wid a paih o' blue duckin's
    on,
  Ain't got no home, ain't got no home.

WATER-BOY

Water-Boy, where are yo' hidin'?
If yo' don't-a come, I'm gwineter tell-a yo' Mammy.

Dere ain't no hammer dat's on-a dis mountain,
Dat ring-a like mine, boys, dat ring-a like mine.
Done bus' dis rock, boys, f'om hyah to Macon,
All de way to de jail, boys, yes, back to de jail.

Yo' Jack-o'-Di'monds, yo' Jack-o'-Di'monds,
I know yo' of old, boys, yas, I know yo' of old.
Yo' robbed ma pocket, yas, robba ma pocket,
Done-a robba ma pocket of silvah an' gold.   10

Water-Boy, where are yo' hidin'?
If yo' don't-a come, I'm gwineter tell-a yo' Mammy.
Oh—o, Water-Boy!

GO DOWN, MOSES

Go down, Moses,
'Way down in Egypt land,
Tell ole Pharaoh
To let my people go.

When Israel was in Egypt's land:
Let my people go,
Oppressed so hard they could not stand,
Let my people go.

Go down, Moses,
'Way down in Egypt land,   10
Tell ole Pharaoh,
To let my people go.

Then spoke the Lord, bold Moses said;
Let my people go,
If not I'll smite your first born dead,
Let my people go.

Go down, Moses,
'Way down in Egypt land,
Tell ole Pharaoh,
To let my people go.

STEAL AWAY

Steal away, steal away, steal away to Jesus!
Steal away, steal away home,
I ain't got long to stay here.

My Lord, He calls me,
He calls me by the thunder,
The trumpet sounds within-a my soul,
I ain't got long to stay here.

Steal away, steal away, steal away to Jesus!
Steal away, steal away home,
I ain't got long to stay here.   10

Green trees a-bending, po' sinner stand a-trembling,
The trumpet sounds within-a my soul,
Oh, Lord, I ain't got long to stay here.

APPENDIX

THEORIES OF POETRY BY SOUTHERNERS

W. G. SIMMS: LETTER TO T. H. CHIVERS

Woodlands, S. C. April 5, 1852.

Dear Sir. I was absent from the city when your letter was received, & other passing causes, have prevented me from answering till now. I have received & read your last volume,* with pleasure and regret. Pleasure, because you have a rare faculty at versification. Regret because you do not do it justice —because you show too greatly how much Poe is in your mind—because you allow your fancies to run away with your muse—because you do not suffer thought to cooperate sufficiently with your faculty for rhyme—and because your rhymes are too frequently iterated, so as to become monotonous. You forget that rhyme is the mere decoration of thought, and not to be suffered to occupy its place. I shall have to say all these things in my notice of your book, and while doing justice to your real endowments, I propose to say these things with some severity. You have too much real ability to be suffered to trifle with yourself and reader; and I shall be severe, simply because I desire to be kind. I have sent you the drama & will send you some other trifles. I am also happy to enclose you the verses you desire. I shall be curious to see your play of C. Stuart & your volume of criticism. You are right to address yourself to labours of length, which may take you out of your mannerisms. Mannerism is a fatal weakness. Give up fugitive verses, which lead only to one form of egotism or another, as Poe, who wrote in jerks & spasms only, & in intervals of passion or drink, contended for fugitive performances. This was his excuse and apology only, for his short-comings. Do not allow his errors to wreck you as they did himself. Give him up as a model and as a guide. He was a man of curious genius, wild & erratic, but his genius was rather curious than valuable—bizarre, rather than great or healthful. You see that I deal with you frankly.

* *Eonchs of Ruby*, by T. H. Chivers.

Do not misconceive what I say, or mistake the feeling which prompts me. I would wish to serve you to promote the exercise of your just faculties. In particular, I would keep you from sinking into this sin of mere imitation. Strike out an independent path and publish anonymously. Your previous writings would surely prejudice your new, if they could be identified, in the estimation of readers & critics. Make your book unique— seek for simplicity & wholeness—avoid yourself in your topics —write no more elegies, and discard all pet words, all phrases —discard all attempts at mysticism. Be manly, direct, simple, natural,—full, unaffected & elaborate. Pardon me this freedom, but a genuine desire to see you successful prompts me to counsel you. I am not well—have been overtasked,—and write with a dizzy brain.

> Very respectfully
> Yr ob. Sert
> W. Gilmore Simms.

T. H. CHIVERS: LETTER TO W. G. SIMMS

> Tontine Hotel, New Haven, Conn.,
> April 10th, 1852.

My dear Simms, For fear that you may probably mistake the purport of my last letter—as it was written in the greatest hurry —permit me to say here that you must disabuse your mind, at once, of the ideas which you entertain of my late book—as expressed in your recent letter.

In the first place, your regrets, as therein expressed, are a "lost fear"—inasmuch as the ornaments about which you speak are the soul of the Poems. I will not stop to prove this here, but merely say you will see it done in my book of *Lectures* entitled *Hortus Deliciarum, or, the Garden of Delights*, in which I have given an analysis of Poetry from its Gothic up to its Greek manifestations. You will therein see a "*New Thing* under the Sun."

Now permit me to say, once for all, that the Poems in that Volume are all original—my own—not only in conception but in execution. There is not a Poem in that book modeled, as you suppose, upon anything that Poe ever wrote. You, no doubt, think that you will have something to harp upon when you come to speak of *The Vigil in Aiden;* but, my dear friend, you will miss it. I am not able at present, to say *what* your talents are in the field of analysis; but I know, very well, that I am able to answer any man on this or the other side of the water, in regard to the originality of Art—and particularly of that Poem. Why, my dear Sir, I do not, like other Americans, steal the old English forms and then send my imitations forth in the world as *something* achieved. I have too much mother-wit to use this *insulting presumption*. There is not a Poem in that book that is not, *per se*, a work of Art—a work of Art not only as an Art-work, but *fortuitously* so—the Existere of it being coeternal with its Esse. This the glorious Poe saw in my first book, but he was too full of envy to express it *fully*—but *he saw it*—and I have now letters in my possession from the first American Literati, which inform me of this fact. Would to God that he were now living here on earth that he could tell it as no one else can.

The Critic *must* be an Artist—he must understand Art. Poetry cannot be criticized by a mere *ipse dixit* (*Verbum sapienti*).

I wrote you in my last that *The Vigil in Aiden* was founded upon Poe himself. But why do you think it is an *"imitation"* of *The Raven?* Because it contains the word *Lenore?* But is not Lenore common property? Mrs. Osgood, as well as the German Poet Korner, made use of it. Is it because I make use of the word *Nevermore?* Is it because it is written in the same rhythm? But all these things are *mine*. I am the Southern man who taught Mr. Poe all these things. All these things were published long before *The Raven*, from which *The Raven* was taken. All these things I will make plain to you in my answer; but do not let this deter you from speaking out—only my answer will go hard with you as a Critic.

But this is what I want to know: Do you conscientiously believe The Raven is to be named in the same century with The Vigil? Look at the Refrains—the every thing—of the two —and answer me. The "monotony" about which you talk is not in the Poem—but in you—as it is always varying to the denouement. Read it, as you ought, and you will see this.

When I show you how that truly great man, Poe, failed in The Raven, in attempting to do what I had already done in the Poem from which he stole, you will then admit that I really "have a happy faculty at rhyming."

"Mysticism." Well, this is necessary in Poetry too—as I will show you in my Lecture on Art. Now if you were as well acquainted with the Jackasses of America as I am, you would know, just as well as I do, what a hold all these new inventions of mine have taken upon them—so that they now stand committed as plagiarists of the blackest dye. I have fifty by me now. Yet, I kept locked up for seven years, and gave only a few friends my Lost Pleiad. Well, this is some consolation—nay, a very great joy to me—proving that *Magnus est veritas, et prevalebit.*

Never talk any more about "fugitive pieces." I have an Epic which you will like—I think. I hope so, at least—for there is no man living whose good opinion I value more than I do yours. God bless you. *Esto perpetua.*

Thos. H. Chivers.

P.S. I have received and read your Drama, and find it the best thing that I have ever seen of yours—in fact, I am now puzzled to know why you should ever have worn out your faculties in writing Novels. I will give you a *just* and a *true* review in my book—not an *ipse dixit* affair with no soul in it but *envy*—but one founded on a close insight into Art. You have shown in this Play that you are not unacquainted with the *true Dramatic Style*—but the next Play you write, meditate a Theme—have it a worthy one, which this is not—then either write a Poem *proper*, or one entirely after the Elizabethan Gods. This you must do, or it will not live. Then, again, it is not *necessary* to the Dramatic colloquy, as you seem to suppose, that you should continually double your syllables at the end of your lines. This, it appears to me, you have studied to do, all along your Play. It also appears to me—(judging from your work)—that you suppose—just as Byron and many others—the Dramatic composition is incompatible with the development of the highest Art. But this is not so—but diametrically opposite to the fact. The truth is, you seem to have a perfect *contempt* for what may be called the *Art of Compostion;* but let me tell you that this is the *glory of all Poetry.* You spoke of my *Lost Pleiad* as being but a feeble exposition of my conception of Art; but you did not know, at that time, that that book was the fulfillment of that wise saying of the Latins—*Ars est celare Artem*—but Poe knew it. Lodovico Carracci could not see all the beauties of his brother Annabale's Paintings, because he was a *rival*. But it has always been my misfortune in life not to have had time to feel this passion—having had so much to think about and suffer.

It would give me great pleasure to receive any thing of yours that you may be pleased to send me. *Do not permit your mind to be abused in regard to me by some of my sap-headed enemies, who bray nonsense to the citizens of Charleston—for they do not know me.*

Yours as above, T. H. C.

T. H. CHIVERS: PREFACE TO *NACOOCHEE*

Poetry is that crystal river of the soul which runs through all the avenues of life, and after purifying the affections of the heart, empties itself into the Sea of God. Now, he who dives the deepest into that mysterious sea, brings up the greatest number of the shells of truth, and is made richer in the lore of the wisdom of the universe. For, the more a man sees of the wise relations that subsist between him and God, the greater number of the strings of joy does he touch, because he is thereby made capable of diving deeper into the perfections of the things that are, and of communing oftener with the Author of those several beauties.

It is, therefore, evident, that the more we investigate the relations that subsist between us and the Creator, the more are our minds expanded, affections matured, and the more are our hopes enlarged in the anticipation of the enjoyment of the fellowship of angels, in that other intellectual world, where happiness survives alone, and where we shall assume those beautiful conformities to God, of which we only dream in this. It is also evident, that, as we have implanted within us, a moral principle of right and wrong—what will benefit us, and what will not— to suffer the advancement of our minds to become sterile, in the contemplation of those things, is to degrade the loftiness of our nature, and trample upon the highest privileges bestowed upon us by the Creator. If we possess faculties unbounded in their nature—deep and unfathomable in their purity—faculties which are capable of thirsting continually for the healing wells of life —we must infer that there are joys in heaven, as far above our aspirations in this world, as our thoughts are acclimated above our petty passions and subordinate desires. It is also evident, that, if the soul of man is so constituted, from the nature of its infinity, that it cannot be satisfied with any thing in this world, it must also follow that there must be a resting-place for it in another state of existence, proportionate to the magnitude of its desires in this.

Poetry is the power given by God to man of manifesting these relations. It is that wave of the soul, in the ocean of life, which washes the shores of the flower-gemmed Elysium. It is that beacon of joy upon the Utopian Isles, which ushers us into the realities of those things which are to be. It is only the susceptible, poetical, and refined mind that can see these things as they are, while others think they only see them as they ought to be.

But that exalted inspiration which a man breathes as he quaffs the wellsprings of the universe, is different from that divine efflux which gushes upon his soul as he tastes of the banquet-bowl of heaven. Poetry is the soul of his nature, whereby, from communing with the beauties of this earth, he is capable of giving birth to other beings brighter than himself; and of lifting up his spirit to the presence of those things which he shall enjoy in another state; and which he manifests to *this* through the instrumentality of certain words and sentences melodiously concatenated; and such as correspond with the definite and wise configurations of the mouth in the communication of thought through language.

There are delineations which grow out of the capabilities of man, which seem to outshine realities, but do not, because they spring from the fountains of things that exist. There is nothing in the world that is not equivalent in brightness to the poetical manifestations of it. People too often mistake the *relations* of things for the *things* themselves. It is thus, from the wellsprings of poetry, we draw the healing fountains of the soul whereby we baptize the passions, purify the sentiments, and cause to spring up in the minds of others the same emotions that live and breathe in our own. It is that essence in the laboratory of the intellect, whereby the soul transmutes the passions and hallows the sentiments of man. It is that divine crucible in which the passionate ore of the heart is fluxed into the refined gold of moral sentiment. It is the outpourings of the skies, and the crystal rivers of the fountain of Religion. It is the Pomona of the soul that presides over the Paradise of the heart. It is the Caduceus of all things.

A man who is setting sail for another country—as all men are—one that is leaving the coral strands of the sea of life for the great ocean of Eternity—would feel very poor at the end of his journey, were he to look back and reflect upon the beautiful shells he had left behind him upon the shore, and have no wherewithal at the great day of accounts to pay his reckoning.

It is therefore gratifying to a man to cull the beautiful flowers from the parterre of life, and feel that he has held familiar intercourse with the wonderful things in Nature, and preserved the spotless jewels of affection in the casket of his heart, as the perquisite of days that are to come; and caught an inspiration from the contemplation of those things, which, in after life, shall become like Gilead to the soul.

As one that is setting out upon a long journey, and having nothing better to bequeath the legatees of his heart, the Author of these poems presents whatever jewels he may have gathered from the regions of his mind, to their especial care.

T. H. CHIVERS: PREFACE TO *MEMORALIA*

It was a wise saying of Lamartine, that "*Poetry is the Guardian Angel of Humanity in all Ages.*" Chapman calls Poetry "*The Flower of the Sun.*" It was the belief of Plato, that the most ancient Poetry was that which was addressed to the Deity under the appellation of Hymns. But this cannot be the case, because the self-love of any probationary being must be antecedent to his universal love—as it is the natural outgushing of that intuitive perception of the influx of the divine life of God into his soul which constitutes true Poetry.

Lyrical Poetry, in its most Gothic state, was, therefore, the most ancient utterings of the God-inspired Prophets of the antediluvian Ages. As man, in the Edenic state, must have incarnated the Will of God, who is love, love must have been the first Theme of all true Poetry. Love-songs must, therefore, have been the very first outpourings of the oversoul of the truly Edenic Man—although it is very probable that Hymns of Adoration soon followed afterwards.

We are told by Isodorus that the most ancient form of writing was in Poetry. This is the reason why the Laws, which were originally written in metre, were called *Canticles*. Poets were not only called wise men, or sages, but the words Poet and Prophet are the same in the Hebrew, Greek and Latin languages.

[Chivers here devotes a page to listing the Hebrew, Greek, and Latin definitions of poet, poetry, music, etc.]

No nation, with the exception of the Hebrews, ever enjoyed so serene a Vision of the Divine Glory as did the Greeks. Their religion was Beauty. It was out of the manifold analyses of Nature that they created their world-renowned Synthesis of Beauty, called *The Venus de Medicis*. For, as there was nothing in Nature perfect enough to represent the Divine Beauty, they had to resort to Art, which is the Synthesis of the highest sensation united to the loftiest thought. Thus, by glorifying sensation, which is finite, into thought, which is infinite, thereby creating an IMAGE, they gave birth to the Apollo—their ideal of the Divine Beauty.

Now, the more palpably this thought is made manifest in the IMAGE, through Art, the more lucid will be the *Revelation of the Divine Beauty*. I speak of this in order to show you what I mean by a perfect unition of Art and Passion in any *crystalline Revelation of the Divine Idea*.

This will reveal to us, at once, why it is that Poets are such great lovers of Beauty. It is not because they are libertines; but because they are the *Revelators of the Divine Idea through the Beautiful*.

Now, the only Arbiter of the Art which could so crystallize this Revelation of the Divine Idea, was Grace—the coeternal with Art—the intuitive supernal Grace. While Taste sat as umpire of the Greek Beauty, the Moral Sense governed the Hebrew mind. The fact is, the Greek mind fulfilled every condition imposed upon it by the Creator in living out the Divine Idea—which is only another name for the Perfect Man—thereby appealing, as a reward for its all-pervading excellence, through the golden Trumpet of its own impassioned lips, to all the Ages for its immortality.

There are, in every true Poem, two beauties (just as there are in the Sacred Oracles, a spiritual and a literal meaning—) an outward and inward beauty—one of Art, the other of Nature, or Passion. Now, the outward form, or Art, of a Poem, is precisely to that Poem what the body is to the soul, or wisdom is to Love—a vehiculum, or *Existere* of its *Esse*, or spirit— just as the Psyche of Man is the involucrum of his Pneuma.

Now, that Poem which consists in a perfect unition of these two—that is, Passion and Art—a pure body united to a pure soul—is a pure Poem; and stands in the same relation to its Author, that Man does to God. Such a Poem would be the truest Revelation of the Perfect, or **Divine Man**—as none but just such a man could write such a Poem.

Art is to the Passion of a Poem precisely what the Cestus was to Venus—that beautifier of its person necessary to enchant the souls of men. The Era of Love Songs is the Golden Age with all true Poets. It is in this epoch that, with the Ithuriel Spear of Genius, the pure Poet can strike out of the adamantine crystal Rock of the Times, cooling and refreshing draughts for the healing delights of the thirsting Nations.

This will reveal to us, at once, why it was that God chose the Poets of old to be the true Revelators of his Divine Will to Man. Thus it is, that the true Poet becomes the crystal-shining Memnon through whose lucid Prism the rays of the Divine Sun are analyzed into the musical Rainbow of his Synthetic Glory. Through this crystalline smile of the weeping Heavens —this Nuncia of the Gods—*Risus plorantis Olympi*—does God come down to dwell among men.

Thus, do all the Correspondences of Heaven, in Nature, have to pass through the soul of man before they can appear in suitable raiment, before the face of God.

I drink Ambrosia out of the Cup of the Gods, in making this declaration to the world—for which I am indebted to no man, but to that Divine Spirit which inundated Heaven with his Glory when the "Morning Stars sang together, and all the Sons of God shouted for joy"—the revelation of which shall make the souls of the God-anointed, in the Golden Years to come, leap like the joyful Antelope on the Hills of Yemen.

Beauty, in its outward manifestation, is the expression of an inward formal grace—just as the body is an outward expression of the soul. This Beauty of form, in the softer sex, when beheld by the true Poet, excites in his mind emotions of admiration— then delight—then love, which eventually, merges itself into an ecstacy, or passionate trance. Now, the reason why this formal grace is beautiful, is, because it is an Image of the Divine Beauty, who is the fountain of all Beauty—that is, Beauty in its *Esse;* and the reason why it is so beheld, is, because he cannot but respond, in perception, to that which fills up the yearning embraces of his soul. This outward manifestation of Beauty, which is so perfectly displayed in the amiable form of woman, is the *Existere* of that inward *Esse*, which is not only the true Image of God in its ipsiety, (wherein consists its beauty,)—but is, ontologically, immortal. Now, the soul could not be the Image of this Divine Beauty, and not admire it—any more than an Æolian Harp could be swayed by the winds of the morning, and not respond in delightful music; and just as the melodiousness of the strings depends upon the perfection of the Harp, so does the perfect recognition, and consequent expression of this Beauty, depend upon the poetical nature of the soul that perceives it. So, the difference between a true Poet and one that is not, depends entirely upon the power which the one has over the other to express his recognition of the Divine Beauty—this expression, at the same time, being always amenable to certain essential laws of Taste, which are just as necessary to a full revelation of it, as its component parts of grace are to itself. This is what constitutes Art.

This is the Art which adorns the intense breathings of Homer and Shakespeare, and is the true Art of the true Poet. Not that the Greek Art was not, in itself, the truest light-garments of the forms of Beauty; but that all Art, whether the true Greek Art or not, must be that which is fortuitous—that which is coeternal with the creation of the Poetical Forms of Beauty—and co-existent with the *Revelation of the Divine Idea*. If the Poet be a true one, the garments will be woven at the moment of the birth of the Angel of Beauty, and not afterwards—leaving her divine loveliness, in the meantime, naked to the vulgar gaze,—so that she will be born, like Minerva, armed, cap-a-pie, from the head of Jupiter—just as it is related of those birds which come forth full-fledged out of their parents' eggs as soon as they are laid. The garments will then be sure to fit the form, as the form will be certain to swell out into the classic folds of the garments. Nor do I mean by this that the Gothic thought should not be able to mould its forms into such beauty as characterized the Greek Art, but that the expression of the soul—the manifestations of the being—the Existere of the creation must be coeternal with its Divine Esse.

A pure Poet is one who makes friends of the Graces—becomes the companion of the Muses—the regrestration of whose thoughts is like the ordering of the Camp of Israel. Living near to Nature, he looks upon her beauties like the great Prophet did when he prayed looking through the windows towards Jerusalem. Such a man as this would write his Poems in Rubies on a diaphanous Tablet of pure Diamond. Feeding on the Apples of Eros, he would grow fat on the white Bread of Heaven—as it is recorded of another great one in Canticles, "Sub arbore malo suscitavi te, ibi corrupta est mater tua, ibi violata est genetrix tua"—"I raised thee under an Apple-tree, there thy mother brought thee forth; there she brought thee forth that bare thee."

The truth is, he is one, who from τὸ βέλτιστον, *the well and fit*, ascends up to τὸ κυζιώτατον, *the highest and best*—thereby becoming the inheritor of that divine promise of God, "*He that overcometh, to him will I give the Morning Star.*"

"Give us the Good through the Beautiful" was the prayer of the Dorians.

"He feedeth among the lilies," because the "lilies drop forth myrrh."

The flowers of his Garden are more beautiful than the purple-streaked Amyrillis of Adowa—more delicious to the soul than the silver honey which beads the white calyx of the Crown Imperial.

In the beautiful language of Solomon, he can truly say, "I am the Rose of Sharon, and the Lily of the valley."

He feeds upon Citrons, Cydonian Apples, and the most aromatic of Cinnamon. Oftentimes it is his lot to pluck bitter fruit—bitterer than Sodom's ashy Apples—off of the pendulous boughs of the Tree of Grief. Blessed is he who tastes only of the Balm of Gilead, or the healing Balsam of Babelmandel.

To him "The vines with the tender grapes give a good smell," because, by the tender refinement of his soul, he becomes susceptible to the most delicate impressions. When it is the least suspected, behold! his soul, like the rod of Aaron, buddeth forth in one night, bringing to light blossoms as beautiful as those which flourish on the wide branches of the green Almond tree. He is one who bindeth his foal unto the vine, and his asses' colt unto the choice vine—"because the right hand of God has exalted him as a Palm tree in Engeddi, or as a Rose-plant in Gardens of Jericho." Like the vine of Cypress which clomb up, by its tentacular ringlets, to the top of the Temple of Diana, at Ephesus; so does his soul climb, from bough to bough, reaching out his tendril-like arms, while twining itself around the great Igdrasil-tree of God.

He lieth down, during the noontide heat of the day, in the

cool, refreshing shadow of the Rock of Rimmon, as Saul did under the Pomegranite-tree in Migron. Like a beautiful Hind of the morning, (Aijeloth Shahor) he maketh his pastime in discursive wanderings among the aboriginal Paradises that Eden the evergreen Savannahs of the meadowy Seas of God.

When his "soul longs for early ripe fruits," God causes the luscious clusters of the Vine to come forth in due season for the satisfaction of his soul. While the souls of others bear only Dahlias—flowers without any odor—on the boughs of his soul may be seen, while others are getting ready to blow, roses of Paradise, Edenic flowers, fragrant, and whiter than Syrian lilies.

Thus does he become the inheritor here, on earth, of the joys which are "undefiled and that fadeth not away" in Heaven— holding within the hollow of his hand not only the rod of Hermes, but the Keys of the doors of the Kingdom of Heaven.

T. H. CHIVERS: *From* PREFACE TO *VIRGINALIA*

... Now, in regard to the Refrain of a Poem, I would merely mention here, that it is not only an ornament, but an essence— a life—a vitality—an immortal soul—not a mere profane appendage, but a sacred Symbolical Ensignium—a crown of beauty, and a diamond of glory, like the Urim and Thummin on the Breastplate of the High Priest—or, those beautiful golden bells which jeweled the hem of his garment—making a pleasant chime. It is to a Poem precisely what Ovid says of the outward golden tire of the many-spoked wheels of the Chariot of Apollo, that makes a continual, ever-recurring Auroral chime at every revolution of the wheels, proportionate to their velocity, which is never lost, or dies away into an echo, but forever returns upon itself, like the menstrual changes of the Moon, but only to make the same sweet Moon—the same sweet Auroral chime. ...

EDGAR ALLAN POE: *From* THE POETIC PRINCIPLE

In speaking of the Poetic Principle, I have no design to be either thorough or profound. While discussing, very much at random, the essentiality of what we call Poetry, my principal purpose will be to cite for consideration, some few of those minor English or American poems which best suit my own taste, or which, upon my own fancy, have left the most definite impression. By "minor poems" I mean, of course, poems of little length. And here, in the beginning, permit me to say a few words in regard to a somewhat peculiar principle, which, whether rightfully or wrongfully, has always had its influence in my own critical estimate of the poem. I hold that a long poem does not exist. I maintain that the phrase, "a long poem," is simply a flat contradiction in terms.

I need scarcely observe that a poem deserves its title only inasmuch as it excites, by elevating the soul. The value of the poem is in the ratio of this elevating excitement. But all excitements are, through a psychal necessity, transient. That degree of excitement which would entitle a poem to be so called at all, cannot be sustained throughout a composition of any great length. After the lapse of half an hour, at the very utmost, it flags—fails—a revulsion ensues—and then the poem is, in effect, and in fact, no longer such.

There are, no doubt, many who have found difficulty in reconciling the critical dictum that the *Paradise Lost* is to be devoutly admired throughout, with the absolute impossibility of maintaining for it, during perusal, the amount of enthusiasm which that critical dictum would demand. This great work, in fact, is to be regarded as poetical, only when, losing sight of that vital requisite in all works of Art, Unity, we view it merely as a series of minor poems. If, to preserve its Unity—its totality of effect or impression—we read it (as would be necessary) at a single sitting, the result is but a constant alternation of excitement and depression. After a passage of what we feel to be true poetry, there follows, inevitably, a passage of platitude which no critical pre-judgment can force us to admire; but if, upon completing the work, we read it again, omitting the first book—that is to say, commencing with the second—we shall be surprised at now finding that admirable which we before condemned—that damnable which we had previously so much admired. It follows from all this that the ultimate, aggregate, or absolute effect of even the best epic under the sun, is a nullity:—and this is precisely the fact.

In regard to the *Iliad*, we have, if not positive proof, at least very good reason, for believing it intended as a series of lyrics; but, granting the epic intention, I can say only that the work is based in an imperfect sense of Art. The modern epic is, of the supposititious ancient model, but an inconsiderate and blindfold imitation. But the day of these artistic anomalies is over. If, at any time, any very long poem *were* popular in reality—which

I doubt—it is at least clear that no very long poem will ever be popular again.

That the extent of a poetical work is, *ceteris paribus*, the measure of its merit, seems undoubtedly, when we thus state it, a proposition sufficiently absurd—yet we are indebted for it to the Quarterly Reviews. Surely there can be nothing in mere *si{e*, abstractly considered—there can be nothing in mere *bulk*, so far as a volume is concerned, which has so continuously elicited admiration from these saturnine pamphlets! A mountain, to be sure, by the mere sentiment of physical magnitude which it conveys, *does* impress us with a sense of the sublime—but no man is impressed after *this* fashion by the material grandeur of even *The Columbiad*. Even the Quarterlies have not instructed us to be so impressed by it. *As yet*, they have not *insisted* on our estimating Lamartine by the cubic foot, or Pollock by the pound—but what else are we to *infer* from their continual prating about "sustained effort"? If, by "sustained effort," any little gentleman has accomplished an epic, let us frankly commend him for the effort—if this indeed be a thing commendable,—but let us forbear praising the epic on the effort's account. It is to be hoped that common sense, in the time to come, will prefer deciding upon a work of Art, rather by the impression it makes—by the effect it produces—than by the time it took to impress the effect, or by the amount of "sustained effort" which had been found necessary in effecting the impression. The fact is, that perseverance is one thing and genius quite another—nor can all the Quarterlies in Christendom confound them. By-and-by, this proposition, with many which I have been just urging, will be received as self-evident. In the meantime, by being generally condemned as falsities, they will not be essentially damaged as truths.

On the other hand, it is clear that a poem may be improperly brief. Undue brevity degenerates into mere epigrammatism. A *very* short poem, while now and then producing a brilliant or vivid, never produces a profound or enduring, effect. There must be the steady pressing down of the stamp upon the wax. De Béranger has wrought innumerable things, pungent and spirit-stirring; but, in general, they have been too imponderous to stamp themselves deeply into the public attention; and thus, as so many feathers of fancy, have been blown aloft only to be whistled down the wind. . . .

While the epic mania—while the idea that, to merit in poetry, prolixity is indispensable—has, for some years past, been gradually dying out of the public mind, by mere dint of its own absurdity, we find it succeeded by a heresy too palpably false to be long tolerated, but one which, in the brief period it has already endured, may be said to have accomplished more in the corruption of our Poetical Literature than all its other enemies combined. I allude to the heresy of *The Didactic*. It has been assumed, tacitly and avowedly, directly and indirectly, that the ultimate object of all Poetry is Truth. Every poem, it is said, should inculcate a moral; and by this moral is the poetical merit of the work to be adjudged. We Americans especially have patronized this happy idea; and we Bostonians, very especially, have developed it in full. We have taken it into our heads that to write a poem simply for the poem's sake, and to acknowledge such to have been our design, would be to confess ourselves radically wanting in the true Poetic dignity and force:—but the simple fact is, that, would we but permit ourselves to look into our own souls, we should immediately there discover that under the sun there neither exists nor *can* exist any work more thoroughly dignified—more supremely noble than this very poem—this poem *per se*—this poem which is a poem and nothing more—this poem written solely for the poem's sake.

With as deep a reverence for the True as ever inspired the bosom of man, I would, nevertheless, limit, in some measure, its modes of inculcation. I would limit to enforce them. I would not enfeeble them by dissipation. The demands of Truth are severe. She has no sympathy with the myrtles. All *that* which is so indispensable in Song, is precisely all *that* with which *she* has nothing whatever to do. It is but making her a flaunting paradox, to wreathe her in gems and flowers. In enforcing a truth, we need severity rather than efflorescence of language. We must be simple, precise, terse. We must be cool, calm, unimpassioned. In a word, we must be in that mood which, as nearly as possible, is the exact converse of the poetical. *He* must be blind indeed who does not perceive the radical and chasmal differences between the truthful and the poetical modes of inculcation. He must be theory-mad beyond redemption who, in spite of these differences, shall still persist in attempting to reconcile the obstinate oils and waters of Poetry and Truth.

Dividing the world of mind into its three most immediately obvious distinctions, we have the Pure Intellect, Taste, and the Moral Sense. I place Taste in the middle, because it is just this position which, in the mind, it occupies. It holds intimate relations with either extreme; but from the Moral Sense is separated by so faint a difference that Aristotle has not hesitated to place some of its operations among the virtues themselves. Nevertheless, we find the *offices* of the trio marked with a sufficient distinction. Just as the Intellect concerns itself with Truth, so Taste informs us of the Beautiful, while the Moral Sense is regardful of Duty. Of this latter, while Conscience teaches the obligation, and Reason the expediency, Taste contents herself with displaying the charms:—waging war upon Vice solely on the ground of her deformity—her disproportion—her animosity to the fitting, to the appropriate, to the harmonious—in a word, to Beauty.

An immortal instinct, deep within the spirit of man, is thus, plainly, a sense of the Beautiful. This it is which administers to his delight in the manifold forms, and sounds, and odours, and sentiments, amid which he exists. And just as the lily is repeated in the lake, or the eyes of Amaryllis in the mirror, so is the mere oral or written repetition of these forms, and sounds, and colours, and odours, and sentiments, a duplicate source of delight. But this mere repetition is not poetry. He who shall simply sing, with however glowing enthusiasm, or with however vivid a truth of description, of the sights, and sounds, and odours, and colours, and sentiments, which greet *him* in common with all mankind—he, I say, has yet failed to prove his divine title. There is still a something in the distance which he has been unable to attain. We still a thirst unquenchable, to allay which he has not shown us the crystal springs. This thirst belongs to the immortality of Man. It is at once a consequence and an indication of his perennial existence. It is the desire of the moth for the star. It is no mere appreciation of the Beauty before us—but a wild effort to reach the Beauty above. Inspired by an ecstatic prescience of the glories beyond the grave, we struggle, by multiform combinations among the things and thoughts of Time, to attain a portion of that Loveliness whose very elements, perhaps, appertain to eternity alone. And thus when by Poetry—or when by Music, the most entrancing of the Poetic moods—we find ourselves melted into tears—we weep then—not as the Abbaté Gravina supposes—through excess of pleasure, but through a certain, petulant, impatient sorrow at our inability to grasp *now*, wholly, here on earth, at once and forever, those divine and rapturous joys, of which *through* the poem, or *through* the music, we attain to but brief and indeterminate glimpses.

The struggle to apprehend the supernal Loveliness—this struggle, on the part of souls fittingly constituted—has given to the world all *that* which it (the world) has ever been enabled at once to understand and *to feel* as poetic.

The Poetic Sentiment, of course, may develop itself in various modes—in Painting, in Sculpture, in Architecture, in the Dance —very especially in Music,—and very peculiarly, and with a wide field, in the composition of the Landscape Garden. Our present theme, however, has regard only to its manifestation in words. And here let me speak briefly on the topic of rhythm. Contenting myself with the certainty that Music, in its various modes of metre, rhythm, and rhyme, is of so vast a moment in Poetry as never to be wisely rejected—is so vitally important an adjunct, that he is simply silly who declines its assistance, I will not now pause to maintain its absolute essentiality. It is in Music, perhaps, that the soul most nearly attains the great end for which, when inspired by the Poetic Sentiment, it struggles —the creation of supernal Beauty. It *may* be, indeed, that here this sublime end is, now and then, attained *in fact*. We are often made to feel, with a shivering delight, that from an earthly harp are stricken notes which *cannot* have been unfamiliar to the angels. And thus there can be little doubt that in the union of Poetry with Music in its popular sense, we shall find the widest field for the Poetic development. The old Bards and Minnesingers had advantages which we do not possess— and Thomas Moore, singing his own songs, was, in the most legitimate manner, perfecting them as poems.

To recapitulate, then:—I would define, in brief, the Poetry of words as *The Rhythmical Creation of Beauty*. Its sole arbiter is Taste. With the Intellect or with the Conscience, it has only collateral relations. Unless incidentally, it has no concern whatever either with Duty or with Truth.

A few words, however, in explanation. *That* pleasure which is at once the most pure, the most elevating, and the most intense, is derived, I maintain, from the contemplation of the

Beautiful. In the contemplation of Beauty we alone find it possible to attain that pleasurable elevation, or excitement, *of the soul*, which we recognize as the Poetic Sentiment, and which is so easily distinguished from Truth, which is the satisfaction of the Reason, or from Passion, which is the excitement of the Heart. I make Beauty, therefore—using the word as inclusive of the sublime,—I make Beauty the province of the poem, simply because it is an obvious rule of Art that effects should be made to spring as directly as possible from their causes:— no one as yet having been weak enough to deny that the peculiar elevation in question is at least *most readily* attainable in the poem. It by no means follows, however, that the incitements of Passion, or the precepts of Duty, or even the lessons of Truth, may not be introduced into a poem, and with advantage; for they may subserve, incidentally, in various ways, the general purposes of the work:—but the true artist will always contrive to tone them down in proper subjection to that *Beauty* which is the atmosphere and the real essence of the Poem. . . .

EDGAR ALLAN POE: THE PHILOSOPHY OF COMPOSITION

Charles Dickens, in a note now lying before me, alluding to an examination I once made of the mechanism of "Barnaby Rudge," says: "By the way, are you aware that Godwin wrote his 'Caleb Williams' backward? He first involved his hero in a web of difficulties, forming the second volume, and then, for the first, cast about him for some mode of accounting for what had been done."

I cannot think this the *precise* mode of procedure on the part of Godwin—and indeed what he himself acknowledges is not altogether in accordance with Mr. Dickens' idea; but the author of "Caleb Williams" was too good an artist not to perceive the advantage derivable from at least a somewhat similar process. Nothing is more clear than that every plot, worth the name, must be elaborated to its *dénouement* before any thing be attempted with the pen. It is only with the *dénouement* constantly in view that we can give a plot its indispensable air of consequence, or causation, by making the incidents, and especially the tone at all points, tend to the development of the intention.

There is a radical error, I think, in the usual mode of constructing a story. Either history affords a thesis—or one is suggested by an incident of the day—or, at best, the author sets himself to work in the combination of striking events to form merely the basis of his narrative—designing, generally, to fill in with description, dialogue, or authoral comment, whatever crevices of fact, or action, may, from page to page, render themselves apparent.

I prefer commencing with the consideration of an *effect*. Keeping originality *always* in view—for he is false to himself who ventures to dispense with so obvious and so easily attainable a source of interest—I say to myself, in the first place: "Of the innumerable effects, or impressions, of which the heart, the intellect, or (more generally) the soul is susceptible, what one shall I, on the present occasion, select?" Having chosen a novel, first, and secondly a vivid effect, I consider whether it can be best wrought by incident or tone,—whether by ordinary incidents and peculiar tone, or the converse, or by peculiarity both of incident and tone—afterward looking about me (or rather within) for such combinations of event, or tone, as shall best aid me in the construction of the effect.

I have often thought how interesting a magazine paper might be written by any author who would—that is to say, who could—detail, step by step, the processes by which any one of his compositions attained its ultimate point of completion. Why such a paper has never been given to the world, I am much at a loss to say—but, perhaps, the authoral vanity has had more to do with the omission than any one other cause. Most writers—poets in especial—prefer having it understood that they compose by a species of fine frenzy—an ecstatic intuition—and would positively shudder at letting the public take a peep behind the scenes, at the elaborate and vacillating crudities of thought—at the true purposes seized only at the last moment—at the innumerable glimpses of idea that arrived not at the maturity of full view—at the fully matured fancies discarded in despair as unmanageable—at the cautious selections and rejections—at the painful erasures and interpolations—in a word, at the wheels and pinions—the tackle for scene-shifting—the step-ladders and demon-traps, the cock's feathers, the red paint and the black patches, which in ninety-nine cases out of the hundred, constitute the properties of the literary *histrio*.

I am aware, on the other hand, that the case is by no means common, in which an author is at all in condition to retrace the steps by which his conclusions have been attained. In general, suggestions, having arisen pell-mell, are pursued and forgotten in a similar manner.

For my own part, I have neither sympathy with the repugnance alluded to, nor, at any time, the least difficulty in recalling to mind the progressive steps of any of my compositions; and, since the interest of an analysis, or reconstruction, such as I have considered a *desideratum*, is quite independent of any real or fancied interest in the thing analysed, it will not be regarded as a breach of decorum on my part to show the *modus operandi* by which some one of my own works was put together. I select "The Raven" as most generally known. It is my design to render it manifest that no one point in its composition is referable either to accident or intuition—that the work proceeded, step by step, to its completion with the precision and rigid consequence of a mathematical problem.

Let us dismiss, as irrelevant to the poem *per se*, the circumstance—or say the necessity—which, in the first place, gave rise to the intention of composing *a* poem that should suit at once the popular and the critical taste.

We commence, then, with this intention.

The initial consideration was that of extent. If any literary work is too long to be read at one sitting, we must be content to dispense with the immensely important effect derivable from unity of impression—for, if two sittings be required, the affairs of the world interfere, and every thing like totality is at once destroyed. But since, *ceteris paribus*, no poet can afford to dispense with *any thing* that may advance his design, it but remains to be seen whether there is, in extent, any advantage to counterbalance the loss of unity which attends it. Here I say no, at once. What we term a long poem is, in fact, merely a succession of brief ones—that is to say, of brief poetical effects. It is needless to demonstrate that a poem is such, only inasmuch as it intensely excites, by elevating, the soul; and all intense excitements are, through a psychal necessity, brief. For this reason, at least one-half of the *Paradise Lost* is essentially prose—a succession of poetical excitements interspersed, *inevitably*, with corresponding depressions—the whole being deprived, through the extremeness of its length, of the vastly important artistic element, totality, or unity, of effect.

It appears evident, then, that there is a distinct limit, as regards length, to all works of literary art—the limit of a single sitting—and that, although in certain classes of prose composition, such as "Robinson Crusoe," (demanding no unity), this limit may be advantageously overpassed, it can never properly be overpassed in a poem. Within this limit, the extent of a poem may be made to bear mathematical relation to its merit—in other words, to the excitement or elevation—again, in other words, to the degree of the true poetical effect which it is capable of inducing; for it is clear that the brevity must be in direct ratio of the intensity of the intended effect:—this, with one proviso—that a certain degree of duration is absolutely requisite for the production of any effect at all.

Holding in view these considerations, as well as that degree of excitement which I deemed not above the popular, while not below the critical, taste, I reached at once what I conceived the proper *length* for my intended poem, a length of about one hundred lines. It is, in fact, a hundred and eight.

My next thought concerned the choice of an impression, or effect, to be conveyed; and here I may as well observe that, throughout the construction, I kept steadily in view the design of rendering the work *universally* appreciable. I should be carried too far out of my immediate topic were I to demonstrate a point upon which I have repeatedly insisted, and which, with the poetical, stands not in the slightest need of demonstration— the point, I mean, that Beauty is the sole legitimate province of the poem. A few words, however, in elucidation of my real meaning, which some of my friends have evinced a disposition to misrepresent. That pleasure which is at once the most intense, the most elevating, and the most pure, is, I believe, found in the contemplation of the beautiful. When, indeed, men speak of Beauty, they mean, precisely, not a quality, as is supposed, but an effect—they refer, in short, just to that intense and pure elevation of *soul—not* of intellect, or of heart—upon which I have commented, and which is experienced in consequence of contemplating "the beautiful." Now I designate Beauty as the province of the poem, merely because it is an obvious rule of Art that effects should be made to spring from direct causes—that objects should be attained through means best adapted for their attainment—no one as yet having been weak enough to deny that the peculiar elevation alluded to, is *most readily* attained in the poem. Now the object, Truth, or the satisfaction of the intellect, and the object Passion, or the excitement of the heart, are, although attainable, to a certain extent, in poetry, far more readily attainable in prose. Truth, in fact, demands a precision, and Passion a *homeliness* (the truly passionate will comprehend me), which are absolutely antagonistic to that Beauty which, I maintain, is the excitement, or pleasurable elevation, of the soul. It by no means follows from any thing here said, that passion, or even truth, may not be introduced, and even profitably introduced, into a poem—for they may serve in elucidation, or aid the general effect, as do discords in music, by contrast—but the true artist will always contrive, first, to tone them into proper subservience to the predominant aim, and, secondly, to enveil them, as far as possible, in that Beauty which is the atmosphere and the essence of the poem.

Regarding, then, Beauty as my province, my next question referred to the *tone* of its highest manifestation—and all experience has shown that this tone is one of *sadness*. Beauty of whatever kind, in its supreme development, invariably excites the sensitive soul to tears. Melancholy is thus the most legitimate of all the poetical tones.

The length, the province, and the tone, being thus determined, I betook myself to ordinary induction, with the view of obtaining some artistic piquancy which might serve me as a key-note in the construction of the poem—some pivot upon which the whole structure might turn. In carefully thinking over all the usual artistic effects—or more properly *points*, in the theatrical sense—I did not fail to perceive immediately that no one had been so universally employed as that of the *refrain*. The universality of its employment sufficed to assure me of its intrinsic value, and spared me the necessity of submitting it to analysis. I considered it, however, with regard to its susceptibility of improvement, and soon saw it to be in a primitive condition. As commonly used, the *refrain*, or burden, not only is limited to lyric verse, but depends for its impression upon the force of monotone—both in sound and thought. The pleasure is deduced solely from the sense of identity—of repetition. I resolved to diversify, and so heighten, the effect, by adhering, in general, to the monotone of sound, while I continually varied that of thought: that is to say, I determined to produce continuously novel effects, by the variation *of the application* of the *refrain*—the *refrain* itself remaining, for the most part, unvaried.

These points being settled, I next bethought me of the *nature* of my *refrain*. Since its application was to be repeatedly varied, it was clear that the *refrain* itself must be brief, for there would have been an insurmountable difficulty in frequent variations of application in any sentence of length. In proportion to the brevity of the sentence, would, of course, be the facility of the variation. This led me at once to a single word as the best *refrain*.

The question now arose as to the *character* of the word. Having made up my mind to a *refrain*, the division of the poem into stanzas was, of course, a corollary: the *refrain* forming the close of each stanza. That such a close, to have force, must be sonorous and susceptible of protracted emphasis, admitted no doubt; and these considerations inevitably led me to the long *o* as the most sonorous vowel, in connection with *r* as the most producible consonant.

The sound of the *refrain* being thus determined, it became necessary to select a word embodying this sound, and at the same time in the fullest possible keeping with that melancholy which I had predetermined as the tone of the poem. In such a search it would have been absolutely impossible to overlook the word "Nevermore." In fact, it was the very first which presented itself.

The next *desideratum* was a pretext for the continuous use of the one word "Nevermore." In observing the difficulty which I at once found in inventing a sufficiently plausible reason for its continuous repetition, I did not fail to perceive that this difficulty arose solely from the pre-assumption that the word was to be so continuously or monotonously spoken by a *human* being—I did not fail to perceive, in short, that the difficulty lay in the reconciliation of this monotony with the exercise of reason on the part of the creature repeating the word. Here, then, immediately arose the idea of a *non*-reasoning creature capable of speech; and, very naturally, a parrot, in the first instance, suggested itself, but was superseded forthwith by a Raven, as equally capable of speech, and infinitely more in keeping with the intended *tone*.

I had now gone so far as the conception of a Raven—the bird of ill omen—monotonously repeating the one word, "Nevermore," at the conclusion of each stanza, in a poem of melancholy tone, and in length about one hundred lines. Now, never losing sight of the object *supremeness*, or perfection, at all points, I asked myself: "Of all melancholy topics, what, according to the *universal* understanding of mankind, is the *most* melancholy?" Death—was the obvious reply. "And when," I said, "is this most melancholy of topics most poetical?" From what I have already explained at some length, the answer, here also, is obvious—"When it most closely allies itself to *Beauty:* the death, then, of a beautiful woman is, unquestionably, the most poetical topic in the world—and equally is it beyond doubt that the lips best suited for such topic are those of a bereaved lover."

I had now to combine the two Ideas, of a lover lamenting his deceased mistress and a Raven continuously repeating the word "Nevermore." I had to combine these, bearing in mind my design of varying at every turn, the *application* of the word repeated; but the only intelligible mode of such combination is that of imagining the Raven employing the word in answer to the queries of the lover. And here it was that I saw at once the opportunity afforded for the effect on which I had been depending—that is to say, the effect of the *variation of application*. I saw that I could make the first query propounded by the lover —the first query to which the Raven should reply "Nevermore" —that I could make this first query a commonplace one—the second less so—the third still less, and so on—until at length the lover, startled from his original *nonchalance* by the melancholy character of the word itself—by its frequent repetition— and by a consideration of the ominous reputation of the fowl that uttered it—is at length excited to superstition, and wildly propounds queries of a far different character—queries whose solution he has passionately at heart—propounds them half in superstition and half in that species of despair which delights in self-torture—propounds them not altogether because he believes in the prophetic or demoniac character of the bird (which, reason assures him, is merely repeating a lesson learned by rote), but because he experiences a frenzied pleasure in so modelling his questions as to receive from the *expected* "Nevermore" the most delicious, because the most intolerable, of sorrow. Perceiving the opportunity thus afforded me—or, more strictly, thus forced upon me in the progress of the construction—I first established in mind the climax, or concluding query—that query to which "Nevermore" should be in the last place an answer—that query in reply to which this word "Nevermore" should involve the utmost conceivable amount of sorrow and despair.

Here, then, the poem may be said to have its beginning—at the end, where all works of art should begin—for it was here, at this point of my preconsiderations, that I first put pen to paper in the composition of the stanza:

"Prophet," said I, "thing of evil! prophet still if bird or
    devil!
By that heaven that bends above us—by that God we both
    adore,
Tell this soul with sorrow laden, if within the distant Aidenn,
It shall clasp a sainted maiden whom the angels name Lenore—
Clasp a rare and radiant maiden whom the angels name
    Lenore."
            Quoth the Raven, "Nevermore."

I composed this stanza, at this point, first that, by establishing the climax, I might the better vary and graduate, as regards seriousness and importance, the preceding queries of the lover—and, secondly, that I might definitely settle the rhythm, the metre, and the length and general arrangement of the stanza—as well as graduate the stanzas which were to precede, so that none of them might surpass this in rhythmical effect. Had I been able, in the subsequent composition, to construct more vigorous stanzas, I should, without scruple, have purposely enfeebled them, so as not to interfere with the climacteric effect.

And here I may as well say a few words of the versification. My first object (as usual) was originality. The extent to which this has been neglected, in versification, is one of the most unaccountable things in the world. Admitting that there is little possibility of variety in mere *rhythm*, it is still clear that the possible varieties of metre and stanza are absolutely infinite—and yet, *for centuries no man, in verse, has ever done, or ever seemed to think of doing, an original thing*. The fact is, that originality (unless in minds of very unusual force) is by no means a matter, as some suppose, of impulse or intuition. In general, to be found, it must be elaborately sought, and although a positive merit of the highest class, demands in its attainment less of invention than negation.

Of course, I pretend to no originality in either the rhythm or metre of the "Raven." The former is trochaic—the latter is octameter acatalectic, alternating with heptameter catalectic repeated in the *refrain* of the fifth verse, and terminating with tetrameter catalectic. Less pedantically—the feet employed throughout (trochees) consist of a long syllable followed by a short: the first line of the stanza consists of eight of these feet— the second of seven and a half (in effect two-thirds)—the third of eight—the fourth of seven and a half—the fifth the same— the sixth three and a half. Now, each of these lines, taken individually, has been employed before, and what originality the "Raven" has, is in their *combination into stanza; nothing even remotely approaching this combination has ever been attempted. The effect of this originality of combination is aided by other unusual, and some altogether novel effects, arising from an extension of the application of the principles of rhyme and alliteration.

The next point to be considered was the mode of bringing together the lover and the Raven—and the first branch of this consideration was the *locale*. For this the most natural suggestion might seem to be a forest, or the fields—but it has always appeared to me that a close *circumscription of space* is absolutely necessary to the effect of insulated incident:—it has the force of a frame to a picture. It has an indisputable moral power in keeping concentrated the attention, and, of course, must not be confounded with mere unity of place.

I determined, then, to place the lover in his chamber—in a chamber rendered sacred to him by memories of her who had frequented it. The room is represented as richly furnished— this in mere pursuance of the ideas I have already explained on the subject of Beauty, as the sole true poetical thesis.

The *locale* being thus determined, I had now to introduce the bird—and the thought of introducing him through the window, was inevitable. The idea of making the lover suppose, in the first instance, that the flapping of the wings of the bird, against the shutter, is a "tapping" at the door, originated in a wish to increase, by prolonging, the reader's curiosity, and in a desire to admit the incidental effect arising from the lover's throwing open the door, finding all dark, and thence adopting the half-fancy that it was the spirit of his mistress that knocked.

I made the night tempestuous, first, to account for the Raven's seeking admission, and secondly, for the effect of contrast with the (physical) serenity within the chamber.

I made the bird alight on the bust of Pallas, also for the effect of contrast between the marble and the plumage—it being understood that the bust was absolutely *suggested* by the bird— the bust of *Pallas* being chosen, first, as most in keeping with the scholarship of the lover, and secondly, for the sonorousness of the word, Pallas, itself.

About the middle of the poem, also, I have availed myself of the force of contrast, with a view of deepening the ultimate impression. For example, an air of the fantastic—approaching as nearly to the ludicrous as was admissible—is given to the Raven's entrance. He comes in "with many a flirt and flutter."

Not the least *obeisance made he*—not a moment stopped or stayed he,
But *with mien of lord or lady*, perched above my chamber door.

In the two stanzas which follow, the design is more obviously carried out:—

Then this ebony bird beguiling my sad fancy into smiling
By the *grave and stern decorum of the countenance it wore*,
"Though thy *crest be shorn and shaven*, thou," I said, "art sure no craven,
Ghastly grim and ancient Raven wandering from the nightly shore—
Tell me what thy lordly name is on the Night's Plutonian shore?"
        Quoth the Raven, "Nevermore."

Much I marveled *this ungainly fowl* to hear discourse so plainly,
Though its answer little meaning—little relevancy bore;
For we cannot help agreeing that no living human being
Ever yet was blest with seeing bird above his chamber door—
Bird or beast upon the sculptured bust above his chamber door,
        With such name as "Nevermore."

The effect of the *dénouement* being thus provided for, I immediately drop the fantastic for a tone of the most profound seriousness:—this tone commencing in the stanza directly following the one last quoted, with the line,

But the Raven, sitting lonely on that placid bust, spoke only, etc.

From this epoch the lover no longer jests—no longer sees any thing even of the fantastic in the Raven's demeanor. He speaks of him as a "grim, ungainly, ghastly, gaunt, and ominous bird of yore," and feels the "fiery eyes" burning into his "bosom's core." This revolution of thought, or fancy, on the lover's part, is intended to induce a similar one on the part of the reader— to bring the mind into a proper frame for the *dénouement* which is now brought about as rapidly and as *directly* as possible.

With the *dénouement* proper—with the Raven's reply, "Nevermore," to the lover's final demand if he shall meet his mistress in another world—the poem, in its obvious phase, that of a simple narrative, may be said to have its completion. So far, every thing is within the limits of the accountable—of the real. A raven, having learned by rote the single word "Nevermore," and having escaped from the custody of its owner, is driven at midnight, through the violence of a storm, to seek admission at a window from which a light still gleams—the chamber-window of a student, occupied half in poring over a volume, half in dreaming of a beloved mistress deceased. The casement being thrown open at the fluttering of the bird's wings, the bird itself perches on the most convenient seat out of the immediate reach of the student, who, amused by the incident and the oddity of the visitor's demeanor, demands of it, in jest and without looking for a reply, its name. The raven, addressed, answers with its customary word, "Nevermore"—a word which finds immediate echo in the melancholy heart of the student, who, giving utterance aloud to certain thoughts suggested by the occasion, is again startled by the fowl's repetition of "Nevermore." The student now guesses the state of the case, but is impelled, as I have before explained, by the human thirst for self-torture, and in part by superstition, to propound such queries to the bird as will bring him, the lover, the most of the luxury of sorrow, through the anticipated answer "Nevermore." With the indulgence, to the extreme, of this self-torture, the narration, in what I have termed its first or obvious phase, has a natural termination, and so far there has been no overstepping of the limits of the real.

But in subjects so handled, however skillfully, or with however vivid an array of incident, there is always a certain hardness or nakedness, which repels the artistical eye. Two things are invariably required—first, some amount of complexity, or more properly, adaptation; and secondly, some amount of suggestiveness—some under-current, however indefinite, of meaning. It is this latter, in especial, which imparts to a work of art so much of that *richness* (to borrow from colloquy a forcible term) which we are too fond of confounding with *the ideal*. It is the *excess* of the suggested meaning—it is the rendering this the upper instead of the under-current of the theme—which turns into prose (and that of the very flattest kind) the so-called poetry of the so-called transcendentalists.

Holding these opinions, I added the two concluding stanzas of the poem—their suggestiveness being thus made to pervade all the narrative which has preceded them. The under-current of meaning is rendered first apparent in the lines—

Take thy beak from out *my heart*, and take thy form from off my
    door!
Quoth the Raven, "Nevermore!"

It will be observed that the words, "from out my heart," involve the first metaphorical expression in the poem. They, with the answer, "Nevermore," dispose the mind to seek a moral in all that has been previously narrated. The reader begins now to regard the Raven as emblematical—but it is not until the very last line of the very last stanza, that the intention of making him emblematical of *Mournful and Never-ending Remembrance* is permitted distinctly to be seen:

And the Raven, never flitting, still is sitting, still is sitting,
On the pallid bust of Pallas just above my chamber door;
And his eyes have all the seeming of a demon's that is dreaming,
And the lamplight o'er him streaming throws his shadow on the
    floor;
And my soul *from out that shadow* that lies floating on the floor
        Shall be lifted—nevermore.

P. P. COOKE: EXTRACTS FROM LETTERS

"What do you think of a good friend of mine, a most valuable and worthy, and hard-riding one, saying gravely to me a short time ago, 'I wouldn't waste time on a damned thing like poetry; you might make yourself, with all your sense and judgment, a useful man in settling neighborhood disputes and difficulties.' You have as much chance with such people, as a dolphin would have, if in one of his darts he pitched in amongst the machinery of a mill. 'Philosophy would clip an angel's wings,' Keats says, and pompous dulness would do the same. But these very persons I have been talking about, are always ready, when the world generally has awarded the honors of successful authorship to any of our mad tribe, to come in and confirm the award, and *buy*, if not read, the popular book. And so they are not wholly without their uses in this world. But woe to him who seeks to *climb* amongst them. An author must avoid them until he is already mounted on the platform, and can look down on them, and make them ashamed to show their dulness by keeping their hands in their breeches pockets, whilst the rest of the world are taking theirs out to give money or to applaud with. I am wasting my letter with these people, but for fear you may think I am chagrined or cut by what I abuse them for, I must say that they suit one half of my character, moods, and pursuits, in being good kindly men, rare table companions, many of them great in field sports, and most of them rather deficient in letters than mind; and that, in an every-day sense of the words, I love and am beloved by them."

"You will find them beneath your sanguine prognostic. They are mere narrative poems, designed for the crowd. Poetic speculation, bold inroads upon the debateable land—'the wild weird clime, out of space out of time'—I have not here attempted. I *will* hereafter merge myself in the nobler atmosphere; in the mean time I have stuck to the ordinary level, and have endeavored to write interesting stories in verse, with grace and spirit. I repeat my fear that in writing for the cold, I have failed to touch the quick and warm—in writing for a dozen hunting comrades, who have been in the habit of making my verse a *post prandium* entertainment, and never endured an audacity of thought or word, I have tamed myself out of your approbation."

... "I detest the law. On the other hand, I love the fever-fits of composition. The music of rhythm, coming from God knows where, like the airy melody in the Tempest, tingles pleasantly in my veins and fingers; I like to build the verse cautiously, but with the excitement of a rapid *writer*, which I reign in and check; and then, we both know how glorious it is to make the gallant dash, and round off the stanza with the sonorous couplet, or with some rhyme as natural to its place as a leaf on a tree, but separated from its mate that peeps down to it over the inky ends of many intervening lines."

HENRY TIMROD: A THEORY OF POETRY

(Timrod gave this address on poetry at Columbia, South Carolina, in 1863. It was edited for publication by Henry Austin, who added items of informatory and refutatory argument in his introductory remarks.)

PART I

[Briefly Timrod considers and dismisses the theory that poetry is simply "the expression in verse of thought, sentiment or passion," and then argues at length against Poe's dogma that a long poem does not exist. He cites Dante's *Divine Comedy* and Milton's *Paradise Lost* as examples showing the value and effect upon the reader of cumulative detail and incident.]

PART II

[Timrod gives various definitions of poetry as understood by people of imagination and insists that Poe's theory is merely "the natural and logical result evolved from his own beautiful and very peculiar genius." Timrod argues that to the element of beauty there must be added "power, when it is developed in some noble shape, and truth, whether abstract or not, when it affects the common heart of mankind."]

. . . I look upon every poem strictly as a work of art, and on the poet, in the act of putting poetry into verse, simply as an artist. If the poet have his hour of inspiration, tho I am so sick of the cant of which this word has been the fruitful source that I dislike to use it, this hour is not at all during the work of composition. A distinction must be made between the moment when the great thought strikes for the first time along the brain and flushes the cheek with the sudden revelation of beauty or grandeur and the hour of patient, elaborate execution. The soul of the poet, tho constrained to utter itself at some time or other, does not burst into song as readily as a maiden of sixteen bursts into musical laughter. Many poets have written of grief but no poet in the first agony of his heart ever sat down to strain that grief through iambics. Many poets have given expression to the first raptures of successful love, but no poet in the delirium of joy has ever bubbled it in anapests. Could this have been possible, the poet would have been the most wonderful of improvisers; and perhaps a poem would be no better than what improvisations always are. It would be easy to prove the truth of these few general remarks by the confessions of the poets themselves. Poe has described to the world how he slowly built up the poem of "The Raven." A greater poet than Poe speaks of himself as

> "not used to make
> A present joy the matter of his song"

and of his poems, which the "Muse accepts, deliberately pleased," as very thoughtfully fitted to the Orphean lyre. The labor through which Tennyson has obtained that perfection of style which is characteristic of his poems must have been almost infinite. And Matthew Arnold, a poet not widely known in this country, but one who, in the estimation of the English critical public, sits not very far below Tennyson, separates, as I have separated, the hours of insight from the hours of labor.

> "We cannot kindle when we will
> The fire that in the heart resides;
> The spirit bloweth and is still;
> In mystery our soul abides;
> But tasks in hours of insight willed
> May be through hours of gloom fulfilled."

Does this fact lessen the merit of the poet, or the charm of the poem? I do not see why it should, any more than, because the "Eve" in your library was once but a beautiful idea in the mind of its creator, was slowly chiseled from a block of shapeless marble, it should deprive the sculptor of his glory, or mar for a single instant the effect of the faultless symmetry and suggestive countenance of the statue. It must not be forgotten that my present aim is to show that a poem, without being all poetry from beginning to end, may be complete as a work of art. Now, there are two classes of poets, differing essentially in their several characters. The one class desires only to utter musically its own peculiar thoughts, feelings, sentiments or passions, without regard to their truth or falsehood, their morality or want of morality, but in simple reference to their poetical effect. The other class, with more poetry at its command than the first, regards poetry simply as the minister, the highest minister, indeed, but still only the minister, of Truth, and refuses to address itself to the sense of the Beautiful alone. The former class is content simply to create beauty and writes such poems as "The Raven" of Poe or "The Corsair" of Byron. The latter class aims to create Beauty also, but it desires at the same time to mold this beauty into the shape of a temple dedicated to Truth. It is to this class that we owe the authorship of such poems as the "Paradise Lost" of Milton, the "Lines on Tintern Abbey," "The Excursion" of Wordsworth and the "In Memoriam" of Tennyson.

The former class can afford to write brief and faultless poems, because its end is a narrow one; the second class is forced to demand an ampler field, because it is influenced by a vaster purpose . . .

. . . A poem may be complete without being in the highest and most legitimate sense poetical in all its parts. If a poem have one purpose and the materials of which it is composed are so selected and arranged as to help enforce it, we have no right to regard it as a series of minor poems merely because there may occur an occasional flaw in the structure. And he who persists in reading such a poem as so many short ones, besides losing the pleasure of contemplating the symmetrical development of a work of art, will fail to grasp the central purpose of the poet. . . .

PART III

[In this section Timrod deals chiefly with truth as a poetic source and pays high tribute to Wordsworth for his appreciation of the commonest things, for his accuracy in the description of them, for his understanding of "something more than meets the senses," and for his love of Nature. In concluding Timrod explains that he is attempting to refute Poe's theory as "too limited" and "most likely to excite interest in an American audience."]

PAUL H. HAYNE: METHODS OF COMPOSITION
(AS REPORTED BY WILLIAM H. HAYNE)

. . . It was notably so in my father's case. The poetic impulse frequently came to him so spontaneously as to demand immediate utterance, and he would turn to the fly-leaf of the book in hand or on a neighboring shelf, and his pencil would soon record the lines, or fragments of lines, that claimed release from his brain. The labor of revision usually followed,—sometimes promptly, but not infrequently after the fervor of conception has passed away. And nobody unacquainted with the artistic side of the poetic temperament can fully understand what such revision means. There is an analogy—strange as it may seem—between the mathematician engaged in the solution of a difficult problem and the poet patiently endeavoring to recast his unsatisfactory lines. The mental strain and expenditure of nerveforce are strikingly similar. There are many people who regard the achievements of imagination as children regard the gifts of some fairy godmother who demands no return for her munificence. Such people are as ignorant of poetry in its relation to intellectual labor as the average Anglo-Saxon is of Sanscrit.

Oliver Wendell Holmes once said to my mother that "poetry takes a great deal out of a man"; and these words express, in a nut-shell, what I mean.

My father's favorite habits of composition were to pace back and forth between the standing-desk in his study and the bookshelves in the library, or beneath the trees surrounding Copse Hill, if the weather was favorable, and with pencil and volume in hand to jot down, on the fly-leaf referred to, the first revision of a poem, or as much of it as the duration of the creative mood would allow. Sometimes he wrote while taking a leisurely horseback ride around the house or through the woods, sometimes while sitting in his armchair of Georgia pine, but generally with greater ease while walking. This was especially true during the early and middle periods of his life, when he found it irksome to sit down for any length of time, and never seemed to weary of those meditative walks.

I have known him to compose the last line, or the intermediate part, of a poem before the beginning. When completed, however, what reader would have doubted that it came into being consecutively?

Occasionally the choice phrasing of a thought that had baffled him for days would visit him in sleep. My mother told me that he awoke one night (he had been very busy preparing his Savannah Sesqui-Centennial Ode) from tranquil slumber, and said suddenly, "Minna, at last, in sleep the thought which has eluded me for days has been captured!"

SIDNEY LANIER: From *THE SCIENCE OF ENGLISH VERSE*

Perhaps no one will find difficulty in accepting the assertion that when formal poetry, or verse,—two terms which will always be used here as convertible,—is repeated aloud, it impresses itself upon the ear as verse only by means of certain relations existing among its component words considered purely as sounds, without reference to their associated ideas. If the least doubt upon this point should be entertained, it may be dispelled by observing that all ideas may be abolished out of a poem without disturbing its effect upon the ear as verse. This may be practically demonstrated by the simple experiment of substituting for the words of a formal poem any other words which preserve the accentuation, alliteration, and rhyme, but which convey no ideas to the mind,—words of some foreign language not understood by the experimenter being the most effective for this purpose. Upon repeating aloud the poem thus treated it will be found that the verse-structure has not been impaired. If, therefore, the ear accepts as perfect verse a series of words from which ideas are wholly absent,—that is to say, a series of sounds,—it is clear that what we call "verse" is a set of specially related sounds, at least in the case of a formal poem repeated aloud.

But a much more sweeping proposition is true. If we advance from the case of formal poetry repeated aloud to that of formal poetry silently perused by the eye of a reader, a slight examination will show the proposition good that here, as before, verse is still a set of specially related sounds. For, in this instance, the characters of print or writing in which the words are embodied are simply signs of sounds; and although originally received by the eye, they are handed over to the ear, are interpreted by the auditory sense, and take their final lodgement, not at all as conceptions of sight, but as conceptions of hearing. The function of the eye is now purely ministerial: it merely purveys for the ear. An analogous process is indicated in the Arabian saw which affirms that "that is the best description which makes the ear an eye." In general, the reader will do well to recall that each sense has not only what is ordinarily called its physical province, but also its corresponding imaginative province; the eye has its imagination, the ear its imagination; and when the term "imagination of the ear" is hereinafter used it must be

understood to suggest those perceptions of sound which come
to exist in the mind, not by virtue of actual vibratory impact
upon the tympanum immediately preceding the perception, but
by virtue of indirect causes (such as the characters of print and
of writing) which in any way amount to practical equivalents
of such impact.   Now these signs convey, along with their
corresponding sounds, the same relations between those sounds
which are suggested to the ear when the sounds themselves fall
upon the tympanum.   It is therefore strictly true that, although
the great majority of formal poems in modern times are perceived by the mind through the original agency of the eye, the
relations indicated by the term "verse" are still relations between sounds.

Nor—to call the briefest attention to the only other case in
which this fundamental proposition could seem at all doubtful
—is this connection of verse with sound less essential when the
formal poem is merely conceived in the thought of its author
without ever reaching either visible or audible embodiment.
For the formal poem is necessarily conceived in words, and in
the imagination of the relations between the sounds, that is,
of verse.

In short, when we hear verse, we *hear* a set of relations between sounds; when we silently read verse, we *see* that which
brings to us a set of relations between sounds; when we imagine
verse, we *imagine* a set of relations between sounds.

Approached in this way, the proposition given below will
probably not seem difficult of acceptance; indeed it is possible
many will be surprised that the ideas leading to it have been
dwelt upon so long.   In point of fact, however, it is the very
failure to recognize verse as in all respects a phenomenon of
sound and to appreciate the necessary consequences thereof
which has caused the non-existence of a science of formal
poetry.   Occasion will presently arise to show how this has
happened, with some detail; meantime, we are now prepared
to formulate a proposition which will serve as the basis of a
science of verse.

The term "verse" denotes a set of specially related sounds.

It is clear that if we can now ascertain all the possible relations
between sounds we will have discovered all the possible deter-
minants of verse, and will have secured physical principles for
the classification of all verse-effects from which there can be no

appeal. This investigation can fortunately be carried on with the confidence attaching to the methods of physical science. For it involves mainly the observation of sensible appearances; and these are, furthermore, in the present instance not complex.

The study of verse must therefore begin with the study of sounds.

Sounds may be studied with reference to four and only four, particulars. We may observe—

(1) How long a sound lasts (*duration*);

(2) How long a sound is (*intensity*);

(3) How shrill—that is, how high, as to bass or treble—a sound is (*pitch*); and

(4) Of what sounds a given sound is composed—for, as in studying colors we find purple composed of red and violet, and the like, so many sounds have been found to be made up of other sounds (tone-color).

These differences in sounds, although really so distinct from each other as to be the origin of some of the most striking and widely-separated phenomena both in art and in our daily life, are so confused by most persons who have had no special occasion to examine them that there are no terms of ordinary use in which they can be expressed with scientific precision. The reader, however, will not only advance with ease, but will win a whole new world of possible delight, by acquiring at the outset such a familiarity with the sound-relations above termed duration, intensity, pitch, and tone-color, that the ear will immediately and intelligently refer every sound heard to all those particulars and measure its relations to the preceding or succeeding sound in terms of them. The remarkable powers which the human ear possesses of making perfectly accurate comparisons of sound with sound in three of these particulars will presently be detailed.

Meantime the reader will receive great assistance towards a clear conception of these differences by observing exactly how they are caused by the vibrating body producing the given sound; that is, by attending to the physical explanation of duration, intensity, pitch, and tone-color.

We have now reached a point where we can profitably inquire as to the precise differentiation between the two species of the art of sound—music and verse. We have found that the art of sound, in general, embraces phenomena of rhythm, of tune, and of tone-color. Many will be disposed to think that the second class of these phenomena just named—tune—is not found in verse, and that the absence of it should be one of the first differences to be noted as between music and verse. Tune is, however, quite as essential a constituent of verse as of music; and the disposition to believe otherwise is due only to the complete unconsciousness with which we come to use these tunes after the myriad repetitions of them which occur in all our daily intercourse by words. We will presently find, from numerous proofs and illustrations which are submitted in Part II. on the Tunes of Verse, that our modern speech is made up quite as much of tunes as of words, and that our ability to convey our thoughts depends upon the existence of a great number of curious melodies of speech which have somehow acquired form and significance. These "tunes" are not mere vague variations of pitch in successive words,—which would deserve the name of tune only in the most general sense of that term,—but they are perfectly definite and organized melodies of the speaking-voice, composed of exact variations of pitch so well marked as to be instantly recognized by every ear. If they were *not* thus recognized a large portion of the ideas which we now convey with ease would be wholly inexpressible. Reserving, then, all details upon this matter until their appropriate place under the head of the Tunes of Verse, in Part II. above cited, it will be sufficient here if the reader is asked to realize them in a practical way by first attempting to utter any significant sentences of prose or verse in an absolutely unchanging voice from beginning to end. This will be found quite difficult, and when successfully executed produces an impression of strangeness which all the more clearly illustrates how habitually and how unconsciously the tunes of speech are used. If, having uttered the sentences in a rigidly unvarying tone, the reader will then utter them in the tunes which we feel—by some inward perceptions too subtle for treatment here—to be appropriate to them, it will be easily seen that definite successions of tones are being used,—so definite that they are kept in mind for their appropriate occasions just as words are, and so regular in their organizations as to be in all respects worthy the name of "tunes," instead of the vague terms "intonation," or "inflection," which have so long concealed the real function of these wonderful melodies of the speaking-voice.

The art of verse, then, as well as the art of music,—the two species of the genus art of sound,—includes all the three great classes of phenomena summed up under the terms rhythm, tune, and tone-color. We will presently find many problems solved by the full recognition of this fact that there is absolutely no difference between the sound-relations used in music and those used in verse.

If this be true,—if the sound-relations of music and verse are the same,—we are necessarily forced to look for the difference between the two arts in the nature of the *sounds* themselves with which they deal. Here, indeed, the difference lies. Expressed, as far as possible, in popular terms, it is as follows:—

When those exact co-ordinations which the ear perceives as rhythm, tune, and tone-color, are suggested to the ear by a series of *musical sounds*, the result is. . . . MUSIC. When those exact co-ordinations which the ear perceives as rhythm, tune, and tone-color, are suggested to the ear by a series of *spoken words*, the result is . . . . VERSE.

But it is necessary to attain a very much more philosophical view of the relation between "musical sounds" and "words" than is generally implied in the popular use of those terms; for a slight examination will show that words are themselves musical sounds. They are capable of the exactest co-ordination in respect of their duration, their pitch, and their tone-color; they are capable of as exact co-ordination in respect of their intensity (loudness or softness) as any other sounds; they give pleasure to the ear by their fall: in short, without here attempting a definition of musical sounds, it must be said that from a scientific point of view there is no incident of them which is not also an incident of words. For all purposes of verse, words are unquestionably musical sounds produced by a reed-instrument— the human voice, that. It must therefore be clearly understood by the reader that, in the above distinction between music and verse, what are called musical sounds are only one set out of the possible body of musical sounds; while what are called words are another set; that is, that "words" (in the sense of the above distinction) means simply one kind of musical sounds, and "musical sounds" means simply another kind. It is to be regretted that our language does not afford us more precise terms for these purposes. Music, although a very old art, has only recently been investigated by exact methods: the same may be said of poetry; and it is probably owing to this circumstance that we have no terms which embody precise relations between spoken words and musical tones. The terms "vocal" and "instrumental" are not satisfactory, because they hide one of the most important facts to be kept in view in all such investigations as the present, namely, the purely instrumental character of the speaking-voice and of its tones (words). "Vocal" here *is* "instrumental." Let the reader always conceive, first, a general body of musical tones; then let the speaking-voice be conceived as an instrument consisting of a tube (the mouth, nose, and throat) and a pair of reeds (the vocal chords), which produces a certain set of these musical sounds. It is true that this certain set has received a special name, "words," because it has come to be used for a special purpose, namely, that of communicating ideas from man to man. It will assist the reader to a clearer conception of this matter, if the fact be called to mind that the selection of vocal sounds for the purpose of communicating ideas was not at all a necessary one. Other sets of musical sounds might have been selected for this purpose, those of whistles or flutes, for instance; or no sounds at all might have been used, and "words" might have been entirely eye-signs, as is actually the case with the deaf and dumb. In fine, when the term "words" is used as describing the peculiar set of sounds used in verse, the reader must understand it merely as a convenient method of singling out that specialized set of musical sounds made by the musical instrument called "the human speaking-voice." . . .

DuBOSE HEYWARD AND HERVEY ALLEN:
From *POETRY SOUTH**

It is a truism that creative art from its very nature must be original, the peculiarly different and unexpected reaction of the artist to his environment. This is especially true of poetry, the least concrete of the arts; and it is this very quality of unexpectedness in the poet, constituting as it does so much of the charm of poetry, that makes an attempt to forecast the reactions of any group or school of poets a task which calls for the prophetic rather than for the merely constructive critic. . . .

Despite some vigorous assertions to the contrary, it seems

*Reprinted from *Poetry*, XX, April, 1922; Southern Number.

as if southern poetry were going to be decidedly regional in spirit, with a quick human appeal but strongly local in tone— poetry of and about places. Much of American verse is city poetry. It is the similarity of our city life perhaps which has given to a great deal of American verse a note of sameness that is too often mistaken for a universal realistic appeal. The city, too, has given American poetry a tendency to mirror back the drab, and accentuated an almost morbid desire for self-expression which the crowd begets. There has been, to be sure, a gain in thought-content and sophistication, but the spontaneous and simple have been sacrificed, while the constant search for the "new" has brought about a ceaseless experiment with alien forms. It seems probable that poetry written from the South will be, in nearly all these respects, the opposite of what has rather arbitrarily been called "city-verse," for the South is still predominantly agricultural. Although industrialism, under the spur of northern capital, has ridden in ruthlessly here and there, the plantation of one kind or another is still the economic, vital unit; and it may be expected that when the plantation poet speaks, it will not be from the necessity of introspectively asserting his existence as an individual apart from the crowd, but of objectively reflecting in simple measures the patriarchal life remnant about him. In this he will very likely be profoundly impressed by his sub-tropical or mountain landscapes, and reflect the spontaneously lyrical and primarily rhythmic melodies of the Negro. Indeed, the effect of the Negro on southern poetry demands a treatment by itself. . . .

The Negro, however, is not the only source of folk-lore in the South. Even richer in poetic material is the lofty back-country of the Appalachians. The rush of American civilization has thus far touched only the fringes of this rugged land. . .

. . . There are certain remote districts in the Black and Great Smoky ranges where life has remained absolutely static for a century and a half. There it is still possible to hear old English ballads and folk-tales which passed from current use generations ago; and one still encounters Elizabethan words. Certainly nowhere else in the America of today can one find conditions so favorable to the development of genuine folk-expression; with the background of an old, but still remembered civilization, and an absolute isolation which encourages the crystallization, by word of mouth, of the idea into the story. . . .

The statement has been made earlier that southern poetry may be largely of and about places. If environment is going to affect our southern poets, if they are going to be at all objective, this will necessarily follow, for there is no other portion of the country so districted—i.e., where sections differ so one from the other as in the South. To pass from the country of the mountain-whites to the Carolina Low Country, for example, is to pass from one world to another, one with a different fauna and flora and a different ethnic background. Here the poets may tell of the sea-islands, with tidal lagoons where the wild-fowl, ducks, marsh-hens, and strange gawky heron feed, and the migrating song-birds pass through each year like a recurring flame. They may speak of magnolia and azalea gardens, ori-ental in a polychromatic spring; of swamps and eerie live-oak forests where the Spanish moss hangs like stalactites in twilit caverns; of the miles of deserted rice-fields where turbaned blacks walk ruined dykes; and of the ancient baronies and manors, each with its legend, where the deer feed around the stately columned houses—shells of a life and an epoch which have passed away.

But if the past does not call the southern poet, the thrusting of industrialism into the Piedmont cotton and tobacco regions, with the rise of the factory system, child-labor, and a burning racial problem, offer a tremendous theme and a possible chance of legitimate propaganda for the present. Then in Florida, at such towns as Miami, a frontier is being peacefully settled, and dotted with villas Roman in their scale and magnificence; while from the Everglades the firelight of the stone-age Seminole glows in the midnight sky when he holds his secret corn-dances. Southward stretch the coral keys, haunted by huge sea-turtles, that crawl out to hide their eggs where pirates once hid gold; and even today the eagle boat of the whiskey-runner shelters there, making for Nassau or Bimini. Then there are the plains of Texas rich with the dusty-golden dreams of Spanish empire, with enchanted mesas, pueblos, Indian stories and cow-boy songs; or the cane-brakes of Louisiana, and faded Creole New Orleans of the old river days.

How absurd to say the South has nothing but genealogy! Who will sing of them, these cities—of Santa Fe or El Paso, San Antonio or St. Augustine, and of old Charleston with her three hundred years of memories? Who is going to write the epos of Coronado, of the lost Fountain of Youth, of De Soto, of the pirates, of Africa transplanted, of the outlandish voodoo that still lingers, and of the strange new Christ the Negroes worship? Is there no one who will tell over again from the clearer light of a better time how the awful, keen sword of civil war struck down these states, how the slave and freedman passed, and how through bitterness they have come to a saner, sweeter life again? Here is a challenge to the American renascence. It is ardently to be hoped that the South will continue to reply to it as she has begun to do, and that she will give us largely of her rich landscapes and historical material, and speak of and from the life of her memory and of her present. And it is also to be hoped that the cleverly inane, or the small accidental dream-life of the individual, so seldom worth uttering—tiny loves and smaller hates, and the baldly phrased usual; above all, the banal echo and the purely sentimental—will be left unsaid. . . .

The last few years have brought a new spirit into the South. With the recovery of her economic life has come the possibility of renewing the old culture, and an opportunity for a leisure not due to apathy and despair. The great war has also stirred and disturbed her subtly and immeasurably, till a vast territory which has for a while lain poetically fallow is now awakening, and from here and there voices, small and inadequate perhaps, but nevertheless earnest and distinctive voices, are giving it utterance.

It is their desire that the rest of the country know and recognize this; for while these voices may utter with a *timbre* peculiarly their own, it is because they are moved, not by a provincial pride, but by the renascence of poetry throughout America; and being so moved by this spirit, they claim to be of it. The South will never express itself in constricted forms; mood, inclination and tradition forbid, nor does it feel the urge completely to slough the old. Here, where the tides of immigration have brought no alien tongues, the grand tradition of English poetry still lingers strongly in an old culture which has survived the wrack of civil war and of reconstruction—a European culture, planted by a strong stock in colonial times; and it is from this tradition and from the descendants of that stock that the southern poetical renascence must come. It will accept with modern spirit the new forms in verse, but accept

them as being valuable for their loosening effect upon the old
rather than as being all satisfactory in themselves; and it brings
to American poetry a little known but tropically rich store of
material, an unurbanized beauty, the possibility of legend, folk-
song, romance, historical narrative, glorious landscape, and an
untired mood; in short, a content which will save it from that
sure sign of literary inadequacy, a too nice preoccupation with
form.

JOHN GOULD FLETCHER: PREFACE TO
PRELUDES AND SYMPHONIES

In one of the Descriptive Catalogues of William Blake there
occurs the phrase, "the productions of our youth and of our
maturer age are equal in all essential points." The author of the
book that follows is unable to apply the comfort of Blake's
maxim to himself, for the reason that, in the opinion of some
discerning critics, he has never equalled the poetry contained
in its pages. And "Preludes and Symphonies" is the book of
my youth; sixteen years having passed since it was conceived
and fourteen since it was finished. Am I to admit that in all
these years that have followed I have wavered in my aim to
write the best poetry of which I was capable, or must I allow
that by some accident, of which I was not conscious and fully
responsible, these productions tapped some inner source in me
that I have since been unable to attain?

The question has more than an academic and a purely personal interest. Most of the critics who hailed these poems when
they appeared liked them precisely because they seemed to do
something not done before. But that point has lost interest for
me, now. We have had so many poets trying to outdo each
other in the search for novel expression, in the last dozen years,
that mere novel expression will not suffice as a criterion for
poetry. But on re-reading the pages herein contained, and particularly in the section entitled "Irradiations," I do feel a certain
freshness of phraseology that at the present day I have to labor
hard to recapture—if indeed I can entirely recapture it. With
"Irradiations" I achieved completely something that I had been
working towards, in obscurity and silence, for about five years:
a presentation of daily life in terms of highly-orchestrated and
coloured words. If poetry is a rendering of moods alone, and
if you have to be in the mood for poetry before poetry can say
anything to you, then "Irradiations" should satisfy many

readers; and the "Symphonies," where each separate mood is not kept distinct but merges into its related and corresponding mood, should satisfy more. Since then I have tended increasingly to hold that poetry is also thought, and that thought and emotion play the part in poetry of counterpoint and melody in the works of musical composers. I still feel, in "Irradiations," the surge of an emotion vital enough to have transformed my existence, but I have to go back sixteen years before I can begin to explain it.

It all happened in the spring of 1913, in Paris. Except for two or three minor pieces, the whole of the first forty pages of this book was written then. At that time, I was just over twenty-six years of age and had spent the last five years of my life in London. "The New Poetry" had just begun to be talked about, on the other side of the Atlantic, and its first heralds, Lindsay, Masters, Sandburg, had scarcely made a stir. The Imagists, with whom later I was to affiliate myself, had not yet attained to the dignity of a collected anthology. I had only read the work of one of them, the pioneer Ezra Pound. During the course of the month in which I was to finish "Irradiations," I was to make his acquaintance. My gods proved to be different from his: I depended on Whitman, Blake, Shelley, and the French Symbolists, while he preferred the remoter and perhaps purer sources of Anglo-Saxon, Provençal, and ancient Chinese inspiration. In "Irradiations" my dependence on the Symbolists is particularly marked. If the reader will turn to the pages of an almost forgotten book of symbolist verse, "Les Fêtes Quotidiennes" by Guy Charles Cros, published by the Mercure de France in 1912, he will find such phrases as "les écharpes violettes de la nuit tombent à plis légers sur les épaules de la terre" and "les petits trilles polychromes des étoiles" which I imitated faithfully in "Irradiations." There are also echoes of Verhaeren strewn up and down these pages. I can only say in extenuation that every poet necessarily borrows something from other poets, just as every man is necessarily influenced in his life by his surroundings; and it is not the fact of such borrowings, but what is made out of them, that is important. In any case, "Irradiations" owes much to the Symbolist school. And the "Symphonies" owe still more.

Like the works of the Symbolists, these poems, despite the fact that they concerned themselves with everyday events and incidents, have all in common a certain aloofness to life. This I realise, though perhaps I did not realise it fully until Conrad Aiken in his "Scepticisms" pointed out their quality of "a detached waver and brilliance," and Edward Garnett in his "Friday Nights" referred to the pitfalls of the allusive method. Had I been left to myself, I might have pursued this pathway to its end in endless heaping up of meaningless colour-patterns; being already encouraged towards that end by my friend, Miss Lowell, whose poetic evolution was, as she confessed herself, largely orientated and directed by the appearance of "Irradiations." Our friendship, indeed, dated from the day I first read her the completed manuscript. I might not have undertaken the "Symphonies" at all had it not been for her sympathy and encouragement. They are, as I have already pointed out, examples of the use, or the abuse, of the *allusive* method (to borrow Garnett's phrase). My aim in them was to describe certain predominant moods in the terms of things happening. Thus one gets expectancy described as a traveller looking at blue mountains in the distance, and despair described in terms of a stoker on board a ship. Each mood was to be presented not as abstract sorrow or joy or rage, but as something seen, heard, felt, and actually happening. By these means, I approached close to that "methodical confusion of all the senses" which was described as the visionary state by no less a poet than Arthur Rimbaud.

In two respects, indeed, these "Symphonies" irritated many worthy critics of the time, and may still irritate some today. That was because to each of them I assigned a colour, and because their form seemed to be entirely shapeless. As regards the colour-title, my intentions in that respect have been greatly exaggerated. My friendly critics might have assured themselves, by a glance at Galton's "Inquiry Concerning Human Faculty" that colour-vision in certain states of excitement, is far more common than most people suppose; and in poetry of this visual type, some indication of the prevailing mood seems to be necessary. My assignment of a colour to each "Symphony" was no more than an indication of my main intention. The charge against the form is less easily rebutted; but I have always felt it more important for a poet to create his form according to the state of his feelings and the condition of his material, than to borrow one ready-made and to attempt to squeeze his feelings in it. Only a few metrical forms are really of universal applicability, perhaps the sonnet and blank verse are the only forms in English that can be used indiscriminately by all poets without loss of quality. I may have pushed metrical variation too far towards anarchy; for having employed it in preference to uniformity, I still feel I owe neither explanation nor apology.

The "Symphonies" have had no direct successors in my later work. With the exception of the love poems contained in "The Tree of Life," upon which I began working before finishing the "Symphonies" and which are so arranged as to make the entire book a symphony, I have felt that this was a type of poetry that I, personally, could not develop farther. I have written since many works in the symphonic form of four or five contrasted movements; attentive readers will find some of them even in my latest book, "The Black Rock"—but I have been at pains to give them a more philosophic structure, and not merely sought to follow my mood wherever it led. That may be because the domain of the subconscious, with which these poems deal, is too readily exhausted, or it may be that the Great War succeeded in modifying my ideas of poetry. In any case I have felt that whatever I succeeded in doing in the "Symphonies" could not be repeated in exactly the same way; which is far from saying that I believed the way partly shown by these poems to be a blind alley.

The value, then, of this book resides rather in its display of lyric temperament than in any ideas it may contain. It does not belong to that main branch of poetry, the branch that is pure folk-song, where are Homer and Chaucer, the authors of the Nibelungenlied and the Song of Roland, many a balladist, Burns and Heine, Wordsworth and Coleridge at their best. Neither can it be classed with the kind of poetry that pre-supposes a steadily-held philosophic background, the kind written by Lucretius and Dante, Goethe and Leopardi, Shelley, Blake, and more recently, Thomas Hardy. But perhaps there is still a third category of poetry, the kind of poetry that has nothing to justify it except its own eagerness for beauty, the kind of which "Endymion" provides a classic example. To that kind this book belongs. And whatever its value, I know that Imagism could not have been what it was, had not these poems been written. With that knowledge I rest content.

ALLEN TATE: *From* NOTE ON SOUTHERN
POETRY

The problem [of what makes a poet Southern] is speculative,
and although the relation of the poet to his world is an aspect
of the significance of scientific ideas in the modern mind, it is
probable that it is only an aspect, a more general fashion of
stating the oldest problem of esthetics. It is fundamentally the
problem of what the poet shall "imitate," and to what end. As
poetry grows increasingly abstract, it competes with science,
or as Aristotle might have put it, competes with some form of
history, and is hence less an imitation of perceived forms than
practicable versions of what happens. The local, immediate,
and the concrete are the take-off of poetry, and the terms of
some long-settled familiarity with concrete features of experience are doubtless the origin of its form. Mr. Ezra Pound has
for years belabored the necessity for the concrete, but he seems
to give his case away to the scientist in not being able to stop
long enough on some few realms of fact to understand them:
the result is that the cosmopolitan Mr. Pound, a very great
artist, is an incomplete scientist.

The historian of Southern poetry must constantly pause to
inquire into the causes of our thin and not very comprehensive
performance, in the past, and it may be, as the next generation
will see us, in the present also. For the thousands who read
William Gilmore Simms' novels and his defense of slavery, a
handful knew his poetry, though by any test it deserved as
much reading as his prose. There was never a profession of
letters in the South. There were, and perhaps here and there
there still are, ladies and gentlemen. It is the English social
tradition. If there had been a Southern Congreve for a Voltaire to visit, he would have been a "man of fashion" first, or
the American synonym for him in the 1840's, and Voltaire
would have been disgusted at his lack of professional pride.
Perhaps this tradition is still active, but it is certainly less so
than it was in the time of Lanier. It may be gone entirely; yet
the Southern man of letters, freed from it, has not seen the
opportunities of his freedom. On the necessity of making
Southern writers, and for that matter American writers, a professional class, bound together by all the ties of a profession
whose ethics consists in devotion to the craft—on the need of

this, some writer should speedily write a tract, and no title could be better suited to it than *Up from Slavery*.

Yet the problem of professional solidarity is not simple. Society in the United States, in this era, is not more concerned about literature than the plantation was: the plantation did not create a great literature, but it read great literature and it had a profound grasp of ideas relevant to its needs—the only kind of ideas any society ever achieves. The industrialist knows little or nothing, neither imaginative literature nor political philosophy. If the modern writer, unlike the old Southern writer, is emancipated from the demands of social conformity, it is not because he has been intelligently emancipated; it is rather that the decay of social standards has left him free, but nevertheless hanging in the air. The place of the old Southern writer was narrow, it hardly existed, but to the extent that it did exist, it was defined. . . .

DONALD DAVIDSON: "THE SOUTHERN POET AND HIS TRADITION"

Ten years ago, in reviewing *Carolina Chansons*, the editor of *Poetry* saw in the joint work of DuBose Heyward and Hervey Allen the promise of a new articulateness for the South. The South had a heroic past; it was rich with legend and fierce with feeling; there was no perceptible reason, Miss Monroe thought, why Mr. Heyward and other Southerners then beginning to write should not make the fullest possible use of the material at hand. Out of the Southern tradition there ought to grow an exciting, possibly a really great Southern poetry which would be a considerable ornament to American letters.

At the time, I was one of a group of poets in Nashville, Tennessee, who though committed to the idea of a distinctly Southern poetry, could not accept Miss Monroe's doctrine. We felt that it was dangerous to prescribe any special subject matter for the new Southern poets; and it was dangerous to tie them up with the sort of local color program that Miss Monroe's remarks seemed to imply. In the columns of *The Fugitive*, then just getting under way, we said as much, and said it with a defiant bellicosity that was quite wasted. If if had been noticed, it might have reminded observers that the picturesque charm of the Carolina Low Country was one thing, but the pugnaciousness of the western South, still "half-horse, half-alligator" and ready to fight all comers, was another thing. . . .

It is time to state Miss Monroe's proposition again, though in slightly different terms. After all, it is a fair question to ask why Southern poets, as artists with a very special local heritage, cannot write like Southerners, rather than like "advanced" Parisians or Greenwich Villagers; and why they cannot, among other things, write about the indubitably Southern themes, even the Southern legends, places, heroes, though that alone, of course, will not make them Southern poets, or in fact, poets of any sort.

Yet this, it seems, is precisely what many of them cannot do, or cannot without falling into grievous error. A young poet "emerging" in the South today is in danger of following one of two courses, both of which are bad. In one case he will utterly divorce himself from all sense of locality and at once begin to write clever but trifling imitations of decadent poetasters in New York, London, and Paris. But, if he is safely illiterate, and so manages to escape the infection of our times, he may then write "Southern" poetry containing very proper local references; and this is sure to be as empty as the other was clever. One tendency gives us modernists of every type— people who begin by grandly renouncing their birthright and by contributing to woolly Messiah magazines of the *Blues* or *Contempo* variety. The other tendency begets local laureates— cheerful infants who commit monstrosities such as songs on the model of Katharine Lee Bates' *America the Beautiful.* This happens too often not to be emphasized as a phenomenon of our times. It can be traced out on a considerable scale in such an anthology as Mr. Addison Hibbard's *The Lyric South.* It appears, though to a less horrifying degree, in the work of some of our best poets. It almost amounts to this: that a poet cannot be "Southern" without behaving like a fool; and if he tries not to be a fool, he will not be recognizably "Southern."

But the malady, if it is such, is not limited to the poets. It may be found in a far more virulent degree among Southern writers of fiction, some of whom have occupied themselves—and with no little success—in getting out "Yankee" novels about the virtues of the downtrodden black man and the vices of the depraved white man in the South. I should be the last to decry the excellence that the better of these writers display. But it is evident that the attitudes underlying their work are too often borrowed from the progressive North and do not belong to the conservative South.

Yet they should not be blamed too harshly. In America—or at least in the progressive America which has been most vocal in recent years—every man who starts out to be an artist is subjected to a subtle but powerful pressure to emancipate himself from his native surroundings. If he is born in Keokuk and wants to do serious writing, his first act must be either to run away from Keokuk or somehow disclaim it. His craft does not come to him as part of a generally diffused tradition which has local roots and which he naturally appropriates as his own. No, he must get out and grab what he can from the set of rapidly shifting formulae spawned from the disorder of a de-localized, vaguely cosmopolitan society, masquerading rather noisily as a civilization. What does this society, loudly proclaiming its devotion to culture and the good life, have to teach the artist? To judge from the evidence, it teaches contempt, suspicion, disillusionment; it has no positive standards to offer, other than a maudlin apostrophe to Beauty, and no loyalties to anything nearer at hand than a somewhat tenuous World-soul. If I may use the words of one of its popular prophets, Everett Dean Martin, it says to the artist, as to all "civilized" persons: "It is nobler to doubt than to believe, for to doubt is often to take sides with fact against oneself." The skeptical, at-cross-purposes tendency of our society was never better epitomized than in this amazing and, I would say, damnable utterance. Whatever it may mean for the scientist, this pronouncement offers a lamentable prospect for the poet, who must believe or perish. It is no wonder that our artists believe nothing; or, by a natural reaction, they turn in and believe too much, trying vainly to rebuild a personal mythology of some kind as a substitute for the tradition that the worshippers of doubt have destroyed.

Southern writers share this malady along with American writers in general, but one nevertheless feels that they ought not to share as much as they do. For Southern society is not yet "American" society. While the North has been changing its apparatus of civilization every ten years or so—this being, I fear, the peculiar curse inherited from that restless haunted soul, Abraham Lincoln—the South has stood its ground at a fairly

safe distance and happily remained some forty or fifty years
behind the times.   Having once got hold of an idea, even
though it be not quite a perfect idea, the South does not hasten
to discard it, but keeps holding on. The South has never been
able to understand how the North, in its astonishing quest for
perfection, can junk an entire system of ideas almost overnight,
and start on another one which is newer but no better than the
first. This is one of the principal differences, out of many real
differences, between the sections—it is perhaps the reason why
the South is not "America the Menace."

One would expect that Southern writers would be responsive
to this stable tradition. The South ought to have an artistic
tradition to fit its social and historical background. One ought
to be able to say of it as Æ said of Ireland, that it is a good
field for the arts, especially for poetry, simply because, in contrast to progressive America, it has long been defeated and poor
and behind the times; or, furthermore, because it offers its people
belief rather than doubt, conviction rather than distrust. There
ought to be something virile and positive in its art, as an art
linked by devotion to a concrete place rather than animated by
a loose enthusiasm for a "national" culture which has no organic
unity behind it. For instance, if a Southerner had written *John
Brown's Body*, one would have expected to find the subject
treated with more conviction and finality than Stephen Vincent
Benét, writing somewhat remotely, could put into it.

Turning to the literary past, I find the evidence on this point
rather confused and not too comforting. I should hardly join
with those determined Rebels who would defend Southern
literature at any cost against the aspersion of Yankee critics. On
the other hand, I should disclaim any agreement with those very
fashionable critics—among them a few Southerners—who
have been issuing passionate and contemptuous repudiations of
the supposedly "sentimental" literature of the Old South. The
literature of the Old South is neither as good nor as bad as
partisans have represented it to be. Vernon Louis Parrington,
at least, has proved that the South shared with the West the
dignity of producing a more respectable body of literature than
the New England Brahmins ever used to allow. The poetry of
the Old South and of the post-bellum South had the virtues
and defects of American poetry in general; it was Romantic, or
was Victorian, with some sporadic excellence but with no con-

certed and general achievement such as existed in New England. In the South there are Poe and Lanier to set off against Emerson and Whitman; there are minor poets like Timrod, Hayne, Russell, Pinkney, or even the newly discovered Chivers. There are also the folk-singers, whose value is only now realized. These anonymous poets—makers of ballads, songs, and spirituals—were and are abundant in the South to a degree which other sections can hardly claim. Yet on the whole one might well say with John Crowe Ransom that the arts of the South in times past took another direction than poetry. They were the eighteenth-century arts of dress, conversation, manners: or, I might add, of architecture, handicraft, oratory, anecdote—all respectable enough and sufficiently recorded to the credit of the South. There is no reason to think that these arts did not express a Southern tradition rather intimately and without any fumbling or debate. Indeed, the problem of the relation of the Southern artist to his tradition did not then arise in its modern form.

Now, however, it has arisen, and the issues it raises are acute. If the South is destined, as so many people are saying, to be "articulate" on a scale never before realized, it would be a strange trick of fate for writers to find themselves, at such a moment, inhibited from a free expression of the Southern tradition, unable to speak for the South as a living historic entity which is separate from America though bound to it, and still abiding to a marked degree by the tenets of a civilization so thoroughly un-American (in the modern sense) that it is in one breath romantically admired and in the next breath harshly deplored by the much interested North.

Yet such is the danger that threatens. Those well-wishers, like Miss Monroe, who are rightly eager to see a Southern poetry arise which is recognizably Southern and not merely a somewhat tropical version of Sandburg, Robinson, or Eliot—those critics must recognize that there is civil strife within the South itself, and because of this civil strife the peculiar dilemma of the American artist, described above, becomes deeply accented.

And how unnecessarily so. Left undisturbed, the Southern tradition would undoubtedly register effectively in art. But it has not been left undisturbed. Instead, the so-called Southern liberal group, who have of late grown much in power, aided by Northern philanthropy and by agitation in Northern journals, have bent every energy to persuade the South to make over its civilization on the progressive Northern plan, largely through the combined agencies of a sweeping industrialization and a large-scale "liberalized" scheme of public education. The effect of this program has undoubtedly been to dislocate many Southern writers from a proper relation to their own people and their own tradition. As studied, for example, in such a center of progressive agitation as the University of North Carolina, the program would reveal on the one hand a determined effort to encourage young Southern writers to be spokesmen for their own section—to produce a modern literature expressive of the South. So far, so good. This would be laudable indeed, were it all.

But there is also the social program that underlies and accompanies the program for the encouragement of the arts. This social program is not native at all. It is foreign to the ideas that are most deeply rooted in the Southern experience and the Southern temperament. It involves a repudiation not only of the Southern past but of the elements of the Southern character that are most firmly ingrained. The progressive leaders, in short, are asking the Southern writer to pay a terrible price for his modernity. They are asking contradictory things, and with such influences beating upon them, Southern artists will escape distortion only by being uncommonly levelheaded and discerning. As long as such a condition endures, the Southern artists who are affected will do their work under the handicap of a painful self-consciousness. Theirs will be the dilemma of the modern artist who in one act must both deny himself and express himself.

There is no remedy, short of the rise to power of a body of Southern writers, economists, politicians, and clergy who will fight to a finish the new order of carpetbaggers and scalawags—or else assimilate them. But even this remedy has much peril for the arts, which do not profit much by contentiousness. It is certain, however, that the well-wishers for the South cannot with one gesture "up-lift" the South into the blessings of modern civilization, and with another demand of Southern writers that they exhibit in their works the virtues of a way of life that they have just been urged to repudiate. Yet if there is hope—and I think there is much hope, in view of the extraordinary confusion into which industrial civilization has got itself—the poets are likely to go further than other writers toward realizing the ideal of a free expression of the Southern character in literature. For the poets are unpopular, the poets are never promoted, they escape the commercial taint that hangs over novelists and playwrights. Let them, then, write what they will, depending on their own integrity for a guide, and if they live like the Miller of Dee, envying nobody and with nobody envying them, they need not fear that their integrity will be impugned or spoiled.

NOTES

1. John Smith (1580–1631), "probably the last professional knight-errant" (Tyler, *History of American Literature*, I, 18) was a daring adventurer, a prolific author, and a noteworthy storyteller, particularly of his own exploits. His *A True Relation of Virginia* (London, 1608) was the earliest book written in America. He frequently interspersed his prose with bits of original verse but "The Sea Mark" is his only known complete poem. It appeared in his *Advertisement for the Unexperienced Planters of New England* in 1631 and was doubtless written after his return to England to live. Though Smith left Virginia in 1609 for England, he made two voyages, in 1614 and 1615, to New England. He is credited with having invented the latter name.

2. This is an unusual and thoroughly Americanized variant of the English ballad, "Lord Thomas and Fair Annet," or, as it is often given in English variants also, "Lord Thomas and Fair Eleanor." Probably the oldest known version is the one which begins

> Lord Thomas and Fair Annet
> Sate a' day on a hill;
> When night was cum, and sun was sett,
> They had not talkt their fill.

The essential parts of the ballad, in almost every variant, remain the same. Reed Smith in *South Carolina Ballads* (pp. 109–20) gives in full or in part five variants.

3. Nathaniel Bacon, a prominent and forceful Virginia colonist, died suddenly of a peculiar illness in 1676, some months after organizing and directing a successful attack on threatening Indian groups. Governor William Berkeley, who had refused the colonists adequate protection, denounced him as a rebel and after his death continued to vent his wrath on all who had followed him, causing King Charles the Second to remark, "that old fool had taken away more lives in that naked country, than himself had taken for the murder of his father."

The "Epitaph," with other anonymous papers dealing chiefly with "Bacon's rebellion," was found by the Burwell family in Virginia (in 1802) and was published by the Massachusetts Historical Society in 1814. The poem is usually credited to one "Cotton, of Acquia Creek, husband of Ann Cotton" (Tyler, *op. cit.*, I, 79), and author of several known letters. The prefacing remarks state that after Bacon's death "he was bemoaned in these following lines, drawn by the man that waited upon his person as it is said, and who attended his corpse to their burial place." Certainly "his man" was no servant, however, but a trusted and faithful lieutenant who attempted by this device to save himself from the certain vengeance of the governor. The dirge in its dignity, stateliness and mournful eloquence has been well compared to the commemorative verse of Ben Jonson.

4. William Byrd (1674–1744) was born in Virginia on his father's estate at Westover but was educated in England. Though he returned to Virginia and spent the greater part of his life there, he ever thought of himself as an expatriated Englishman. His writings, almost entirely in prose, were the journals he kept on his several expeditions to various parts of Virginia and North Carolina.

The bit of verse given here is from "The History of the Dividing Line, April 1728" (J. S. Bassett's *The Writings of Colonel William Byrd*, 101) and endorses Governor Spottswood's efforts to Christianize the Indians, though Byrd's own opinion was that intermarriage rather than education was the proper procedure. "The care Colo. Spotswood took to tincture the Indian children with Christianity produc'd the following Epigram, which was not publisht during his Administration, for fear it might then have lookt like flattery." (Bassett, *op. cit.*, 101). Byrd gives the poem no title.

5. *Poems on Several Occasions, by a Gentleman of Virginia*, from which this poem is taken, was published in 1736 by William Parks, the first printer in the state; it was the first volume of poetry to be published in Virginia. Its author's anonymity is complete, though it has been conjectured that he was a professor in the College of William and Mary. The one volume of the poems known to be extant today was in the possession of George Washington, whose signature on the title page is that used by him about 1780. It was left at Mount Vernon by his heirs until 1848 when through various transactions it was presented to the Boston Athenaeum. Mr. Earl Gregg Swem, librarian of William and Mary, prepared an edition of 68 copies in 1920 for the Heartman Historical Series. In 1930 the Facsimile Text Society issued an edition with a bibliographical note by Ralph L. Rusk.

6. This anonymous ballad celebrates the victory of a small American force (principally composed of mountaineers under the officers named) over a larger band of English regulars on October 7, 1780. The engagement took place on a rugged height near the northern border of South Carolina. The victory, though a minor one in the war as a whole, was especially valuable to heighten the morale of the countryside and to dampen the ardor of the American Tories who had favored the British.

7. John Shaw (1778–1809) was born in Annapolis and, after studying medicine in Philadelphia and Edinburgh and traveling as ship and troop surgeon, practiced medicine in Baltimore. His death from consumption

followed chemical experiments in which he heedlessly exposed himself. His poems were collected and published the year following his death.

8. St. George Tucker (1752–1828) was born in Bermuda and emigrated to Williamsburg at the age of 20. After his graduation from the College of William and Mary he entered the legal profession; his writings in that field gained him the title "the American Blackstone." For some years he taught law at William and Mary and later served with distinction on the bench of both State and Federal courts. His poems, chiefly fugitive pieces of a patriotic or sentimental nature, have not been collected. "Resignation" (sometimes miscalled "Days of My Youth") and "The Belles of Williamsburg" (written in collaboration with Dr. James McClurg) are best known.

9. Francis Scott Key (1779–1843), a native of Frederick County, Maryland, was educated at St. John's College in Annapolis and practiced law in Frederick, Maryland, and in Washington.

According to his brother-in-law, Chief Justice Roger B. Taney, "The Star-Spangled Banner" was composed while Key was detained on an American ship during the British attack on Fort McHenry, Maryland, April 13–14, 1814. It was written from memory on an envelope while he was on his way to shore the next morning and was printed and sold on the streets of Baltimore as a broadside the following day. Set to the music of "Anacreon in Heaven" (the official song of the Anacreontic Society in London), it attained nationwide popularity and has been adopted by the Army and Navy as the national anthem.

10. "Stanzas" (sometimes called "The Lament of the Captive") was written between 1812 and 1814 and was first printed about 1818, without the knowledge or consent of the author. It was republished frequently in this country and appeared in one or more Scottish journals as well; in 1823 it was printed in the Cork (Ireland) *Mercantile Chronicle* and later in other Irish papers. Sometime during the 1820's also it was translated into Greek and published as a newly discovered fragment of the poetry of Alcaeus. By 1830 many people were persuaded that Mr. Wilde had plagiarized either from the Irish poet, Daniel O'Kelly (whose version appeared between 1824 and 1831), or from Alcaeus. In the first issue of the *Southern Literary Messenger* (August, 1834) the poem is given with the editorial comment that it is "very generally ascribed to the pen of the Hon. R. H. Wilde." The discussion continued, however, and in October, 1856, the same magazine reprinted from the Columbia, S. C., *Examiner* an article by James Wood Davidson which reviewed the history and notoriety of the poem and refuted the charges of plagiarism. Mr. Davidson quoted entire a letter, dated December 31, 1834, from Mr. Wilde to the editor of the *State Rights' Sentinel*, in which Mr. Wilde admitted authorship of the poem.

As "My Life is Like the Summer Rose" the poem was set to music by Charles Thibault about 1822 and was popular as a song. Aubrey H.

Starke (*American Book Collector*, January, 1934) lists six other known musical settings, including an unpublished one by Sidney Lanier.

11. "To the Mocking Bird" may have appeared anonymously in a magazine. The subject is a favorite one with Southern poets.

12. "To Lord Byron" was printed in the *Southern Literary Messenger*, November, 1834. Byron's works were widely read in the South and his influence on the poets was strong. See W. E. Leonard, *Byron and Byronism in America.*

13. "A Farewell to America" seems to have appeared first in *Poets and Poetry of America* (1842), edited by Rufus W. Griswold. The date of composition is given, however, as June, 1835, at the time the author was sailing for several years' stay in Europe.

Wilde's verse ("mostly written when he was a member of Congress during moments of relaxation") has never been collected. He contributed frequently to the *Southern Literary Messenger*, in whose success he was enthusiastically interested, to *Graham's* and quite probably to other magazines. Griswold includes seven poems by Wilde and a brief account of the author in *Poets and Poetry of America.*

14. *Poems*, by Edward Coote Pinkney, was published in 1825. In October of that year the *North American Review* published a long review of the book, fairly complimentary in general, but containing the significant sentence: "We do not like the moral tone of this poetry. It is too close and too loud an echo to that of Byron."

Edgar Allan Poe in "The Poetic Principle" says "It was the misfortune of Mr. Pinkney to have been born too far south. Had he been a New Englander, it is probable that he would have been ranked as the first of American lyrists, by that magnanimous cabal which has so long controlled the destinies of American Letters, in conducting the thing called the *North American Review.*"

The song "We Break the Glass" was probably addressed to Miss Mary Hawkins, who did not return the affection of the poet.

15. In "The Voyager's Song," the second line of the second stanza has been compared to Shakespeare's line in *Richard II*, II, i, 46: "This precious stone set in the silver sea."

16. "Serenade" addressed to Miss Hawkins, and probably written in 1822, has been set to music by at least four composers. I have followed Mabbott and Pleadwell (*The Life and Works of Edward Coote Pinkney*) in using the words of the first edition of the song, as published under the title "Look Out Upon the Stars, My Love, A Serenade," Baltimore, 1823.

17. "A Health," dated August 10, 1824, in her album, was most probably written to the author's wife, née Georgiana McCausland, whom he married October 12, 1824. Various traditions name other ladies who believed the lines were written in their honor.

18. "Day Departs" was set to music and published as a serenade in 1844.

19. Mabbott and Pleadwell (*op. cit.*, 125) suggest that "The Widow's Song" may commemorate the affection of the poet's mother for his father. They give the following note: "The Afghans have all a great reverence for burial grounds, which they . . . call . . . Cities of the Silent, and which they people with the ghosts of the departed, who sit each at the head of his own grave, invisible to mortal eyes, and enjoy the odors of the garlands which are hung on their tombs, and of the incense which is burned by their surviving relations." (Mountstuart Elphinstone, *An Account of the Kingdom of Caubul*, London, 1815, Book I, chap. V.)

20. The lines now entitled "Self-Esteem" were written in Pinkney's notebook but given no title, in 1826, at a period when prejudice against a poet-lawyer combined with ill health was making it difficult for the author to make a living. (Mabbott and Pleadwell, *op. cit.*, 51.) This is the only poem given in this group not included in *Poems* (1825). Cf. Wordsworth's "My Heart Leaps Up."

21. "On Parting" was written in the album of Miss McCausland in 1823.

22. Note given by Mabbott and Pleadwell (*op. cit.*, 170), on "Melancholy's Curse of Feasts": "Under this title Rufus Dawes printed the following lines in *The Emerald and Baltimore Literary Gazette* of November 15, 1828 . . . with a note signed 'ed.' to the effect that they were 'Never before published,' and 'By Edward C. Pinkney.' There can be little doubt that Dawes obtained the poem from the Pinkney family direct, but there is a chance that he added the title himself, since the classical setting and references to the East in the third stanza suggest that the poem may be connected with *Cleonice*. . . . The verses are among the most powerful that Pinkney ever wrote."

l. 3. Cf. Revelation 8: 10–11, for the star "Wormwood."

l. 5. Small glass vases found in ancient tombs were believed to be for holding the tears of mourners. (Mabbott and Pleadwell, *op. cit.*, 171.)

l. 9. The Egyptians at banquets introduced a reminder of Death, probably really in the form of a mummy case.

l. 11. See Daniel 5, for the handwriting at the feast of Belshazzar.

l. 16. The apples of Sodom were fabled to be fair to view, but to turn to ashes when bitten.

23. Cf. Bryant's "Song of Marion's Men." Bryant appends the note, "The exploits of General Francis Marion, the famous partisan warrior of South Carolina, form an interesting chapter in the annals of the American Revolution. The British troops were so harassed by the irregular and successful warfare which he kept up at the head of a few daring followers, that they sent an officer to remonstrate with him for not coming into the open field and fighting 'like a gentleman and a Christian.'"

24. W. P. Trent (*William Gilmore Simms*, 100) says "The Edge of the Swamp" describes "the uncanny place [on Simms's South Carolina plantation] with some little power." The cayman is a native crocodile.

25. The mythological story of the pleiad which disappeared seems to have affected the imagination of many poets about this time; Byron's line "Like the Lost Pleiad seen no more below" (*Beppo*, xiv) certainly furnished the inspiration for Mrs. Hemans and probably for Simms, Chivers, Henry B. Hirst, and others. The Pleiads were the seven daughters of Atlas and Pléioné. They were transformed into stars, one of which, Electra, is invisible; some said out of shame for having married a mortal, others, from grief for the destruction of Troy. It is said she disappeared a little before the Trojan war. Note also Job 38: 7, "When the morning stars sang together."

"The Lost Pleiad" given here is the earlier version of Simms's poem from *Poems* (1853) rather than the later, longer, and decidedly weaker one given in *Areytos*, as revised and enlarged in 1860. The poem first appeared in *Cortes, Cain, and Other Poems* (1829).

In connection with Simms's use of the word *Areytos*, it is interesting to quote Sir Philip Sidney in "An Apologie for Poetrie" (1595): "Even among the most barbarous and simple Indians where no writing is, yet have they their Poets, who make and sing songs which they call *Areytos*, both of theyr Auncestors deedes, and praises to theyr Gods."

26. Cf. Samuel Minturn Peck's "The Grapevine Swing."

27. Cf. Tennyson's *Ulysses*, "I am a part of all that I have met."

28. "Faith," written in 1827, is the earliest work by Chivers to be preserved; it was included in *Nacoochee*, in 1837.

29. "Georgia Waters" was written in April, 1829, just after Chivers had completed his thesis at Transylvania University on "Intermittent and Remittent Fevers." A revised version was published in *Nacoochee;* I have followed Damon in using a later revision published in the *Georgia Citizen* under date of February 10, 1854.

30. "Song of Adoration to God" appeared in *Nacoochee*.

31. "The Crucifixion" is quoted from *Virginalia*.

32. "Grief," dated New York, May 23, 1841, is from *Virginalia*.

33. "Isadore" published as early as 1841, is considered one of the most probable sources of Poe's "Raven." Damon (*op. cit.*, 211) notes: "Here we have the fundamental idea of 'The Raven,' and something of its atmosphere as well. Moreover, we have the repeated line with the repeated rhyme; and the shortened line always ending on 'Isadore.' Is Poe's 'Lenore' so different? And this *ore* rhyme here (as in 'The Raven') is carried throughout the poem.

"Chivers's priority in these things—idea, meter, refrain, and something of the atmosphere—is unquestionable."

The name Politian, however, was evidently borrowed by Chivers from Poe, and is used here, perchance, in compliment to Poe. The poem was included both in *Eonchs of Ruby* and *Memoralia*.

34. The elegy, "To Allegra Florence" was written to commemorate the death of Chivers's daughter of that name on October 18, 1842. "The Lost Pleiad," the title poem of the book by that name, is "eight hundred and twenty-three lines of agony over Allegra Florence." (Damon, *op. cit.*, 142.)

35. "Mary's Lament for Shelley" (first published as "The Wife's Lament for Her Husband Lost at Sea") seems to have been included in three volumes, *The Lost Pleiad*, *Eonchs of Ruby*, and *Memoralia*. It drew praise from Poe in a letter to its author, June 6, 1842, and was quoted by Poe in his favorable review of *The Lost Pleiad* for *Graham's Magazine*. (Damon, *op. cit.*, 128–30.)

36. "Song to Isa" (frequently called "Song to Isa Singing" to distinguish it from "Sonnet to Isa—Sleeping") was included in *The Lost Pleiad and Other Poems* (1845). Cf. Poe's "Israfel," p. 66, above. A. G. Newcomer ("The Poe-Chivers Tradition Re-examined," *Sewanee Review*, January, 1904) uses this poem in showing the influence of Chivers on Swinburne.

37. "The Chaplet of Cypress" was published in *Eonchs of Ruby* and in *Memoralia*.

38. "Apollo" (*Virginalia*), according to Bayard Taylor, contains "one of the finest images in modern poetry" in lines 12 and 15. (Damon, *op. cit.*, 230.)

39. "The Voice of Thought" appeared in *Eonchs of Ruby*.

40. Chivers wrote two poems entitled "Rosalie Lee" and two called "Lily Adair" repeating in each almost the same refrain. The version used here appeared both in *Virginalia* and *Memoralia*. A. G. Newcomer (*op. cit.*) suggests that it is a continuation of the earlier poem published in *Eonchs of Ruby*. Chivers's explanation of the title of the latter book is given in the *Georgia Citizen* (June 28, 1851): "The word *Eonch* is the same as *Concha Marina*—*Shell of the Sea*. *Eonch* is used instead of Concha, merely for its euphony. It is the same as the *Kaur Gaur* of the Hebrews. Ruby signifies, in the language of Correspondence, *Divine Love*. The word *Eonch* is used, as a title, by metonymy, for *Songs*. The meaning of the title is, therefore, apparent—namely, *Songs of Divine Love*. The clouds, I hope, are now dispelled; and the mystery, I presume, evaporates. I hope the day will continue clear." (Quoted from Damon, *op. cit.*, 181.)

41. We have followed the Stedman and Woodberry edition of Poe in choice of texts. The first three poems in this selection, though published earlier, were not included by Poe in _The Raven and Other Poems_ (1845); the last three were written after that volume appeared.

"To Science (A Prologue to 'Al Aaraaf')" appeared in _Al Aaraaf, Tamerlane and Minor Poems_ (1829) and in _Poems_ (1831). "Al Aaraaf. A star was discovered by Tycho Brahe which appeared suddenly in the heavens—attained, in a few days, a brilliancy surpassing that of Jupiter—then as suddenly disappeared, and has never been seen since." [_Poe's note_ (1845).]

42. "Romance" is almost identical with the first and fifth stanzas of "Introduction" as given in the 1829 and 1831 volumes.

43. "To Helen," was probably inspired by Mrs. Jane Stanard, the mother of one of Poe's friends at the academy in Richmond. This lady became the recipient of his boyish confidences and her early death affected him greatly. Lines 9 and 10 in the 1831 version read:

> To the beauty of fair Greece
> And the grandeur of old Rome.

Nicæan probably refers to the city built by Alexander the Great on the Hydaspes River in India. Here he constructed a fleet to convey a portion of his army home to Greece, by way of the Red Sea, the "perfumed sea" of tradition.

44. Poe used "The City in the Sea," with slight rewording, as "The Doomed City" in _Poems_ (1831); as "The City of Sin," in the _Southern Literary Messenger_, August, 1836, and as "The City in the Sea," in the _American Whig Review_, April, 1845, and in _The Raven_ (1845). Killis Campbell (_The Mind of Poe_, 154) compares the mood and style to Coleridge's "Kubla Khan."

45. An earlier version of "Israfel" was included in _Poems_ (1831). After appearing in the _Southern Literary Messenger_ in August, 1836, and in _Graham's Magazine_ in October, 1841, it was revised before being placed in _The Raven_. The earlier version has the quotation from the "Preliminary Discourse" in Sale's translation of the Koran but Poe later interpolated the words "whose heartstrings are a lute." The motto was probably taken from _Lalla Rookh_, by Tom Moore. Cf. Chivers's "Song to Isa." Campbell (_op. cit._, 155) speaks of the "Shelleyan ideality of the poem."

46. "To One in Paradise" was first printed in _Godey's Lady's Book_, Jan., 1834, and reprinted in the _Southern Literary Messenger_, July, 1835; the title of the story in which it appeared was "The Visionary." It was changed slightly before appearing in _The Raven_.

47. "The Coliseum" was printed in the _Southern Literary Messenger_ in August, 1835.

48. "The Haunted Palace" appeared in the Baltimore *Museum* in April, 1839. Griswold included it in his 1846 edition.

49. "The Conqueror Worm," which was first published in *Graham's Magazine* in 1843, shows elements of similarity to Chivers's "The Death of Time," printed in *Nacoochee* in 1837.

50. "The Raven" was first published in the New York *Mirror*, January 29, 1845, and made Poe "the literary hero of the hour." R. Brimley Johnson in the Oxford edition of Poe's poems gives three more or less authenticated traditions of the date and manner of composition, the earliest placing the poem in 1842 or 1843; the weight of evidence, however, suggests that the poem was printed soon after its composition. Damon (*Thomas Holley Chivers*, 210–4) asserts that Chivers's "To Allegra Florence in Heaven" and also "Isadore" were sources for this poem, but he clears Poe of the charge of positive plagiarism. Campbell (*op. cit.*, 154) traces the melody and internal rhymes to Coleridge's "Ancient Mariner" and points out the unmistakable similarity to Mrs. Browning's "Lady Geraldine's Courtship"; Poe not only praised this poem highly in a review of *The Drama of Exile and Other Poems* in the *Broadway Journal*, January, 1845, but dedicated *The Raven and Other Poems* to Elizabeth Barrett Browning. It should be noted also that Dickens in *Barnaby Rudge*, which was reviewed by Poe for *Graham's Magazine* in February, 1842, makes much use of a raven. Poe's essay "The Philosophy of Composition" deals almost entirely with the method of writing "The Raven."

51. "Lenore" was probably inspired by the death of his friend, Mrs. Stanard (see "To Helen").

52. "Ulalume" appeared with slight variations and an additional (tenth) verse in the *American Whig Review*, December, 1847. Quinn, Baugh, and Howe (*The Literature of America*, I) give an excellent explanatory note: "Probably written after Virginia's death in 1847. It represents the struggle between the physical and spiritual passion, the Phoenician form for the Babylonian goddess of fertility, Ishtar. She is associated with the planet Venus in Babylonian astrology and later with the moon goddess Selene, which causes some confusion in 'Ulalume,' where there is a contrast between the star Astarte and Diana, the moon goddess. Curiously enough, both Venus and the Moon would be crescent in the early morning during the month of October and would be in conjunction with the constellation of Leo ('the Lion'). The poem may be an explanation of Poe's various sentimental affairs from which he was recalled by the memory of Virginia, his 'lost Ulalume'."

"Nacoochee," by Chivers, and "Endymion," by Henry Beck Hirst, have elements of similarity with "Ulalume." See also F. L. Pattee's "Ulalume" (in *Sidelights on American Literature*), an elaborate interpretation of the poem as subjective.

53. "Annabel Lee," which perhaps refers to the author's wife, was printed in the New York *Tribune*, October 9, 1849, two days after Poe's death; it was reprinted in the *Southern Literary Messenger* for November, 1849.

54. "Florence Vane" was accepted by Poe, as editor, for publication in *Burton's Gentleman's Magazine*.

55. "Life in the Autumn Woods" was printed in the *Southern Literary Messenger*, December, 1843.

56. These stanzas were quoted in a review of *Froissart Ballads* in the *Southern Literary Messenger*, July, 1847.

57. G. W. Ranck, *The Bivouac of the Dead and Its Author*: "It was written in August, 1847, for the dedication of the chaste and beautiful military monument erected in the State Cemetery at Frankfort, to the memory of the gallant Kentuckians who fell in the Mexican War." The poem was read by the author at that dedication.

58. These lines, dated June 21, 1843, were written in memory of the author's illustrious cousin, Hugh Swinton Legaré, who had died the previous day.

59. "Flowers in Ashes" was published in the August, 1847, issue of the *Southern Literary Messenger;* J. M. Legaré was a frequent contributor that year.

60. Timrod's sonnets show the influence of Wordsworth, who was a favorite author of the American poet. G. A. Wauchope (*Henry Timrod*, 20) writes: "Timrod has interpreted with insight, delicacy, and enthusiasm the haunting grace and incarnate loveliness of the world of nature."

61. "Ethnogenesis," written in February, 1861, during the meeting of the First Confederate Congress at Montgomery, Alabama, expresses the hope and confidence of Southerners at the opening of the war.

62. Wauchope, *op. cit.*, 27: "Next to Lowell's Commemoration Ode . . . 'The Cotton Boll' is the noblest ode in American literature." Cf. Lanier's "Corn."

63. Henry Austin has compared "A Cry to Arms" to a drum beat; "Carolina" to a cannon roll.

64. "Carolina" was adopted by the General Assembly of South Carolina, on February 11, 1911, as the state song; it was set to music by Miss Annie Curtiss Burgess. Wauchope (*op. cit.*, 28) calls it "the most fervid war-lyric in our whole literature" and says, "It should never be read except aloud, and it can hardly be sung except standing." Paul Hamilton Hayne said the "lines are destined perhaps to outlive the political vitality of the state, whose antique fame they celebrate."

65. "Charleston" was written before the attack by sea and land early in April, 1863.

66. "Christmas" "passed the borders of conflict and was re-echoed throughout the North." The noble invocation to Peace in the final stanzas has "often stirred and hushed at once the heart of the South." (Quoted by Thompson, *op. cit.*, 114.)

In the second stanza there is a reference to the tower of St. Michael's Church of Charleston; the historic bells of this church were in Columbia for safekeeping during the war.

67. The "Ode," written in 1867 shortly before the poet's death, is "the most perfect thing of its kind in conception, tone, and technique in our national literature" (Wauchope, *op. cit.*, 29). It was sung on the occasion of decorating the graves of the Confederate dead, at Magnolia Cemetery, Charleston, S. C., 1867. Cf. William Collins's "How Sleep the Brave."

68. "My Study" was written before the poet's home and valuable library were destroyed by fire during the bombardment of Charleston.

69. Robert S. Henry (*Story of the Confederacy*, 252–65) gives a brief and vivid account of the siege of Vicksburg. The traditions of the bravery and gallantry of the citizens and soldiers of Vicksburg are numerous.

70. Daniel Decatur Emmett (1815–1904), the son of Abraham Emmett of Staunton, Virginia, and of Sarah Zerick Emmett of Fredericktown, Maryland, was born in Mount Vernon, Ohio. His education was very scanty and was mostly obtained during his apprenticeship to a printer (1828–1832). When he was seventeen, he joined the army as a fifer, but was discharged three years later "on account of minority." He sang and played various musical instruments and from 1842 to 1888 he was connected with minstrel troupes, writing "gags" and songs (mostly "walk-rounds") and planning much of the business as well as performing. He was the author of numerous songs, many of which became popular but most were never collected and are now forgotten; his earliest success was with "Old Dan Tucker," written in 1830 or 1831. "Dixie" was written one rainy Sunday in New York (September, 1859) in answer to a demand for a new walk-round for Monday's show of Bryant's Minstrels. It was sung in New Orleans during the winter of 1860–61 and was immediately adopted by the South as its own. The phrase "I wish I was in Dixie" was a common one referring to the South but the stories of its origin are all speculative.

The original words of the song were hastily written and were later modified; new stanzas were added by Mr. Emmett and probably by others also. The version here printed is that of the autograph copy of "Dixie's Land" in the Ohio State Archaeological and Historical Society. A first stanza which was discarded on suggestion of the Bryants that it might give offense read:

> Dis worl was made in jiss six days,
> An finished up in various ways;
>   Look away! Look away! Look away! Dixie Land!
> Dey den made Dixie trim an nice,
> But Adam call'd it "Paradise."
>   Look away! Look away! Look away! Dixie Land!

The *Confederate Veteran* (III, 266–9, September, 1895) has an account of a visit to Mr. Emmett by S. A. Cunningham, editor of the magazine; there is also a facsimile letter from Mr. Emmett to Mr. Cunningham, dated July 31, 1895, which contains these words: "In compliment to you and the messages of good will you bring, I hand you to engrave for the *Confederate Veteran* the original copy of Dixie, made on that rainy Sunday in New York City in 1859." The words of this autographed manuscript copy read:

> I wish I was in de land ob cotton,
> 'Cimmon seed an' sandy bottom,
>   Look a-way, look way a-way! Dixie Land!
> In Dixie Land whar I was born in,
> Early on one frosty mornin',
>   Look a-way, look way a-way, Dixie Land!

Chorus:

> Den I wish I was in Dixie! Hooray! Hooray!
> In Dixie's Land we'll take our stand, to lib an' die in Dixie.
> Away! away! away down South in Dixie.
> Away! away! away down South in Dixie.

> Ole missus marry Will de Weaber;
> William was a gay deceaber;
>   Look a-way, look way a-way, Dixie Land!
> When he put his arm around 'er,
> He look as fierce as a forty-pounder;
>   Look a-way, look way a-way, Dixie Land!

> His face was sharp like a butcher's cleaber;
> But dat did not seem to greab 'er;
>   Look a-way, look way a-way, Dixie Land!
> Will run away Missus took a decline, O'
> Her face was de color ob bacon rhine, O'
>   Look a-way, look way a-way, Dixie Land!

> While Missus libbed, she libbed in clover,
> When she died, she died all ober,
>   Look a-way, look way a-way, Dixie Land!
> How could she act such a foolish part, O'
> And marry a man to break her heart, O'
>   Look a-way, look way a-way, Dixie Land!

Buckwheat cakes and stony batter,
Makes you fat or a little fatter;
   Look a-way, look way a-way, Dixie Land!
Here's health to de next ole missus,
An' all the gals dat want to kiss us;
   Look a-way, look way a-way, Dixie Land!

Now if you want to drive 'way sorrow,
Come an' hear dis song tomorrow;
   Look a-way, look way-way, Dixie Land!
Den hoe it down an' scratch yo grabble,
To Dixie's land I'm bound to trabble;
   Look a-way, look way a-way, Dixie Land.

Percy M. Boynton in "Patriotic Songs and Hymns" (*Cambridge History of American Literature*, III, 496) makes the distinction: "They stand in deference to the tradition of 'The Star-Spangled Banner' but they rise to 'Dixie' itself."

71. Of the numerous attempts to write a literary "Dixie," the one of Albert Pike is the most successful and best known. It appeared first in the Natchez *Courier*, April 30, 1861.

Albert Pike (1809–1891), whose paternal ancestor came from England in 1635, was born in Boston and educated in Massachusetts schools. In 1831, in search of adventure, he went as far west as New Mexico, but he soon returned to settle in Arkansas. He became publisher of the Little Rock *Gazette* and studied law, and during his active life combined the professions of journalism and law in Little Rock, New Orleans (1853–57), Memphis (1867–68), and Washington (1868–91). From 1850 on he was active in Freemasonry, rewriting the rituals, and rendering services recognized both at home and abroad. Though opposed to slavery and to secession, he accepted a commission in the Confederate Army rather than desert friends and property. As his command of the Indian Territory was unsatisfactory to his superiors, however, he saw but little service; his loyalty was suspected by both South and North and his property was confiscated in 1865. His books of poems (*Nugae*, 1854; *Hymns to the Gods and Other Poems*, 1872, enlarged in 1873 and in 1882), with additional uncollected items, have been edited by his daughter in three volumes: *General Albert Pike's Poems* (1900), *Hymns to the Gods and Other Poems* (1916), and *Lyrics and Love Songs* (1916).

72. James Ryder Randall (1839–1908) was born in Baltimore of English and Irish stock which reached America in the seventeenth century; his mother was a descendant of Acadian exiles who settled in Baltimore in 1755. Randall was prepared by private tutors and entered Georgetown College at ten; illness prevented his graduation and after voyages to Brazil and the West Indies and short periods of employment in Baltimore, Florida and New Orleans, he began teaching in Louisiana in 1860. His

health prevented active service in the war. After 1865 he was associated with the Augusta *Constitutionalist* and other newspapers. *The Poems of James Ryder Randall*, edited in 1910 by M. P. Andrews, include "The Unconquered Banner," one of the many replies to Father Ryan's "The Conquered Banner."

F. F. Browne (*Bugle Echoes*, 23) gives the following note on "Maryland, My Maryland": "This poem is probably the most famous, as it is the most stirring in its martial tone, of all that the war evoked. Its form is doubtless suggested by Mangan's 'Karamanian Exile':

> I see thee ever in my dreams,
>   Karaman!
> Thy hundred hills, thy thousand streams,
>   Karaman, O Karaman!
> As when thy gold-bright morning gleams,
> As when the deepening sunset seams
> With lines of light thy hills and streams,
>   Karaman!
> So now thou loomest on my dreams,
>   Karaman, O Karaman!

... From his editorial desk in Augusta, Ga., he [Randall] has sent a corrected version of 'My Maryland,' with these interesting particulars of its history: 'In 1860–61 he who pens these lines was, though very young, a professor at Poydras College, upon the Fausse Rivière of Louisiana. There, a stripling, just from college in Maryland, full of poetry and romance, he dreamed dreams, and was only awakened by the guns of Sumter. At an old wooden desk, in a second story room of Poydras College, one sleepless April night in 1861, the poem of 'My Maryland' was written. ... And now the desk is ashes, and the building too.'" The poem first appeared in the New Orleans *Delta*, Sunday, April 26, 1861, and was immediately reprinted over the South. The words were adapted to an old German song by the Misses Jennie and Hetty Cary of Baltimore.

73. "The Bonnie Blue Flag" was first sung at the secession convention in Jackson, Mississippi, January 7, 1861, at which time the first flag of the Confederacy was displayed. The words, with music, were published in the *Confederate Veteran*, May, 1895. The issue of the magazine for July contained a letter from William Fort Smith of Texas, describing the stirring scenes when a large body of troops on their way to the front first heard the song in New Orleans on September 18, 1861. Dr. A. J. Thomas wrote from Indiana (*Confederate Veteran*, October, 1895), "In September, 1861, I was marching through Missouri, Northern Arkansas and the Indian Territory, to the inspiring notes of the 'Bonnie Blue Flag.' It was sung every night at every campfire of the Army of Ben McCulloch and 'Old Pap' Price."

Little is known of the author, Harry McCarthy, except that he was an

Arkansan and that both he and his wife were members of a traveling troupe of entertainers. He died in his native state in 1874. Unsubstantiated claims were made by his friends that he was the author of "Dixie" also; his troupe sang the song frequently. No other writing of McCarthy's is known.

74. Innes Randolph (1837–1887) was born in Winchester, Virginia, and from early youth showed ability in both music and art. After service in the Confederate Army, however, he practiced law in Baltimore and contributed occasional poems and sketches to local newspapers. For some years before his death he devoted his time to editorial writing for the Baltimore *American*. His poems were collected and published by his son in 1898.

75. Francis Orray Ticknor (1822–1874) was born in Fortville, Georgia, a few months before the death of his father, Dr. Orray Ticknor, a native of Connecticut. His brilliant and capable mother (née Harriot Coolidge) sent her son to college in Massachusetts, to New York and Philadelphia for medical training, and for semi-internship with a physician in her ancestral home, Norwich, Connecticut. In 1842 young Dr. Ticknor became a country practitioner in Georgia. Lonely for intellectual companionship and for music, he devoted his spare moments to "verse-making" or to playing the flute. His marriage to Rosalie Nelson of Virginia was felicitous. During the war he was in charge of hospitals in and about Columbus and gave of his skill and energy without stint. His friend, Paul Hamilton Hayne, wrote an appreciative sketch of him for the first collection of his poetry (*Poems*, 1879).

"The Virginians" was inspired by William Norbonne Nelson, the author's dearest friend and later brother-in-law.

76. "Little Giffen" was first printed in *The Land We Love* in November, 1867; the last verse was entirely rewritten and a few other slight changes were made before it appeared in *Poems*. Miss Ticknor, in *Poems of Francis Orray Ticknor*, gives a review of its changes. Isaac Newton Giffen, son of a blacksmith in the Tennessee Mountains, was found by Mrs. Ticknor in an improvised hospital in Columbus and, at her request, was brought to their home by Dr. Ticknor. The boy remained with them from September, 1863, to March, 1864.

77. Henry Lyndon Flash (1835– ?), of English descent, was born in Cincinnati, but was reared in New Orleans. He graduated from the Western Military Institute of Kentucky in 1852, and, after some time spent in travel, went into business in Galveston, Texas. During the war he served as an aide on the staffs of General William J. Hardee and General Joseph Wheeler. At its close he was acting as editor of the Macon, Georgia, *Confederate*. Soon afterward he removed to New Orleans and was in business there until his retirement in 1887; during the remainder of his life he lived in Los Angeles. A small volume of lyrics was published in New York in

1860 but his later verse appeared primarily in newspapers, frequently under a pen name. He wrote rapidly and rarely changed a phrase of his original draft. His collected *Poems* appeared in 1906.

Brig.-Gen. Felix Kirk Zollicoffer, C. S. A., was killed while reconnoitring during the battle of Fishing Creek, Kentucky, January 19, 1862. A powerful Whig leader in Tennessee, he had opposed secession and worked ardently for peace. Though he had rejected the major-generalship of the Tennessee forces because of lack of military experience, his loss was a severe blow to the Confederacy.

78. John Reuben Thompson (1823–1873) of Richmond, Virginia, received his A.B. degree and his legal training at the University of Virginia. His interests were mainly literary, however, and as part-time proprietor and editor of the *Southern Literary Messenger* from 1847 until his retirement in poor health in 1859, he did able editorial work and gave much encouragement and assistance to Southern writers. Trips to Europe proved beneficial to him and from 1863 until after the close of the war, he lived in London, contributing to various magazines. Returning to the South, ill and dispirited, he soon accepted a position as literary editor of the New York *Evening Post*, with which he was connected until his death.

F. F. Browne (*Bugle Echoes*, 216) gives the following note on "Lee to the Rear": "Founded on an incident in one of the battles of the Wilderness, when General Lee seized the colors of a Texas regiment to lead a charge against a well-nigh impregnable position. The colonel promised to carry the position if Lee would go to the rear; and when the soldiers heard the promise and expostulation, they repeated it, and 'Lee to the rear!' was shouted down the line."

79. John Williamson Palmer (1825–1906) was the son of Edward and Catherine Croxall Palmer of Baltimore; after education in Maryland schools, he completed his medical training at the University of Maryland in 1846. The gold rush of 1849 took him to California; for several years he cruised, usually as ship's surgeon, around the Orient. Returning to America, he devoted his time to writing, mainly travel sketches; *Folk Songs* (verse) appeared in 1856. During the war he served as aide to Gen. J. C. Breckinridge and was correspondent for the New York *Tribune*. After active medical service in the cholera epidemic of 1866, he again turned to writing, contributing essays and reviews to periodicals, and editing various books; his special interests centered in the social life of Maryland and the old South, and in engravings and etchings.

Palmer's most famous poem, "Stonewall Jackson's Way," appeared in *In Vinculis, or The Prisoner of War* (1866), by Anthony M. Keiley, and by some collectors was accredited to Mr. Keiley. W. G. Simms included the poem in *War Poems of the South* (1867), noting: "These verses, according to the newspaper account *may* have been found in the bosom of a dead rebel, after one of Jackson's battles in the Shenandoah Valley; but we are pleased to state that the *author* of them is a still living rebel and able to write even better things." *Bugle Echoes* (1886) states that "they were unquestionably written by Dr. J. W. Palmer of Maryland."

The dramatic death of General Thomas Jonathan Jackson, "more than any other [event] pierced the heart of the South and called forth scores of poems from all sections. . . . No other poem gives anything like so adequate an expression of Jackson—his personal appearance, his religious faith, his impressive commands, his almost magical control of his men—as *Stonewall Jackson's Way*." (Mims, "Poets of the Civil War, II," *Cambridge History of American Literature*, II, 307.) The nickname "Stonewall" was given the General at the Battle of Bull Run in July, 1861, when Brig.-Gen. Barnard E. Bee commented, as his own troops retreated, "There is Jackson standing like a stone wall." In vain Jackson protested that the name belonged to his men, rather than to himself.

80. Margaret Junkin Preston (1820–1897) was the daughter of Rev. George and Julia Rush Miller Junkin and was born in Milton, Pennsylvania, while her father was pastor of the Associated Reformed (Presbyterian) Church there. Rev. Junkin served as president of Lafayette College (Pennsylvania) and of Miami University (Ohio) before becoming president of Washington College (now Washington and Lee) at Lexington, Virginia, in 1848. Margaret, an ardent student and the author of *Silverwood* (1856), married Major John T. L. Preston, a professor at Virginia Military Institute, in 1857. Her father went North in 1861 but Mrs. Preston chose to remain in the South. Her husband, after distinguished service in the Army of the Confederacy, returned to his teaching position at V. M. I.; their home was in Lexington until his death in 1890. Mrs. Preston lived with her son in Baltimore during the remainder of her life.

"The Shade of the Trees" is founded upon the words of General Jackson in delirium just before his death: "Order A. P. Hill to prepare for action; . . . pass the infantry to the front; . . . tell Major Hawks . . ."; his voice failed, but in a few minutes, he murmured quietly, as if in relief: "Let us cross the river and rest under the shade of the trees." These were his last words.

General Jackson's first wife, Eleanor Junkin, the sister of Mrs. Preston, died in 1854.

81. John Esten Cooke (1830–1886), the younger brother of Philip Pendleton Cooke, was born and educated in Richmond. He was admitted to the bar in 1851, but neglected his practice for writing: fugitive poems, essays, stories, and seven volumes of fiction were published before 1860 and gave him a nationwide reputation. An ardent secessionist and a friend and admirer of Stuart, Cooke served throughout the war and was Lee's Inspector-General of Field Artillery when the South surrendered. After his marriage to Mary Frances Page in 1867, he retired to an estate near his ancestral home and devoted himself to writing. *The Virginia Comedians*

(1854), *My Lady Pocahontas* (1885), *Stories of the Old Dominion* (1879), and the history, *Virginia* (1883), are his best known books; his poetry has not been collected. John O. Beaty, his biographer (*John Esten Cooke, Virginian*, 1922), calls him "a chivalric Cavalier who idealized the past and was unreservedly devoted to Virginia. His books are what he wished them to be—interesting and pure."

His exquisite and haunting lyric, "The Band in the Pines," was written as a memorial to Major John Pelham, C. S. A., killed at Kelly's Ford, Virginia, in March, 1863. Cf. J. R. Randall's "John Pelham," also called "The Dead Cannoneer."

82. John Dickson Bruns (1836–1883) was born in Charleston and was prepared for college by his father, a man of fine scholarship. After graduating with first honors from the University of Charleston in 1854, he attended medical lectures in Philadelphia but received his M.D. degree from the Medical College of Charleston, again winning high honors. He was editor of the Charleston *Medical Journal* until 1861; during the war he served as surgeon of a general hospital; and from 1866 until his death he was professor of physiology and pathology in the New Orleans School of Medicine. The occasional prose and verse which Dr. Bruns contributed to periodicals and newspapers evinced literary facility and a wide range of interests; his favorite authors were Shakespeare, Wordsworth, Tennyson, and Timrod. Although he was the author of a considerable body of poetry, mainly lyric, no collection of his work has been made. "The Foe at the Gates" is dated Charleston, 1865.

83. Joseph Blyth Allston (1833–1904), the son of Gen. Joseph Allston, was born at "Waverley," his father's plantation near Georgetown, South Carolina; after his parents' early death, he was reared by his uncle, Gov. R. F. W. Allston. After his graduation from South Carolina College in 1851, he read law under Judge James L. Petigru and was admitted to the bar in 1854. He then spent several years in travel and study in Europe but was practicing law in Charleston when the war broke out. He volunteered immediately and served throughout the war, attaining the rank of captain. From 1865 until his retirement a few years before his death, he practiced law in Georgetown and in Baltimore. His numerous poems, contributed to newspapers and magazines, have not been collected.

"Stack Arms" was written shortly after the close of the war while Mr. Allston was still a prisoner in Fort Delaware, Delaware.

84. William Gordon McCabe (1841–1920), the son of Rev. John Collins McCabe, an Episcopalian minister and a poet, was born in Richmond. He graduated from Hampton Academy with highest honors at seventeen, and was a tutor for some months before entering the University of Virginia in 1860. Immediately after the secession of Virginia, he joined a student company at Harper's Ferry and served with distinction, first under Gen. Albert Sidney Johnston and later under Division Commander John

Pegram. In October, 1865, he opened the famous University School (which he moved to Richmond thirty years later) in Petersburg, Virginia. His fame as an inspiring teacher and brilliant Latinist and as a gifted administrator is second to none. His poetry, written almost entirely during the war and published for the most part in the *Southern Literary Messenger*, has never been collected. His prose, essays on literary, historical and military topics, appeared in foremost English and American magazines; he was a frequent contributor to the publications of the Virginia Historical Society and the Southern Historical Society, both of which organizations he served as an officer.

85. Daniel Bedinger Lucas (1836–1909), the son of William and Virginia Lucas, was born at Rion Hall, near Charles Town, Virginia (now West Virginia), and was named for his maternal grandfather, a man of position and some poetic talent. An injury to his spine during infancy kept him physically inactive but gave him an unusual opportunity for reading in his father's valuable library and for study under private tutors. At the University of Virginia he excelled in oratory. After his graduation in 1854, he studied law at Lexington and completed the course with honors in 1859. He volunteered immediately for service in the Civil War but was soon released on account of physical disability. For some years he was disbarred from law practice by the "test oath," but in 1889, he became a member of the State Supreme Court of Appeals. From 1893 until his death, he lived quietly, writing intermittently on a life of Lincoln. His verse was collected by his daughter, Virginia, in 1913.

"The Land Where We Were Dreaming" was written soon after Lee's surrender while the author was in Canada on a mission to aid a friend held on a charge of treason. It was first published in the Montreal *Gazette.*

86. "The Conquered Banner" was first printed under the pen name "Moina." W. G. Simms in his *War Poetry of the South* attributed it to Mrs. Anna Peyre Dinnies of New Orleans, who had published poems under that *nom de plume;* other collectors have given it as anonymous. The authorship of Father Ryan has been established, however. F. F. Browne (*Bugle Echoes*, 278) quotes from a letter written to him by Ryan: "I wrote 'The Conquered Banner' at Knoxville, Tennessee, one evening soon after Lee's surrender, when my mind was engrossed with thoughts of our dead soldiers and dead cause. It was first published in the New York *Freeman's Journal*. I never had any idea that the poem, written in less than an hour, would attain celebrity. No doubt the circumstances of its appearance lent it much of its fame. In expressing my own emotions at the time, I echoed the unuttered feelings of the Southern people; and so 'The Conquered Banner' became the requiem of the Lost Cause."

87. "The Jacquerie," inspired by the chronicles of Froissart, was begun while Lanier was in college and was partially completed in 1868; it was a subject of interest to the poet ever after though he never found time to

complete it. In a letter to Judge Logan E. Bleckley of Georgia, November 15, 1874, Lanier explained his purpose to write "a long poem, founded on that strange uprising in the middle of the fourteenth century in France, called 'The Jacquerie.' It was the first time that the big hungers of *the People* appear in our modern civilization; and it is full of significance. The peasants learned from the merchant potentates of Flanders that a man who could not be a lord by birth, might be one by wealth; and so Trade arose, and overthrew Chivalry. Trade has now had possession of the civilized world for four hundred years: it controls all things, it interprets the Bible, it guides our national and almost all our individual life with its maxims; and its oppressions upon the moral existence of man have come to be ten thousand times more grievous than the worst tyrannies of the Feudal System ever were. Thus in the reversals of time, it is *now the gentleman* who must rise and overthrow Trade." (Quoted by Mims, *Sidney Lanier*, 158.)

88. The writing of "The Symphony" was described by Lanier in a letter to Peacock, March 24, 1875 (*Letters of Sidney Lanier*, 12): "About four days ago, a certain poem which I had vaguely ruminated for a week before took hold of me like a real James River ague, and I have been in a mortal shake with the same, day and night, ever since. I call it 'The Symphony.' I personify each instrument in the orchestra, and make them discuss various deep social questions of the times, in the progress of the music." The poem was published in *Lippincott's Magazine* in June, 1875, and was received by critics most favorably. The theme is much like that planned for "The Jacquerie."

89. F. V. N. Painter in *Poets of the South* (1903) gives an earlier and less artistic version of "Song of the Chattahoochee"; he notes that it appeared in *Scott's Magazine* (Atlanta, 1865–1869). I have not been able to locate this version, and Mrs. Lanier dated the poem 1877. The poem in its present form was published after the author's death in the *Independent*, December 20, 1883. Lanier grouped this poem with "The Waving of the Corn" and "Clover" in planning a volume of his poetry, since the three poems teach the same lesson "of art, not for art's sake but for the sake of love." (Starke, *op. cit.*, 263.) Cf. Tennyson's "The Brook."

90. "The Stirrup-Cup" was written in Tampa, Florida, in 1877, and printed in *Scribner's Magazine* in May of the same year.

91. Starke (*op. cit.* 310) says that this poem was based on an incident in William Black's *Macleod of Dare*, a contemporary magazine novel; it was Lanier's first experiment in writing in logaoedic (or English as opposed to classical) dactyls. Dated Baltimore, 1878, it was first published in *Appleton's Journal*, 1878.

92. Only three "Hymns of the Marshes" ("Sunrise," "Individuality," and "The Marshes of Glynn") of a projected volume of six hymns were completed before the poet's death. "Marsh-Song—At Sunset" was

included in the sequence in *Poems*, edited by Mrs. Lanier. *Poem Outlines by Sidney Lanier* (Scribner, 1908), 3, gives the following description for "Hymns of the Marshes": "The courses of the wind, and the shifts thereof, as also what way the clouds go; and that which is happening a long way off; and the full face of the sun; and the bow of the Milky Way from end to end; as also the small, the life of the fiddler-crab, and the household of the marsh-hen; and more, the translation of black ooze into green blade of marsh-grass, which is as if filth bred heaven:

'This a man seeth upon the marsh.' "

93. "Sunrise" (written in Baltimore, December, 1880, and printed in the *Independent*, December 14, 1882) was the last poem written by Lanier; at the time he had a fever of 104 degrees and was unable to feed himself (*Poems*, xxix). Cf. Wordsworth's "Evening of Extraordinary Splendour and Beauty."

94. Mims (*op. cit.*, 316–7) quotes from a letter of Lanier to J. F. Kirk, June 15, 1880: "I have been studying science, biology, chemistry, evolution, and all. It pieces on, perfectly, to those dreams which one has when one is a boy and wanders alone by a strong running river, on a day when the wind is high but the sky clear. These enormous modern generalizations fill me with such dreams again.

"But it is precisely at the beginning of that phenomenon which is the underlying subject of this poem, 'Individuality,' that the largest of such generalizations must begin, and the doctrine of evolution when pushed beyond this point appears to me, after the most careful examination of the evidence, to fail. It is pushed beyond this point in its current application to the genesis of species, and I think Mr. Huxley's last sweeping declaration is clearly parallel to that of an enthusiastic dissecter who, forgetting that his observations are upon dead bodies, should build a physiological conclusion upon purely anatomical facts.

"For whatever can be proved to have been evolved, evolution seems to me a noble and beautiful and true theory. But a careful search has not shown me a single instance in which such proof as would stand the first shot of a boy lawyer in a moot court, has been brought forward in support of an actual case of species differentiation.

"A cloud (see the poem) *may* be evolved; but not an artist; and I find, in looking over my poem, that it has made itself into a passionate reaffirmation of the artist's autonomy, threatened alike from the direction of the scientific fanatic and the pantheistic devotee."

The poem was written in Baltimore in 1878–79 but was not published until it appeared in the *Century Magazine* in December, 1882. See P. E. Graham, "Lanier and Science," in *American Literature*, IV, 288–92 (Nov. 1932).

95. "Marsh Song—At Sunset" was written in Baltimore in 1878–79 and appeared in *Our Continent*, February, 1882.

96. "The Marshes of Glynn" was written in Baltimore in 1878 for the *Masque of Poets* (1878), a volume of one hundred seventy-five poems, all published anonymously but many by well-known authors. It describes the sea marshes of Glynn County, Georgia, immediately around the sea-coast city of Brunswick, which Lanier had visited in 1875 (*Poems*, 253).

97. "A Ballad of Trees and the Master" was first planned as an interlude in "Sunrise" and in the author's first copy of the "Hymns" it was incorporated following the invocation to the trees (*Poems*, 255) which ended with the lines

> "And there, oh there
> As ye hang with your myriad palms upturned in the air,
> Pray me a myriad prayer."

It was written as it now stands in fifteen or twenty minutes and handed to Mrs. Lanier to take on a visit to a sick friend. The lines were printed in the *Independent*, December 23, 1880.

98. "Aubade" has been set to music by Emma Hanson Bartmess.

99. James Barron Hope (1829–1887) was the son of Wilton and Jane A. Barron Hope of Norfolk, Virginia. After graduating from the College of William and Mary, he served as secretary to his uncle, Commodore Samuel Barron, for a year while he read law. After several years of practicing law in Hampton, Virginia, he was elected commonwealth's attorney in 1856. From 1861 to 1865 he served in the Army of the Confederacy, surrendering as major with Gen. Joseph E. Johnston at Greensboro. He was engaged in newspaper work in Norfolk from then until his death.

Hope's early poems (*Leoni di Monota and Other Poems*, 1857) show much influence of Tennyson and Keats. Of his later writings the metrical address, "Arms and the Man," written by invitation of Congress for the Centennial Celebration of Cornwallis's surrender, is best known.

100. William Hamilton Hayne, the son of Paul Hamilton and Mary Michel Hayne, was born March 11, 1856, in Charleston, South Carolina. He was educated privately at Copse Hill, Georgia, and lived quietly then and in Augusta, Georgia, most of his life. A book of poems, *Sylvan Lyrics*, was published in 1893.

101. John Moore was born in Marion, Alabama, August 26, 1858; he assumed the name "Trotwood" after that *nom de plume* became famous. He graduated from Howard College, edited the Marion *Commonwealth* for one year and taught school for six years, before moving to Columbia, Tennessee. His poems and stories of that region (to which he referred as "the dimple of the universe"), especially *The Bishop of Cottontown* and *The Ole Mistis*, won him fame. After his appointment as state historian, he wrote a history of Tennessee, and several volumes of fiction—his last novel, *Hearts of Hickory*, which dealt with Andrew Jackson's time, being especially popular. Also, with Governor Bob Taylor, he edited the *Taylor-Trotwood Magazine*. He died in Nashville, May 10, 1929.

102. Walter Malone was born in De Soto County, Mississippi, February 10, 1866, but spent most of his active life in Memphis, Tennessee, practicing law. From 1905 until his death in 1915 he served as judge of the Second Circuit Court of Shelby County. Of his eight volumes of verse, the poems "Opportunity" and "October in Tennessee" are best known.

103. Olive Tilford Dargan (Mrs. Pegram Dargan) was born at Tilford Springs, Kentucky, the daughter of Elisha Francis and Rebecca Day Tilford. She began teaching at the age of thirteen, interrupting her teaching career to attend the University of Nashville and Radcliffe College. Subsequently she lived abroad for several years but she has now decided that she prefers "dirt farming" and is living on an estate near Asheville, North Carolina. Mrs. Dargan has published several volumes of poetry and has been the recipient of various prizes for her work.

104. James Branch Cabell, a descendant of colonial families of Virginia, was born in Richmond, April 14, 1879. His early education was in private schools; before his graduation from the College of William and Mary in 1898 with high honors, he was instructor there in Latin and Greek. After several years in newspaper work he settled down to writing books and stories, building them gradually into a series dealing with Dom Manuel, Count of Poictesme (a perfectly constructed medieval country), and tracing the lineage to his Virginia descendants. Mr. Cabell is interested also in genealogical and historical research and is genealogist for several organizations. While he has published only one volume of poems, his prose is frequently interspersed or illustrated with fragments of verse, usually ascribed to imaginary medieval poets. Cabell's theory of escapism is outlined in his *Beyond Life*. For his practices as a novelist, see H. Hartwick's *The Foreground of American Fiction* (1934), 177–186.

105. Alec Brock Stevenson, the son of James Henry and Evelyn (Sutherland) Stevenson, was born in Toronto, Canada, December 29, 1895. He was educated in Nashville, graduating from Vanderbilt University in 1916. He served in France as sergeant and lieutenant of artillery. He is in business at Nashville. Stevenson's poems have appeared in *Fugitives* (an anthology) and in various magazines. "Icarus in November" was published in *Hound & Horn*.

106. It is interesting to note that Mr. Fletcher's father bought for a residence the house built by General Albert Pike. This house is more fully described by Fletcher in a series of poems, "The Ghosts of an Old House," in *Goblins and Pagodas*, and reprinted in *Preludes and Symphonies*.

107. "Ode to the Confederate Dead" was first written in 1926, and was revised and printed on several occasions, before the author was satisfied with his work. For an earlier version see *Mr. Pope and Other Poems*.

108. Mr. Warren used the same general title for a later series of poems, subtitled "The Owl," "The Cardinal," and "Watershed," which appeared in *Poetry*, May, 1932.

INDEX

Individual titles of poems and critical essays are in small capitals; if the selection is given in this volume, the page on which it begins is shown in black-faced type. Selections from the various authors are also shown under the names of the authors in black-faced type. Titles of books and magazines are italicized. First lines of poems are in their alphabetical order, and in quotation marks. Books listed in the bibliography are not included in the index.

"A dirge for the brave old pioneer!" 91

"A little while (my life is almost set!)," 134

"A white tomb in the desert," 246

ABOU BEN ADHEM, civ

Adams, John Quincy, 18

Addison, Joseph, xxiii, xlii

Aeschylus, l

"After the whistle's roar has bellowed and shuddered," 258

"Ah, broken is the golden bowl! the spirit flown forever!" 77

AHAB-MOHAMMED, civ

Aiken, Conrad, cxxii, 366

"Alas! our pleasant moments fly," 24

Alcaeus, 13, 379

Alcott, Bronson, xcviii

"All the here and all the there," 273

Allan, John, 60–61

Allen, G. W., lxxv, c

Allen, Hervey, lxxvii–lxxviii, cxxiv, 234, **360–364,** 369

Allston, Joseph Blyth, **157,** 394

Allston, Washington, lxxxvii

"Aloof, aloof, and come no near," 3

Anacreon, lxxxiv, 379

"And owe we not these visions," 87

ANNABEL LEE, **81**

Anonymous, **4, 5, 7, 154, 315, 316, 318, 319**

APOLLO, **57**

APRIL WEATHER, **215**

Aristocracy, xviii–xix

Aristotle, 336, 368

Arnold, Matthew, lxviii n., 352

"As if the sun had trodden down the sky," 256

"As the uncertain twittering of the birds," 43
ASPECTS OF THE PINES, 128
AT THE HOUR OF THE BREAKING OF THE ROCKS, 308
AUBADE, 223
AUTUMN LOVE, 275
"Awake! the dawn is on the hills!" 223

Babbitt, Irving, lxxiii n.
"Back to the primal gloom," 205
Bacon, Nathaniel, xx, 377
BACON'S EPITAPH, MADE BY HIS MAN, lxxxiv, 5
BALLAD OF TREES AND THE MASTER, A, cxvii, 201
BAND IN THE PINES, THE, 155
Barclay, Anthony, 13
Bassett, John Spencer, xxviii, 378
Bates, Katherine Lee, 370
BATTLE OF KING'S MOUNTAIN, THE, 7
"Beautiful as the flying legend of some leopard," 271
"Because they thought his doctrines were not just," 125
Beddoes, Thomas L., xcv
BELLES OF WILLIAMSBURG, THE, lxxxvii, 379
BELLS, THE, lxiv, c
Benét, Stephen Vincent, 372
Berkeley, Sir William, xx, xxiii
BEYOND CONNECTICUT, BEYOND THE SEA, 277
"Beyond the wrack and eucharist of snow," 308
Bishop, John Peale, lxxx, cxxviii, 276, 277–280
BIVOUAC OF THE DEAD, THE, cviii, cxi, 89
BLACK ROCK, THE, 263
Blair, Robert, lxi
Blake, William, xcv, 365, 367
BLESSING ON THE DANCE, A, 208
BLUE GIRLS, 273
BOLL WEEVIL SONG, THE, 316
BONNIE BLUE FLAG, THE, cx, 142
Boone, Daniel, cviii–cix, 246
Booth, John Wilkes, xxxviii
Bourne, Randolph, xlix
Bradstreet, Anne, lxxxv
"BRIGADE MUST NOW KNOW, SIR!, THE," 154
Brooks, Van Wyck, xlix
BROWN GIRL OR FAIR ELLENDER, THE, lxxxii n., 4
Brown, John, xxxvi–xxxvii, 304
Browning, Elizabeth Barrett, 385
Bruns, John Dickson, ciii, 156, 394

Bryant, William Cullen, l–li, xcix, 27, 125, 381
BURDENS OF UNREST, MARY'S LAMENT FOR SHELLEY LOST AT SEA, 52
Burns, Robert, cxix, 367
Burton's Gentleman's Magazine, 61, 83
Butler, General Ben F., xxxviii
"By night they haunted a thicket of April mist," 270
Byrd, William, xviii, xix, xxv, lxxxiii, lxxxvi, 6, 378
Byron, Lord George, li n., lxxxix, xc n., xci, xcii, xcvi, 324
"Byron! 'Tis thine alone on eagles' pinions," 15

Cabell, James Branch, cxxiii, 242, 398
Calhoun, John C., xxvii, xxxi, xxxii–xxxiv
"Calm as that second summer which precedes," 117
CAROLINA, cvii, cxi, 112
Carew, Thomas, xci
Carnegie, Andrew, xli
Carr, Peter, xxiii
Catullus, xci, 100
Cawein, Madison, cxx, 222, 222–228
Centennial Cantata, 169
CHAPLET OF CYPRESS, THE. AN ELEGY ON THE DEATH OF MY SISTER, 55
Chapman, George, lxxxiii, 327
CHARLESTON, cvii, cxi, 117
Chastellaux, F. J. de, xlvii
Chaucer, Geoffrey, 367
Chivers, Thomas Holley, xvii n., xviii n., lii–liii, lv–lviii, lxix, xciv–xcvii,
    c–ciii, cxii, 38, 40–60, 62, 321, 322–332, 373, 382–385
CHORUS, 231
CHRISTMAS, 119
CHRISTMAS-NIGHT IN THE QUARTERS, cxix, 206
Cicero, xxiv
CITY IN THE SEA, THE, 64
Civil War, The, xxxvi–xxxviii
Clark, Emily, cxxiii
CLOVER, cxvi–cxvii
Coleridge, Samuel Taylor, lix, xcv, xcvi, xcvii, xcviii, lxiii, lxiv, lxvii n.,
    lxix, 367, 385
COLISEUM, THE, 61, 68
"Come, men, stack arms! Pile on the rails," 151
COMPENSATION, 203
CONFEDERATE DEAD, ODE TO THE, cxxvii, 301
Congreve, William, 368
CONTESSA TO HER JUDGES, THE, 248
CONQUERED BANNER, THE, cxi–cxii, 162
CONQUEROR WORM, THE, 71

Cook, Eben, lxxxvi
Cooke, John Esten, 83, **155**, 393
Cooke, Philip Pendleton, liv–lv, cii, 83, **84–88, 349–351,** 393
Cooper, James Fenimore, lii
CORN, cxvi, 169
COTTON BOLL, THE, cvii, cxi, **106**
Crafts, William, lxxxviii, xcii
Crane, Hart, cxxvi
Crittenden, George B., xxxvii
Crockett, David, xxxiii
Cros, Guy Charles, 365
CROSS, THE, **304**
CRUCIFIXION, THE, **43**
CRY TO ARMS, A, cxi, **110**

Dabney, Richard L., xliv
Damon, S. Foster, lvii, ci n., cii n., 38, 382–383
DANIEL BOONE'S LAST LOOK WESTWARD, **246**
Dante Alighieri, xcv, 351, 367
Dargan, Olive Tilford, cxx, **240**, 398
Darwin, Charles, xliii, lxxi
Davidson, Donald, lxxviii, cxxiv–cxxvii, 280, **281–296, 369–375**
Davies, John, xvii n.
"Dawn of a pleasant morning in May," 148
"Day departs this upper air," 23
"Days of my youth," 9
"Death, thou'rt a cordial old and rare," 182
"Death, why so cruel? What! No other way," 5
DECAY OF A PEOPLE, **37**
Deism, xxi
DEPARTED, THE, **203**
DESERTED, **227**
De Soto, cxx
Dial, The, cxxiii
Dickens, Charles, 338, 384
Dickinson, Emily, cxviii
Dickson, Samuel Henry, lxxxviii, ciii, 16, **17–18**
DIXIE, cix, cx, cxi, **136, 138, 388**
"Do not suppose that I confess," 248
Donne, John, xci, xcv
Double Dealer, The, cxxiii
Douglas, Stephen A., xxxvii
DOWN THE MISSISSIPPI, **256**
Drayton, Michael, lxxxiii
DREAMING IN THE TRENCHES, **158**

Dreiser, Theodore, xliii
"Drifting, groping," 233
Dryden, John, xviii n., xxiv, lxxxiii n., lxv–lxvi, xciii
"Dull masses of dense green," 256
DUSK, **235**

EARTH, cxxii, **259**
"Earth, let me speak to you," 259
"Easter thaws no overwintered mind," 275
EDGE OF THE SWAMP, THE, xciii, **31**
Education, xxii–xxiv, xliii
ELDORADO, **82**
Eliot, George, lxx
Eliot, T. S., lxix n., lxxx, cxiv n., cxxiii, cxxv, cxxvii, cxxviii, 373
EMBARKATION, **256**
Emerson, Ralph Waldo, xcvii, lxiv, c, cxviii, 373
Emmett, Dan D., cix, **136**, 387
English Novel, The, lxix–lxx, lxxi n., 169
EPIGRAM, **7**
ETHNOGENESIS, cxii, cxi, **102**
EVOLUTION, **204**

"Faint as the far-down tone," 58
"Fair were our nation's visions, and as grand," 159
FAITH, **40**
"Faith is the flower that blooms unseen," 40
"Far, far from here the church bells ring," 231
"Farewell, my more than fatherland!" 15
FAREWELL TO AMERICA, A, lxxxix, **15**
Fielding, Henry, xxiv, lxx n.
FIRE ON BELMONT STREET, **289**
FIRST BANJO, THE, **212**
"First in the fight, and first in the arms," 148
Flash, Henry Lyndon, **148**, 391
Fletcher, John Gould, xvii n., lxxx–lxxxii, cxxii–cxxiii, cxxv, cxxvi, 249,
   250–269, 364–367
"Flinging its arc of silver bubbles, quickly shifts the moon," 257
FLORENCE VANE, cii, 83, **84**
Florida, lxxvi
FLOWERS IN ASHES, **97**
FOE AT THE GATES, THE, **155**
Foerster, Norman, lx
"For sixty days and upwards," 127
"Forlorn and white," 250
Forrest, Nathan Bedford, xxxix

"Forth from its scabbard pure and bright," 164
Franklin, Benjamin, xxix
Franklin, State of, xx, xxvi
Freneau, Philip, lxxxvi
Friend, Julius, cxxiii
"Frieze of warm bronze that glides with catlike movements," 258
Froissart, Jean, liii–liv, 83
FROM A FELUCCA, **246**
"From the Temple torn asunder," 43
Frontier, xix–xx (F. J. Turner's definition of, xix n.)
Frost, Robert, cxxiii, cxxvii
Fugitive, The, cxxix, 269, 280, 306
Fugitives, The, cxxiv–cxxviii, 269, 280, 300, 306
FULL MOON, **257**
Fuller, Thomas, xviii n.
"Furl that Banner, for 'tis weary," 162

Gaines, Francis Pendleton, xxxv
Garnett, Edward, lxxxi, 366
"Gayly bedight," 82
Gentleman of Virginia, A, lxxxiv–lxxxv, xlvi, **7,** 378
Georgia Citizen, cii n.
GEORGIA WATERS, ci, **41**
Gildersleeve, Basil L., ciii, 100
Gilman, D. C., lxx
"Glooms of the live-oaks, beautiful-braided and woven," 197
"Go bow thy head in gentle spite," 95
GO DOWN, MOSES, **318**
"Go 'way, fiddle!—folks is tired o' hearin' you a-squawkin'," 212
Godwin, William, 338
Goethe, J. W. von, 367
GOING BLIND, **205**
Goldsmith, Oliver, xxiv
"Good is the Saxon speech! clear, short and strong," 236
Gosse, Sir Edmund, cxx, 222
Grady, Henry, xli–xliv, lxxviii
GRAPE-VINE SWING, THE, **36**
Graves, Robert, 269
Grayson, William J., lxv–lxvi, ciii
Griswold, Rufus W., 62, 380

Hardy, Thomas, cxxvi, 367
Harrington, James, xxiv
Harris, Joel Chandler, xliv, lxxvii, cxix, 206
"Hath not the morning dawned with added light?" 102

HAUNTED PALACE, THE, **70**

HAW-BLOSSOMS, **95**

Hawthorne, Nathaniel, xcvi n.

Hayne, Paul Hamilton, liii, ciii, cv–cviii, cxii–cxiii, 17, 27, 100–101, 124, **125–136, 353–354,** 373, 386, 387, 391

Hayne, Robert Young, ciii n., 124

Hayne, William Hamilton, cxix, 125, **237, 353–354,** 398

"He leans far out and watches: down below," 228

"He was a worthy citizen of the town," 289

HEALTH, A, xc n., **22**

HEAT, **256**

Heine, Heinrich, 169, 367

"Helen, thy beauty is to me," 63

Henry, Patrick, xxiv

Herder, J. G von, 169

"Here is no easy fate, nor may you find," 268

HERE LIES A LADY, **271**

"Here lies a lady of beauty and high degree," 271

Hesperia, xlix, lxxxix, 13

Heyward, DuBose, lxxvii–lxxviii, cxxix, 234, **235–236, 360–364,** 369

Hibbard, Addison, 370

Higginson, Thomas Wentworth, cv

HISTORY AMONG THE ROCKS, **309**

"Ho! woodsmen of the mountain side!" 110

Holmes, Oliver Wendell, 125, 354

HOME, **233**

Homer, xlviii, xcv, 330, 332, 367

Hooker, Richard, xxiv, xxix n.

Hope, James Barron, **236,** 397

Horace, xxiv, xlii, lxxxv

HOUSE TO THE MAN, THE, **268**

"How grace this hallowed day?" 119

"How like a mighty picture, tint by tint," 133

"How many an acorn falls to die," 203

"How still Earth lies!—behind the pines," 98

Howells, William Dean, 222

Hume, David, xxiv

Hunt, Leigh, lv n., lxviii n., civ

HYMNS OF THE MARSHES, lxxvi, **188**

"I burn no incense, hang no wreath," 23

"I came the Womack Road from Sandy Bridge," 310

"I cannot think of any word," 216

"I fill this cup to one made up of loveliness alone," 22

"I have a need of silence and of stars," 233

"I have grown weary of the open sea," 229
"I hear thy spirit calling unto me," 52
"I heard a bird at break of day," 229
"I know not why, but all this weary day," 101
"I know that perfect self-esteem," 24
"I loved thee long and dearly," 84
"I picture her there in the quaint old room," 158
"I see an Eagle winging to the sun—," 94
"I SIGH FOR THE LAND OF THE CYPRESS AND PINE," 17
"I sometimes think Thou art my secret love," 232
"I think it is over, over," 135
"I walk down the Valley of Silence,—" 166
"I wish I was in de land ob cotton," 136, 388
ICARUS IN NOVEMBER, cxxviii, 244
I'M A GOOD OLD REBEL, 144
"I'm only four score year, my sons, and a few," 246
Imagists, The, cxxii–cxxiii, 249
IN HARBOR, 135
"In Heaven a spirit doth dwell," 66
"In my sleep I was fain of their fellowship, fain," 188
IN NEW YORK, 231
"In the greenest of our valleys," 70
IN THE NIGHT, 233
Indian poetry, xvii
INDIVIDUALITY, 194
"Into the woods my Master went," 201
Irving, Washington, 99
"Is there but emptiness from sky to sky," 218
ISADORE, 44, 385
ISRAFEL, 66, 383
" 'It is long since we met,' she said," 242
"It matters not that Time has shed," 237
"It was a hunter's tale that rolled like wind," 281
"It was many and many a year ago," 81
"It was three slim does and a ten-tined buck in the bracken lay," 183

Jackson, Andrew, xxxii–xxxiv, 26
Jackson, George Pullen, 313
Jackson, Gen. Thomas Jonathan, 393
Jefferson, Thomas, xxii–xxiv, xxix–xxx, xxxiii, xlvii–xlviii, lxxxvi
JOHN BROWN, 304
"John Brown of Ossawatomie," 304
JOHN HENRY, 315
Johnson, Andrew, xxxviii
Johnson, Guy B., 314

Johnson, James Weldon, 313, 314
Johnson, Samuel, xxiv, xlvii, xlviii, l, liii, 27
Jones, C. C., xlv
Jonson, Ben, lxxix n., lxxxiv, xcv, 168
JUDITH OF BETHULIA, 271

Keats, John, 350
Kennedy, John Pendleton, 61, 83
KENTUCKY MOUNTAIN FARM, 308
Key, Francis Scott, cviii, cxi, 11, 379
KILDEE, 203
"Kildee! Kildee! far o'er the lea," 203
Kipling, Rudyard, ci n.
Krutch, Joseph Wood, lix
KU KLUX, 225
Ku Klux Klan, xxxix

LAND WHERE WE WERE DREAMING, THE, 159
LAND WITHOUT RUINS, A, cxii, 165
Lanier, Sidney, xliv, lxix–lxxvii, xc n., cvii, cxiii–cxix, 168, 170–201, 202,
    355–360, 368, 373, 395–397
Lee, Robert E., xxxiv, xxxvii
LEE IN THE MOUNTAINS, cxxvii, 281, 292
LEE, THE SWORD OF ROBERT, 164
LEE TO THE REAR, 148
Legaré, Hugh Swinton, l–lii, liv, lv, lxxxviii n., xcii, ciii, civ, 93, 386
Legaré, James Mathewes, liii, liv n., ciii–civ, 93, 94–99, 386
LENORE, c, 77, 382
Leopardi, Giacomo, 367
Lessing, Gotthold E., lxxiii
Lewisohn, Ludwig, lxii–lxiii, 93
LIFE IN THE AUTUMN WOODS, cii, 85
LILY ADAIR, xciv, 58
Lincoln, Abraham, xxxvi–xxxviii, 371
Lindsay, Vachel, cii, 365
"Listen! the somber foliage of the Pine," 126
LISTEN TO THE MOCKING-BIRD, cx
"Lithe and long as the serpent train," 36
LITTLE GIFFEN, 146
LITTLE WHILE I FAIN WOULD LINGER YET, A, 134
"Lo! Death has reared himself a throne," 64
"Lo! 'tis a gala night," 71
Locke, John, xxiv, xxix, xxx
"LONG HAS THE FURIOUS PRIEST," 6
Longfellow, Henry Wadsworth, c n.

"Look out upon the stars, my love," 21
"Lord! in the Temple of thy love," 41
LORENA, CX
LOST PLEIAD, THE, xciii, **33**
Lowell, Amy, cxxii, 250
Lowell, James Russell, 386
Lucas, Daniel Bedinger, **159**, 395
Lucretius, 367
LUTE AND FURROW, **240**
Lyric, The, cxxiii

McCabe, William Gordon, xliii, **158**, 394
McCarthy, Harry, **142**, 390
McClure, John, cxxiii
McClurg, Dr. James, lxxxvii, 379
Macy, John, cxviii
Magazines, Southern, xlix–l, lii n.
Malone, Walter, cxx, **239**, 398
MAN HUNT, THE, **226**
MARGINALIA, (quoted) lxii
MARSH SONG—AT SUNSET, cxvii, **197**
Marshall, John, xxii, xxxii
MARSHES OF GLYNN, THE, cxvii, **197**
Martin, Everett Dean, 371
MARYLAND, MY MARYLAND, cix, **140**
Masters, Edgar Lee, cxxiii, 365
Mather, Cotton, xxi
MATINS, **205**
MELANCHOLY'S CURSE OF FEASTS, **24**
Memoralia, Preface to, **327–332**
Mencken, H. L., cxxiii
METHODS OF COMPOSITION, **353–354**
Meynell, Alice, 202
Millay, Edna St. Vincent, cxxiii
Milton, John, l, lvi, lix, lxvii, lxxx, xci, 205, 332, 340, 351, 353
Mims, Edwin, cxiv
Monroe, Harriet, lxxvii n., 369–370, 373
MOON'S ORCHESTRA, THE, **257**
MOONSHINER, THE, **228**
Moore, John Trotwood, cxix–cxx, **237**, 306, 398
Moore, Merrill, cxxiv–cxxv, 306, **306–307**
Moore, Thomas, xc n., xci, 99, 337, 384
More, P. E., xcvi n.
Morris, William, cvii, 125
"Most men know love but as a part of life," 102

"Mother, dear mother, come riddle to me," 4

MOTHERS, THE, **279**

MOUNTAIN STILL, THE, **228**

MR. POPE, **300**

Music and Poetry, lxx n., cvii, cxvi

"My life is like the summer rose," 14

MY SECRET, **204**

MY STUDY, **126**

Nacoochee, Preface to, **325–327**

Neal, John, 18

Negro songs and spirituals, 313–315

New South, The, xli–xliv

Newton, Isaac, lxxi

"Night and the mountain road: a crag where burns," 228

NIGHT LANDING, **257**

NOISE THAT TIME MAKES, THE, **306**

"Not in the sky," 33

NOTE ON SOUTHERN POETRY, **368–369**

"Now are the winds about us in their glee," 37

"Now on you is the hungry equinox," 308

Nullification, xxvi–xxvii, xxxi

"O I'm a good old rebel," 144

"O Mahsr! let dis gath'rin' fin' a blessin' in yo' sight!" 208

"O! say, can you see, by the dawn's early light," 11

"O thou, whose potent genius (like the sun," 133

" 'O Trade! O Trade! would thou wert dead!' " 171

ODE ("Sleep sweetly in your humble graves"), cviii, cxi, **123**

ODE TO THE CONFEDERATE DEAD, cxxvii, **301**

"Off the long headland, threshed about by round-backed breakers," 263

"Oh, band in the pine-wood, cease!" 155

"Oh, de boll weevil am a little black bug," 316

"Oh, hush, my heart, and take thine ease," 215

O'Hara, Theodore, cviii–cix, cxi, 88, **89–93**, 386

O'Kelly, Daniel, 13, 379

OLD PIONEER, THE, 89, **91**

OLD SAUL, **216**

ON PARTING, **24**

ON SUNDAY MORNING, **231**

"On the beryl-rimmed rebecs of Ruby," 58

ON THE DEATH OF A KINSMAN, **94**

"On thy waters, thy sweet valley-waters," 41

"Once upon a midnight dreary, while I pondered, weak and weary," 72

ONE END OF LOVE, **242**

OPPORTUNITY, **239**

Ossian, xlvii

OUR ANGLO-SAXON TONGUE, **236**

OUR TWO WORTHIES, **273**

"Out of the dusk a shadow," 204

"Out of the focal and foremost fire," 146

"Out of the hills of Habersham," 181

"Over the monstrous shambling sea," 197

OVERTONES, **229**

Ovid, *Metamorphoses*, trans. by George Sandys, xviii, lxxxiii n.

Page, Thomas Nelson, xliv

Page, Walter Hines, xli–xliv, lxxviii

Paine, Robert Treat, lxxxviii

"Pale, funeral flowers," 24

Palmer, John Williamson, 151, 392

PARADISE LOST, lxvii, 332, 340, 351, 353

Parrington, Vernon Louis, xxvii, 372

Pepys, Samuel, 168

Percy, William Alexander, cxxi, 229, **229–234**

Petigru, James L., ciii, 100

PHILOSOPHY OF COMPOSITION, THE, lx–lxi, c, **338–349**

Physiocrats, xxix–xxx

Pike, Albert, cx, **138**, 249, 389, 399

Pinckney, Gen. Charles Cotesworth, xci

Pinckney, Josephine, cxxix, 296, **297–300**

Pindar, l

PINE'S MYSTERY, THE, **126**

Pinkney, Edward Coote, xc, xciii, 18, **19–25**, 373, 380–381, 386

Plato, lvii, 327

Poe, Edgar Allan, l, lv, lvi, lvii, lviii–lxix, lxxiii, xc n., xciv, xcvi–cii, cv, cxi, cxii, cxiii, cxiv, cxviii, 38, 39, 60, **62–83**, 321, 322, 323, **332–349**, 351–353, 373, 380, 384–386

POETIC PRINCIPLE, THE, lx, **332–338**

POETRY SOUTH, **360–364**

Pope, Alexander, xviii n., xxiii, xxiv, xlvi, lviii, lxv–lxvi, lxxxvi, lxxxviii

Populists, The, xlv–xlvi

Pound, Ezra, cxxiii, 250, 365, 368

POWER OF THE BARDS, THE, (selection from) **87**

Preludes and Symphonies, Preface to, **364–367**

Preston, Margaret Junkin, **153**, 393

Prior, Matthew, lxxxvi

PRODIGAL, cxxix, **236**

PROTOTYPES, **224**

PSALM OF THE WEST, CXV

Quarles, Philip, xvii n.

RAILROAD SONG, ci
Raleigh, Sir Walter, xvii n., lxxxiii
Randall, James Ryder, cix, **140**, 389
Randolph, Innes, **145**, 391
Randolph, Thomas, xxiii
Ransom, John Crowe, lxxviii–lxxx, cxxiv–cxxviii, 269, **270–276**, 373
RATIONALE OF VERSE, lxv, c
RAVEN, THE, c, **72**, 338–349, 382
REAPER, THE, **98**
REBUKE OF THE ROCKS, **308**
Reconstruction, xxxvii–xl, 169
REDIVIVUS, **281**
Reese, Lizette Woodworth, cxx–cxxi, 214, **215–221**
Religion, xx–xxii
RESIGNATION, lxxxvii, **9**
REVENGE OF HAMISH, THE, cxvii, **183**
Reviewer, The, cxxiii
Rice, Cale Young, cxx–cxxi, 245, **246–249**
Rich, Richard, xviii, lxxxii
Richardson, Samuel, lxx n.
Rimbaud, Arthur, cxxviii, 366
"Ring round her! children of her glorious skies," 155
Robinson, Edwin Arlington, cxxiii, 373
ROMANCE, **63**
"Romance, who loves to nod and sing," 63
Rossetti, D. G., ci n.
"Row after row with strict impunity," 301
Russell, Irwin, lxxvii, cxix, 205, **206–214**, 373
Russell, John, ciii
Russell's Magazine, ciii n., 100, 124
Ryan, Abram Joseph, cxi–cxii, cxviii–cxix, 162, **162–168**, 390

"Sail on, sail on, fair cousin Cloud," 194
SAM DAVIS, **237**
Sandburg, Carl, cxxiii, 365, 373
Sandys, George, xviii, (contemporary ballad on, quoted) xviii n., lxxxiii
"Scaurus hates *Greek*, and is become," **7**
Schiller, J. C. F. von, civ, cxxi
Schlegel, A. W., lxi
Science, xliii
Science of English Verse, The, (quoted) lxxii–lxxiii, lxxvi, 169, **355–360**
"Science! true daughter of Old Time thou art," 62
Scott, Sir Walter, xlii, liii, liv n., xcii

SEA-DRINKING CITIES, **299**

"Sea-drinking cities have a moon-struck air," 299

"Sealights reflected on the rocks," 279

SEA MARK, THE, **3**

SELF-ESTEEM, **24**

SERENADE ("Look out upon the stars"), 18, **21**

Sevier, John, xx, xxvi

SHADE OF THE TREES, THE, **153**

SHADOW AND SHADE, **305**

Shakespeare, William, xxiii, xliii, xlvi, l, lii, lxxix n., lxxx, xcv, cxvi–cxvii, cxxi, 330, 350

Shaw, John, lxxxvii, **9**, 378

Shelley, Percy Bysshe, xcv, xcix, 365, 367

SHELLEY, **125**

SHERIFF, THE, **228**

Sherman, Gen. W. T., xxxviii

SHOT WHO? JIM LANE! **307**

Sidney, Sir Philip, lvi, 382

SILENCE, THE, **259**

Simms, William Gilmore, xvii n., lii–liv, lv, lvii, lviii n., xci–xciii, cii, ciii, 17, 25, **28–38**, 100, 125, **321–322**, 322, 368, 381–382, 392, 395

"Sleep sweetly in your humble graves," 123

Smart Set, The, cxxiii

Smith, Captain John, xvii, xviii, lxxxii, lxxxiii, **3**, 250, 377

Smollett, Tobias, lxx n.

SNOW, **222**

SNOW-BIRD, THE, **204**

SNOW-BOUND, cxix

SNOW-MESSENGERS, THE, **129**

Solomon, 331

"Some day, when the stern seeker in my brain," 236

SONG ("Day departs"), **23**

SONG for "The Jacquerie," **170**

SONG ("We break the glass"), **19**

SONG ("Who has robbed"), **9**

SONG IN MARCH, **37**

SONG OF ADORATION TO GOD, **41**

SONG OF THE CHATTAHOOCHEE, lxxvi, cxvii, **181**

SONG OF THE MYSTIC, **166**

SONG TO ISA, **54**, 384

SONG YOU LOVE, THE, **232**

SONNET: GRIEF, **43**

SONNET: I KNOW NOT WHY, cvii, **101**

SONNET: MOST MEN KNOW LOVE, cvii, **102**

SONNET—TO SCIENCE, xcviii, **62**

SONNET ("We are a part"), **38**
SONNETS OF THE BLOOD, cxxvii
"Soul of the sunny South! thy voice is heard," 60
"Sound trumpets, ho!—weigh anchor—loosen sail—," 19
Southern Literary Messenger, cii n., 61, 83
SOUTHERN POET AND HIS TRADITION, THE, **369–375**
Southern Review, I
"Southrons, hear your country call you!" 138
SOUTHWARD RETURNING, **292**
SPECTRAL LOVERS, **270**
Spencer, Herbert, lxxii
Spenser, Edmund, lxxx
SPICEWOOD, **216**
SPRING, cviii, cxi, **115**
"Spring, with that nameless pathos in the air," 115
STACK ARMS, **157**
" 'Stack Arms!' I've gladly heard the cry," 157
STANZAS ("My life is like the summer rose"), lxxxviii, **14**
STAR-SPANGLED BANNER, THE, cviii, cxi, **11**
STEAL AWAY, **319**
"Steal away, steal away, steal away to Jesus," 319
Stephens, Alexander, xxvi, xxxi, xxxiv
Sterne, Laurence, lxx n.
STEVEDORES, THE, **258**
Stevens, Thaddeus, xxxix
Stevenson, Alec B., cxxiv, cxxviii, **244**, 399
"Still sing the morning stars remote," 205
STIRRUP-CUP, THE, **182**
STONEWALL JACKSON'S WAY, **151**
STREET CRIES, **297**
Stuart, Jesse, cxxviii, 310, **310–313**
"Summer has gone," 85
Sumner, Charles, xxxix
SUNRISE, cxvii, **188**
"Surely in no benignant mood," 231
SWAMP FOX, THE, **28**
SWAN, THE, **262**
Swift, Jonathan, xxiii, xxiv
Swinburne, Algernon, ci n., cxiv n., cxviii
SWORD OF ROBERT LEE, THE, cxii, **164**
SYMPHONY, THE, cxiv–cxv, cxviii, 169, **171**

Tabb, John Banister, cxviii–cxix, 169, 201, **202–205**
TALL MEN, THE, **281**, epilogue to, **289**
"Tall, sombre, grim, against the morning sky," 128

Tate, Allen, lxxviii–lxxx, cxxix–cxxviii, 300, **300–305, 368–369**

Taylor, Bayard, 169, 383

Taylor, John, xxx

TEARS, 214, **215**

" 'Tell me his name and you are free,' " 237

Tennyson, Alfred, lv n., civ, cvii, cxv, 352, 353, 396

"The despot treads thy sacred sands," 112

"The despot's heel is on thy shore," 140

"The dreamer turns," 297

"The hound was cuffed, the hound was kicked," 170

"The knightliest of the knightly race," 146

"The moon, like a round device," 222

"The muffled drum's sad roll has beat," 89

"The noise that Time makes in passing by," 306

"The old house leans upon a tree," 227

"The pine-trees lift their dark bewildered eyes—," 129

"The rain is plashing on my sill," 121

"The shadow streamed into the wall—," 305

"The skies they were ashen and sober," 78

"The spicewood burns along the gray, spent sky," 216

"The winter has grown so still," 240

"The woods stretch deep to the mountain side," 226

THEORY OF POETRY, A, **351–353**

"There are many ways to die," 309

"There is a place that some men know," 304

"There is a moment blind with light, split by the hum," 244

"There is a silence I carry about with me always," 259

"They cannot wholly pass away," 203

"They do me wrong who say I come no more," 239

"They swear the dead come back at night," 216

"They tell me she is beautiful, my city," 235

"Thin lips can make a music," 281

"This is my world! within these narrow walls," 126

"This the true sign of ruin to a race—," 37

Thompson, John Reuben, 27, **148**, 392

"Those hewers of the clouds, the Winds,—that lair," 224

"Thou wast all that to me, love," 67

Ticknor, Francis Orray, **146–147**, 391

Tiger Lilies, lxxvi, 169

Timrod, Henry, liii, lxi n., lxv–lxix, xc n., ciii–cviii, cxi, cxii–cxiii, cxviii, 13, 17, 28, 99, **101–124**, 124, 125, **351–353**, 373, 386–387

" 'Tis not what I am fain to hide," 204

" 'TIS TRUE THAT LAST NIGHT I ADORED THEE," **35**

" 'Tis a wild spot, and even in summer hours," 31

TO A LILY, **95**

TO ALLEGRA FLORENCE IN HEAVEN, **49**, 385

TO HELEN, **63**

TO IDEALON, **60**

TO LONGFELLOW (ON HEARING HE WAS ILL), **133**

TO LORD BYRON, lxxxix, **15**

TO MY FATHER, **237**

TO ONE IN PARADISE, **67**

TO SCIENCE, **62**

TO THE MOCKING-BIRD, lxxxix, **14**

"To you, Virginia, Tennessee," 292

TO W. H. H., **133**

TODAY, **218**

Trent, William P., xxviii

Tucker, St. George, lxxxiii, lxxxvii, **9**, 379

Turner, Nat (Rebellion), xxxv–xxxvi

" 'Twas on a pleasant mountain," lxxxvi, **7**

"Twirling your blue skirts, travelling the sward," 273

Tyler, Moses Coit, lxxxiv

"Type of the antique Rome! Rich reliquary," 68

ULALUME, c, **78**

Uncle Remus, xliv

"Under a wall of bronze," 262

UNKNOWN DEAD, THE, cxi, **121**

Untermeyer, Louis, xvii n.

"Up through the hyaline ether-sea," 55

"Upon thy lips now lies," 54

Vergil, xlii, xliii

VICKSBURG, **127**

Views and Reviews, lii

Virginalia, Preface to, **332**

VIRGINIA BANISHING TEA, lxxxvi

VIRGINIANS OF THE VALLEY, THE, **146**

VISION OF POESY, (quoted) civ

VOICE OF THOUGHT, THE, **58**

Voltaire, 368

VOYAGER'S SONG, THE, **19**

Wagner, Richard, lxxiv

WAITING, **216**

"Walking into the shadows, walking alone," 292

WANDERER, THE, **229**

Warren, Robert Penn, lxxix n., cxv, cxxiv–cxxviii, 307, **308–310**

Washington, George, lxxxiii, lxxxvi
WATER-BOY, **318**
"Water-Boy, where are yo' hidin'?" 318
"We are a band of brothers, and native to the soil," 142
"We are a part of all things that we see," 38
"We break the glass, whose sacred wine," 19
"We follow where the Swamp Fox guides," 28
"We have sent him seeds of the melon's core," 225
WEARINESS, **232**
Webb, W. R. (Sawney), xliii
Webster, John, lxxxiv, xcv
"What are stars, but hieroglyphics of God's glory writ in lightning," 57
"What are the thoughts that are stirring his breast?" 153
"When Alexander Pope strolled in the city," 300
"When he was shot he toppled to the ground," 307
"When I consider Life and its few years—," 215
"When I have sung the sweet songs and the sad," 232
"When I look into my sons' eyes I see," 277
"When John Henry was a baby," 315
"When merry Christmas-day is done," 206
"When snow, like silence visible," 204
"When the moon lights up," 257
"When thy soft round form was lying," 49
"Where, with unruffled surface wide," 97
"Whether it be that we in letters trace," 224
"While I recline," 106
"While the world lay round me sleeping," 44
"While yesterevening, through the vale," 95
WHITE SYMPHONY, **250**
Whitman, Walt, c, ci, cxviii, 365, 373
Whittier, John Greenleaf, cxix
"Who has robbed the ocean cave," 9
" 'Who've ye got there?' 'Only a dying brother," 154
"Why am I silent from year to year?" 101
WHY SILENT, **101**
WIDOW'S SONG, THE, **23**
Wigglesworth, Michael, lxxxv
Wilde, Richard Henry, xlviii–xlix, liv, lv, lxxxviii–xc, 12, **14–16**, 379–380
William and Mary, xxii n., xxiii, 378
WINDS, THE, **224**
"Winged mimic of the woods! thou motley fool!" 14
Wordsworth, William, lxiii, lxiv, lxvii n., lxviii n., lxix, xc n., xci, xcii, civ, cvii, 353, 367, 386, 397
Wythe, George, xxii–xxv, lxxxvi

Yeats, William Butler, lxix n.
"Yes, give me the land where the ruins are spread," 165
Young, Edward, lxiii
YOUNG KENTUCKY, 310

ZOLLICOFFER, 148
Zollicoffer, Brig.-Gen. Felix Kirk, 148, 392

Luc — 222 — 229 Percie
Deboise # 234 — 236

med. single poems — no
Rice 245
20 Ransome 269

Then Ransome — 276

296 — 319

helped found Fugative soc.)

John Crow Ransom

Donald Davidson
allen Tate.

merrill moore (an early member)